The Living Goddess

T0352871

The Living Goddess

A JOURNEY INTO THE HEART OF KATHMANDU

ISABELLA TREE

ELAND
London

First published by Viking/Penguin Books, India 2014

First published in Great Britain by Eland Publishing Ltd,
61 Exmouth Market, London EC1R 4QL in February 2015

ISBN 978 1 78060 046 8

Cover design: *Patan Kumari* © Panni Bharti
Cover photograph: Narendra Shrestha
Maps courtesy of The Rough Guide to Nepal 2012

Text set in Great Britain by James Morris
Printed in England by Clays Ltd, Elcograf S.p.A.

To Living Goddesses, past, present and future

Look upon a woman as a goddess
Whose special energy she is,
And honour her in that state.

Uttara Tantra

Contents

PART THREE

Timeline

100,000 BCE	The Kathmandu Valley is formed as a huge lake drains away.
c. 563 BCE	Siddhartha Gautama, the Buddha, is born in Lumbini in southern Nepal.
300–879 CE	The Licchavi kings rule Nepal.
7th–13th centuries CE	Nepal's 'dark ages', or 'Transitional Period'.
11th century	The *Samvarodaya Tantra*, the first known text recording Buddhist tantric worship of a Kumari, is composed in Nepal.
1097	King Nanyadeva founds the city of Simraongarh in Tirhut, a Hindu kingdom to the south of Nepal.
1325	Sultan Muhammed bin Tughluq sacks Simraongarh, forcing King Harisimha and his court to flee.
1326	King Harisimha dies en route to Nepal but his wife Devaldevi and son Jagatsimha find sanctuary in Bhaktapur, establishing the cult of Taleju in the city.
1349	The Muslim armies of Sultan Shams-ud-Din plunder the Kathmandu Valley, destroying the stupa at Swayambhu and many other temples.

r. 1382–1395	Devaldevi's grandson-in-law Jaya Stithi Malla unites the valley and codifies its laws.
1428-82	Rule of Yaksha Malla, Jaya Stithi's grandson. His death results in the valley being split between his six sons into three rival Malla kingdoms of Kathmandu, Patan and Bhaktapur.
1491	The joint kings of Bhaktapur establish the first 'royal' Kumari.
1559-1570	Dravya Shah, prince of Lamjung, becomes first king of Gorkha, a hill kingdom 80 miles to the west of the Kathmandu Valley.
r.1560–74	Mahendra Malla establishes Taleju Temple and other temples around Kathmandu's Durbar Square.
r.1619–61	Siddhirasimha Malla establishes Taleju in Patan, where he becomes king.
1641-74	Pratap Malla, king of Kathmandu, dancer, poet and devotee of Guhyeshvari, presides over an era of artistic patronage, substantially rebuilding the palace of Hanuman Dhoka and raising devotional pillars in front of Taleju Temple.
1735	Jaya Prakasha Malla succeeds to the throne of Kathmandu.
1744	Prithvi Narayan Shah, king of Gorkha, seizes the Malla fort of Nuwakot – the first target in his campaign to conquer the valley.
1757	Jaya Prakasha Malla builds a special temple

establishes Nepal's modern boundaries
and gives Britain the right to recruit
Gorkha soldiers in Nepal and maintain a
residency in Kathmandu.

1846   The Kot Massacre eradicates the cream of
the court aristocracy, ushering in the Rana
era and reducing the Shah kings to puppets.

1934   A massive earthquake destroys much of
the Kathmandu Valley.

1951   King Tribhuvan and the Nepal Congress
Party, with Indian support, overthrow the
Rana regime and establish a new coalition
government. Nepal opens its doors to the
outside world.

1953   Everest is conquered by New Zealander
Edmund Hillary and Nepali Tenzing Norgay.

1955-72   Rule of King Mahendra sees the
introduction of elections which are then
declared void as the *panchayat* system of
government is restored.

1960   Malaria eradication programme opens the
Terai to industry, intensive agriculture,
and rapid population growth.

1975   Birendra is crowned king in Kathmandu's
Hanuman Dhoka.

1990   The mass demonstrations of the Jana
Andolan, the People's Movement, force
King Birendra to accept a new
constitution, restoring democracy and
relegating the king to the role of
constitutional Hindu monarch under a
multiparty democracy.

1996-2005   A decade-long Maoist insurgency brings
the country to its knees and results in the
death of 13,000 Nepalis. Development
projects stall and tourism plummets.

2001   Prince Dipendra massacres ten members
of the royal family, including his father,
King Birendra, before shooting himself.
Birendra's brother, Gyanendra, inherits
the throne.

2005   King Gyanendra dismisses the
government and assumes direct control
of the country in a state of emergency,
citing the need to crush the Maoist rebels.

2006   After weeks of protests involving
hundreds of thousands of people, King
Gyanendra reinstates parliament, which
votes to curtail his emergency powers.
Maoists and government officials sign a
peace agreement and the Maoist rebels
enter an interim government.

2007   The 250th Sri Kumari Anniversary
Celebrations mark Jaya Prakasha Malla's
founding of the Living Goddess's
residence in Kathmandu's Durbar Square
and her first jatra around the city.

2008   Nepal abolishes the monarchy and
becomes a federal democratic republic,
with former Maoist guerrilla leader
Pushpa Kamal Dahal ('Prachanda') as the
first prime minister. Prachanda resigns a
year later. After three years' investigation
the Supreme Court rejects the claim that
Kumaris are exploited and recommends
increased pensions for ex-Kumaris.

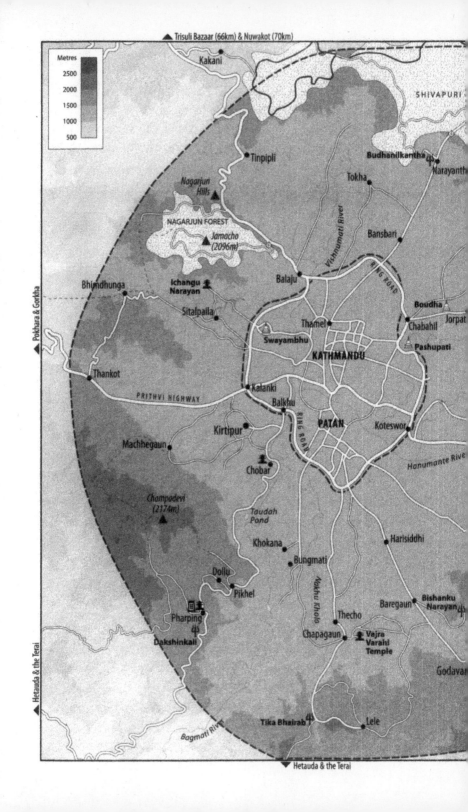

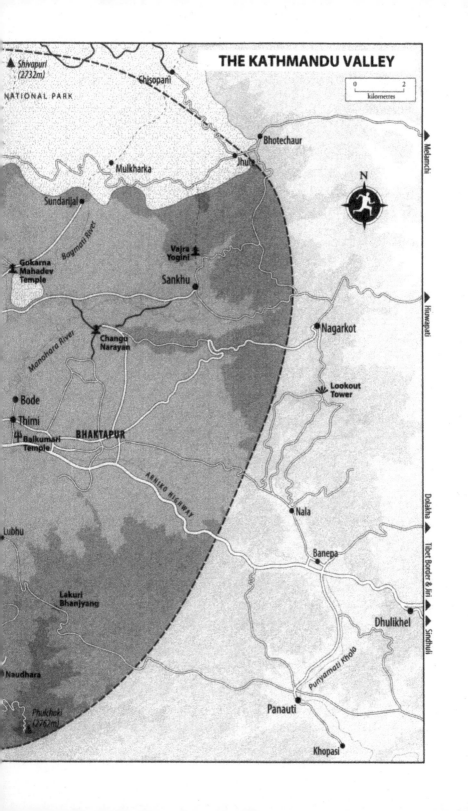

THE KATHMANDU VALLEY

PART ONE

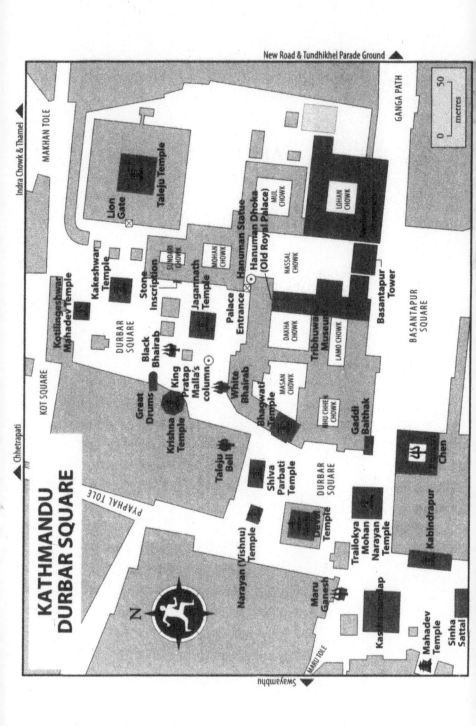

Chapter 1

A Living Goddess

A hush descends on the tiny stone courtyard. A footfall, a cough, the beating of a pigeon's wings resound like a thunderclap in the silence. Outside, the jangling of rickshaw bells and motorbike horns belongs to another world.

Without warning, a child appears at an ornately carved window on the second floor. She could be six, eight or nine years old. It is impossible to tell. She gazes sternly down on the assembled foreigners, pouting slightly, looking mildly inconvenienced. Her eyes are huge, exaggerated with thick lines of kohl reaching all the way to her temples. She is dressed entirely in red, her lips bright red; her hair bound up tightly in a topknot; gold ornaments around her neck and bangles on her wrists. Her tiny fingers, their nails painted red, clasp a wooden rail across the bottom of the window with the command of a captain at the ship's helm.

There are awed murmurs and even some applause. The child's expression does not falter. Lowering his voice the guide explains, 'She does not smile. If she did, it would be an invitation to heaven and you would die.'

Just as suddenly, the child is gone, reabsorbed into the shadows, leaving only a flutter of red curtains.

The little girl is Nepal's 'Living Goddess', one of the sightseeing landmarks of Kathmandu, the face in every guidebook and on every tourist poster. To Nepalis she is known as 'Kumari' – the word for a virgin or unmarried girl. She is believed to manifest a powerful Goddess who protects Kathmandu and watches over the country and all its citizens. All-seeing, all-knowing, she is said to have eyes in the past and the future, and to see everything that goes on in the present. She has the power to cure illnesses, to remove obstacles in the way of happiness, to bestow immeasurable blessings on those pure of heart. She is said to punish the wicked with a single withering stare.

I was eighteen the first time I saw her, fresh out of school, travelling with three friends on a gap year in South Asia. For several months in the summer of 1983 we rented a couple of rooms in Freak Street, a fading hippy colony in the heart of old Kathmandu. Our shutters opened on to the southern facade of the old royal palace and, on the other side of Basantpur Square, an imposing three-storey building made of red brick with a deep, clay-tiled roof and wooden lattice windows – the palace of the Living Goddess.

The 'Kumari Ghar', or 'Kumari Chen' – the Kumari House – was a hive of activity, the entrance around the corner in Durbar Square guarded by a pair of magnificent stone lions. Every day devotees would climb the short flight of steps between the lions and, ducking their heads beneath the ornate wooden doorway, carry plates of offerings inside. Across the little courtyard they entered a door tucked away in a corner marked 'Hindus ONLY'.

This was as far as we could go, the building itself being strictly closed to foreigners. But devotees themselves can only venture as far as the Kumari's public puja room upstairs, behind the window where the little goddess occasionally appears for tourists. The rest of the building remains a mystery to them. In particular, we were told, there is one room where no one outside the Living Goddess's inner circle can go. On the top floor, directly above the main entrance, is an elaborate five-section window looking out on to the pagoda temples of Durbar Square. The central section is bronze-gilt and framed by golden dancing goddesses. It is a window fit for a queen. Only the Living Goddess can look through it. Behind it is her throne room, the most powerful place in the whole building – a ceremonial chamber reserved for rituals conducted by tantric priests and attended by the king.

A certain amount is widely known about the Living Goddess. For most of the time, our neighbours told us, she is restricted to the inside of the Kumari Chen. She leaves the building only to attend festivals, a dozen or so times a year. In order to maintain her purity her feet must never touch the ground, so on most occasions she is carried out of the house in the arms of one of the male members of her household and then borne aloft in a handheld palanquin. For three days in September, during the festival of Indra Jatra, she is pulled around the city on a massive golden chariot.

A special female caretaker and her family are responsible for looking after her and preserving the conditions that allow the Goddess to reside inside her. The Kumari's own family lives elsewhere. Her parents hand over their daughter to the Kumari Chen when she is selected for the role, around the age of three or four. Though they can go and see her they cannot embrace her or speak to her. They simply touch their foreheads to her feet like other devotees. She will be their daughter again only on the cusp of puberty, when she rejoins the world of mortals and leaves the Kumari Chen for good.

Another stipulation is that the Kumari must not bleed. If she cuts or grazes herself accidentally – if she suffers so much as a scratch – then the spirit of the Goddess inside her will disappear. So special care has to be taken to protect her from injury. When she shows signs of reaching puberty, before she can experience the blood loss of her first menstruation, the Kumari is dismissed and another little girl takes her place.

This much is popular knowledge. But much of what goes on inside the Kumari Chen is highly secret. The Kumari belongs to a belief system based on esoteric tantric rituals. Rumours and speculations are rife, even among Nepalis who worship her. There are stories of dark initiations at the dead of night: a terrifying ordeal in which the little Goddess walks barefoot through bloody courtyards scattered with the severed heads of goats and buffaloes while men dressed as demons leap and howl in the shadows. She is said to spend the night alone, shut up in a room with ghosts and rats. If the child shows no fear, our neighbours explained, it proves the Goddess has accepted her.

How the Kumari is selected is also a mystery. Some say it is a mystical process, the work of astrologers and tantric priests – like the selection of Tibet's Dalai Lama. Some say she is stripped naked and subjected to an intimate physical examination. There are certain signs the priests are said to look for. She has to be exceptionally beautiful, with radiant 'golden' skin, no blemishes, birthmarks or scars, and no indications of smallpox that, until recently, blighted the complexions of so many children in Nepal. She is said to be blessed with thirty-two *lakshina* – the physical perfections of a *bodhisattva*. She has to have the chest of a lion, for example; a neck like a conch shell; eyelashes like a cow; body like a banyan tree; the thighs of a deer; small and well-recessed sexual organs; a voice clear and soft like a duck's. Sometimes, mothers are said to dream of the Goddess when they are pregnant – a sure sign they are bearing a Kumari. Sometimes a snake – generally considered a good omen in Nepal – enters the house shortly after a future Kumari is born.

The child Goddess exhibits almost superhuman patience and poise. She is often required to sit motionless on a simple throne or cushion for hours at a time. Even when she is carried outside in her palanquin her demeanour remains sublimely calm, at odds with the thronging, excitable crowds around her. To westerners familiar with demanding toddlers her placidity is inexplicable. At Indra Jatra, her chariot processions last the best part of a day, during which time she does not touch a morsel of food or a drop of water, or absent herself to go to the lavatory. It was rumoured in the shady cafés of Freak Street that the caretakers use hypnosis, or strong alcohol or drugs – the only way, our hippy neighbours claimed, a toddler can ever possibly be this compliant. One old *dharma* bum was convinced, not without envy, that the Kumari is given *soma* – the legendary narcotic mentioned in the Rig Veda.

What happens to a Kumari after her dismissal is also a matter of conjecture. Former Living Goddesses are said to be extremely dangerous and capable of wreaking bloody accidents wherever they go. No one would ever want to marry an ex-Kumari, Nepalis told us. Snakes slither out of her vagina, threatening to emasculate any man foolish enough to try to deflower her. Some, on the other hand, insisted that sex is the only way these degraded goddesses can earn a living and claimed that ex-Kumaris are trafficked, along with thousands of other girls from Nepal, to brothels in Mumbai or Bangkok.

~

As we settled into life in Durbar Square the enigma of our neighbour became all-engrossing. We dropped in on her courtyard almost every day. Often she would grace us with an appearance at her window but some days we would wander away disappointed. At night we would catch a glimpse of a little figure in red flashing past the windows of her house. Her presence, like an occlusion in the mind's eye, trailed us on our excursions around the valley. We began to see the name 'Kumari' everywhere we went – on signs for shops, banks, travel agents, as the brand name of beauty products. On quiet afternoons in our flat I would write about her in my journal, wondering where she came from, what life was like for her inside the Kumari Chen, whether she was happy, where she would go when she was dismissed, if there was any truth to the darkest of the rumours.

I realized my framework for understanding what she represented was very limited. I found myself likening her to a 'Christ-child –

innocent, vulnerable'. 'Perhaps,' I scribbled in my notebook, she stood for 'some kind of sacrifice, atoning for the sins of the world'. Or, being virginal, she was a version of the Madonna – 'meek and submissive', 'without sin', 'untainted by adult desires'. But deep down, I knew my theorizings were wide of the mark. The Kumari's expression as she gazed down on us from her window – defiant, sultry, provocative – kept pulling me up. It warned me not to take anything about her for granted.

I was particularly intrigued by the notion of her power. I lived in a world where the omnipotent deity, if one still believed in his existence, was incontrovertibly male. The idea of a supreme female being was inconceivable. Yet to Nepalis the Goddess residing in this little child was regarded as sovereign, pivotal to the very existence of their kingdom. Every year, at the festival of Indra Jatra, the king of Nepal would come to the Kumari's house, kneel at the feet of the Living Goddess and beg her blessing to rule. If the Kumari was happy with him, she would dip her fingers in a dish of vermilion by her side and place a red *tika* on his forehead. If the king did not receive this blessing, his reign was doomed. The Kumari's displeasure, people said, might even signify his death.

The tradition requiring the king of Nepal to submit himself to the divine will of a female child originated in the time of the Mallas – the Hindu kings who had ruled the Kathmandu Valley before the present Shah dynasty. The Mallas were names still on everyone's lips. Their influence was everywhere in the valley, but their showmanship was concentrated in the spectacular buildings they had created around their *durbars* and the votive pillars they had erected in front of certain temples with golden statues of themselves on top, kneeling in prayer.

The Mallas had originally fled to the Himalaya to escape the Turkish invasions of India, eventually coming to power in the Kathmandu Valley around 1200 CE. Their provenance is illustrious. They are mentioned in the *Mahabharata* and in early Buddhist texts. As with all Hindu kings, their subjects had considered them to be divine. Once established in the 'Valley of Nepal' they ushered in an era – lasting over five and a half centuries – of extraordinary prosperity and by the fifteenth century had established three separate dynasties in the valley ruling from three kingdoms centred on the cities of Bhaktapur, Kathmandu and Patan. Like the city states of ancient Greece each Malla kingdom was independent yet intimately connected to the others, bound together by an endless cycle of kinship and enmity, alliances and competition. At its height, under their auspices, the wealth of the Kathmandu Valley reached mythical proportions. Rumours of a lost Shangri-La, abounding in rivers of gold and untold treasure, tantalized the outside world as the Malla kings embellished their palaces and temples with golden doors, gigantic bronze gongs and bells, copper roofs and golden roof-finials.

The Mallas had derived their wealth from two vital trade routes traversing the valley: one running south–north from India to Tibet and, beyond, to China; the other east–west from Bhutan and Sikkim to Mustang and Kashmir. The city of Kathmandu lay at the centre of this lucrative crossroads. Sitting high on the steps of the pagoda temples, watching the world go by, the magnetism of this spot continues to be overwhelming. The same criss-crossing traffic passes by the old royal palace, skirting the temple plinths and the ancient pilgrims' rest house of Kasthamandap (the building that gave Kathmandu its name) as it has for over a millennium. Coin dealers and money changers vie for passing trade as dark-skinned hawkers from the Terai wheeling bicycles loaded with apples and oranges intersect the passage of Sherpas from the hills staggering full tilt, heads bowed under some monstrous load like an oven or fridge. In the tight alleyways around Durbar Square, alongside shops selling motorbike parts and pirated cassette tapes, merchants deal in the same commodities that have filled their coffers for centuries – silk, musk, salt, wool, red coral, turquoise, lapis, silver, gold, rubies, yaks' tails, spices, sandalwood, vermilion, cotton, tea.

But locals have another way of explaining the centripetal pull of Kathmandu's ancient centre. According to legend the city had been founded in Satya Yuga, the Golden Age, by Manjushri – a great *bodhisattva*, or enlightened being – in the shape of his sword. Manjushri was the central figure in the Buddhist creation myth of the valley. The crux of his sword marks the crossroads that is now the heart of the city. It is a sacred place, a magical apex that generates prosperity for the kingdom and bestows blessings on everyone who passes through it.

~

In Kathmandu, we discovered, all the stories of the past are suffused with myth, and legends run circles around historical facts. To Nepalis this is natural, as if facts alone cannot reveal all the hidden meanings and deeper relevances. Myths are living things, stories to live by. As familiar as close friends, they permeate dreams and waking thoughts, evoking comparisons. Reminiscences and coincidences tumble about, instructive reminders that the present dances hypnotically to the rhythms of the past.

Nowhere are the boundaries between myth and reality more blurred than around the origins of the Living Goddess. The most popular story attributes the last Malla king of Kathmandu with establishing the first Kumari. Jaya Prakasha Malla, a king reigning in the first half of the eighteenth century, had instituted the practice of worshipping a living child after falling foul of a goddess with whom he used to spend afternoons playing dice. Though little more than two centuries ago, this was in the days when gods and goddesses still frequented the valley, consorting with mortals. But he did not worship her for long. In the middle of the eighteenth century an ambitious Hindu raja from the small hill kingdom of Gorkha, some eighty miles to the west of Kathmandu, set his sights on conquering the valley. In a campaign that lasted twenty-five years, Prithvi Narayan Shah – ancestor of the modern royal dynasty of Nepal – began attacking the Malla forts on the valley rim, capturing them one by one, cutting off the valley's vital trade routes, and slowly starving the population into submission. His aim was to bring the Malla kings to their knees – a goal he ultimately achieved with the Living Goddess's blessing.

Everyone in Nepal knows the story of how the Gorkha conqueror and his troops stole into Kathmandu at night during the festival of Indra Jatra while the population of the city was riotously drunk and Jaya Prakasha Malla was accompanying the Living Goddess on her procession in her temple chariot around the city streets. In the mayhem that followed, the Malla king was separated from the Kumari and forced to flee. The Kumari returned to Durbar Square in her chariot, took up her throne on the dais outside the Kumari Chen and, seamlessly, Prithvi Narayan Shah stepped up and knelt at her feet. In front of the astounded crowds the Living Goddess planted her *tika* on the forehead of the Gorkha conqueror.

From all we heard about this story and its enduring power in the community around Durbar Square it was clear that to Nepalis the fortunes of the Shah dynasty, sealed on that fateful night in 1768, depended on the reigning monarch's continued devotion to the Living Goddess. More than two centuries on, Prithvi Narayan Shah's descendant still came to the Kumari Chen every year, climbing the stairs to the Kumari's throne room behind the golden window, seeking her blessing, securing his rule over the kingdom. As teenagers we had hoped, in vain, to catch a glimpse of him. King Birendra Bir Bikram Shah, the only remaining Hindu king in the world, crowned in 1975, was, like his predecessors, considered to be a god – an avatar of Vishnu, the great preserver. Seeing him, we were told, would wash away any sins committed that day.

The old royal palace of Hanuman Dhoka threw its shadow over our little flat. Its presence was a brooding legacy of palace intrigues and royal coups. A tangled knot of medieval towers, dark passages, long low-ceilinged halls and hidden courtyards, it had been vacated by the royal family at the turn of the twentieth century when they moved to a modern mansion, the Narayanhiti Palace, where they still lived. But the influence of Hanuman

Dhoka remained. This was where the kings of Nepal came to be crowned and where the sword representing their power was kept. King Birendra was said to come at the dead of night, sometimes, to perform secret *pujas* at shrines in the palace's courtyards. And in moments of uncertainty or danger, his priests would send offerings to the Kumari Chen, or the king might come himself to supplicate the Living Goddess.

~

I found this idea, that the existence of the king of Nepal still depended on the performance of a child, compelling, and even more, the fact – not acknowledged in the guidebooks or other western accounts – that the little girl with the power to grant or withhold her blessing from the Hindu king was a Buddhist. The 'Hindus ONLY' sign by the door in the courtyard of the Kumari Chen was, in essence, misleading. Nepali Buddhists also come regularly to worship the Kumari. Her caretakers are Buddhist, and a royal Buddhist priest comes every morning to perform his worship at the Buddhist shrines in the Kumari Chen while the royal Hindu priest performs parallel pujas to the Kumari in her throne room.

The blending of Hinduism and Buddhism, and the religious tolerance it demonstrates, was, to me, one of the most beguiling aspects of Nepal. It had been fostered by an extraordinary coincidence of geography and climate. For millennia, this small, fertile basin in the steep southern ridges of the Himalayan foothills had been accessible only by footpaths winding through the mountains. Pilgrims and traders journeying to the sacred sites and lucrative markets of the fabled 'Valley of Nepal' had to brave high passes and swaying rope bridges over vertiginous chasms the mere sight of which caused one tenth-century lama travelling from Tibet to 'tremble more than quicksilver'.

On reaching the valley visitors were compelled to stay for months, waiting for the change in seasons. For nearly six months of the year, during the summer monsoon, the valley was cut off from the Indian plains to the south because of the swollen rivers and the malaria-ridden jungles of the lowland Terai; during the winter, the northern passes were closed by snow. This enforced mingling of travellers from different cultures created a society that was extraordinarily tolerant, open-minded and self-confident – one that promoted the valley as a repository of artistic and religious ideas, and an important destination for great teachers, artists and gurus of every persuasion.

Early on, Shiva had become the dominant Hindu deity of the valley, his temple by the burning *ghats* of Pashupati on the Bagmati – where the kings of Nepal were cremated – an important pilgrimage site, and most of the valley's first rulers were, ostensibly at least, Shaivas – followers of Shiva.

Buddhism had also made an early entrance, the Buddha himself having been born in Lumbini in what is now southern Nepal. The great Indian emperor Ashoka, or at least his daughter, was thought to have journeyed to the Kathmandu Valley in the fifth century BCE, founding some of the earliest Buddhist stupas in the subcontinent.

In the melting pot of the Kathmandu Valley these two strands of belief grew so entwined as to be profoundly confusing to outsiders. While Nepalis might describe themselves as Shivamargi (Hindus, or 'followers of the path of Shiva') or Buddhamargi (followers of the Buddhist path), in practice there is often little distinction. The two faiths borrow practices and ideas from each other, worship each other's deities, only with different names, and lend each other priests. The Living Goddess, worshipped by both Hindus and Buddhists, and served by both a Hindu and a Buddhist priest, seemed to me the ultimate expression of this unique blend of religious cooperation.

Nepal's remoteness not only created a nursery for religious ideas and practices, it also safeguarded it from the great empires flexing their muscles on its doorstep. There was no whiff of colonialism here, a feature that made Kathmandu all the more appealing in my eyes. The Muslim invasions that transformed the Indian subcontinent failed – apart from one singularly destructive raid in the fourteenth century – to make inroads this far. Similarly, for Chinese imperialist ambitions, Nepal, on the other side of the inhospitable plateau of Tibet, was an impossible goal. Even the British East India Company in the eighteenth century, headquartered 350 miles away in the Bay of Bengal, was forced, after several attempts, to accept the futility of taking over the prosperous little 'Kingdom of Nepaul'.

The valley remained true to its inherent nature, its culture both insular and traditional, yet also malleable and open-minded. Over the centuries it became the natural refuge for non-conformist spiritual practices and philosophies, especially those antithetical to the rising mainstream religions of brahmanical Hinduism, Islam and Christianity.

The valley threw a lifeline to Buddhism as, under pressure from Muslim conquest, it entered its death throes in India. Buddhist monks, scholars and tantric priests with artefacts and sacred texts secreted in their robes fled up the mountain paths to Nepal following the destruction of the great Buddhist monasteries and the scholastic university of Nalanda in the twelfth century. To Buddhists the valley became known as 'punya bhumi' – the sacred land.

The branch of Buddhism that ultimately prevailed in Nepal was Mahayana and it was to this school of Buddhism that the children chosen to be Living Goddesses belonged. To me, as a teenager, with only the vaguest notions of Buddhism, Mahayana was a revelation. Instead of the purist focus on a single Buddha, Nepali Buddhists worship a bewildering proliferation of gods and goddesses, *yakshas*, *yoginis* and flying *dakinis*. There are even additional historical Buddhas who, according to Mahayana, lived prior to the fourth-century BCE Buddha Shakyamuni, as well as Buddhas who are destined to come in the future, and five Transcendent Buddhas, or 'Jinas', residing in other dimensions.

Mahayana evolved around the beginning of the Common Era in a famous split from the Theravada doctrine of conservative monasticism propounded by Buddha's disciples. Unlike Theravada, established in countries like Sri Lanka, Cambodia and Thailand, Mahayana – the 'Great Way' – threw its doors open to everyone. Instead of focusing on personal salvation in isolated monasteries, relying on the charity of others, Mahayana Buddhists focus on a more altruistic goal – the liberation of all sentient beings – and choose to remain in the swim of life where they can help everyone. In Nepal, as in Tibet, Buddhists worship gods and goddesses as celestial '*bodhisattvas*' – meritorious beings destined to achieve enlightenment who have delayed their attainment of Buddhahood in order to assist others along the same path.

But it was not only Buddhism that flourished in the sanctuary of the valley. Boosted by the Himalayan practices of animism and spirit possession, cults of goddess worship and Shaktism (worship of the supreme feminine principle) found refuge here as the patriarchal religions engulfed the subcontinent. The Living Goddess is a reflection of these older influences, too, and her roots lie deep in the misty origins of the valley itself, in the story of Nepal's beginnings.

Chapter 2

The Jewel of Beginnings

In the morning of time, in the golden age of Satya Yuga, when the mountains and plains and forests of the world were newborn, there was a lake – the most beautiful lake the world would ever know. It sparkled like liquid gold. Into it poured the clearest streams from the glaciers of the surrounding Himalaya. Its surface mirrored the sky. Every day as the sun rose and set it blushed the colour of roseate coral. At midday it turned the thundering blue of lapis lazuli. And at night the stars set themselves in the surface like glittering diamonds. The lake was at one with the heavens, a vessel of wealth and tranquillity upon the earth.

There were many strange and beautiful spirits in the lake, and their watery domain was governed by the snake gods known as Nagas. Crowned with precious jewels in their heads, the Nagas guarded the fabulous riches of the lake. Foremost among the Nagas were King Karkotak and his beautiful queen. The lake became known as Nagahrada – Lake of the Nagas.

As the aeons passed, the lake also drew to its shores *siddhas*, accomplished sages, who would meditate upon the waters from the surrounding hilltops. The first such sage to arrive at the lake was Vipashvin, the first of the seven historical Buddhas – the first human being to attain enlightenment.

As Vipashvin sat high atop Nagarjun Mountain, with eyes half-closed, hands resting lightly on his thighs, contemplating the sacred nature of the water before him, a lotus seed miraculously appeared and hung suspended in the air before him. Softly, like a moth, Vipashvin spread his right hand so that the seed might drift down on to his palm.

Then in his wisdom, Vipashvin knew what he must do. He closed the seed in his fist and raised himself to his feet and circumambulated the lake three times; and he threw the lotus seed high into the air so that it spun in a rainbow arc out into the middle of the water where it landed with an almost imperceptible splash. He recited charms over it, and a wondrous prediction came to him, and he began to chant: 'When this lotus shall flower, the primordial Buddha, Swayambhu, the Self-Existent One, shall be revealed as a flame.' And in his mindfulness he also predicted that in a forthcoming era a great *bodhisattva* called Manjushri – 'He of Great Majesty' – would come from China and he would drain the water in the lake, thereby leaving a fertile valley fit for human habitation.

And so, over the years, the seed drifted down into the silt at the bottom of the lake and in the era of the second historical Buddha, Shikhin, it began to germinate. The lotus seed had taken root at the site of an eternal spring, source of the Goddess herself, hidden deep in the earth. It was the secret opening, the womb, from which all life began, a hidden source of the Goddess known as Guhyeshvari – 'Mistress of the Secret'.

Drawing thus upon the source of all things, the lotus sent its stem steadily upwards from the *pitha*, the seat, of Guhyeshvari through the murky depths to the clear waters above where, reaching the air and sunlight at last, it burst into a flower as large as the wheel of a chariot. The flower was wondrous to behold. It had ten thousand petals with diamonds sparkling on their upper sides, pearls shimmering beneath them, and rubies gleaming in their centres. The pollen of the flower was golden, the seed lobes were emerald, and the stamens, lapis lazuli. From the centre of the flower radiated a gigantic flame one cubit high and of such brilliance it transformed all those who saw it. The flame itself was the Adi Buddha 'Swayambhu' Jyotirupa – the Primordial Buddha Self-Originated Light-Form – and its light consisted of rays of five colours, white, blue, yellow, red and green, which were the essence of the five Transcendent Buddhas who personify the five knowledges of a fully enlightened being.

In time, the third Buddha, Vishvabhu, came with his disciples to pay homage to the sacred flame of Swayambhu in the great lake of serpents, and he stood on Mount Phulchok to take *darshan* of the primordial light, and offered his *puja* in the form of a hundred thousand flowers. And in the presence of his disciples he confirmed that the time had almost come when the great *bodhisattva*, sweet-voiced Manjushri, would come.

Indeed, at the very same time, in faraway China, on the five-peaked mountain of Wu-tai Shan, the *bodhisattva*, sweet-voiced Manjushri, entered into a deep meditation and became aware of the existence of the primordial Adi Buddha in the form of a flame on the other side of the Himalaya in the lake known as 'The Abode of Serpents'. So he took upon himself human form and left China to take *darshan* of this place, carrying in his left hand the book of wisdom and in his right a shining sword called Chandrahas (Moon Derider).

As soon as the *bodhisattva* came upon the great lake of serpents he circled it three times leaving soft indentations with his feet in the surface of the water. Then he made a circuit of the holy mountains around the lake. Taking each peak in one stride, his silken robes fluttering like prayer flags, he went first to Mount Nagarjun; and then to the peak of Mount Phulchok; and then he strode on to Mount Champadevi; and finally, alighting on the peak of Sengu which rose like an island in the middle of the lake, he paid homage to the sacred flame of Swayambhu.

And as Manjushri gazed upon the lake stretching in all directions around him, it occurred to him that the primordial flame could be venerated more easily by men if the lake was drained. So he decided

to expose the flame of Swayambhu and all the sacred locations
that were still underwater and entered into a deep meditation on
how best to do this. And when he had seen how he could do it, he
summoned all his strength and with a mighty roar raised his shining
sword above his head and brought it down upon Kotval Mountain,
cleaving it in two. Then he slashed further clefts at Chobar, Gokarna
and Aryaghat and the water began gushing out, crashing in silvery
cascades towards India.

The Nagas, great snake kings, realizing that their precious home
was being destroyed, came to Manjushri in despair. Manjushri told
them he wished them no harm and was sorry that, for the greater
good of men and all sentient beings, it had been necessary for him
to drain the lake, and he implored the Nagas not to leave the valley
but to take up residence in a special pond he would create for them
instead; and he assured them that here they would receive worship
from humankind henceforth and forever. For Manjushri knew that
the Nagas were very auspicious beings who knew the secrets of rain
and wealth and many other things that would be of great assistance
to the future inhabitants of this land.

The Nagas acquiesced and slithered into their new home in
Taudah pond. Here great Karkotak, king of the Nagas, constructed a
magnificent underwater *durbar*, and Karkotak's queen sat on a throne
studded with jewels, shaded with three umbrellas of white diamonds
one above the other. And though, in years to come, men tried to
drain this pond in order to find this *durbar* and steal its treasures,
none has ever succeeded. The pond of Taudah is where Karkotak
and his beautiful queen dwell to this day.

When, at last, the great lake had disappeared, Manjushri received
darshan of the Swayambhu Adi Buddha on the full moon of the
month of Karttika and for the first time the mysterious root-source
of the thousand-petalled lotus that had once lain at the bottom
of the lake became visible. The site was wondrous to behold.
The lotus seed, with its three corners deep inside the earth, had
lodged around a deep, dark opening in the shape of a triangle,

like the entrance of the female sex. The site reeked of liquor and foamed with the froth of flowers and incense. This was the *yoni* of Guhyeshvari, the Goddess's lower mouth, her sex, the essence of her being.

But now a whirlpool was beginning to rise at this spot and, fearing that it might once again fill the entire valley with water, Manjushri took in one hand a mighty diamond thunderbolt called a *vajra* and began to meditate deeply on what he had seen. He visualized the luminous form of the Goddess, seeing it in the form of water, visible everywhere, and as he achieved this visualization, he rejoiced and worshipped it with deepest reverence and thus restrained the upsurging torrent.

So pleased was the Goddess with Manjushri's devotion and his recognition of her hidden source that she gave *darshan* to him in her universal form. First, she revealed herself to him in peaceful aspect, as a young girl, sixteen years of age, with round breasts and firm thighs, naked but for her beauteous adornments, dancing with her face towards the north. On her head she bore a magnificent crown of the Five Buddhas; her earrings were the sun and the moon. She had three eyes, lovely as lotus petals; and she played entrancingly with a cleaver and a skull-cup in her hands. As she danced, her girdle of bone and the garland of human heads around her neck swung hypnotically to the rhythm of her body.

Then, as Manjushri gazed in wonderment, the apparition of the Goddess began to change. Flowers rained down from the sky, tremors shook the earth, and the Goddess transformed herself into her wrathful form. Her eyes became the sun and moon; her third eye, aeon-ending fire. Intoxicated with the five forbidden nectars and dressed in a tiger's pelt with garlands like lightning flashes, the Goddess began to dance. Blasts of heat and searing cold began to emanate from her body. Suddenly she had a thousand faces. Two thousand arms fanned out from her sides, each wielding a weapon or instrument of destruction more fearsome than the next. The constellations orbited in her hair; her earrings were wailing ghosts. As she danced, surrounded by a whirling chorus of skeleton devotees, waves of vibrations rippled through the universe. Fearlessly she trampled upon the mighty forms of the great gods Brahma, Vishnu and Shiva, beating them to her will with the pounding of her feet.

When, in the midst of this terrifying performance, the Goddess spoke, her voice bayed like the howling of a hundred jackals sending shivers through the viscera of Manjushri's being. Roaring like thunderclouds and gnashing her teeth, with her eyes bulging and her black tongue projecting horrifyingly from her mouth, the Goddess began to impart her secrets to Manjushri. And Manjushri observed her, as calmly as he could, opening his heart and receiving the awesome knowledge into his soul with perfect stillness.

After displaying her single-faced form followed by the thousand faces of her most terrifying aspects, the Goddess transformed herself into water and disappeared back inside her *pitha*. This was on the ninth day of the waning half of the month of Marga.

On the next day, the tenth of the lunar calendar, Manjushri prepared a suitable conduit for the Goddess's emissions. He covered the opening with a triangular stone slab. In the centre of the stone was a hole through which the water could safely issue forth.

Then Manjushri took his principal disciple, a great *yogin* called Shantikar Acharya, to a deep cave on Sengu hill and initiated him into the esoteric teachings of the Vairochana and Akshobya cycles and the Chakrasamvara Tantras, just as they had been revealed to him by the Goddess. And so Shantikar Acharya became the valley's first *vajra*-master, or Vajracharya priest. And in time, Shantikar Acharya passed on this knowledge to others who, in utmost secrecy and after rigorous training, also became Vajracharya masters, living among the people and using their powers to invoke the deities for the benefit of all sentient beings.

So now the lotus of Swayambhu was exposed on a hillock where all could come and worship it; and around the hillock, where once there had been water, lay a great valley of rich and fertile land. And soon the valley filled with Manjushri's disciples, and he designed a glorious city for them in the shape of his sword. He sited this city in a most auspicious place, at the confluence of the Bagmati and Vishnumati, rivers fed by the waters that issued from deep inside Guhyeshvari *pitha*.

He called the city Manju (sweet) Pattana (city) and enthroned one of his devotees, Dharmankara, as king. And he taught the people who inhabited the city the fundamentals of civilization and culture, and of farming and husbandry, and also the art of ritual including the Ten Rites of Passage, and devotion to the five Transcendent Buddhas, the Three Jewels and the Ten Perfections, as well as worship of the seven historical Buddhas, and all the attendant *bodhisattvas* and other gods, and the Astamatrika – the eight mother goddesses, protectoresses of the eight directions. And for those citizens whose *dharma* it was to live as monks or priests he created monasteries and temples.

He also taught the people of Manjupattana how to venerate the tree spirits in the mighty forests at the edge of the valley, so that they might cut down the trees with impunity; and he showed them how to carve the wood and give it new life. He taught them how to mould and bake the red clay that had once lain at the bottom of the lake so that even the humble house-brick would be blessed and become strong as iron. They learnt how to make roof tiles like the scales of a Naga, with dragon's heads at the roof corners, and to imprint the clay with flowing waves and mythical beasts for cornices in memory of this watery pre-existence; and in no time their craftsmanship was sought after across all the other kingdoms of the Himalaya, and far, far beyond.

For their own city, they built beautiful, many-tiered pagodas, with dancing deities carved on the roof struts and monasteries with latticed peacock windows, and Buddhas and *bodhisattvas* in elaborate wooden shields called *toranas* above the doors. Soon they were carving devotional plaques and friezes and reliefs and guardian lions from stone.

But most magnificent of all was the work they fashioned from gold and silver and bronze. For Manjushri taught the people the magical secrets of metallurgy, and from crucibles of molten fire they began to pour and cast images of the gods that were so beautiful they could move the heavens. And the work of these divinely inspired bronze- and gold-smiths would become much sought-after throughout the world.

After he had taught the inhabitants of Manjupattana all these wondrous things, Manjushri made ready to return to his abode on the five-peaked mountain of Wu-tai Shan in China. But before he left, he enshrined an aspect of himself in an image on the western peak of the hillock of Swayambhu from where he rains down countless blessings upon the inhabitants of the valley to this day.

So pleased were they with all this work of devotion established in the valley by sweet-voiced Manjushri that from time to time the gods and goddesses themselves would descend from their residences in the Abode of Snows to dwell among the people of Manjupattana and their kings, delighting in the earthly pleasures of the beautiful settlements there and vying for the attention of their illustrious devotees. And in time, Manjupattana came to be known as Kathmandu; the valley, Nepal; and its inhabitants, the Newars.

Chapter 3

The Newars

I left Kathmandu at the end of that summer in 1983 with regret, feeling as though something had slipped through my fingers. Back at home, life took over and the Living Goddess became a retreating memory, the questions about her receding to the back of my mind.

Fourteen years later, however, in 1997, an opportunity presented itself that catapulted the Kumari back into the forefront. A friend, recently married to a colonel in the British Gurkhas, had just moved out to Kathmandu and invited me to stay. She suggested coming in October, in time for Dasain, the biggest festival in the Nepali calendar. The traditional marker for the end of monsoon and the opening of the season for military campaigns, Dasain is celebrated with particular gusto by the Nepali army. It is also one of the most important festivals for the Living Goddess. It is the occasion on which a new Kumari – if one is called for – is installed. It is also the moment when, every year, the reigning Kumari is rumoured to be subjected to terrifying initiation rituals among severed buffalo heads in a courtyard in the old royal palace.

~

Laxminath Shrestha welcomed me into his house in an affluent suburb of Kathmandu and showed me to a bright, modern sitting room. At first I could see nothing about him to distinguish him from any other well-to-do Nepali. He made his living teaching Nepali to expats, including the friend I was staying with, and, in his smart blazer and buckled brown shoes, comfortably at home with foreigners, he clearly considered himself a man of the world. As we began to talk, though, something seemed to stir inside him. There was a sense that, away from the coffee table strewn with grammar textbooks, Laxminath's allegiances lay elsewhere, deep in the recesses of old Nepal.

Dasain is a festival of reunions and new beginnings, when the Nepali diaspora comes home from abroad and foreigners descend on the capital to witness the festival, and to Laxminath this was a natural time for me to be returning to Kathmandu. But he also assumed a stronger pull. In Laxminath's eyes, my standing in the Kumari's courtyard, seeing the Kumari fourteen years earlier, had ignited a connection with the Goddess. He referred to it as *darshan* – 'seeing' – a term loaded with meaning for both Hindus and Buddhists.

The notion of vision, of eye contact, as an opening to the divine is evident in every aspect of life in Kathmandu. There are eyes painted on the tailgates of trucks, on rickshaws and buses, on the wheels of bicycles, and on the great solid wooden wheels of the Living Goddess's golden chariot. These are watchful eyes, the oversight of protective deities saving passengers from accidents. Then there are eyes indicating sacred space – at the entrances to temples and monastic courtyards, and on either side of the narrow entrance to the old royal palace, where the monkey god Hanuman guards the gate, or *dhoka*. Inside Hanuman Dhoka itself, in Nasal Chowk, the palace's central courtyard, great wooden eyes with wooden eyelashes and eyebrows guard doors leading off into inner chambers.

For visitors to Nepal the most characteristic of all are the great sloping eyes on the *harmikas* of the Buddhist stupas at Swayambhu and Boudha – the eyes that are reproduced everywhere on tourist T-shirts and posters. Half-closed, as if in a meditative trance, these gigantic eyes gaze out across the valley through the veils of the beyond.

In sacred paintings – of the kind sold in artists' shops around Durbar Square and in the tourist enclave of Thamel – the eyes of deities are invariably huge. Some, like the Buddhist goddess Saptolochana, have eyes in the palms of their hands and feet. The god Indra, king of Heaven, has a thousand eyes over all his body. The intention is to draw the mind of the beholder into the paintings through visual contact, energetically connecting them with the deities themselves.

Nowhere is this notion of spiritual vision more powerful than in the third 'fire eye' located in the sacred spot in the centre of the forehead of some of the more ferocious deities. All-seeing, all-knowing, all-encompassing, the fire eye can either radiate bliss or reduce the object of its gaze to a heap of smouldering ashes. The Living Goddess herself has a fire eye, or *drishti* – a golden eye with a black pupil that she wears on special occasions like Indra Jatra or Dasain when she is at her most powerful. To have *darshan* of the Kumari when she is wearing her third eye is, Nepalis believe, to receive the most powerful connection with the Goddess.

But just catching a glimpse of the Living Goddess at her window on a normal, non-festival day, as tourists do, can have lasting repercussions, Laxminath said; it can open channels of communication with the deity even if you have no inkling of it at the time.

Laxminath swept aside the grammar books on the coffee table as his wife, Belayati, brought in Nepali tea and we began to talk about the days ahead. He had agreed to guide me through the climax of Dasain, and in particular the great ninth day, or Navami – a day of animal sacrifices. The reason I had solicited Laxminath's help for this was that he was, specifically, a Newar.

The significance of the Newars had eluded me on my last visit, as it often does first-time visitors to Kathmandu. This is partly because, physically at least, it is often difficult to distinguish Newars from other Nepalis. Some ethnic groups are more obvious – like the Thakalis, Tamangs and Sherpas from the hills; the Rais and Limbus from eastern Nepal; the Gurungs and Magars, Tibeto-Burmese peoples from the central midlands to the west; or the dark-skinned Tharus from the southerly Terai. Newars, on the other hand, embrace a range of different ethnic origins from both Mongoloid and Caucasian roots; and the wide spectrum of Newar castes are often characterized by different physical characteristics, with levels of education and prosperity varying enormously between them.

Newars, though, are central to the culture that developed over centuries in the Kathmandu Valley, and they are key to understanding the Living Goddess. The belief system to which the Kumari belongs is Newar – as is the Kumari herself.

For centuries Newars have been the majority in the Kathmandu Valley but the ratio has been declining steeply over the past three decades owing to burgeoning immigration. Now, less than 30 per cent of the total valley population of 2,600,000 are Newars, with around 650,000 Newars living elsewhere in the country.

It is at the cultural and historical levels that the most important distinctions exist between Newars and the other inhabitants of the valley. The difference is particularly significant between Newars and the Indo-Nepalese, or 'Parbatiya' – with whom Newars often feel a particular cultural, political and commercial rivalry.

Parbatiya is the collective name for Bahuns (the Brahmin priest caste) and Chettris (the Kshatriya warrior caste) – the ethnic group that makes up 30 per cent of Nepal's population. The Parbatiya are exclusively Hindu and associated with orthodox Hindu Brahmins and the military aristocracies of the Indian Rajputs. Preoccupied with military chivalry and Hindu concepts of purity, these warlike rajas had, by the sixteenth century, carved out for themselves numerous petty hill states around the Kathmandu Valley. Parbatiya itself means 'hill-people'. It was from one of these small Parbatiya hill states that the conqueror Prithvi Narayan Shah, the founder of the present dynasty of Nepali kings and the unifier of Nepal, had come.

Newars, on the other hand, are not natural warriors. Principally artisans, farmers and merchants by profession, Newars consider themselves the true custodians of what it is to be Nepali. They are the original inhabitants of the 'Valley of Nepal' – or believe themselves to be. They are thought to be descended from the Kirata, a Himalayan people referred to in great Indian epics like the *Mahabharata* and the sacred texts of the Puranas. Over time, waves of immigrants descending on the Kathmandu Valley had added to their genetic mix. The Newars had absorbed these new influences while strongly adhering to their own traditions.

Newars are bound together by a strong sense of community focused on the old city centres and towns in the valley. While most of the modern commercial areas of Kathmandu have been colonized by Indian and non-Newar traders, the original courtyards around Durbar Square are still principally inhabited by Newars, descendants of communities who have lived there for centuries. Newar daily life is defined by ritual and every day, somewhere in the valley, a Newar festival is going on, often several at once. They also observe elaborate life-cycle rituals for both sexes marking the important stages of life from birth to death, known as the Dasa Karma Vidhi (*Samskara* in Sanskrit), or Ten Rites of Passage.

Originally, it seems, Newars were predominantly Buddhist. But over time and with increasing Hindu influence in the valley, the balance shifted, and at some point, probably around the fourteenth century, Newars adopted the Hindu caste system. Now, half of all Newars claim to be practising Buddhists, and half are Hindu. Many Newars, however, especially those of the middle and lower castes, practise aspects of both religious paths. A popular joke, Laxminath said, is that a Newar is 60 per cent Hindu and 60 per cent Buddhist.

There have been moments in valley history of friction between

Buddhists and Hindus – flare-ups over land rights, money or precedence in some ritual performance – but these tended to be localized disputes of the kind that inevitably arise in close-knit communities. The sort of entrenched and radical opposition such as exists between Christianity, Judaism and Islam, or that came to exist between Hinduism and Islam in India, is anathema to the Newar way of thinking. Coexistence and assimilation have always been the Newar ethos, and harmony and balance, empathy and compassion remain goals every good Newar should strive for.

When the Malla kings arrived in the valley they were soon seduced by the culture of the Newars and adopted, or imitated, many of their rituals and practices. They employed Newar architects to build palaces and temples, and, fuelled by their intense rivalry with each other, commissioned works of art from Newar sculptors, painters, carpenters and bronze-casters. Under the influence of the Newars, the Hindu Mallas became far less orthodox in their outlook, subscribing to their melange of localized Buddhist and Hindu practices – some kings venturing so far down the Buddhist path, wearing Buddhist insignia and ornaments, and reading Buddhist texts, that outsiders often mistakenly considered them to be Buddhist.

The turning point came in the eighteenth century when the Kathmandu Valley was conquered by Prithvi Narayan Shah, the Parbatiya king of Gorkha. The Gorkha conquest of the valley tipped the scales in favour of brahmanical Hinduism as the religion of authority in Nepal. The trend towards what Newars considered the 'Indianization' of the valley had begun.

Nowhere is this process of cultural tension more clearly felt than in the battle for language. Newari – a Tibeto-Burman language – had originally been the language of the valley, and was adopted by the Malla kings. It is known as *Nepal bhasha* – 'the language of Nepal'. Parbatiya, on the other hand, speak Nepali – formerly known as Gorkhali – which is Indo-Aryan in origin and closely related to Sanskrit and its offshoot Hindi. Following Prithvi Narayan Shah's conquest Nepali became the favoured language of government and Newari began to be sidelined. In the 1920s Nepali became the official state language and today few foreigners are aware of another language in the valley, let alone that it was once the most widely spoken.

Though he was a Nepali teacher by profession, Laxminath's first language was Newari. It was a matter of enormous cultural pride to him, as it is to all Newars. Under Rana rule, from the mid-nineteenth to mid-twentieth century, Newars had been outlawed from writing or publishing in their own language. The movement to reinstate Newari on an equal footing with Nepali – to have it taught in schools and spoken on radio and TV – has grown increasingly vociferous in recent years.

'Some of the most senior Newar citizens speak only Newari,' said Laxminath. 'But most Newars speak Newari and Nepali as well. We have to, from the moment we go to school. But at home we always prefer to speak Newari. As children it is the first language we hear. It is a playful language, very expressive, but also polite and considerate.' Few Parbatiya, on the other hand, can speak Newari – a fact that suggests a one-way turnstile of cultural understanding.

A further distinction, and one that had caused me particular headaches in preparation for this trip, are the two calendrical systems. There is the date according to the solar calendar of the Parbatiya – which has become the secular calendar of commerce and government. Known as Vikram Samvat, its starting point is 57 BCE and it is the system promoted by the Shah kings.

And then there is the date according to the Newars – Nepal Samvat – which started in 879 CE and was the calendar that had been favoured by the Malla kings. It is based on the phases of the moon, each month having two halves: the dark fortnight with the waning moon leading up to the new moon day and the bright fortnight with the waxing moon leading up to the full moon day. Nepal Samvat is regarded as the sacred calendar and is still used to chart all the religious and ceremonial events in Nepal.

Several Nepali newspapers carry three dates at the top of their pages – Vikram Samvat, Nepal Samvat and the Gregorian date. All three calendars have different numbers of months, all with different names, and different starting points for the year. While the western calendar begins in January, the New Year for Vikram Samvat is in April, and for Nepal Samvat, New Year is in November.

This means that planning for a particular event in advance, especially if it involves international flights revolving around a religious festival, as my trip did, is an exercise requiring several calendars, a calculator and the inside track from an astrologer.

Though Newars are now in the minority their influence in the corridors of power and business nevertheless remains considerable. They share this position with the Bahuns and Chettris – the elite, wealthy Parbatiya castes into whose hands posts in the government and the army, in particular, naturally fall.

Laxminath, himself, was a Shrestha – the largest and most influential of the Newar castes, and the best educated. Shresthas tend to be civil servants, businessmen and professionals. They are the most westernized of the Newar castes and the one most closely influenced by the Parbatiya. Yet, though they are also ostensibly Hindu, the Shresthas adhere to a far less orthodox, Newar brand of Hinduism. Traditionally their caste includes the astrologers and Karmacharyas – Shaivite tantric priests – for whom worship of the Goddess, over the traditional Hindu gods Brahma, Vishnu and Shiva, is the primary focus.

'In Nepal we honour the Devi. The Goddess is regarded above all others,' said Laxminath. 'We believe it is the Goddess's *shakti* – her creative energy – that brings everything into being, makes it live. Without *shakti* there is nothing. That is why we worship the Kumari. She is *shakti* in human form.'

Unlike male gods – who are generally conceived as having separate identities and specific attributes – the Goddess, he explained, is fluid and all-encompassing. Different goddesses are regarded as emanations of the same Universal Devi, a Mother Goddess who manifests herself in innumerable ways and who can transform from one idol to another – from wrathful to benign and back again – in the blink of an eye. The Living Goddess is one such manifestation, and a particularly powerful one since she materializes in human form. Worshipping the Kumari is widely considered to bring the most immediate results.

Laxminath had taken offerings to the Kumari on several occasions, but it was usually his wife or mother-in-law who went when a member of the family was sick or having problems getting a promotion at work. The Kumari is renowned as a 'remover of obstacles'.

'We worship the Kumari on a simple level,' he said. 'I have seen only the public *puja* room on the second floor. The audience room at the front of the Kumari Chen with the golden throne and the golden window overlooking Durbar Square is where the king comes to worship her. This is where powerful *pujas* take place. But the deeper practice of Kumari worship is kept secret from everyone, even ordinary Newars.'

The rituals investing the Goddess inside the living child, and keeping her there, can be witnessed by no one other than the Kumari priests and the caretakers themselves. The priests, Laxminath said, belong to the highest Newar caste and receive secret initiation and empowerments.

The Newar caste system is unusual in the fact that it is twin-headed. There are two competing priestly or religious castes at the top of the tree – the Rajopadhaya Brahmans and the Karmacharyas, custodians of Hinduism, on the one side; and the Vajracharyas and Shakyas, who are the guardians of Newar Buddhism, on the other. The administration of the Kumari tradition rests exclusively in the hands of these high Newar priestly castes. Daily *pujas* are performed by two royal priests – a Vajracharya, from the Buddhist side, and a high-caste Karmacharya on the Hindu side. All practices of Kumari worship conducted by the priests are intensely secret. Laxminath had no idea what went on in them. Though esoteric practices are conducted by the Newar priestly castes in most of Kathmandu's temples and shrines, nowhere are these performances more closely guarded than at the Kumari Chen.

'The Kumari caretakers and priests are wary of outsiders,' Laxminath said. 'They do not like speaking to anyone. They are cautious because they believe they are protecting someone very important and very powerful. If harm comes to the Living Goddess, or if they fail to perform the *pujas* properly, then there could be disaster for the king, for Kathmandu, for the whole country.'

The festival of Dasain is crucial. Ostensibly a Hindu festival re-enacting the victory of the Hindu warrior Goddess Durga over the buffalo demon Mahisasura, Dasain – or Dussehra, as it is known in India – is, typically, in Nepal, embraced by both Hindus and Buddhists. Every performance conducted during the festival, Laxminath explained, has to be followed to the letter if the rituals of empowerment and protection are to succeed.

Over the days since my arrival the spirit of Durga had been slowly, inexorably, taking possession of Kathmandu. On Ghatasthapana – the first day of Dasain – a sacred *kalash*, or water vessel, made out of clay had been placed in temples throughout the valley and in the prayer room of every home. The clay pots had been sown with barley seeds and the seeds invoked with the spirit of the Goddess. Every morning since, traditional Nepalis – including Laxminath and his family – had worshipped the *kalash* in their prayer room, sprinkling it with drops of pure water and keeping it shielded from the light. As the barley shoots grow, the physical presence of Durga intensifies. On the tenth day of Dasain, the shoots would be five or six inches tall and the sacred yellow *jamara* would be cut, distributed as Durga's blessing, to be worn in the hair or tucked behind the ears as decoration.

'To understand the Kumari, you need to understand the story of Durga, the Supreme Goddess – how she came into being,' said Laxminath. 'To us, these are not merely myths and legends – these are influences that live with us, that come into being over and again. This is what Dasain is about.'

In Nepal, Laxminath suggested, history as westerners understood
it – essentially the surface notions of cause and effect – is subservient
to the deeper workings of supremely powerful influences. The gods
and goddesses, the planets, the laws of karma are omnipresent agents
of action affecting daily happenings and influencing decisions. In
the same way, the myths and stories these deities generated are
wellsprings of interaction and inspiration in daily life. Newars access
these influences through dreams and visions. The subconscious,
encouraged by practices of ritual and meditation, plays a dynamic
role in giving these influences expression.

These notions, challenging though they might be to my own
perceptions, are, Laxminath insisted, fundamental to understanding
the enigma of the little girl who had once been my next-door
neighbour.

'This is an important time for the Kumari, and for the country,'
Laxminath concluded. 'What happens now will affect us for the rest
of the year. We will see on Navami. At Dasain the Living Goddess
takes on her most powerful form. She becomes the Goddess Durga
herself.'

Chapter 4

Supreme Goddess

In the stillness of time, before end or beginning, Adi Shakti Maha Maya, Supreme Power Great Illusion, created existence.

As she thus felt moved to create, Adi Shakti Maha Maya took her true form, becoming Parama Prakriti, the Goddess, Supreme Force of Creation, and there was the quality of sound alone. It began as a single resounding syllable, OM, a deep vibration of thought.

As the sound rushed through the great sky, wind was created for the first time – so now there were two qualities, sound and touch. And with touch came form, and with form, a great brightness that the Supreme Goddess formed into the sun. After these four qualities of sound, touch, form and brightness, came water. On this expanse of water, known as Jalamaya, *sattva, rajas* and *tamas*, the three qualities of intelligence, emotion and darkness, came into being. And these qualities the Supreme Goddess formed into three gods, Brahma, Vishnu and Shiva, and to each of these forms she assigned duties.

To Brahma she gave the job of creation, giving him the five elements of sky, wind, light, water and earth with which to create. Then she addressed Vishnu. 'At the time that the world is being created by Brahma,' she warned him, 'many demons will also be created and cause much oppression. True religion will be lost. *Sadhus* and good people will be afflicted with terrible pain and suffering, sin

will increase, and there will be a heavy burden upon the world. At
this time you must take various avatars in order to kill these demons,
and to restore true religion and protect *sadhus* and all good people.'
So saying she made Vishnu the Sustainer.

Then, turning to Shiva, she said, 'I will give you the job of
Destroyer.' But Shiva replied, 'O Ishvari, I don't like that kind of
work! I don't want to destroy whatever Brahma creates. All the blame
of killing will be given to me!' But the Supreme Goddess answered,
'O Maheshvara, destruction is but another force for creation. But
if you are unwilling to be known for such work then first create
Yamaraja and Kala and to these two gods give the burden of death.
Then create all kinds of sickness such as phlegm, wind, bile and
fever – and then no blame for killing will befall you.' And so Shiva
was reassured.

Shining with the brightness of a thousand suns, the Supreme
Goddess blessed the three gods and they bowed before her and sang
in her honour. Then, placing the three gods in a flowery chariot,
the Supreme Goddess bid them farewell and sent them speeding
on their way.

When the chariot came to rest Brahma began his wondrous job
of creation. He created eight mountain ranges including the Kailash
and the Himalaya and sowed them with trees, shrubs, grasses and all
kinds of flowering plants. Then he created the seven world planes
of existence; the seven upper realms, including heaven; the seven
lower realms of the underworld; and between them, in the middle
realms, he created Martyaloka, the realm of mortals.

Then Brahma created the eight directions, with a great city
in each; and above, he created a luminary circle of stars, shaped
like a dolphin, called Sishumara, and heaven – Swargaloka – and
the multitude of stars. He made a place for Shiva to live and a
place for Vishnu, and a place where he himself might live. And
he also made places for the *yakshas*, *gandharvas*, *kinnaras* and all
the other gods to live. And he created tens of millions of other
universes, or Brahma eggs; and within this world mandala he

created gods, people and all creatures and jungle dwellers, moving and unmoving.

In order to protect and sustain the lives of all these creatures, and in order to provide food for them all, Brahma created all kinds of medicines and edibles, greens, fruits and roots, along with various other edible things and all kinds of flowers. Thus he created all living things born from the earth itself.

From Brahma's right foot a great hero named Daksha Prajapati, brilliant as the sun, was born, and from Brahma's left foot a young woman named Virani, like a candescent moon, and these two were made husband and wife and had thirteen daughters who, in turn, gave birth to Indra and the 330 million gods, and all the *danavas* and *rishis*, the Nagas, *apsaras*, the *hahas* and the *huhus*, and all the *gandharvas*, winged beings, two-legged beings, human beings, lions, elephants and other forest dwellers, and all kinds of fish and aquatic life.

Then the 330 million gods went to the mountains of the Himalaya to perform austerities and Shiva, happy to see this, granted them boons. He made Indra guardian of the east, king of the gods and lord of heaven; he made Agni, god of fire, guardian of the south-east and protector of all beings; Yamaraja he made guardian of the south, to make trouble for all sinners; Nirrti, he made guardian of the south-west and king of the *rakshasas*; Varuna, guardian of the west and king of the Nagas; Vayu, guardian of the north-west and breath of all living beings; Kubera, guardian of the north and lord of wealth; and Vishvakarma, guardian of the north-east, lord of all craftsmen.

In this manner all the gods were granted boons, crowned rulers in the localities assigned to them; and each was given his own rightful place and his own responsibility.

But then it came to pass, just as Adi Shakti Maha Maya had predicted, that the world was disturbed by the emergence of demons. These *asuras* grew in strength and number, destroying everything in their path.

Vainly the gods attempted to vanquish these beings but, as fast as the gods destroyed them, more demons sprang up in their place. War raged between the gods and *asuras*, fierce and relentless, for a hundred years until the gods began to weaken and the Lord of the Asuras – the evil demon Mahisasura – overcame Indra, the Lord of Heaven himself, banishing him and the other *devas* from Amaravati, their Abode of Bliss.

Seeing the heavenly gods' humiliation, Shiva, Vishnu and Brahma's rage began to mount and a great light issued from their bodies and flames projected from their mouths. Looking on, the other gods grew angry, too, contributing to the blaze. And as the light intensified it combined into a fiery cloud that swirled up into the atmosphere, its brilliance pervading the Three Worlds. From this great fire took shape a female form, a dazzling numen dancing to the beat of time – a Goddess, mightier than the forces of all the gods combined, beautiful and awful to behold.

The splendour of Shiva formed her face, her tresses were the splendour of Yama, her arms the splendour of Vishnu. Her two breasts were born from the splendour of the moon; her waist from the splendour of Indra; her legs and thighs from the splendour of Varuna; and her hips from that of the earth. Her feet were formed from the splendour of Brahma and her toes from that of the sun; the fingers of her hand from the splendour of Vasus and her nose from that of Kubera. Her teeth were formed from Prajapati's splendour, the lord of all beings; and the triad of her eyes was the splendour of fire. Her eyebrows were the splendour of the two twilights, her ears that of the wind.

As her body blazed golden with the splendour of all the gods, piercing light radiated from her three eyes and all the immortals who were oppressed by Mahisasura found themselves filled with inexpressible joy and they fell before her, presenting her with offerings. Shiva drew forth a trident from his own trident; Vishnu, a discus from his own discus; Yama, a staff from his own staff of death. Indra gave her a thunderbolt, and his elephant Airavata gave her a bell. Varuna, the lord of waters, gave her a noose; Agni, a spear; Vayu, a bow; Kala, a sword; and Vishvakarma, a most brilliant axe and impenetrable armour. Mountainous Himalaya gave her a lion to ride upon; and Surya, the sun, his own rays that poured forth like arrows from every pore of her skin. Brahma gave her a rosary and a *kalash*; the milk-ocean gave her a pure necklace and undecaying garments, shining anklets and armlets, beautiful rings and a divine crest jewel; and the ocean presented her with garlands of unfading lotuses. The lord of wealth, Kubera, gave her a drinking cup, eternally filled with wine; and Sesa, the lord of all serpents, who supports this earth, gave her a serpent necklace bedecked with the finest jewels.

When all the gods had honoured her, showering her with their gifts, the Goddess gave out a giant roar that filled the sky and rocked the mountains. And the gods, delighted, cried 'Victory!', calling the Goddess 'Mahakali', Great Goddess of All Time, and 'Durga', which means Beyond Reach.

Taking up her weapons in her thousand arms and standing fearlessly on her lion, Durga flew into battle. The world shook and trembled beneath her. And the demon Mahisasura, hearing her mighty roar, cried out in anger and rushed towards her, surrounded by innumerable *asuras*.

When he saw Durga – the earth bending beneath her lion leaps, her diadem scraping the sky, the netherworlds trembling with the twang of her bowstring – Mahisasura hurled all his armies with their horses, elephants and chariots against her.

The *asuras* attacked her with swords, axes and halberds. Some fired arrows or threw spears; some swung clubs and iron maces; yet others hurled spears and nooses. But the *Devi*, as if in play, fell upon the *asuras*, killing hundreds with ease by her trident, club and showers of spears. Some were stupefied by the sound of her bell; others she dragged to the ground with her noose. Some were split into two by the sharp slashes of her sword; others, smashed by the blows of her mace. Some, hammered by her club, vomited blood.

Her lion, too, roaring and tossing its mane, stalked among the *asuras*, trampling them to death.

As Durga fought, her sighs breathed life into battalions of goddesses who leapt to her aid. As swiftly as fire consumes tinder, the battalions of goddesses laid waste to the armies of *asuras*, falling upon them with their deadly weapons, cutting off arms, breaking necks, ripping out entrails, severing heads.

Soon the battleground was choked with bodies and broken chariots, the blood from the *asuras*, elephants and horses flowing between them like rivers. And watching this, Indra and the other gods, restored to heaven, joyfully showered down flowers upon the scene.

But the battle for the earth was far from won. Mahisasura assumed the form of a water buffalo, a terrifying guise in which he focused all the forces of darkness. Bellowing and snorting, he charged the troops of the Goddess, trampling battalions of *devis* beneath his thundering hooves, goring and tossing them with his horns.

The earth began to crumble under his hooves and, lashed by his tail, the ocean ran everywhere in flood tide. Clouds were shredded by his swaying horns, and mountains, cast up by the blast of his breath, collapsed in fragments.

The Goddess then withdrew to a place where she summoned up all the powers from the origins of her being. For nine days she sat upon the tip of a needle. In the first three days she meditated as Mahakali, drawing upon the powers of *tamas*, the nature of darkness. For the next three days she meditated as Mahalaxmi, drawing upon the powers of *rajas*, the nature of passion. And for the final three days she meditated as Mahasaraswati, drawing upon the powers of *sattva*, the nature of goodness.

On the ninth day, the great Goddess Durga took up a skull-cup and drank from the nectars it contained. As she drank she grew steadily more intoxicated with her own strength, and she began to laugh a terrible laugh, and her eyes and face grew blood-red. And Mahisasura, eager to fight, roared back.

Then, flying from the tip of the needle, swelling to a size that shrank mountains, Durga bore down upon the buffalo-demon and with one mighty swipe of her cleaver severed the head from the buffalo-demon's body. The spirit of the demon fled out of the gushing neck of the beast, howling with anguish, never to be seen again.

So the world was relieved of the presence of Mahisasura and the vile impeding armies of *asuras*; and Shiva, Vishnu and Brahma, and all the other gods, overbrimming with joy, bowed before the Goddess and worshipped her.

Chapter 5

The Glorious Ninth

Walking through Durbar Square in the half-light of dawn was eerily disembodying. The pagoda temples floated through the mist like tall ships in a sea fog; hand-bells awakening the gods thudded in blind directions.

Kot Square, the courtyard of the Old Royal Armoury and venue for the Royal Nepal Army's Dasain celebrations, was a short distance from Hanuman Dhoka, beyond Mahendreshvar Temple. The small 'Visitors' Balcony' up a narrow flight of steps was already, at 6 a.m., packed with photographers. Hari Bahadur Limbu deftly manoeuvred me into a position with full view of the parade ground.

Hari had served in the 10th Gurkha regiment in the British army, graduating to the rank of Captain. Retired now and running a trekking outfit in the eastern foothills, he was still every bit the soldier, his ramrod back and square shoulders straight off the parade ground; the polished brogues, tweed jacket and cap giving him the air of an English country squire. The military sacrifice at Kot kicked off the celebrations of Navami, the climax of Dasain, and Hari had offered to lead me through the official proceedings before Laxminath took me on to other sites in the city to show me the Newar perspective.

'In India they don't perform sacrifice like this any more,' said Hari, peering over my shoulder on tiptoe. 'People are becoming very "PC". They can't stomach the sight of blood. They don't like to look death in the face. They have forgotten the proper worship of Durga.'

Dotted around the square beneath us were clusters of regimental colours and beside them, sacrificial posts. Clay pots, like the ones I had seen at Laxminath's house containing shoots of yellow-green barley, nestled at the base of the flags. Now tall and sword-like, the shoots bore witness to the past nine days as, slowly and deeply, Kathmandu had become possessed with the spirit of Durga.

Today, Maha Navami – the Glorious Ninth – marked the final day of Durga's great battle against the buffalo-demon Mahisasura. There would be sacrifices all over Nepal to mark the Goddess's victory and the restoration of the world. One hundred and eight goats and one hundred and eight buffaloes – an auspicious number – were gathered outside the parade ground awaiting their fate. All the animals were male and entirely black, like Mahisasura himself.

Similar sacrifices would be taking place today in army barracks across Nepal. In Pokhara, at a parallel ceremony performed by the British Gurkhas, a buffalo would be sacrificed for every one of the eight or more regiments serving overseas. To all Nepali soldiers, the mass sacrifice at Dasain is critical. They believe their lives depend on it. Proper worship of the Goddess during this, her moment of supreme power, secures her blessing on the army for the coming year.

The ritual release of blood on the soldiers' weapons guarantees the efficiency of knives and bayonets, *khukuris* and *khoras*; guides the aim of guns and artillery; protects soldiers from accidents and ill judgement, and from defeat or death on the battlefield. Any slip-up in the ritual process can have disastrous consequences. A soldier failing to decapitate an animal in one fell swoop in the time-honoured Gorkhali way is a particularly bad omen. The previous year, according to Hari, a British Gurkha who had failed to kill his buffalo cleanly at Dasain had died a few months later when his platoon was ambushed in the jungles of Kalimantan in Borneo.

Kot Square itself is an appropriate place for the country's largest ritual sacrifice. In 1846 there had been a famous massacre here, a bloodbath that had wiped out fifty-five members of the Nepali nobility and established the autocratic regime of the Ranas, a second 'royal family' in the kingdom that seized control from the Shah kings and kept them virtually captive in their palace for over a century.

The sun had shredded away the mist by the time the military band struck up and officers in full dress uniform marched into the arena with their troops. A current of excitement ran through the spectators as the king of Nepal made his appearance on the stand. His Majesty King Birendra Bir Bikram Shah Dev, decked with medals and ribbons, took the salute standing stiffly to attention beside his son Crown Prince Dipendra and a cluster of dignitaries.

In his trademark shades, worn even at this unearthly hour, he was unmistakable though this was the first time I had seen him in the flesh. His photograph, and that of the queen, hung in pride of place behind every office desk and hotel reception in Nepal, garlanded with fresh flowers every day. With his tight-lipped smile and neat, arching moustache, he looked every bit the monarch, serenely self-conscious, stiffly unresponsive to all the gazes riveted upon him.

It was impossible not to be struck by a sense of living history. Here was the world's only Hindu king; tenth in the line of Shah kings; direct descendant of the conqueror Prithvi Narayan Shah; and, in the eyes of the majority of his subjects, an incarnation of the great god Vishnu. His grandfather, King Tribhuvan, had seized back the throne from the Ranas in the 1950s in a dramatic coup involving a daring escape to Delhi in a Dakota. It was Tribhuvan who had embarked on the modernization of Nepal; his grandson King Birendra who had, after a democratic uprising forty years later, followed it through.

The process towards democracy had been a turbulent one,

however, and there had been political unrest in the country for decades. Strict censorship had been in force throughout the 1960s, '70s, and the '80s, when I had been living on Durbar Square, and the arrest and torture of political activists had been common practice as the Democratic Movement, spearheaded by the Nepali Congress party, pushed for change.

Despite King Tribhuvan's intentions of creating a modern, democratic state after seizing back power from the Ranas in 1951, Nepal had slid back into the old ways. It had returned to a feudal, village-council-operated system of government – the *panchayat* system – with the king in overall control. In 1979, riots led by democratic hopefuls had broken out in the capital and King Birendra had been forced to agree to a referendum whereby the country could decide between the old tradition of *panchayat* and a more democratic form of government involving elected parties. The result had been 55 per cent to 45 per cent in favour of retaining the *panchayat* system.

The hopes of the reformers had been bitterly frustrated. To many, particularly those among the foreign-educated, aspiring middle classes in the Kathmandu Valley, the disappointing outcome of the referendum was yet further evidence of the corruption entrenched in the *panchayat* system.

The simmering discontent had erupted again in 1989, as revolutions ignited across the world. The year that sparked the fall of the Berlin Wall and bloodshed in Tiananmen Square saw similar scenes in Kathmandu. Tens of thousands took to the streets and hundreds were shot. Eventually, though, the persistence of the protesters was vindicated. In April 1990 King Birendra announced he was lifting the ban on political parties and conceded his willingness to accept the role of constitutional monarch. In May 1991, the year in which the Soviet Union collapsed, Nepal held its first general elections.

This milestone in Nepal's political evolution had been applauded in India and the West but the situation in the country remained far from rosy. Nepal's conversion to democracy had not been anywhere near a complete process. Since 1991, governments in Nepal had come and gone with unsettling frequency, there had been numerous unstable coalitions, and opportunism and corruption were rife.

The poor, isolated in the remote countryside, remained dislocated from the seat of power in the Kathmandu Valley. Promises of water, electricity, health centres and schools in remote areas remained unfulfilled despite massive injections of funding from international aid agencies. At one point Nepal was receiving more charitable contributions per capita than any other nation in the world. Most of it failed to reach its intended destination. Frustration began mounting in villages in the distant hills and down in the Terai, providing fertile ground for rebellion.

Eighteen months before my visit, on 13 February 1996, the Maoist branch of the Communist Party of Nepal had declared a 'People's War'. The insurgency was rooted in the impoverished regions in the far west and south of the country – far enough away to seem, as yet, unreal to those living in the bubble of the Kathmandu Valley. To the affluent middle classes of Kathmandu the homegrown revolutionaries presented no more of a threat than the remote but ever-present possibility of an earthquake. Only at the airport – where the Nepali army, taking no chances, had posted sandbag sentry posts along the runway – was there any outward sign that the country was now, effectively, at war.

Despite his initial reluctance, Birendra's surrender of power had done much to restore his reputation in the eyes of the people. To the majority of his subjects the king had accepted his reduced authority with dignity. Now, even some of those who had been ardent supporters of 'demo-crazy' – as it had come to be known – were beginning to wonder if they had made a grave mistake: whether continuing under a benign dictatorship, as in the neighbouring kingdom of Bhutan, might not, after all, have been the wiser option. At very least, King Birendra's avuncular presence was now regarded by many in the valley as a vital force for stability in an increasingly unpredictable and dangerous world.

There were rumours, Hari said, that at home – in the modern royal palace – the formidable Queen Aishwarya held sway, and that the Crown Prince was a bit of a tearaway, a playboy with a passion for women and guns. But Dipendra was young. In time his father would see him right. An appropriate Nepali wife with the proper royal connections and auspicious horoscope would be found for the future king of Nepal and he would settle down. Until then the spirit of the nation, at least, was safe in his father's hands.

~

Across the parade ground guns cracked in unison. The first water-buffalo was led out to one of the wooden posts. A priest in white stepped forward to whisper a *mantra* into the buffalo's ear. He sprinkled its brow with water and the buffalo tossed its head and twitched its ears. With a few more sprinklings, it shook itself briefly down the length of its back.

'That's a good sign,' whispered Hari, 'it shows the spirit of Durga has entered its body.'

It is crucial, he explained, that every animal gives its consent by shaking in this way. The animal has to be seen to go willingly to its death, to volunteer its life for the greater good, accepting its part in honouring the great Goddess. As a reward for its selflessness Durga blesses the animal with a better incarnation in its life to come; it may even return to this world as a human being. If the animal does not consent, then it is simply led away, reprieved. But this rarely happens.

'We have ways to encourage the animals to shake,' said Hari grinning, 'if they're a bit slow we flick some cold water on their testicles – that will usually do the trick.'

The ritual blessings for this buffalo were over swiftly. Soldiers stepped forward, one to rope its head to the post, another holding it firmly by the tail, carefully aligning it so it faced east, towards the rising sun, the auspicious direction of rebirth. A third soldier took his stance, feet apart, knees bent, and, raising his sickle-shaped *khora* with both hands above his head, swiped it down with a mighty blow straight through the animal's neck. On the ground a block of wood cushioned in straw safely received the slicing blade of the *khora* as the severed head rolled to one side, ears still twitching.

At the instant the knife made contact with flesh a volley of gunshots burst into the air. Blood ejaculated from the animal's trunk in long, hot jets, splattering the surrounding offerings of rice and flowers, the sacred *kalash* and regimental flags and the soldier's pristine sports kit.

With barely a pause the next animals were led forward and one by one they were blessed, shook themselves and went to their death. To the triumphant blasts of a military band the headless bodies were dragged at a run by one leg, drawing protective circles in blood around the standards, before being hauled off the parade ground to be butchered for a huge feast at army headquarters the following day. Soon the sand of Kot was stained deep red. The severed heads accumulated at the foot of the flags, nuzzling together in a cluster of toothy grimaces.

Amazingly, the waiting animals seemed barely affected by the whole performance. Despite the smell of blood and rapid-fire decapitations, the blaring brass band and the intermittent volleys of rifles, they behaved almost as if nothing was happening. They chewed nonchalantly on offerings of grain and grass, calmly twitching away flies while their fellows met their end. When it was the goats' turn, soldiers carried them forward in their arms and then squatted on their haunches behind them, holding them still with steadying scratches. At the end of the sacrifice there would be a massive feast for the soldiers, and every officer would receive a generous portion of meat for his family.

For the Nepali army, just as for the British Gurkhas, there is an added bonus to this annual sacrifice. Killing animals provides invaluable military training.

'It is important for a soldier not to be afraid of blood,' said Hari. 'You need to know how to take a life with confidence and precision. Often in battle there is no second chance.'

Thanks to their celebrations at Dasain, Nepali soldiers enter battle already well accustomed to the sight of blood and guts, to the feel of steel on sinew and bone; they know what it is to extinguish a life, and the force it requires. Every one of them has overcome a living being larger and stronger than themselves. This is a long way from bayoneting hay bags. The lethal reputation of the Gurkha warrior begins here.

'It's dishonourable for a Gurkha to draw his blade from its sheath without drawing blood,' added Hari. 'If you ask to see a Gurkha's *khukuri*, he will have to cut himself, or take the head off the nearest chicken.'

Every weapon honoured with blood on the day of Navami is believed to be charged with the *shakti* of Durga. Unsheathing a *khukuri* is like igniting a flame – not something one does without due respect or intent. When Gorkhas storm into battle, screaming their bloodcurdling battle cry 'Jai Durge!' – 'Victory, Durga!' – they do so with the conviction that the Goddess's energy is surging through them.

After the fanfare of military theatre and the nationalistic trumpeting of king and country at Kot, permission was given for sacrifices across the country to begin. Laxminath was waiting for me impatiently by the gates of New Road. I found myself suddenly shifting perspective, slipping from orchestrated military efficiency and regal pageant into the swirling currents of indigenous valley tradition.

'In Newari, the day of Maha Navami is also called "Syako Tyako",' Laxminath shouted above the tumult as we hurried towards Bhadrakali Temple, an island in the middle of a traffic intersection on the other side of Tundhikhel parade ground. 'It means "the more you kill, the more you gain".'

The grass parade ground that had, for the last week, been heaving with livestock was now an empty expanse of droppings and litter. The animals had all been led off and were awaiting dispatch at numerous Goddess shrines in the city.

The Newar celebration of Dasain is no less bloodthirsty than the performance at Kot but its intentions are different. Here, Durga's victory is taken at a more metaphysical level – the enemies to be engaged are not men and guns on the battlefield but invisible foes in the form of destructive emotions or negative thoughts. In the Newar context the Hindu story is suffused with Buddhist compassion for all. Worshipping Durga is a way of exhorting the Goddess to purge the world of bad intentions, to get rid of all evil influences for the coming year.

Five types of animals are traditionally offered up for sacrifice to the Goddess. Each represents a different vice. Buffaloes are anger; goats, lust; sheep, stupidity; chickens, fearfulness; ducks, apathy. As an individual householder, you sacrifice what you can afford; but taken together, the communal slaughter of these five embodiments is a collective effort to wash away all the bad deeds and experiences of the past year and establish good intentions, blessings and prosperity for the next.

A long line of middle-aged ladies, gorgeously attired in their best red saris, were queuing up outside Bhadrakali's shrine. They were holding *puja* plates loaded with rice, vermilion and flowers. Some of them had live chickens or ducks under their arms; others were tugging odiferous black billy goats along by a string.

Bhadrakali's shrine, like many Goddess shrines, is in the open air, in a sunken pit; the image of the Goddess a simple, aniconic stone. Such *pithas*, Laxminath explained, are regarded as power-places of *shakti*; they are the seats of the dangerous, bloodthirsty aspects of the Goddess known as the Astamatrika, the 'Eight Mothers'.

The Eight Mothers are the guardians of the eight directions and their *pithas*, located outside the boundary of the old city walls, are believed to form a protective ring around Kathmandu, defending it from all kinds of threats such as earthquakes, disease and invasion. Being emanations of Durga, the Astamatrika are wild and ferocious, an indomitable battle line standing between the forces of anarchy and chaos, and the safe ground of civilization.

Like hungry lionesses they demand blood and are energized with regular transfusions. Sacrificing to the Astamatrika, particularly on the super-charged ninth day of Dasain, protects the city. Similar rings of Astamatrika pithas protect Patan and Bhaktapur, the other 'royal' cities in the valley, and there would be sacrifices there today, too.

Even though the city walls of Kathmandu had disappeared some time ago Newars are still conscious of what is 'dhvaka dune' – the area lying 'inside the gates' – and what is 'dhvaka pine' – the area outside the old city walls where the Astamatrika *pithas* are located. Traditionally, for a Newar, passing through the city gates, crossing that notional boundary means stepping from the safe, civilized world into the wild and dangerous regions beyond.

Down in the sunken *pitha*, the shrine stone was dripping red and devotees were slithering up to a priest through pools of blood, their bare feet leaving skid-marks on the white ceramic floor tiles. The killing here was harder to watch, the clinical precision of the *khora* replaced by the laborious sawings of a kitchen knife. The priest took a firm grip on a goat and cut through the jugular, holding its head back so that blood jetted from the vein in pulsing fountains over the shrine, filling the mouth of the thirsty Goddess. A rich, iron smell rushed the nostrils, charging the brain with a visceral hit.

The sacrifices are, ostensibly, a Hindu performance, but even Newar Buddhists are complicit in the climax of Dasain. Though they usually – but not always – refrain from blood sacrifice, the Buddhists enact similar rituals, cracking an egg over an image of Durga and drinking the yolk as *prasad*. Strict vegetarians take a cleaver to a pumpkin. The symbolism is the same. Everywhere the Goddess, the great Mother, is celebrated and vivified; the loss of life, her gain; her thirst sated by blood; her protective energies recharged for the year ahead.

Laxminath took me to other Astamatrika shrines around Kathmandu. Originally sited just outside the city walls, the *pithas* had in recent years become engulfed by traffic and urban sprawl as the city spilled out of its ancient boundaries.

Two of the Astamatrika *pithas* – belonging to the goddesses Indrayani and Kankeshvari – in the west of the city, on the banks of the sacred Vishnumati river, are located in traditional charnel grounds. The bodies of Newar Jyapu (farmer) and Chitrakar (painter) castes are still brought here for cremation. There is a dark, brooding atmosphere at these *pithas* that is more than the sum of blood running into the drains or the twitching mats of fur and feathers amassing flies. Many *pithas*, if not all, are commonly believed to have also once been sites of human sacrifice. There are rumours that the practice persists in some shrines in the valley to this day, with stories of street kids disappearing in mysterious circumstances and wild sects of tantric *sannyasins* hiding out in the forest.

'Even today, there are some places in the valley I don't like to go to, especially at night,' said Laxminath. 'Like Dakshinkali near Pharping, and the village of Harisiddhi on the road to Godavari.'

Descriptions of human sacrifice feature prominently in Nepali chronicles and in reports of nineteenth-century observers, as well as in the oral traditions of the valley. The victims were often prisoners convicted of particular crimes against the Goddess; captives from the battlefield, sometimes procured specifically for the purpose; or even, some commentaries suggest, children snatched at random by masked dancers.

And it was the terrifying warrior Mother Goddesses who most commonly demanded propitiation with human flesh. In the late eighteenth century, the last Malla king of Kathmandu, Jaya Prakasha – the king responsible for building the Kumari Chen in Durbar Square – is described by the chronicles as having had several men, who had been caught in the act of trying to empower themselves by impersonating certain Mother Goddesses, sacrificed at the relevant *pithas* in order to return the stolen *shakti* to the Mother Goddesses. In the reign of Girvan Yuddha Vikram

Shah (1806–37), the chronicles describe an 'insane Brahman' who sacrificed a horse, a Kusle (a descendant of the Kanphata and allegedly the class of persons most commonly victimized for this purpose) and – an unparalleled abomination – a Brahman woman at the *pitha* of Guhyeshvari.

The Vamsavalis, or dynastic genealogies, also record a bizarre and violent custom in Kathmandu in which the inhabitants of the northern half of the city used to assemble in the dry bed of the Vishnumati to fight the inhabitants of the southern half, thereby providing an opportunity for both sides to capture prisoners to sacrifice. The fighting was with stones and buffalo bone clubs so as to minimize the pre-sacrificial loss of blood. Prisoners seized by the northern faction were sacrificed at the *pitha* of the goddess Kankeshvari and those of the southern faction, in their territory, at the *pitha* of Luti Ajima.

According to the Vamsavali known as Wright's Chronicle, the custom ceased in the mid-nineteenth century when Jang Bahadur Rana abolished the practice 'on the occasion of the British Resident, Colvin, being struck by a stone whilst looking on'. But as late as 1905 the respected French historian Sylvain Levi reported that Kankeshvari was still claiming human victims.

The Mother Goddess legends of the Kathmandu Valley often involve tales of human sacrifice, or at least describe how Mother Goddesses were persuaded away from the practice. At the festival of Naradevi, or Svetakali – one of the Astamatrika of Kathmandu – her devotees perform a drama recalling how Naradevi was given a sheep instead.

In Bhaktapur, one of the most prominent features of Dasain is the dance of the Navadurga – the Nine Durgas. Every year nine men, ritually invoked with the *shakti* of the nine aspects of Durga, dance through the streets. Part of their performance – called '*nya layegu*', 'catching fish' – involves pretending to seize little children.

'Nowadays it's good fun – all the children laughing and falling over themselves to run away,' said Laxminath. 'But people believe that, not so long ago, the children were seized for real, as sacrifices for the Navadurga.'

Many people, he went on, are still anxious for the safety of their children; they are afraid that if the Mother Goddesses are not satisfied with the blood of the animals they are given, they might demand human sacrifice again, or take away the lives of their loved ones with some sickness or accident. Blood sacrifice could be made to a Mother Goddess at any time – Tuesdays and Saturdays were the most auspicious – but making a sacrifice during Dasain, on the day of Navami, is considered to be the best guarantee of their loved ones' safety.

The men, women and children offering their *pujas* at these gore-dripping stones seemed to be enjoying every minute of it but I was glad to leave. I felt I had had enough of blood. It was not easy, though, to sidestep the carnage on a day like today. Sacrifices on the 'Glorious Ninth' are not confined to *pithas* and temples. We passed people spraying motorbikes, bicycles and rickshaws with blood from the jugular of goats and ducks. The wheels of cars were bloodied, too, and the bonnets of buses and trucks.

Even the airplanes out at Tribhuvan airport received a blessing, their nose-cones anointed with blood sprayed from a black water-buffalo. Implements and mechanical appliances, too, and students' books, surgical instruments, carpenters' saws, chisels, photocopiers, printing presses, fuse boxes, computers, every kind of blade or tool in every workshop, house and office were being daubed with blood, imbued with the protective energy of Durga, with the power to work safely and to perfection.

At last we completed the circuit of the bloodthirsty Astamatrika, finding ourselves back where we started, a stone's throw from Kot. As always I felt the restorative effect of being back on home turf. Durbar Square felt like a fulcrum. The frenetic comings and goings of the city, the violent assaults of noise and colour and smell seemed to fall into some sort of abeyance here, at the centre.

Chapter 6

The Goddess's Yantra

After her great victory over the demon Mahisasura, the Goddess retreated into a thought-form of herself, a sacred shape or *yantra* in which she would reside and from which she could be pulled in times of need, whenever mankind or the gods needed her protection.

This *yantra* was powerful beyond all imagining, for the Goddess created it in the shape of a *yoni*, the secret place of all women – a perfect triangle with three equal sides, tip pointing downwards. In the centre was lodged the seed of life, the *bindu*, single point of all beginnings.

This most beautiful shape, the fount from which life was aroused, became the refuge of the Goddess's being, her *bhaga*, the prism from which she would take form. From this *yantra* all things began; to it all things return.

Indeed, so precious was this *yantra* that Shiva entrusted it to the safekeeping of Indra, the king of Heaven, who installed it in the heavenly city of Amarapur. There Indra worshipped and nourished it with a secret *mantra*, a sound so powerful it could not be uttered by men. It was the sound-vibration that generated the cosmos; it was an encrypted word, the resonance of the organ of the female sex – *Tala*.

And while the Goddess's *yantra* remained safe in Indra's heaven, properly worshipped, all was well with the worlds.

However, in the Treta Yuga, or Silver Age, a terrible war was stirred up by a mighty demon, Ravana, the king of Lanka. Ravana was fearful to behold. He had ten heads and twenty arms, a body like a mountain and complexion of lampblack. He was the enemy of all gods and men, and a burden to the earth, setting his dark heart on stealing the *yantra* for himself.

With hordes of evil *rakshasas*, Ravana attacked heaven and, amid the chaos of that mighty battle, Ravana's son Meghanada stole the *yantra* from Indra's custody and carried it away to Lanka. The whole world was plunged in shadow and the seas churned and the skies rained down Indra's anger.

Whereupon Vishnu incarnated a great warrior prince called Rama, who rose up on behalf of men to fight the evil Ravana. And Rama rallied mighty hosts of bear- and monkey-gods and, after a fierce and arduous battle, defeated the demon king and retrieved the *yantra* from the dread city of Lanka and brought it back to Ayodhya, his beautiful capital in the country of Koshala.

With the *yantra* restored to his safekeeping, Lord Rama recommenced the proper worship for he knew the secret sound, the *mantra* that must be uttered in order to activate its power; and he also venerated the *yantra* with blood, knowing the Goddess's wish for the offering that is the very essence of life.

And so harmony returned to the earth and men lived for a thousand years, and due rains fell, and the winds were favourable, and there was no distress from sickness or from wild beasts or from invasion, and all men were prosperous and happy.

Then at last, when the hero Rama himself drew close to death, the Goddess appeared to him in a dream and told him he must throw the *yantra* into the Sarayu, the river which flowed past the city of Ayodhya, because no one would know how to worship it after he was gone; for the world – she told him – was about to enter its fourth age, the Kali Yuga, an age of discord, when the Goddess's very name would be forgotten. Few would be the men of this era who would know how to honour and worship her.

So, with sadness in his heart, the dutiful Rama threw the Goddess's *yantra* into the river.

From time to time, kings of Ayodhya came across the Goddess's *yantra* in the river and, though they desired it, none of them could keep it, for they did not know how to worship it properly.

But then there came to the country of Koshala a noble king, Nanyadeva, of the Solar dynasty from Karnataka in southern India who had lost his kingdom to the warlike Mlechhas, and the Goddess knew that here, at last, was a king who could keep the flame of her being in his heart and whose lineage would be worthy of her patronage.

So, one day, as the exiled king was wandering restlessly here and there, the Goddess caused him to stop and rest on the bank of the Sarayu river. As he lay exhausted from his wanderings in the generous shade of a sal tree his eyes began to close and a dream came to him of a beautiful girl, sixteen years of age, who said to him, 'Oh, King Nanyadeva, your lineage deity is in the Sarayu river. You must find her in order to worship her. I am she, your lineage goddess. Bees will be flying around the surface of the river where I am hidden.'

The king awoke immediately and found a cloud of black bees hovering over the water. From the bottom of the river he pulled out a copper casket inside which was a smaller box of gold. On the golden box was an inscription: 'Herein lies the secret of the thrice-blessed Goddess, a treasure retrieved and protected by Lord Rama, and destined for the hands of King Nanyadeva.' The treasure contained within the box was none other than the Goddess's *yantra*, and the king, filled with joy, clasped the *yantra* to his breast.

In the still, deep moonless night, the Goddess appeared again to Nanyadeva in a dream and whispered to him her *mantra*, warning him that it was so powerful it would render to ashes any man who uttered it without permission, for it was the echo bound to the *yantra* itself; and without one, the other was nothing.

The Goddess told Nanyadeva that she bequeathed her *mantra* to all the subsequent kings among Nanyadeva's descendants, that they should whisper it to the next generation at the moment of death; for with this *mantra* they would gain infinite knowledge and pass on the mantle of kingship; and the *yantra*, activated by the secret *mantra*, would bring them untold power. Henceforth, the kings of the Solar dynasty took the Goddess for their lineage deity, calling her Taleju Bhavani: 'Taleju', after the sound that was her *mantra*, and 'Bhavani', as the giver of existence.

Taleju then told the exiled king to establish a temple to her in the forest near Janakpur and that she would build a city for him not far away, in Tirhut, in a place which today is in the Terai in southern Nepal. For this purpose she summoned an ingenious architect called Mayavi who had magical powers. She instructed Mayavi to build the city according to the protective design of a *mandala* and warned the architect that, since he must keep this construction secret, he should work under cover of darkness in the course of one night.

So, as dusk fell, Mayavi began to lay out a wonderful city according to the design of the Goddess, with fifty-four wells drawing sweet water, and seven water tanks crowded with red lotus, fish and waterfowl, and 108 square courtyards with 60,000 houses, and gardens full of flowers and singing birds to rival the gardens of Indra in heaven. At the centre the architect built a marble palace for the king with eleven large gates, and a temple five stories high, mighty as Mount Meru itself, to house the Goddess's *yantra*. Around the city he constructed seven walls so thick and so high neither beasts nor enemies would be able to penetrate them, and the final wall was defended by four towers, each with four ramparts at its angles; and beyond this were twenty-one ditches in concentric circles, filled with water and edged with trees.

As day began to lift the veil of night, Mayavi hurried to complete the last section of the ramparts along the city wall. At last, when the sun rose and the first cry of the peacock was heard, the architect put down his trowel and, standing back to admire his work, congratulated himself for he had left none but a tiny portion of the fortifications unfinished.

Then Taleju summoned King Nanyadeva and said to him: 'Let the world behold you today installed within your city like the radiant midday sun. None but you, beloved Nanyadeva, can bear the heavy burden of kingship. No more will you dwell in lonely places, but you shall sleep and rise to the sound of music and the twinkling of women's anklets. And you and your descendants shall rule the people as long as the sun endures and as far as the earth extends.'

And Nanyadeva said, 'So be it.' He called the great city Simraongarh and dedicated a special horse sacrifice in honour of the Goddess who had bestowed her authority upon him.

So, with blood sacrifice and secret *mantra*, King Nanyadeva worshipped the *yantra* of his tutelary goddess all the days of his life, mounting the steps to the shrine at the top of her temple at the centre of the city of Simraongarh first thing every morning.

So high was her temple that, from its peak, the raja could see laid out before him the magnificence of India – to the south the holy confluence of Jamuna and Ganga, to the west the deserts of noble Rajasthan, to the east the deep jungles of Bengal and to the north the wooded plains of the Terai leading up to the foothills of the Mahabharat range and, far beyond that, the snowy peaks of the mighty Himalaya, Abode of the Gods.

King Nanyadeva rewarded the Goddess's favour, for he was a moon among stars, a true upholder of the law; and his people were righteous and happy, well provided with goods, self-restrained and truthful, charitable and full of faith. He had many wise counsellors and saintly priests and his ministers were such men as could keep their counsel and judge things finely, for they were well versed in the arts of policy and ever fair-spoken. The court of Simraongarh became famous throughout India for music and drama and poetry composed in the beautiful language of Maithili. The domain of Simraongarh stretched wide and glorious, and the royal coffers filled with booty captured from distant and neighbouring lands.

When it came King Nanyadeva's time to leave this life, as he lay on his bed of death, he whispered the secret *mantra* of the Goddess into the ear of his son Gangadeva, and entrusted to him the Goddess's *yantra*, and Gangadeva in turn became king and his son after him, and so on through the generations. And the kings of Simraongarh presided over their lovely city, keeping the wheel of society spinning smoothly and evenly; and the rains fell and the sun shone and crops grew in due season, for they were kings among kings.

So it was through the cycle of years until the present time of troubles began. A storm blew into India from the north-west as first Mamluks, then Khiljis, and then Tughluqs engaged the Hindu kings in war. Across the plains of the Punjab, mighty armies clashed together; temples and monasteries were destroyed; and the great libraries and universities – Nalanda, Vikramshila, Ratnagiri, Oddantapuri, Somapuri – where students and *siddhas* the world over had come to bathe their souls in the sacred texts, were consigned to flames, the wisdoms of seven hundred years, the philosophies of great minds, the fruit of lifetimes' meditations, a conflagration of palm leaves.

As men rushed to kill one another, the Goddess watched the tide of destruction in her beloved land with sadness in her heart, for she knew that now the era of wrong-mindedness had come to pass, a time when mankind would turn away from her. So she searched for a refuge where the essence of her being could be safeguarded. She visited all the places where she was yet worshipped, from the palm-fringed coasts of southern India to the steamy jungles of Bengal, but none seemed safe from the gathering clouds of ignorance.

Then, casting her eyes towards the high Himalaya, her gaze fell upon the sweetest place of all, a place of origin, her deepest centre, where, many aeons ago, her *shakti* had risen in the *pitha* known as Guhyeshvari at the bottom of a wondrous lake known as Nagahrada, Lake of the Nagas, where she had revealed her secrets to the *bodhisattva* Manjushri. Here the people held the Goddess in their hearts and would continue to do so for aeons to come for they were close to her source.

So the Goddess shepherded her devotees, the *siddhas* and the *tantrikas*, as they scattered from the storm and guided them north up treacherous mountain paths and over high passes until they reached the clear air and emerald terraces of the Valley of Nepal, home of the Newars, who gave them refuge.

Then Taleju turned her thoughts to the city of Simraongarh in the kingdom of Tirhut where her *yantra* remained in the possession of the noble king Harisimha, descendant of Nanyadeva; and with vivid dreams and portents she tried to alert the raja to the approaching danger and to urge him to save the prism of her being.

Chapter 7

Taleju Temple

I sat down with Laxminath in the shade, on the steps of Kageshwar Temple, by the north-west corner of the old royal palace. Out of the beating sun the air was cool and reviving. On the carved roof struts above our heads a fluster of pigeons was gently cooing. Slowly I felt the violent tempo of our *pitha* tour begin to ease, the joyful atmosphere of festival reasserting itself.

Opposite us was the colourful Singha Dhoka, the Lion Gate of Taleju Temple, set in a high brick wall. The gate was an ornate arch of symbols flanked by pillars, painted orange, featuring *kalashes* of abundance and the ever-present, watchful eyes. On either side stood a pair of white guardian lions, two-metres high, gaudily painted, with bulging eyes and red cheeks, and ears like elephants. A long, patient queue of devotees was passing beneath the arch into the temple precinct on the other side, carrying *puja* plates of flowers, rice and vermilion. I was relieved to see there were no goats or chickens with them.

At the apex of the arch a little figure was seated cross-legged on a throne inside a blue and white pavilion, looking out at us. This was Jaya Prakasha, the last Malla king of Kathmandu, who had built the Living Goddess's residence just across the square.

'Navami is the only day in the year that Taleju Temple is open to ordinary Hindus and Buddhists for worship,' said Laxminath. 'Usually only the tantric priests are admitted. But even today foreigners are not permitted inside the shrine itself.'

Taleju Temple was magnificent. The giant three-tiered edifice, rising twenty-five metres high, way above the exterior walls and the palace rooftops, was once the tallest temple in Kathmandu. This, Laxminath said, was so that the people of Kathmandu, wherever they were, could have *darshan* of the temple.

'Before modern times it was forbidden by the kings to build anything taller than this,' said Laxminath. 'They said the Goddess Taleju would strike such buildings down with lightning or an earthquake.'

From where we were sitting the main temple could be seen clearly above the precinct walls. It was mounted on a twelve-stage pediment, with twelve small, two-tiered subsidiary temples surrounding the main structure at one level, and four others on a higher stage. All the doors and *toranas* and even some of the carved roof struts were gilt, and the topmost roof was surmounted by a spectacular golden finial under a golden parasol.

The temple had been built by Mahendra Malla in the sixteenth century. Legend had it that Taleju had revealed the plan of her temple to King Mahendra in a dream but it was so complicated none of the builders in Kathmandu could fathom how to build it. But then a famous *sannyasin*, who was living in a cave near the *pitha* of Guhyeshvari, showed them how. When the temple was finished, Taleju entered the shrine at the very top in the form of a bee.

Taleju is not in the common pantheon of Hindu deities. She had arrived in the Kathmandu Valley in the fourteenth century as the lineage goddess of the Malla kings. Though the Mallas had broadly embraced the traditions of the valley – worshipping other deities in their local incarnations, extravagantly donating to temples and subsidizing indigenous festivals, and generally falling in with Newar practices – Taleju had remained apart: a secret entity, the Malla kings' personal guardian, the key – so they believed – to their power.

On his deathbed a Malla king would pass on the *mantra* of Taleju to his heir, handing on the baton of the Goddess's authority. Without the *mantra* of Taleju a king's ability to rule was severely compromised. Once, in an effort to gain power for themselves, ruthless courtiers had imprisoned a Malla king – Laxminarasimha – in a tower in Hanuman Dhoka where he had languished and died without being able to pass on the *mantra* to his son. The *mantra* – it was said – had curled away from the dying raja's lips, slipping through the lattice shutters of his cell and flying upwards into the sky. It was spotted, blazing across the heavens like a comet, by another Malla king, over in Patan, who, with the help of a powerful *siddha*, managed to recapture it.

It was Mahendra Malla's great devotion to Taleju, epitomized by building this magnificent temple, that – Laxminath said – had been the secret of his success. Mahendra Malla had become one of the valley's wealthiest kings, the first king to mint coins in Kathmandu and, ultimately, to mint coins for Tibet.

Two centuries later, when Prithvi Narayan Shah conquered the valley, he, too, adopted Taleju as his protectoress, worshipping her as his personal deity, just as the Mallas before him. History did not relate how the Shah conqueror had learnt the *mantra* of Taleju – if indeed he had – but as a young man, Prithvi Narayan was known to have stayed for several years as a guest of the Malla king in Bhaktapur. Popular belief was that the ambitious Gorkha prince had stolen the *mantra* then – knowledge that ultimately gave him the power to conquer the valley.

The bond between Taleju and the ruling kings of Nepal remained to this day. For 364 days of the year her temple in Kathmandu is the preserve of royal priests and specialist attendants who come and go through an entrance connecting the temple with a secret courtyard in Hanuman Dhoka. No one else is allowed inside. But once a year, on this super-charged ninth day of Dasain, the doors of her shrine are opened.

'Taleju is the highest form of Durga,' Laxminath said. 'You have to be a *tantrika* to worship her properly. She is difficult to reach. That is why we cannot worship her every day. Only kings and the priests of Taleju Temple have this knowledge.'

High in the atmosphere, almost beyond reach of the human ear it seemed, floated the tinkling of a bell. On the *toranas* and roof struts, golden images of the Goddess slaying the buffalo-demon lift Durga, the warrior protectoress, up towards the ethereal heights of Taleju's shrine. The golden finial on the temple peak points to the pinnacle of existence, that existential pinprick of transcendence – like the tip of the needle on which the Goddess herself had meditated for nine days as she summoned the power to slay the buffalo-demon. For the worshippers threading their way up the levels of the temple to the top, it is like scaling Mt Meru, ascending from the world of matter to the highest spiritual plane.

Though she was now back on her elevated seat Taleju had also recently descended to receive blood sacrifice. Unbeknownst to most Nepalis, Laxminath explained, the first sacrifice of Dasain is not the ritual I had witnessed with full fanfare early that morning at the old armoury of Kot. The first sacrifice happens here, at midnight, in secret, in a courtyard called Mul Chowk on the far side of the main courtyard in Hanuman Dhoka. Mul Chowk had been built by King Mahendra. It has an entrance connecting it with the precinct of Taleju Temple. Inside Mul Chowk, on the first floor, is another shrine to Taleju. The previous night, on the cusp of the last hour of the eighth day of Dasain and the dawning of the Glorious Ninth, the priests had brought Taleju down from the top of her temple in a sacred *kalash*. This midnight hour is known as Kalaratri, the Black Night – the definitive moment of the great Goddess's triumph.

Last night, away from the public gaze, the priests had installed Taleju in her secondary shrine with a powerful *puja*. A tantric number of goats and buffaloes would have been sacrificed at stone pillars in the courtyard. They had been killed by Khadgi men, from the low caste of butchers, who pierced the animals' throats so that the blood jetted out in gigantic fountains, spraying the courtyard. They had cut off the heads and the priests had taken them as offerings to Taleju's shrine.

When the killing was over the Living Goddess herself had come to Mul Chowk, led out of the Kumari Chen by the priest of Taleju along a white cloth that was unfolded in front of her. She had entered Hanuman Dhoka and, walking through the courtyard where the animals had been sacrificed, she had entered the shrine of Taleju which had been sprayed with blood.

This is not a rite of initiation, Laxminath said. This is a ritual of empowerment. No one other than the tantric priests know what happens inside the shrine of Taleju. This is the most secret part of the ritual, when the Living Goddess receives the *shakti* of Taleju.

I was beginning to feel light-headed. Too much blood and too much sun, perhaps, on an early start and an empty stomach. But the entrance of the Living Goddess into the gory scenes of Dasain had my mind spinning. I had dismissed the bloodthirsty stories, the tales of gruesome initiations, as fallacious rumours but now I wondered if there might be some substance to them after all.

'We think of blood as the energy, the force of life,' Laxminath said. 'Blood is very important for the Kumari because it contains the *shakti*, the creative energy, of the great Goddess. But since she is a child and she is also a Buddhist, she doesn't see the sacrifices herself. The sacrifices are performed before she arrives, to the goddesses inside her.'

The Kumari, pure and virginal though she is, and though she is never a witness to sacrifices, has an affinity with blood. In the context in which she is worshipped, blood is not polluting – as it is in orthodox Hindu belief. The reason the Kumari herself cannot bleed is not because blood would contaminate her, but because the Kumari contains all the power of life inside her. All her blood has to remain inside her body; not a drop of it should be spilt. Though she is a child, the Kumari contains the full potential of a woman. The forces of female creativity and sexual energy are fully present inside her. The fact that she has not yet menstruated or lost so much as a drop of blood by any other means concentrates that creative power within her.

Had she been pure in the sense of being purely spiritual, not of this world – the stainless innocent I had originally supposed her to be – she would have been dressed in the *sattva* colours of white, yellow or saffron, like priests, monks and ascetics. But the Living Goddess is always dressed in red – in the full-bodied *rajas* colour of energy and fertility, with all the jewellery and make-up of a bride. The virginity of the Living Goddess does not make her neutral or passive. It is what gives her power. Her relationship with blood, and particularly the blood of sacrifice and menstrual blood, makes her part of this world, identifies her as the vital, dynamic force within it.

'That is why people go to the Kumari especially when they have blood disorders like haemorrhaging or menstrual problems or when they are coughing blood,' said Laxminath. 'My auntie did *puja* to the Living Goddess when she suffered miscarriages.'

Laxminath got to his feet. 'Come,' he said.

He led me back across the square, past the pagoda temple of Jagannath and the royal palace balcony, to the familiar facade of the Kumari Chen. We stood in front of the steps facing the Kumari's proprietorial stone lions. Above us was the Living Goddess's golden window with the lovely golden goddesses on either side. Laxminath pointed to the doorway beneath it, or more specifically to the *torana*, the wooden shield mounted directly above the entrance. Like a coat of arms, or a plaque on a historic building, the central *torana* of a temple entrance is a mark of identity, the signature of the deity inside.

At first glance the entrance *torana* to the Kumari Chen was similar to the *toranas* above the outside windows of the house: it was minutely carved and teeming with symbols – snarling aquatic *makaras* with monstrous curling elephant trunks, tiny seated Buddhas and floating *apsaras*, and at the apex a '*chhyepu*', or 'face of glory', hungrily devouring its bottom jaw – an allusion to the folding of time.

But it is the figure in the centre that is key. Ducking beneath the entrance *torana* on my previous visits to the Kumari courtyard I had never stopped to examine it. The tiny, exquisitely carved figure has eighteen arms fanning out around her, most of them brandishing a weapon – sword, arrow, bow, discus, club, thunderbolt. Her feet are braced apart in the fierce stride of a warrior, one foot standing on her lion mount, the other stamping on the body of a buffalo. One of her many hands holds a demon by the hair, dragging him out of the buffalo's body through the severed neck. The head of the buffalo lies upturned between her feet, its muzzle and floppy ears in an endearing gesture of worship. The Goddess's face, minutely observed in the midst of this frenzied wheel of motion, is a picture of loveliness – fresh, calm, serene.

Laxminath led me through into the familiar little courtyard. 'You see: Durga – Taleju – Kumari,' he said conclusively, 'they are one and the same.'

As if on cue, at the triple window above us, a tiny hand with scarlet fingernails pulled back the curtain.

Chapter 8

Taleju's Flight from India

As the priests and monks and *sadhus* and *tantrikas* fled along the mountain paths away from India, a blaze of conquest began to rise from Delhi. Yet Harisimha, descendant of Nanyadeva, King of Simraongarh, like a child playing in a forest inhabited by tigers, refused to see the danger, even though Taleju sent portents to warn him. The walls of her temple began to crack, bells rang in her shrines at the dead of night, beads of sweat broke upon the face of her golden image – all in vain. In vain Taleju tried to plant the thought of Nepal into Harisimha's dreams, hoping he would be entranced by these visions of the emerald valley and inspired to move there to safety, for she knew that Simraongarh was soon destined to fall. But Harisimha, proud in the palace that had housed the kings of the Solar dynasty for centuries, would not be moved.

So the Goddess conceived a different plan. She sent the lofty King of Simraongarh a beautiful wife from the Valley of Nepal – a seventeen-year-old girl called Devaldevi, from the city of Bhaktapur, whose brother was the ruler Rudra Malla – in the hope that a woman might at last knock some sense into him. Devaldevi was lovely to behold, with lotus eyes and a reed-like waist, strong of heart and with a fiery spirit. In time she bore him a son, Jagatsimha.

Yet even the charms of Devaldevi could not prevail over the stubborn raja. In vain the young queen tried to persuade Harisimha that they should flee to her brother's court in Bhaktapur where they would be safe, where the mountains of the Valley of Nepal would protect them. But whenever Devaldevi entreated him the king would grow impatient. 'Are you so homesick that you would persuade me to abandon my glorious city?' he would protest. 'Do you expect me to run from my birthright like a hunted hare? Do you not know the strength of the walls that were built by Mayavi in the time of King Nanyadeva? Here they have stood for two hundred years and no army has ever breached them. Let the Sultan of Delhi attack. He will find Simraongarh and its Hindu king his undoing.'

Then the sultan, Malik Ghuyas-ud-din Tughluq, hearing of the defiance of King Harasimha, turned his engines of war towards Mithila, determined to crush him and the beautiful city of Simraongarh. Like an angry swarm of bees the army of Turks appeared over the horizon. As their horses and war elephants broke into a charge towards the city it was as if an earthquake was let loose across the plains. Thunder rolled around the hills; trees shook; water in the tanks and moats began to tremble. Reaching the forest that surrounded Simraongarh, and finding it difficult to penetrate, the sultan took an axe and began, himself, to fell trees. His soldiers followed suit and soon not a tree was left standing. Then the sultan ordered his army to fill in the ditches. Soon the Muslim catapults and fire-throwers reached the outermost wall. Again and again they attacked. But the Maithili archers loosed showers of arrows down upon them from the towers and the mighty walls of the fortress of Simraongarh stood firm.

It was only as evening approached and the sun began to slide from the sky that one of the Turk masters of horse happened by chance to notice a strange aberration in the long, dark shadow thrown by the city across the ground. So ingenious was the design of Simraongarh that to look at it directly, nothing seemed amiss. But down below, in the city's shadow, a chink in the fortifications revealed itself, as eye-catching as a missing tooth. This was the place where the demon architect Mayavi, not quite finished, had been compelled to hang up his trowel at the first light of day. Swiftly, the Turk commander called for ladders and stone-flingers to assail this vulnerable spot.

Over the walls swarmed the heavy-armed soldiers of Malik Ghuyas-ud-din Tughluq and they poured into the city through the courtyards and palaces of Simraongarh and when they found King Harisimha seated on his golden throne beneath his royal parasol in his audience chamber, they did not fall to their knees and honour him, but dragged him out and presented him to the sultan who took him prisoner and brought him in ropes along the road to Delhi.

The Goddess Taleju, outraged at the desecration of Simraongarh and the cruel treatment of her beloved king, soon brought retribution down upon the sultan. Several days later, at a victory parade, the sultan's own son brought about his death, goading an elephant to push against a weakened beam jutting out from a special wooden kiosk in which his father was standing. The building collapsed on top of the Sultan of Delhi, breaking every bone in his body.

Then his son, Muhammed bin Tughluq, now sultan himself, ignobly led the Hindu king Harisimha to Delhi as his prisoner, with a rope around his neck. At last he agreed to set him free, provided Harisimha return to Simraongarh and pay him heavy tribute. King Harisimha declared he would but returned to Simraongarh with no such thought in mind and instead determined to resist and urged other Hindu kings to revolt against the sultan.

And so Muhammed bin Tughluq launched another army into the northern frontier of his empire to subdue the king of Simraongarh, only this time he vowed the assault would be bloodier than his father's and he would show no mercy, ensuring that not a citizen nor any member of the royal household be spared nor any Hindu shrine or temple remain standing.

And as the sultan's army stormed once again towards Simraongarh, Taleju knew that the end was, indeed, near for the kings of the Solar dynasty and she appeared to Harisimha in a dream. 'Make haste, Harisimhadeva,' Taleju urged. 'It is not yet too late. A glorious future is yours, you have only to take it in your hands. Follow your queen Devaldevi. It is my wish that you should bring the dynasty of Nanyadeva to Nepal and worship me there, in the place of my origin, in the valley of my sacred *pitha*, where I am honoured and cherished.'

Now at last Harisimha felt the hand of destiny upon him and straightway he entered Taleju's inner shrine and fell to his knees before her. 'Now I see the tears that fall from your eyes like raindrops and your golden face cracked with concern,' he cried. 'I have been blind. And you sent me lovely Devaldevi, my queen, whose advice I failed to hear. Forgive me, thrice-blessed Taleju, and if it indeed be your will, escort the king of Simraongarh away from here to safety.'

Though he trembled with sorrow at the thought of leaving Simraongarh, he took the precious *yantra* of the Goddess from its golden box and hid it in his robes. Then, assembling his queen, his son, his priests and ministers, the king of Simraongarh fled through a secret tunnel and rode under cover of darkness out into the hills.

The path through the jungle thickets on the edge of the Terai was treacherous and under the moonless sky it was difficult to see. Jackals howled and birds screeched; leopards snarled in the rocks; poisonous snakes slithered across their path. But Taleju urged them on and, with Devaldevi leading the way, courageous as a tiger, her son on the saddle before her, the band of refugees were soon within reach of the Mahabharata hills.

Only King Harisimha seemed to lose heart, his spirit flagging with every step that took him further away from Simraongarh. As dawn broke and they reached the top of the first hill he turned to look one last time on his beloved city. Through his tears he could see the thin, far plumes of smoke rising from the parapets and the blazing roofs of his palace and temples, and the army of Muhammed bin Tughluq razing the mighty walls.

On the sorry band of refugees went for many days and as they slowly wound their way up through the forest into the foothills they began to grow weak with hunger. So King Harisimha meditated on the *yantra* of Taleju and the Goddess duly appeared to him and told him they should eat whatever he saw first the next morning. At dawn, when he opened his eyes, Harisimha saw a wild buffalo. He had it caught and brought it before the Goddess who gave instructions as to how to choose a qualified slaughterer. Such a man was found in their party who was at that moment defecating with his face towards the east – which was a sign that he was not of twice-born status – and he was brought forward to slaughter the animal. This man was to be the ancestor of the Khadgi, the Newar butcher caste. He duly immolated the animal, offering it up to the Goddess and the Goddess allowed the flesh to be eaten. Henceforth all Newars, both Buddhists and Hindus, would eat buffalo meat in this way, in honour of Taleju.

And so the refugees continued along the Marin river, through Sindhulimadi until, twenty-five days after leaving Simraongarh, they reached the valley of Tinpatan in the Chure hills. But here the king, having lost sight of his city forever and feeling his life's will slipping from his grasp, could continue no more. Like a great sal tree felled by the woodman's axe, Harasimha collapsed to the ground and, with his heart ready to break, called for his queen.

Devaldevi heard his cry and, with tears falling down her lovely cheeks, dismounted and ran back down the path with her son at her side. 'My queen,' King Harisimha said, 'I can scarcely see your beautiful face – my senses are no longer keen. I am like a smoking lamp that burns low when there is but little oil remaining. Bring me my son so I might give him what now should be his.'

Drawing his son close, King Harisimha pressed the Goddess's *yantra* into his son's hand, and with his dying breath whispered the *mantra* of the Goddess in Jagatsimha's ear, thus conferring upon the young boy the authority of the Solar kings.

Having consigned to flames the noble body of Harisimha, the

refugee court of Simraongarh pressed on with heavy step towards the Valley of Nepal with Queen Devaldevi leading Jagatsimha on his father's horse.

A little further on, however, they arrived at the village of Rajgram in the district of Ramechhap and there the evil village leader, Majhi Bharo, having heard of the procession of the court of Simraongarh and the riches they were carrying with them, robbed them of all their gold and jewellery and fine ornaments. But he did not find the most precious thing of all, the *yantra* of the Goddess, which was cleverly concealed in the waistband of the young prince Jagatsimha.

At last, the band of refugees reached a pass overlooking the emerald Valley of Nepal. The woods around the valley, full of tall trees bearing fruits and flowers, rang with the cries of cuckoos and the belling of deer. Winding rivers and lotus ponds shone like silver, and gold glinted from the finials of Hindu temples and the rings above the domes of Buddhist stupas. And dotted here and there across the valley, raised on hillocks like gems in a necklace lay Bhaktapur, Lalitpur, Kirtipur, Kathmandu, Sanku and the other lovely towns of the Newars.

As Devaldevi and her entourage descended into the valley, messengers from outlying villages ran ahead to alert Rudra Malla that his sister had returned to the place of her birth, bringing with her from Simraongarh the *yantra* of Taleju. And as the weary band approached the lion gates of Bhaktapur, flags were hoisted, the roads were swept before them and flowers showered upon them and Rudra Malla came out on his white horse to welcome them.

And so the *yantra* of Taleju that had once resided in Indra's heaven, that was rescued by Lord Rama from the demon Ravana, that was revealed to the wandering King Nanyadeva at the bottom of Sarayu river, that for centuries presided over the fortunes of the rajas of Simraongarh in Mithila, came to the Valley of Nepal, to the land of the Goddess's secret *pitha*, and found sanctuary in Bhaktapur, City of Devotion. There Devaldevi's brother installed it in a secret shrine in Mul Chowk, the innermost courtyard of Bhaktapur palace, and instructed the royal priests to worship it with blood.

As young Jagatsimha knelt before the *yantra* and spoke the *mantra* his father had passed to him with his dying breath, Taleju herself appeared as a beautiful young girl, sweeter than the dawn, and declared herself well pleased with her new abode.

Seeing that the great Goddess herself had come to live in their midst, all the other gods in the valley – Brahma, Vishnu and Shiva at the fore – came to welcome her and shower her with gifts. And such was Taleju's influence that all Bhaktapur's former enemies were destroyed and good men were exempted from being reborn.

In time the Malla kings of Bhaktapur came to rule all the Valley of Nepal, establishing three dynasties descended from Devaldevi's line who ruled from the cities of Bhaktapur, Patan and Kathmandu. Each dynasty established a temple to Taleju in the heart of their city, within the confines of their royal palace where they worshipped their lineage goddess, passing on her *mantra* to the next generation. As their fortunes grew and prospered each successive king in each of the three cities tried to outdo his cousin-kings in his devotions to Taleju.

And Taleju, for her part, was enchanted by the Malla kings. How she delighted in their donations of blood sacrifice and the costly fire sacrifices and the dances and theatre performed in her honour, and the sound of her *mantra* surging through the land! Taleju watched over the Malla kings as a lioness watches over her cubs tumbling and competing with each other in the safety of their den; and she strengthened them in everything and protected them from their enemies; for the valley was her *mandala*, the triple kingdoms the three corners of her *yantra*, and her presence blazed like a thousand suns within it.

Chapter 9

Rashmila, ex-Kumari

Dasain was over and Laxminath had come up with a suggestion. A cousin of his lived near an ex-Kumari. He would see if he could arrange a meeting.

The idea astounded me. The rumours I had heard about the fate of ex-Kumaris had assigned them to oblivion, but Laxminath was clear. There were at least half a dozen former Kumaris, a reign's length apart in age, living normal lives in and around Kathmandu. They had simply returned to their families when their tenure as Living Goddess was over, at around twelve years old. Several of them lived within a few minutes' walk of the Kumari Chen.

As we negotiated muddy potholes in the unlit backstreets somewhere beyond Kasthamandap, trying to find the way to Rashmila Shakya's house, I felt my pulse racing. The Great Ninth was just days ago and my mind was filled with thoughts of bloodthirsty goddesses. I was still coming to terms with the notion that the little Kumari I had nurtured in my memory so fondly all these years was bound up with a voracious, demon-slaughtering Goddess. The prospect of meeting an ex-Kumari now seemed distinctly alarming. What kind of person could she be after all she had seen – the midnight rituals, severed buffalo heads, the ailing, blood-spitting devotees – and after all she believed herself to have been, a manifestation of Durga, protectress of the nation, *shakti* of the king? How, moreover, would she have reacted to her dismissal as she returned to the world of mortals?

The ex-Kumari we were about to meet was the youngest of eight surviving generations of ex-Kumaris in Kathmandu. Rashmila Shakya had been selected in 1984 when she was four years old. She had replaced the Living Goddess I had first seen when I was a teenager. Her term in office had come to an end eight years later, in 1991, when she was twelve. She was now, after all that had happened to her, only seventeen.

The caste the Kumaris come from – the Shakyas, householder monks – are conservative, devout, well educated and relatively prosperous. As members of the Newar religious caste, at the top of the tree, second only to the priestly Vajracharyas, Shakyas are highly respected in Nepali society. They claim lineage from Shakyamuni, Sage of the Shakyas – the Buddha himself – who had been born at Lumbini in southern Nepal.

Traditionally most Shakyas enter the trade of their forebears as goldsmiths, working in small courtyard foundaries, creating exquisite bronze and gold figures and statues of the gods for temples and household shrines using the ancient and highly specialized 'lost wax' technique. Nowadays, however, Shakyas have branched out and often also take jobs as teachers, politicians and businessmen. The father of the ex-Kumari we were about to meet worked as a government officer in the Ministry of Education.

The strong religious nature of the Shakyas means they are also among the most traditional of the Newars. While other castes have begun to move away from their old neighbourhoods into the sprawling modern suburbs, the Shakyas of Kathmandu continue, for the most part, to live in residential areas attached to *bahals* – traditional monastic courtyards in the old city centres.

Though by no means closed to passersby, *bahals* retain an aura of mystery about them. Their entrances – often guarded by lions, like the Kumari Chen – are sometimes a little daunting. Stepping inside is like slipping into a parallel universe. Conventionally *bahals* are two storeys high with clay-tiled roofs and deep eaves supported by carved wooden roof-struts in the classic Newar style, and centred on a paved courtyard – again, like the Kumari Chen – with a plinth raised a foot or more above this pavement and running around all four sides of the ground floor.

Inside the courtyard, opposite the entrance, is the ground floor shrine, the *kvahpah dya*, containing an image of one of the Buddhas – usually Shakyamuni or one of the Transcendent Buddhas. In the centre of the courtyard there is invariably a *chaitya*, a miniature of the great stupa at Swayambhu. Some *bahals* have numerous additional *chaityas*, offered down the centuries by pious patrons, while some have votive pillars and *mandalas* raised on plinths, the courtyard erupting in an imbroglio of devotional tributes.

Residential courtyards have attached themselves to the main *bahal* like cells around a nucleus and the alleys connecting these courtyards with the streets outside are often so tiny as to be lost to the eye.

Today's *bahals* have lost some of their traditional features – the long halls and lattice-shuttered balconies around the courtyard converted into domestic housing with additional storeys, often in concrete with modern glass windows. But the ground floor shrine remains sacrosanct, binding the community to their historic role as temple guardians and keepers of the *dharma*.

There are eighteen principal *bahals* – or Maha Viharas – in the vicinity of Durbar Square. It is one of the strict rules of Living Goddess selection, Laxminath told me, that candidates must come from a pure Shakya lineage attached to one of these *bahals*. And it is here, to her parents' house in their lineage *bahal*, that a Kumari returns after her dismissal.

We stopped at last at a door in a tiny courtyard down a dead-end street. Laxminath called up to a third-floor window. After a moment there was a rustle behind the shutters and a chink of light threw its blade into the darkness. For a split second the face of the ex-Kumari passed above us before vanishing behind the curtains. She was breathtakingly beautiful, unmistakable though I had never seen her before.

Surya Ratna Shakya, the ex-Kumari's father, opened the old wooden front door, turning an iron lock and leading us past a couple of motorbikes, up a flight of steep, dark, wooden stairs. The house was a traditional building about two hundred years old. Though the family now lived in a modern style, some taboos still applied. As we progressed up the stairs we paused on the landings, allowing one person at a time to continue to the next level, calling out 'binabi!' – 'be aside!' – as we went, to avoid crossing beneath one another or intercepting someone else coming down the stairs, and keeping the sacred space above our heads free from the pollution of someone else's feet. Leaving our shoes beside an array of footwear on the landing, we ducked our heads to cross the threshold and stepped into the family living room.

There was no doubt this was an ex-Kumari's house. In the corner was a glass cabinet full of expensive foreign dolls and toys; and on the wall beside it a poster of Rashmila – a beautiful, serious-looking child in full Indra Jatra regalia with her tall, golden, bejewelled crown and her bronze eye staring obliquely from a scarlet forehead. Beneath it was a sticker in English – 'Smile on face, cry in heart'.

Laxminath and I were shown to low armchairs at a formica coffee table while her father, affable, relaxed and beaming from ear to ear, called for his wife. A cosy, plump woman in a sari – Rashmila's mother – came in carrying a tray of Nepali tea. We sat and drank, waiting amicably. 'The candidates for Kumari have to be from a Shakya family with no inter-caste marriages in its lineage,' Surya Ratna's wife said. 'They must be very young, between about three and five years old. They must have no blemishes, or smallpox scars. Also, they cannot have undergone *ihi* yet.'

Ihi – also known as *bel biha* – is the most highly regarded and sacred of all Newar domestic rituals and is undertaken by all young Newar girls before reaching puberty, usually between the ages of four and ten. Marked by the ritual exchange of a wood-apple, or bel fruit, *ihi* symbolizes marriage to a god. The ceremony is a joyful occasion. The prepubescent Newar girls are dressed in red like brides with large red *tika* marks painted on their foreheads, and gold jewellery. Their feet and hands are painted red and their hair parted with vermilion powder or tied with a red bow.

As a rite of maturity, *ihi* grants a Newar girl full membership of her father's caste, reaffirming her ties with her father's family – a position that girls in the orthodox Hindu tradition are usually forced to surrender when they marry and become subservient to the family of their husband. As a 'mock' betrothal *ihi* also grants a young Newar girl the status of a married woman, protecting her position in the future. Being married to a god sends a strong signal to the man the girl eventually marries – who is, in a sense, her second husband: if he lifts a finger against her, he will have the anger of her first husband – and a god at that – to contend with.

The status conferred on a woman by *ihi* is particularly significant when it comes to widowhood. If her husband dies, a Newar woman is regarded as still being married and cannot, therefore, incur the kind of stigma a widow in orthodox Hindu communities has to endure.

The same applies to a Newar woman who remains unmarried. *Ihi* reinforces the message that a woman does not belong to a man, but to a deity. It is consequently perfectly respectable for a Newar woman to lead her life as a spinster; while in orthodox Hinduism spinsters are regarded as on a par with untouchables. Divorce and separation are still frowned upon by Newars but, thanks to *ihi*, it is nowhere near as difficult for a Newar woman to sever ties with her husband. Newar women are also much freer to remarry, or to marry outside their caste, for love.

As a kind of mock marriage ceremony it also implies that the girls who have undergone the ritual are no longer virgins – which helps to dispel the prejudices often attached to the issue of defloration in other cultures and the ideas of pollution that are traditionally associated with virginal blood. However, this symbolic defloration also means that girls who have undergone *ihi* are not eligible to be Kumari.

'Of all the girls who were the right age and had not done *ihi*, there were four the Kumari caretaker thought were suitable,' her mother went on, ' – Rashmila, her younger sister Samjhana, and two others. Many people thought Samjhana would be chosen, even though she was only three years old, because she was the most beautiful but at the time of selection the weather was very hot and she had a rash.

'But Rashmila was also beautiful and very calm and contented. She was always a very generous little girl and would give away everything she had. She never cried. She was very dreamy and often seemed to be in another world. When the royal astrologer came and checked her horoscope, he could see it was ideal. It had all the positive signs and, most important of all, it matched the horoscope of the king. So the search went no further. Rashmila was clearly the one.'

Rashmila had been taken to the house of the Mul Purohit – the royal priest – for the physical examination. This had been conducted by the priest's wife and her daughter; with Rashmila's mother in the room with her all the time. Rashmila's mother had removed her daughter's outer garments but left her underwear on. There was no truth to the claims that the Kumari was naked for this examination, she said. The check was simple, just a matter of the priest's wife confirming that there were no birthmarks or scratches, and that Rashmila hadn't lost any of her teeth yet.

After that, Rashmila had been taken to Narayanhiti Palace to be introduced to the king. As Kumari-elect she had offered the king a coin, which he had accepted, thereby agreeing to her appointment. A week later, Rashmila was installed at the Kumari Chen.

While we talked, Rashmila Shakya had slipped unobtrusively into the room, quietly taking up the space on the sofa that her parents, I could see now, had left for her between them. She was wearing a purple *kurta* pinned at the neck with a tiny brooch and a black hand-knitted waistcoat. But it was an effort to notice these things. Rashmila's shyness and her beauty were intoxicating. At first she averted her eyes from us, gazing bashfully at her fingers as they twisted nervously in her lap. But when she heard Laxminath translating my questions in Newari, she lifted her head and flashed us a smile of heart-warming sweetness. Her face had a clarity and openness that seemed almost luminous.

I had scarcely embarked upon my questions, however, when Rashmila's two older sisters, Sharmila and Pramila, entered the room and began to take over. They were only a few years older than Rashmila, attractive and intelligent, but beside their ethereal younger sister they were conspicuously extrovert and garulous. This was an opportunity to practise their English and they intercepted my questions with lightning reflexes.

They told me how they used to visit Rashmila at the Kumari Chen after she had become the Living Goddess, how they would bow and call her 'God-sister'. How, as a Goddess, Rashmila had learnt to expect everything to be done for her, to have special dishes cooked for her, to win every game, to wake up when she felt like it, and this had made her spoilt and bossy and difficult to live with when she came home. When Rashmila realized she couldn't be as bossy with her sisters at home as she had been with everyone as Living Goddess, they told me, she had resorted to playing with her dolls all day.

I sensed a touch of sibling satisfaction as the sisters described Rashmila struggling to deal with simple daily tasks after her life of conspicuous privilege, but their tales were not without sympathy or tenderness. The family shared Rashmila's destiny and Pramila and Sharmila clearly felt, above all, hugely honoured to have a Kumari as a sister. It was hard for her, they said, getting used to living with them all again. While they chattered away, Rashmila looked passively on.

Eventually, Pramila and Sharmila got up and left. They had studies to attend to. I thought at last this would leave Rashmila free to talk. But I was wrong. Her sisters, it emerged, had been playing a role that had evolved out of necessity. They had fielded my questions because Rashmila, it seemed, had lost the ability – or at least the inclination – to speak for herself.

Unused to the give and take of normal conversation, to the very concept of having to explain herself, Rashmila had fallen into the habit of allowing others to speak for her. Now, left on her own in the spotlight, with the attention of strangers focused upon her, she looked bewildered and lost. I tried to soften my approach, to temper my eagerness, but the more I tried to coax her, the less the beautiful young woman seemed able to utter a word.

It was her parents, now, who picked up the threads of her story. Yes, sometimes – they told me – when Rashmila was living in the Kumari Chen she had wanted to play outside, to run and skip with other children, but she was a Goddess – she knew she was different and couldn't do this.

What did she do when she wasn't receiving worshippers, I asked. She played with the caretaker's children or with her dolls, they said. Rashmila was still very fond of dolls. She had a huge collection given to her by devotees.

Occasionally, her mother said, Pramila and Sharmila would go to the Kumari Chen and Rashmila could play with them if she wanted. But she didn't usually want to – she used to say her natural sisters seemed strange to her, and that sometimes they didn't respect her enough. She preferred to play with the children she was familiar with in the Kumari household, who knew how to behave in the company of a Goddess.

Had Rashmila missed her parents? Rashmila stared into her lap while her mother replied. 'She didn't really remember us as her parents then,' her mother said, her sadness almost palpable. 'The caretakers at the Kumari Chen became her family. I used to go every week to worship her, and though I could speak to her when she was not on her throne, I could not cuddle her. The first time I went to worship her was very hard. I wanted to rush up and hold her but I couldn't.'

The main caretaker, Gyan Devi Shakya, then in her late forties and with four grown-up children of her own – three of them living at the Kumari Chen with their own small children – had taken the place of Rashmila's mother. The relationship between Gyan Devi and Rashmila had become that of a surrogate mother and daughter, though here the daughter could make demands that the parent was obliged to fulfil. Beyond the constraints imposed upon her by her office, a Living Goddess's whims were to be indulged at every turn. The caretakers could advise and exhort a Kumari to behave well, and encourage her to conduct herself in a manner befitting a Goddess, but they could never scold or punish her. A Goddess always knew best.

Even though she regarded Gyan Devi as her mother – her parents told me – Rashmila did not call her 'ma' (mother) or 'aji' (grandmother) as Kumaris usually did, because Gyan Devi was, in reality, her aunt – Rashmila's father's sister. So Rashmila called her 'phuphu', Nepali for 'auntie'. A Kumari's family is often closely related to the family of Kumari caretakers because they are from the same close-knit Shakya community. It is, they explained, like being brought up by extended family.

The position of Kumari's caretaker is hereditary and held by a woman. It is passed down the line from the caretaker to the wife of her eldest son, with the caretaker's husband and other family members playing a de facto role in the caretaking system. After Gyan Devi, the chief position would pass to her daughter-in-law, Kamaltara Shakya. The role had evolved out of a need for continuity and specialist management. If there was a break between Living Goddesses – if the Kumari throne was empty for any length of time – the king and the country would be at risk. The Goddess would not be there to protect and empower them. In order to keep it running smoothly the Kumari tradition required specialists practised in the complex rituals and purity constraints, who were also versed in royal protocol, and who could mediate between the Living Goddess herself, the royal priests and astrologers, and the palace.

But the caretakers are also guardians, Rashmila's father said, drawing on generations of experience of caring for Kumaris, smoothing over the transition from mortal to deity and back again. Devout and conscientious, they know how to look after the chosen ones; how to lead the little girls through their life as a Goddess. Gyan Devi – or one of her daughters, Durga or Sita – had attended to Rashmila's every need. They had watched her closely, sometimes even sleeping on the floor beside her bed if Rashmila requested it. It was Sita who had usually bathed Rashmila and helped her to get dressed on festival days and who had tied her hair up on her head.

Because she was only four at the time Rashmila couldn't remember the separation from her parents. But it had clearly been hard for her mother.

'Rashmila always seemed to feel uncomfortable when I visited her at the Kumari Chen,' her mother said. 'She didn't know how to behave with me. It was better when I brought Rashmila's baby brother with me. He was born a few years after Rashmila became Kumari. Rashmila loved playing with him. He is the sixth child in the family and our only son. We thank the Goddess for giving him to us. The same thing happened to the family of the Kumari before Rashmila. They were also blessed with a son when their daughter became Kumari.'

Rashmila seemed to be growing used to our presence. While her mother had been talking her hands had relaxed a little and she had raised her head to observe our responses. I ventured to direct another question at her. How had she felt as a Goddess? Had she felt different?

With an effort, Rashmila let slip a few words, soft whispers that had Laxminath and me leaning forward in our chairs. Her parents, listening closely, translated for her, expanding her utterances. The communication between them seemed almost telepathic.

She had felt different as the Kumari, of course – Rashmila intimated in this convoluted way. She had felt like a Goddess. Whenever she put on the *naga mala* – her serpent necklace – Rashmila responded obliquely, she had felt different. She had felt stronger, bigger. She never felt like smiling then, or talking. She had felt the Goddess's power inside her. Had she ever been frightened? No, she said. The Goddess does not feel afraid.

'What did Rashmila think about the foreigners coming to see her in the little courtyard?' I asked.

A faint smile appeared on Rashmila's face. She leaned in and murmured to her mother. She was always very curious about them, her mother said. They seemed to be dressed very strangely. She thought their hair was wild and odd because it was all different colours and often untidy. Sometimes she was tempted to call down to their Nepali guide to ask where these strange people came from, why they came to see her – didn't they have Goddesses in their own land? But she knew she had to stay silent and, specifically, not to smile or she might visit some terrible misfortune upon them.

Sometimes the foreigners would do *namaste* when she appeared. Some would just stand and stare. She thought these were very rude. Of all the foreigners who had come to see her she liked the ones she was told came from Japan the best. They did not look so very different and they had always politely applauded when she came to the window.

She had never had to come to her window if she didn't want to but she had felt it was her duty. Sometimes she would stay for longer if she found the foreigners interesting to look at. At other times it had been annoying to have to interrupt what she was doing, especially if she had been busy playing with her dolls.

Emboldened by Rashmila's increasing participation, I ventured to probe deeper, into the more delicate matter of the rumours I had heard. What about the sacrifices at Dasain and the rituals at Mul Chowk, and had Rashmila undergone any other kind of test, I asked; were there any other indications to prove that she was a Goddess; was she given alcohol or anything else to calm her down then, or to keep her quiet when she was on her throne or in her chariot?

But I had gone a step too far. Rashmila flashed me a look of irritation. She had had enough of this crass questioning. She resorted to a blank glare, withdrawing as if to some safe redoubt. For the first time I sensed the heat of a Kumari's anger.

'She does not remember the details,' her father interjected, smoothing over his daughter's hostile reaction. 'When she left the Kumari Chen, a special *puja* was performed which took away her memory of such things. These things must always be kept secret. Even if she could remember, she would not be able to say.'

The most difficult thing after her dismissal had been simply walking outside. Until then she had only walked the length of the rooms and narrow corridors inside the Kumari Chen. For eight years she had not worn shoes. Whenever she had been taken out from the Kumari Chen she had been carried in the caretaker's arms or in a palanquin, or, if it was Indra Jatra, in her chariot. On only one occasion did she walk any distance. That was at Dasain, when she was led by hand across the square to Taleju's shrine in Hanuman Dhoka. Because her feet could not touch the ground, a white cloth was laid out before her as she walked.

Rashmila had found shoes painful and awkward the first time she wore them after her dismissal – her sisters used to tease her saying she clomped about like a horse – but this was nothing compared to the difficulty she found negotiating uneven surfaces, potholes, and crowds of people and traffic. Climbing even a gentle incline was tiring and made her dizzy. Even now, when she tried to keep up with her sisters as they pelted around playing games and chasing each other, she constantly found herself off balance, falling over, and they would laugh at her. Life as a mortal was, literally, about finding one's feet.

She was at school now and finding it difficult. Traditionally a Living Goddess was considered to be omniscient and it was thought bad luck to try to teach a Kumari to read and write. Things had changed a little recently and she had received some rudimentary schooling from her caretaker, and in her last years a private tutor had come every morning to the Kumari Chen to give her maths, English and Nepali lessons. But this had not been enough to meet the challenges of ninth grade. Rashmila had found herself several years behind her peers academically and she felt distant and removed from the rest of her class in other ways. The principal still deferentially addressed *namaste* to her first; still called her '*Dyu Maiju*' – God-Miss; and many of the other children were wary of her. She found it hard to join in. Even now, no questions were ever directed specifically to her and she never put her hand up to volunteer an answer. She was still painfully embarrassed at having to sit in the same room with boys.

She felt happy at home now, though she had felt angry and miserable at first. She hadn't understood she was returning home for good, even though the caretakers and her own family had tried to explain what was about to happen to her. When the priests and the caretaker's son had brought her here, on the eighth day of Dasain, five years ago, she had imagined it was for some private ritual. Dressed in all her Indra Jatra finery she had been welcomed into the house by her mother and upstairs, in this sitting room, they had given her *sagun*, ritual food to indicate that she had finished her journey. After she had tasted the boiled egg and dried fish and taken the customary three tiny sips of the rice wine they had given her, everyone had taken photos of her. She only realized why afterwards, when the priests began to remove her heavy crown and all her golden necklaces and bracelets and anklets. This was the last time she would ever wear the ornaments of a Living Goddess.

Then the priests and the caretaker's son, whom Rashmila thought of as a brother, had returned to the Kumari Chen without her. Abandoned to her natural parents and siblings, she had felt desperately alone, isolated among strangers, and had begged to be taken back to the Kumari Chen. She thought she must have done something wrong.

Four days later the caretaker and the priest returned and she had thought at last they had come to take her back. But instead they took away the remaining gold ornaments and her red dress and, in a final act of dissolution, they released the Kumari topknot and let down her hair.

She had wept inconsolably and stayed in her bedroom for days, her mother said, refusing to eat or talk to anyone. Rashmila had felt outraged that she was now expected to eat with everyone else, humiliated to have to use the same lavatory when she had been used to having her own. It was an unhappy time. Everything was new for her. Even the tears on her cheeks felt strange. As a Goddess she had cried very rarely, and never for long. There was always someone, or something, to placate her. 'She smiles now,' said her mother gently, 'but still she has not learnt to laugh – at least on the outside.'

Once, her mother said, on a family outing, Rashmila had even run away and returned to the Kumari Chen. They had been having dinner at a cousin's house and were walking back through Durbar Square when Rashmila realized where she was and made a rush for her old home. The door was bolted for the night and Rashmila had hammered on it with her fists, begging to be let back in.

'We didn't try to bring her back,' said Rashmila's father. 'We knew it was going to be difficult for her, adjusting to life outside, and to us – that it might take a long time.'

Rashmila had stayed at the Kumari Chen for an entire week on that occasion. During that time Rashmila said she had never begrudged the little Kumari who had taken her place. She had even shared her old room with her, though now it was Rashmila sleeping on the floor, with the new Kumari tucked up in the bed, in red sheets, on a red pillow, with all her expensive new dolls around her. Rashmila was just pleased to spend time with her old family, and to talk and joke with them again.

By the end of the week, when her mother finally came to get her, Rashmila had changed. She seemed to have accepted her situation.

Her real family loved her, she realized, and she had a new life ahead of her. She considered it as being reborn.

Ex-Kumaris often go to stay at the Kumari Chen, explained Rashmila's father. They go as often as they need to. It is part of the process that helps them adjust to the outside world. Every time they go back they are warmly welcomed by the caretakers but inevitably, as time goes on, the Kumari Chen feels less and less like home. Eventually they no longer feel the need to go. But still, every year at Dasain, ex-Kumaris are reunited at the Kumari Chen, some of them staying the night if they live far away. This time is important, and not just for the occasion that links them with their past existence as the goddess Durga; they all seem to enjoy it, and it is a chance for the older ex-Kumaris to share their wisdom with the younger ones. Rashmila had just come back from staying at the Kumari Chen.

I looked at her mother, smiling proudly on the sofa next to her daughter and felt a sudden onrush of sympathy for Rashmila and the tangible chasm still yawning between them. I felt I had, in a minor way, experienced something similar myself. I looked at Rashmila and remembered, just several years earlier, sitting on a sofa next to the stranger I knew to be my natural mother. My situation, though, had been different from Rashmila's in a crucial respect. I had sought out the woman who had given me life entirely of my own volition, and after our meeting and all the empty spaces it had filled, I had returned to my adoptive parents, to my childhood home, to everything I loved and knew as my own, to the world I felt had made me the person I was.

For Rashmila, though, there was no going back. Her place was here, now, in the house of her birth. I wondered how long it would be before the kind, conciliatory woman sitting on the sofa next to Rashmila would seem like her mother again; or this house, her home.

There were still some days when Rashmila was in low spirits, her father said, and it was hard for anyone to communicate with her. But she was never sad for long now. And she was doing much better with her studies. She had a natural affinity for maths. She even had a friend or two at school.

And what of the future? Presumably marriage was out of the question? 'It is not true what they say that no one is willing to marry an ex-Kumari,' her father patiently corrected me. 'There are many rumours about this. Mainly it is because journalists who write about the Kumari talk to non-Newars who do not know about it.'

Every ex-Kumari older than Rashmila was married, he said, except for Anita, the one before Rashmila, who was still in her twenties. The oldest living ex-Kumari, Hira Devi Shakya, was over eighty years old and still with the husband she had married at fourteen. Rashmila's father smiled, 'We have never heard of an ex-Kumari's husband dying in some terrible way, like some people say. There are no dead persons being carried away from wedding-beds in the middle of the night.'

And what about Rashmila, I asked, would she like to marry some day? Rashmila blushed and stared back at her hands. It was too soon for her to consider such a step, her father said gently. 'She wants to go to college,' he added, 'she wants to study architectural engineering.'

Laxminath looked at his watch. We had imposed ourselves long enough. It was time to go.

'One last question,' I begged. 'If Rashmila had a daughter, would she be happy for her to be a Living Goddess?'

Rashmila smiled and a few precious words fell into her lap.

'If she was given a better education, so she could go straight into school with no problem,' her father expanded, 'Rashmila says "yes" – it would be a blessing if a daughter of hers became Kumari.'

'And what about you?' I asked her father. 'Would you give her up to be a Living Goddess if you had to do it again?'

Her father spoke softly but his reply was firm. 'It was hard, especially for her mother. But for us, it was our *dharma*. To have your daughter chosen by the Goddess, this is something wonderful, something we are all thankful for. We did not do it, as some people say, because of the privileges or the pension she gets afterwards. These are not so much when all is said and done. And there are many disadvantages, and problems to come afterwards. Getting used to normal life is hard for Rashmila but it will get easier. She is happy to have been Kumari and in time this happiness will lead her through the rest of her life.'

Rashmila leaned towards her father and whispered something. Her father nodded and added, 'She says the Living Goddess is for everyone. It is important we continue to worship the Kumari. It is important for all of us.'

Outside on the street, as Laxminath led us back the way we had come, the world seemed a sordid, troubled place. A drunken youth tried to beg money off us. Dogs copulated on a mound of rubbish. Thunder rolled around the mountains where, in distant and desperate villages, Maoist rebels were inexorably gathering force. My trip to Nepal was over. Despite the good fortune of meeting Rashmila, and seeing her in the gentle lap of her family, I felt saddened and frustrated, as though I had missed the main part of the film, arriving in time to catch only the closing credits. The deeper secrets of the Living Goddess – what went on in the tantric rituals, behind her golden window in the shadows of her Lion Throne Room – remained hidden from view, locked away inside the walls of the Kumari Chen.

As we passed through Durbar Square I stopped for a moment, near the great resting-pavilion of Kasthamandap, at a familiar shrine – the miniature gilded temple to Ganesh – where people paused every day for blessings on their way to work. Leaving a modest offering of coins and ringing the heavy bronze bell I pressed my hands together and bowed what I thought were my final goodbyes. The true significance of my gesture, however, eluded me. I was doing what Nepalis do, not at the end but at the start of a journey or undertaking. I was summoning the attention of the kindly Elephant God worshipped by both Buddhists and Hindus as the Gate-Keeper, Lord of Wisdom, Remover of Obstacles and Master of New Beginnings.

PART TWO

PART TWO

Chapter 10

A Kingdom in Mourning

Four years later, news broke upon the world that the entire Nepali royal family had been massacred. The story took several days to materialize but when it did, the events seemed beyond the realms of comprehension.

On the evening of 1 June 2001, it emerged, the king and queen of Nepal and their immediate family had gathered at Narayanhiti Palace for their customary fortnightly soiree. Crown Prince Dipendra had been hosting the evening and the intimate group of twenty or so family members had been received in his private quarters in grounds at the back of the palace.

The guests had been served drinks in the billiard room while they waited for the king who, adhering to royal protocol, was always last to arrive. Their host, the crown prince, had appeared heavily intoxicated. That, in itself, was not unusual – the prince was known for his excessive use of alcohol and drugs. In the moments before the king had arrived, however, he had seemed on the verge of passing out, so his younger brother, Prince Nirajan, and his cousin Paras had helped bundle him out of sight into his bedroom, away from his father's wrath, to sleep it off.

When Dipendra had suddenly reappeared at the door of the billiard room barely half an hour later, wearing combat fatigues, black jackboots and gloves, it had looked at first like he was playing some kind of practical joke. He seemed to have completely recovered. Entering the room with a look of intense concentration on his face, he had walked straight up to his father, released a blast of gunfire from a sub-machine gun, then turned and left the room.

The king had sunk slowly to the floor, blood drenching his starched white *kurta suruwal*. There were screams and calls for an ambulance as members of the family rushed to his side. The room was still in confusion when, seconds later, the crown prince had reappeared, looking – as one witness described later – like the many-armed goddess Kali wielding numerous terrifying weapons. He had walked back to his father, now lying wounded on the floor, and fired off another round, this time from an assault rifle, into the king's body at point-blank range.

As the king's youngest brother, Prince Dhirendra, reached out to try and grab the gun, Dipendra had cut him off with a burst of automatic fire through the chest. Behind him, the king's son-in-law was caught in the fusillade. Princess Shruti, rushing to her husband's aid, was also gunned down. Then the spotlight from Dipendra's M16 began scanning the room and one by one other people had begun to fall – the king's sister-in-law Princess Komal; his sisters, Princesses Shobha, Shanti and Sharada; Princess Sharada's husband; the king's cousins Princesses Ketaki and Jayanti.

The killer had moved methodically about the room, picking out the wounded, taking aim and shooting them again. Then he went outside. Queen Aishwarya and Prince Nirajan, so far unscathed, had pursued him into the garden. The other survivors, cowering behind a sofa in the billiard room, had heard a long burst of automatic fire, followed by another; and then a single pistol shot.

When rescuers finally arrived on the scene they had found Prince Nirajan's body so riddled with bullets they had trouble lifting it intact. The queen was lying face down on some steps, her red sari blasted to shreds, her skull blown to pieces. Fragments of her brain, jawbone and teeth, earrings and red glass bangles, even the red *tika* ornament from her forehead, had scattered over the area where she fell.

Dipendra himself was found lying by the edge of an ornamental fishpond, groaning loudly, the entry wound of a single bullet in the left side of his head.

~

Western commentators likened the massacre to an ancient Greek or Shakespearean tragedy. But in Nepal people looked to the laws of *karma*. Such a violent and seemingly inexplicable event, they believed, had to be mired in some deeper malaise.

Nepal was no stranger to bloodshed. Over centuries the *durbars* of Kathmandu, Patan and Bhaktapur had witnessed numerous murders, plots and coups. Accounts in the Nepali press inevitably recalled the infamous massacre at Kot, 150 years earlier, when over fifty members of the Nepali aristocracy had been gunned down in cold blood at the instigation of the ruthless and ambitious Shah queen, Rajya Laxmi, and her chief minister, Jung Bahadur Kunwar, the first of the Rana oligarchs.

Other commentators recollected the curse said to have been visited on the first Shah king, Prithvi Narayan, by the divine sage Goraknath. The legend was famous in Nepal and had cast a shadow over the Shah dynasty, threatening to limit their reign to ten generations. Birendra had been the tenth king descended from the Shah conqueror.

As I tried to digest the shocking news I remembered the king, less than four years earlier, taking the salute during the army sacrifices at Dasain. Images of the blood-soaked parade ground of Kot, associated in my mind at the time with the nineteenth-century massacre of the nobility, were now gruesomely entwined with the bloodbath of the twenty-first. I thought of Birendra and all I could see was blood.

Footage on the TV news revealed something of the scale of the tragedy unfolding in Nepal. Processions of stretchers draped with garlands and prayer scarves passed, one after another, through stunned and silent crowds as they wound their way from the military hospital in Chhauni, around the base of the great Buddhist stupa of Swayambhu, through the winding streets of old Kathmandu, past Narayanhiti Palace, and down to the Hindu cremation grounds at Pashupati. The bodies were wrapped in saffron cloth. King Birendra's stone-grey face had been anointed with vermilion. For decency's sake, the queen's missing face had been replaced with that of a china doll. In all, eleven members of the royal family died of their wounds. Not since Kot had so many funeral pyres smoked alongside each other on the royal *ghat*.

Three days after the main funeral another body was carried down to Pashupati. Crown Prince Dipendra had at last succumbed to the bullet lodged in his brain. He had been king of Nepal, in an irreversible coma, for three days.

The official thirteen days of mourning were barely over before it became clear that the country was spiralling into chaos. On the news, images of mourners lining up at barbers' shops to have their heads shaved, women lighting butter lamps in front of portraits of the dead king and queen, schoolchildren laying flowers at the gates of Narayanhiti Palace, boys scrambling up *stupas* with bundles of prayer flags, devolved rapidly into scenes of angry mobs hurling rocks, setting fire to cars, overturning rickshaws, uprooting trees, sealing off the main thoroughfares of Kathmandu with cavalcades of motorbikes and stacks of burning tyres. Riot police stormed the streets firing tear gas and rubber bullets.

King Birendra had celebrated his fifty-fifth birthday earlier in 2001. Only a few months before his murder thousands had taken to the streets of Kathmandu to wish him long life and happiness.

His loss had a profound emotional impact but there were spiritual implications, too. To the majority of Nepalis, the murder of their king was not simply regicide, it was deicide. That his son Crown Prince Dipendra may have been the perpetrator was almost impossible to countenance. As rightful heir to the throne Dipendra had been semi-divine himself; for three days he had, in effect, been king. It was bad enough to consider the son killing his father; but what did it say for the balance of the cosmos if one god had killed another?

Online blogs were abuzz with conspiracy theories. The Maoists insisted the massacre had been an Indian plot to destabilize the country. Indian commandos, they asserted, had broken into Narayanhiti Palace that night in a daring raid that had eliminated the entire royal family, successfully framed the crown prince, and then escaped back into the night during the ensuing chaos. Some pointed the finger at Chinese operatives. Others, at the CIA. Yet others turned the blame on the Maoists, with or without foreign support.

Whichever agents were thought to have been responsible, a popular theory was that an unknown man, or perhaps several men, posing as Dipendra, had broken into the palace wearing look-a-like rubber facemasks. One site even gave the name of the factory in China where these Dipendra masks were supposed to have been manufactured.

A strong argument was levelled in the crown prince's defence. How – the bloggers demanded to know – could Dipendra have possibly carried, let alone fired, all the weapons that had been used against his family – an M16 assault rifle, an MP5K sub-machine gun, two Franchi twelve-bore pump-action shotguns and a 9mm Glock pistol – when official reports claimed he was drunk and high on drugs? The massacre bore all the hallmarks of a commando-style operation; hardly – they argued – the work of a man who, only an hour earlier, had been staggering about the place incapacitated. And another question – how could Dipendra have shot himself in the left side of the head when everyone knew he was right-handed?

The most popular assertion by far, however, was that the massacre had been orchestrated by those who stood to benefit directly from it. King Birendra's brother Gyanendra – third in line for succession – had been away in the trekking capital Pokhara and had not attended the palace for the fated Friday soiree. His wife, Komal, had attended and had also been wounded – the bullet she received in her lung had missed her heart by centimetres – but this alone was not enough to deflect suspicion from Gyanendra. The fact that Gyanendra's son, Paras – now heir to the throne – had also attended the dinner and yet was one of the few to survive the massacre without a scratch seemed, to the online theorists, to prove that there was blood on Paras's as well as Gyanendra's hands.

Neither Gyanendra, his wife, Komal, nor their son, Paras, was popular in Nepal. Birendra's brother and his wife rarely appeared in public. He was – like his younger brother who had been exiled to London some time ago for his misdemeanours – rumoured to be involved in serious fraud and to have lined his pockets with revenues from the sale of stolen deities, a particularly unpalatable crime considering he was now a god-king himself.

Gyanendra had also, by a bizarre twist of fate, been 'king' – or at least puppet king – before. The Rana regents had bundled him on to the throne when he was a three-year-old, in 1950, after his grandfather King Tribhuvan had fled the country accompanied by almost every other significant member of the royal family.

Gyanendra's infant 'reign' had been short-lived. Within three months King Tribhuvan had returned to Nepal and, with backing from India, ousted the Ranas and restored power to the monarchy. But according to Gyanendra's detractors, this little spell in his grandfather's shoes had whetted his ambitions. Who knows what resentments he had nurtured for all these years, they argued; what envy must he have felt for the elder brother who had succeeded to a throne that he, Gyanendra, had occupied, centre of attention for once, dangling his little legs from the golden *asan* in the main courtyard of Hanuman Dhoka?

If Gyanendra was widely distrusted, Paras was positively despised. A drug-taking, gun-toting playboy by reputation, the *bête noire* of bars and clubs in Kathmandu, he had already been publicly blamed for causing two deaths – in front of a number of witnesses – in hit-and-run car accidents. One of the men he was alleged to have killed was a famous Nepali pop-singer. Only the year before – in August 2000 – half a million people had petitioned King Birendra to bring his nephew to justice. Paras was never charged; but in the eyes of many, he was a murderer.

In the aftermath of the massacre, grief and suspicion made an angry cocktail. As Gyanendra drove around town, rocks were thrown at his royal-number-plated car and furious youths shouted, 'Gyanendra, thief!' 'Leave the country!' 'Death to Gyanendra!' 'Hang the Murderer!' It seemed no one in Nepal was ready to welcome their new king.

~

In early July, five weeks after the massacre, the foreign pages of one of the British newspapers ran an arresting headline – 'NEPAL'S KING TURNS TO GIRL, AGED FOUR, AND HER MAGIC POWDER'. The news set my heart racing. In the thick of the events unfolding in Kathmandu was the little Kumari:

> Nepal's new 'Living Goddess' was installed in an ancient villa in the heart of Kathmandu yesterday ... three months ahead of schedule as a traditional way of allaying the Nepalese people's doubts about the legitimacy of their new king, Gyanendra.

A change of Living Goddesses after a king had died was normal procedure but this haste was unusual. The auspicious time for installing Kumaris is the Black Night of Kalaratri, between the eighth and ninth days of Dasain, when Taleju manifests herself in the Living Goddess amid the blood sacrifices in the secret courtyard of Hanuman Dhoka. Dasain, though, is in late October – still several months away. The powers behind the throne had, for some reason, decided to pre-empt this most important of ceremonies and install a new Goddess as quickly as possible.

Nepal was now focusing on the festival of Indra Jatra in early September, the critical moment when the Kumari could give her *tika* of authority to the king. The little Goddess in Durbar Square clearly continued to wield considerable influence over public opinion. The eyes of the entire country were now upon her. Her blessing on the new king was an issue of national significance, a question, perhaps, of war or peace.

But why, I wondered, was it not possible for the authorities to wait for Dasain to change Kumaris? Was her horoscope incompatible with that of the new king? Was that significant enough in itself to warrant this haste? Or had the outgoing Goddess intimated in some way that she would refuse to give the new king her blessing? And what if this new Kumari, too, refused to give her blessing to Gyanendra? Would it be his downfall?

There were larger questions still. If the Living Goddess was believed to protect the king and to provide him with *shakti*, with divine power, what was the explanation for what had happened at the time of the massacre? Had the Living Goddess withdrawn her protection from her patron?

The Maoists had been quick to make capital out of the tragedy. Already news was crossing the airwaves that a Maoist bomb had detonated – mercifully without casualties – in Kathmandu. The fate of the Nepali monarchy was clearly hanging in the balance.

But if the monarchy were indeed to be overthrown, I wondered, what was the future for the 'royal' Kumari? If atheist revolutionaries stormed the city and took over, what would that mean for the religious traditions in the valley? What was the Maoist position on living deities? Was the Living Goddess tradition itself now in danger?

The death of Birendra seemed to have done more than deprive a nation of a god and a king: it had set two worlds – ancient and modern – on a collision course. As the sense of political urgency grew, it dawned on me that now might be my last chance to revisit the Living Goddess. This time, I decided, I would not rest, even if it took numerous trips over many years, until I had found answers to all my questions.

Chapter 11

Gorakhnath's Prophecy

One day, in the hills to the west of Nepal, near the village of Lamjung, a young boy called Dravya Shah was watching over his father's cows when a mendicant appeared in his pasture. Being pious and dutiful the young boy went to fetch some milk for the beggar even though the man was one of the filthiest creatures he had ever encountered.

The young boy's forebears were the rajas of Chittor, proud warriors and pious Hindus from northern India, kings of the lineage of Gopalas, the Cow Protectors who were descended from the moon. When their great citadel fell to the Turks they had fled to the Himalaya, preferring exile to the ignominy of living under the rule of cow-killers and beef-eaters. For many years they had wandered the narrow tracks of the Himalayan foothills, crossing treacherous passes, until they had found refuge in the province of Palpa, country of the Magars – where Dravya Shah was born.

The malodorous beggar received the bowl of milk and so pleased was he with the boy's kindness that he revealed to him who he really was.

'I am Gorakhnath, Lord of the Cow Protectors, Sage of Sages,

Lord of Yogins, avatar of Shiva,' the mendicant proclaimed as the boy stood there, struck dumb with astonishment.

'O noble son of the Gopalas,' the sage continued, 'your deed is most handsomely done. In return for this milk, I grant you a boon – a city of your own and a glorious destiny. You will find a fortress not far from here, on a hill well protected and supplied by a fertile plain. This fortress belongs to the raja of the Khas. Take it for yourself and your people will be proud warriors once more.

'And for your generosity I promise you this, also: one day a descendant of yours will conquer the unconquerable – the Valley of the Goddess, home of the Malla kings. One day your kingdom will echo greatness through the Himalaya like the rolling of thunder, and the name of your warriors will strike fear into the hearts of enemies.'

So saying the sage disappeared, leaving only the impression of his footprints behind him, steaming in a cowpat.

As Dravya Shah grew to manhood the prophecy stirred within him. Marshalling a band of warrior kinsmen, he captured the fortress near Lamjung, slaying the Khas raja with his own hand, and renaming it 'Gorkha' after the divine sage.

Soon the fortress of Gorkha, like an eagle's nest in a forest teeming with other birds, held sway among the Twenty-Four Kingdoms of the region; and Dravya's descendants, the Shah rajas of Gorkha, grew in strength and ambition and began to cast their eyes further afield. They began to think about conquering the great Valley of Nepal, for they were envious of the Malla kingdoms with their golden-roofed palaces and temples and their sophisticated ways.

But try as they might, the Gorkha kings were unable to make any headway with their ambition, for the valley was protected by the Goddess. So instead, they entered into alliances with the Malla kings, trying to pit one against the other. Yet still the valley would not yield.

One day, a young prince of Gorkha, Prithvi Narayan Shah, sat on a high rocky bluff not far from the *durbar* of Gorkha, pondering these things. His father, Narbhupal Shah, had tried – and failed – to seize a fortress from the Mallas and now the raja lay in his chamber in the *durbar* a broken man, his ambition like a gasping fish upon a riverbank.

As the young prince sat upon his stone seat on the ridge, gazing out upon the ice-blown peaks of Annapurna and Ganesh Himal, possessed by resentful thoughts, a *sadhu* in filthy rags approached him.

At first the prince tried to ignore him but the *sadhu* was insistent and so, eventually, Prithvi Narayan Shah went back to the palace, his mind still taken up with thoughts of conquest, and returned with the *sadhu's* begging bowl brimming with curd. The *sadhu* received the bowl wordlessly from the prince's hands and began to drink it down in greedy gulps; but no sooner had the *sadhu* finished the curd than he was overcome by convulsions, his wasted stomach began to churn and in great heaving gobbits he vomited the curd back into the bowl.

Wiping the vomit from his lips the *sadhu* handed back the bowl to the prince, indicating that he should drink it. Disgusted, Prithvi Narayan Shah hurled the bowl back at the filthy old man, soiling the *sadhu's* outstretched hands.

Then the *sadhu*, drawing himself up to his full height, revealed his identity to the hapless prince.

'Oh prince of Gorkha,' the *yogin* cried, his words echoing around the rocks, 'descendant of the noble Gopalas! Know that I am Gorakhnath, Sage of Sages, Guru of Gurus, from whom your kingdom claims its name. I have come to tell you that the time is ripe to fulfil my promise to your noble ancestor Dravya Shah – that his lineage will conquer the Valley of Nepal, home of the Malla kings.'

Then Gorakhnath recalled himself to the gobbits of curd dripping from his hands and the empty bowl cast aside on the ground.

'But oh, rash prince, see what you have done!' – and as the great *yogin's* rage began to mount, his voice thundered over the ridge, sending small avalanches of rocks down the mountainsides – 'had you but swallowed your pride I would have granted your line glory in perpetuity. Instead – oh ingrate! – you have rejected my *prasad*. So now I tell you – ' and he shook his curd-splattered fingers before the prince's face, 'this is how many generations of your lineage shall rule Nepal – ten. This many and no more. Mark you well. The tenth of your descendants will be the last Shah king.'

Chapter 12

The Way of the Diamond Thunderbolt

The atmosphere in Nepal was still extremely tense when I arrived back in December 2001 though, six months after the royal family massacre, the immediate crisis for the monarchy seemed to have been averted. The new Living Goddess – a three-year-old – hastily installed in July, had given the new king her blessing at the September festival of Indra Jatra.

The event had been splashed across the front of every newspaper in Kathmandu. King Gyanendra had emerged from the throne room of the Kumari Chen on the last day of the Living Goddess's festival with the distinctive red *tika* on his forehead and the country had breathed a sigh of relief. When the festival of Dasain in October also passed without incident, with the mass sacrifice at Kot duly conducted and all the Mother Goddess shrines around the valley propitiated with blood, a nervous public was further assuaged.

The Maoists, though, were continuing to take advantage of the anger and uncertainty and, for the first time, their presence was clearly evident in the vicinity of Kathmandu. In the week preceeding my arrival Maoists had started to target multinational companies based in the valley. Unilever and Coca-Cola factories on the outskirts of the capital had been planted with incendiary devices. Though not on the scale of major terrorist events (the devices were more like glorified fire-crackers than car bombs), the explosions, nonetheless, had significant psychological impact and most large businesses, including hotels, were now paying the Maoists protection money. The Maoists had just called for a nationwide *bandh* – a general strike – forbidding people to go to work on pain of reprisals. The use of cars, buses, trucks and non-emergency journeys would be banned. They were flexing new muscles, and the Nepali army were flexing back in response. The sandbag sentry posts that had been visible only at the airport on my last visit were now a feature of every crossroad and entry-point into the city. Kathmandu was readying itself for war.

Gyanman Pati Vajracharya's house was in a small, quiet courtyard on the northern side of Durbar Square, just beyond the temple of the Navadurga – more popularly known as Shiva-Parvati Temple after the amorous deities gazing, arms around each other, out of its top window. The courtyard itself was called Layku Bahil after its proximity to the *layku*, the old royal palace.

A member of the priestly caste of Vajracharyas, Gyanman Pati's lineage was the one from which the 'Raj Gubhaju' – the royal Buddhist priest officiating for the Living Goddess – came. Gyanman Pati was in close touch with the Kumari Chen, and his elder brother, Yagyaman Pati, was keeper of an important collection of original family documents pertaining to the Kumari tradition.

I had been given the introduction by a Nepali friend, Prem Basnyet, who had directed a film in the 1970s – the first colour movie ever made in the country – about the Kumari. Though his film had been a work of pure fiction – an adaptation of a Nepali novel that, he confessed, took as its premise the wildest of the Kumari rumours – Prem had made friends with Gyanman Pati and his family in the process and had recommended them as a first base. I was hoping, in particular, they would be able to provide insights into the Kumari's role as protectoress of the king and the tantric beliefs that bound them together, as well as the circumstances surrounding the Kumari's dismissal shortly after the massacre.

Gyanman waved me through into the little courtyard with a

characteristic large stone *chaitya* in the middle and two smaller ones beside it. Despite the modern buildings with flat roofs that had replaced the old brick and timber constructions on three sides, the courtyard retained a reassuring sense of timelessness and tranquillity.

The main shrine of the courtyard, the *kvahpah dya*, remained true to the original, its entrance – on the eastern side – marked by two stone lions, an old carved wooden *torana* and an arch of blackened oil-lamps. Inside was a statue of the Buddha Akshobhya, one of the Transcendent Buddhas. The shrine was open to worship by anyone – even foreigners – but only initiated members of the *sangha*, like Gyanman Pati, could enter the shrine itself.

When it was his turn as guardian, Gyanman Pati would rise shortly after sunrise and open up the shrine to perform *nitya puja*, awakening the Buddha with offerings to arouse his senses; the sounding of a gong and the ringing of a bell to awaken his hearing; incense and flowers for their evocative smell; a light to open his eyes; food to taste; a ritual sprinkling of water for the Buddha's morning wash. He would recite hymns or selections from the *Sutras*, and at night he would put Akshobhya to bed with the evening *arati* – an offering of light.

But there was another kind of worship in this *bahal* – also fundamental to Newar Buddhism – that was conducted behind closed doors. Above the *kvahpah dya* shrine was an ornately carved fivefold casement window just like the one in the courtyard of the Kumari Chen at which the Living Goddess appeared. Behind this window, in a small closed room, was the *agam* – a private shrine where the esoteric deities of the courtyard were worshipped. Entrance to the *agam* was restricted to members of the Vajracharya community who had undergone special initiation – like Gyanman Pati himself. The initiation qualified Gyanman as a practitioner of Vajrayana – the complex, secretive practice of Newar Buddhists.

Vajrayana is key to understanding worship of the Living Goddess from the Buddhist side. It is the esoteric strand of the Mahayana school of Buddhism – the branch of Buddhism that had ultimately prevailed in the Valley of Nepal.

Vajrayana – the 'Way of the Vajra' – derives its name from a powerful tantric symbol equated with the Diamond or Thunderbolt. Vajrayana is also sometimes called simply 'Mantrayana', the Way of the Mantras; or 'Tantrayana', the Tantric Way. Heavily influenced by Hindu tantric ideas, it evolved as a specialized path within the Mahayana school offering practitioners the experience of enlightenment within this lifetime and the acquisition of extraordinary powers.

No one knows how old the philosophy of Tantra is, though there are hints of it in India's oldest literature. It was already well established in Bengal, Assam, Kashmir and part of southern India by the sixth century CE. It is not known exactly when it took root in Nepal though it was probably around the seventh century; and it was certainly a dominant force in the Kathmandu Valley by the twelfth century. It is still a living cult in all these places. True to its radical nature, Tantra thrived on the periphery, off the beaten track, away from the centres of empire or the great dominions. It was, historically, a grass-roots reaction to the established conventions of Hinduism: patriarchy, the caste system and notions of ritual purity.

The tantric practitioner had, therefore, theoretically at least, to commit to acts that were deliberately polluting and broke social conventions and taboos. A vegetarian would eat meat, a teetotaller drink alcohol. The left hand, normally reserved for wiping away excrement, would be used for eating – which was why tantric practices were often known as *vamachari*, 'left-handed practices'. A *tantrika* would have sex with his wife while she was menstruating, and drink her menstrual blood, or his own semen; or eat the brains from the skull of a corpse. While these practices are still believed to go on among the wild *sadhus* and *sannyasins*, in Newar tantric practice, under the influence of Buddhism, most of these acts have become ritualized and are internalized as visual meditations.

The intention, however, is the same. Unlike mainstream religions that regard the abnegation of the flesh as the means to redemption, in Tantra it is the body itself, its desires and sensations, that is the key. The sexual urge is considered to be one of the most powerful of all the body's impulses. It represents the overpowering instinct for unity – for the male and female to be drawn together, entering a state beyond polarity. The moment of sexual climax is a moment of physical transcendence, when the mind becomes empty of thoughts and the ego is extinguished by an experience of supreme bliss. This is the moment that Tantra aims to expand. Gradually, through meditation and control of desire, the *tantrika* has to learn to reach that same experience without releasing energy or becoming a slave of lust. Theoretically, he, or she, can eventually perform this act of rocket-fuelled transcendence on his or her own, through visualizations alone.

In Hindu Tantra, it is *shakti*, the female principle, that is considered to be the empowering force. In Vajrayana, it is the male principle – *pragya*, sometimes translated as 'compassion' or 'compassionate means' – that brings to life the fundamental feminine principle of wisdom – *upaya*. Another distinction is the goal: the Hindu *tantrika* seeks union with an all-pervading cosmic consciousness; while the Buddhist *tantrika* seeks immersion in the ultimate reality of emptiness. The underlying philosophy of Hindu and Buddhist Tantra, however, is the same: the attainment of the great bliss – *mahasukha* – of enlightenment is only possible through the resolution of polarity; through bringing together and reuniting the cosmic aspects of male and female.

Crucially, since sexual experience is fundamental to tantric practice, Vajrayana took the extraordinary step of converting the traditional vows of the Mahayana monk into a new set of vows, regarded as being higher and much more powerful than those of the Mahayana school. The young Vajrayana monk is, after a brief spell of conventional monasticism, required to renounce celibacy, to re-enter the world of the householder and, ultimately, to seek a sexual partner with whom he can practice the transformative art of Tantra. A wife who can participate in all the rituals on equal terms as a catalyst for her husband is essential for tantric Buddhist practice.

This move away from celibacy and renunciation contributed to, if not determined, the survival of Buddhism in Nepal. By 1200 CE – the time of the early Malla kings – almost all of the monastic courtyards in towns around the valley had converted to Vajrayana principles and the Buddhist monks who lived in them had begun to marry and have children.

They had also, thanks to the strong influence of their kings, fallen into step with the Hindu caste system, an anomalous situation whereby Buddhists – who were by definition egalitarian and non-discriminatory – found themselves accepting hierarchical status. Buddhist monks and priests – the Shakyas and Vajracharyas – were designated high caste, at the top of the pile, on a par with Hindu Brahmins.

While the Mahayana school of Buddhism expanded successfully into China, Japan, Indonesia and Korea, it was only in the Himalaya – in Nepal and Tibet – that the Vajrayana strand of Buddhism fully flourished. Here, like Hindu Tantra, Vajrayana progressed from being a rebellious movement on the periphery into mainstream practice and eventually became institutionalized, its intense, complicated, subversive systems once again the preserve of a spiritual elite. In the Kathmandu Valley, Vajrayana – though in theory open to anyone – came to be practised almost exclusively by the high Newar caste of Buddhist religious specialists – the Shakyas and Vajracharyas – who received tantric initiation by dint of their birthright and through instruction by elders of their own caste.

Adopting the practice of Vajrayana, however, had not meant that the 'Great Way' of Mahayana was in some way negated or eclipsed – rather that now, with a tantric *agam* established above the *bahal's* public shrine, a powerful new current of Buddhism was being discharged through the old. Vajrayana is the invisible backbone running through the visible body of Mahayana belief.

With the introduction of Vajrayana, deities could be worshipped on different levels at once – in public, with their exoteric names and faces; and in private, with identities they revealed only to the initiated. This concept of simultaneous inner and outer worship extends through every devotional performance in the valley. Every festival or public ceremony is supported in some way by accompanying esoteric rituals. This is true, too, for the Living Goddess. The Kumari is worshipped publicly by lay people in one way; and she is worshipped in private, in a different way, with a secret identity known only to initiated priests.

Like all Shakyas and Vajracharyas – ex-Kumari Rashmila's father, Surya Ratna Shakya, included – Gyanman Pati Vajracharya had undergone the rite known as *bare chuyagu* – the making of a traditional Buddhist monk. With the subsequent 'Laying Aside of the Robes' ritual, Gyanman and his fellows then passed from Theravada into Mahayana Buddhism and became officially engaged in the *sangha* as 'householder monks'.

A further rite of passage only for Vajracharyas – called '*acharya (achah) luyegu*', the 'Making of an Acharya, or spiritual teacher' – was conducted immediately after the boys had disrobed. It was the ritual that formally enrolled them in a Vajracharya *sangha* and entitled them to perform the fire ritual and to act as family priests if they wished.

The 'Making of the Acharya' initiation is performed in the *agam* of the main lineage *bahal* and only initiated Vajracharya members of the *sangha* can witness it. During the ritual the young Vajracharya novices are presented with all the paraphernalia of a priest of tantric Buddhism, the most important of which is the bell – or *ghanta* – and the *vajra*.

The *vajra* is generally made of bronze, and shaped like a knot with inverted prongs at either end. It is a symbol that appears at all Buddhist sites in the valley. It represents the power of the thunderbolt and the lightning speed at which the holder of the *vajra* can attain enlightenment. It also conveys the 'adamantine' qualities of a diamond – clarity, brilliance, rarity and indestructibility, qualities that are considered to be the mark of a *siddha*, an enlightened being.

The *vajra* represents the male principle and is always held in the right hand; the bell is female, symbolic of the transcendent, salvific principle of wisdom, and always held in the left. The Vajracharya priest employs these two objects in every ritual he performs. Used together, they embody the coming together of male and female, the union of opposites and resolution of duality.

In addition to these socially mandated life-cycle rituals, however, there is another, more highly charged initiation. It is taken voluntarily, later in life, and is open to Shakyas and Vajracharyas, as well as Tuladhars – members of the middle-ranking merchant caste. This is *diksha* – the stage that passes on the knowledge of Vajrayana, the Way of the Tantras.

'*Diksha* is highly secret,' Gyanman said. 'It is even longer and more complex than the other steps. It demands great application and mental energy. It has to be taken with a partner, a man and a woman together. My wife and I took *diksha* as soon as we were married, when I was twenty-three years old. We took special training and studied under a guru for several months. The ceremony itself lasted five days.

'There were forty-eight members in the group altogether – my wife and I, my two sisters and their husbands, my brother Shyamman and his wife. Thirty-eight of us were from Vajracharya families and four were Shakya. The initiation was conducted by Jogmuni Vajracharya, one of the greatest tantric gurus at the time.'

Unsurprisingly Gyanman would not discuss the nature of the initiation itself as it involved secret rituals including – at least symbolically – sexual practice, but he was enthusiastic about the effects.

'*Diksha* is a good thing,' he said, 'and very powerful. It is important to continue the practices of our ancestors. This wisdom, passing down the generations, is very precious. These are things we cannot learn from modern life.'

Diksha took Gyanman to the level of a *tantrika* who could now enter the *agam*, the secret tantric shrine behind the fivefold window above the shrine to Akshobhya. It also meant he could perform daily worship to the tantric deities in his own household *agam* – a shrine room hidden away on the top floor of his house that only other initiated members of the family could enter.

~

Gyanman steered me towards his front door and through a dark ground-floor storeroom to the staircase. Though modern, the house conformed to the traditional notions of a protective *mandala*. As we progressed up the stairs we were, in Newar terms, ascending in stages closer to the gods. The ground floor, with its bicycles and motorbikes, tools and storage containers, was the worldly level. The first floor, divided into bedrooms, was for sleeping. The second floor, with a large convivial room was for work and recreation. The kitchen where '*jaa*' – boiled rice – the 'purest' and most sacred of foods to Newars, was prepared and eaten was on the top floor, closest to heaven. Even though now, like most Newars, Gyanman freely admitted guests from other castes and even outsiders into his house, he was still selective about whom he invited into the family kitchen. Next to the kitchen was the household *agam* which was still strictly taboo, open only to family members who had received *diksha*.

Gyanman's elder brother Yagyaman Pati was waiting in the sitting room on the second floor, along with another younger brother, Shyammam Pati – a cosmetics dealer. Yagyaman rose to his feet to welcome me. He was wearing traditional *suruwal* and a colourful Nepali *topi*. There was a distinct family resemblance between all three brothers with Yagyaman assuming the gravitas of the eldest.

'Please come, sit,' Yagyaman said, inviting me to some cushions on a woven rice-mat facing the windows.

A small sofa and coffee table nodded to western convention but the family still generally preferred to sit crossed-legged on the floor. At the other end of the room a dresser showcased trophies of imported whisky and gifts of exotic bottles of perfume. In pride of place on top of the dresser, garlanded with fresh marigolds, were photographs of the murdered King Birendra and Queen Aishwarya. There were no pictures yet, I noticed, of Gyanendra and his wife.

Although he was the eldest, and had undergone further rigorous training and initiations as a Vajracharya, Yagyaman had decided not to take up the profession of an acting priest. Instead he had spent his working life as a controller in the government's Finance Department. But since his retirement he had taken on a number of Newar students interested in Newar Buddhism and had given consecration to around thirty of them. He had taken part in several big tantric *pujas* and reconsecrations of temples. He was deeply concerned about the declining number of practising Vajracharyas and what he saw as the erosion of spiritual discipline.

Neither Yagyaman nor his younger brother Shyamman lived in Layku Bahil any longer. The family had grown too large for the house here so the eldest and the youngest brothers had moved with their families to modern houses in outlying neighbourhoods of Kathmandu. The bond with Durbar Square, though, was still strong. Whenever there was a major festival the entire family descended on the old family house. The rooftop provided a grandstand view of all the great events – Ghode Jatra (the festival of the horse), Gai Jatra (the festival of the cow), the chariot-pulling festival of Seto Macchendranath and Indra Jatra – the festival incorporating the great chariot procession of the Living Goddess. The little courtyard of Layku Bahil tied the family to their ancestors, to the navel of the Newar universe and the spiritual orbit of the gods.

'The centre of Kathmandu is like a mirror,' Yagyaman said, as I followed his gaze out of the windows on to Durbar Square.

'Everything that goes on in the rest of Nepal, especially inside the valley, is reflected here. It makes an echo. I don't mean just the political demonstrations and protests that have been going on here recently, but the omens the gods show us. Things that happen here, in the centre of Kathmandu, echo what is going on elsewhere in the country – or tell us what may be about to happen.'

The sun was throwing purple shadows across the flagstones and the last of the marigold sellers were packing up their baskets on the lowest plinth of Maju Deval temple. The rickshaw rank by the temple to Narayan was doing swift end-of-day business. *Sadhus*, waiting for photo-snapping tourists on the steps of Navadurga temple, were ready to call it a day, heading back towards the *ashrams* at Pashupati. Across the way the golden finials on the rooftop of the Kumari Chen glinted in the evening rays.

'Most of these temples here were constructed in the time of Mahendra Malla, in the sixteenth century,' Yagyaman said. 'They were built according to the tantric code.'

Tantra became fundamental to the authority of kings. The powers it conferred could be used not just for spiritual ends but for material benefit, including the acquisition of worldly power. It became essential to the king's ability to rule – could be key to his very survival. Through tantric practice the body of a king could become one with his kingdom. He could exert power over his dominion and his subjects, he believed, by harnessing the divine energy within his own body. He could extend this energy, and the powers of protection it conferred, to the very borders of his kingdom. It was, however, particularly important for a king to exercise supreme self-control, so that he used his powers for the good of his people rather than for himself.

The Malla kings had all been *tantrikas*, and several of them, like Pratap Malla, the king of Kathmandu, or Siddhinarasimha, the king of Patan in the seventeenth century, became famous for having acquired the attainments of a *siddha* through the practice of *shakti* tantra. It was said they could walk through walls, be in two places at once, survive extreme temperatures of heat and cold, survive assassination, resist the strongest poison, fill the treasuries with vast fortunes, bend the Nagas to their sway and force them to release the rains.

Tantric powers were particularly desirable in war. The inner sight, the *dhyan drishti*, of the tantric raja was believed to bring heightened powers of perception whereby he could master the elements, visualize distant terrain and predict the movement of his enemy.

In Kumari worship the Mallas believed they had found the most powerful, immediate method of acquiring tantric powers. By identifying their own body with the living body of the child Kumari they had hotwired themselves to the *shakti* of the Goddess. Not only did the Living Goddess confer on them remarkable powers of their own, with her third eye she could see beyond the valley wall and signal approaching danger.

When Prithvi Narayan Shah had embarked on his campaign to conquer Nepal he had also turned to *shakti* tantra. He had consulted the *Svarodaya*, a tantric manual that showed him how to connect his body and the rhythms of his breathing with the energy of the Goddess and project it into the body of his army. But he also knew he could only defeat the Mallas and take their lands if he learnt their particular tantric secrets. Copying their worship of the Living Goddess and adopting Taleju as his personal goddess had been the key to his success. It was also, he believed, crucial to the survival of his dynasty and every Shah king since, including King Birendra, had been a *shakti tantrika*.

The temples around the royal palace, Yagyaman went on, are prisms of tantric energy founded by the kings not just for worship, but for empowerment and protection. Like lightning conductors they absorb surges of activity in the atmosphere. It is not unusual for temple buildings to reverberate with disturbances felt – or about to be felt – in the valley or even in the rest of the country. A battle or a famine affecting people miles from Kathmandu could result in cracks or falling masonry in a temple in the city centre. The house of the Living Goddess is the most reactive building of all.

'Recently, night watchmen at the Kumari Chen have been hearing the sound of distant gunfire inside the courtyard,' said Yagyaman. 'The caretakers have been woken by it too. It's Maoist activity they can hear, even though it's happening far away in the hills.'

Not only temple buildings but the images of the gods inside them could communicate impending disaster, their bronze faces breaking out in beads of sweat or cracking under the strain. No deity is more expressive than the Living Goddess herself.

'The Kumari, because she is flesh and blood, reacts very swiftly,' said Yagyaman. 'Her face, her body and her mood change according to what is happening around her.'

This could be on a personal level, in response to individual worship by lay devotees. Supplicants, seeking a particular boon, watch her closely to see how she responds to the offerings they give her.

'If the Kumari is happy,' he said, 'things are good. The caretakers do their utmost to make sure she remains content. But if she falls ill or if she becomes angry, something is going wrong. If she fools around or behaves in some strange way when she is on her throne, especially during *nitya puja* or some big worship, then that is a sign that something bad is on its way.'

There are specific signs to look out for, he went on.

'If the Kumari has a very gloomy face during the moment of worship, and particularly if she looks to her left and her right, that means there will be quarrelling at the worshipper's home. If she trembles then the worshipper will go to jail – for how long depends on the length of the tremble. If she claps her hands, the worshipper should fear that something bad will be coming his way from the king. If she makes a sort of drumming with her fingers, then there will be a theft in the worshipper's house.'

If she only picks at the food she is offered, Yagyaman went on, the person offering it will lose money. If she kicks the ground or rubs her foot on the floor, the worshipper will need to leave his house. If she pinches her lips with her nails, or bows her head without speaking, or winks without speaking, or looks sideways at the worshipper, this indicates that she is not satisfied and the worshipper will have to begin his *puja* all over again.

Worst of all, he said, is if the Kumari cries during the time of worship. This very rarely happens. If it does, the worshipper will fall seriously ill. If the Kumari weeps and rubs her eyes at the same time, the worshipper will die very soon. If the Kumari refuses to eat and begins to talk, then the worshipper's spouse will die.

'But if the Goddess remains in a good mood throughout the *puja* and shows none of these signs,' Gyanman said, 'then we know the worship has been successful and the Kumari will fulfil our wishes.'

The Kumari's passivity is not a cause for concern but – on the contrary – a sign that all is well.

More dramatic mood swings or upsets, however, particularly if they are prolonged and unrelated to any individual puja, are believed to indicate a broader malaise, something threatening the country as a whole – an impending disaster like a drought, perhaps, or an earthquake, or civil unrest. This inevitably implicated the king as the body of state, the *chakravartin* – turner of the wheel, responsible, through his own devotional practice, for maintaining harmony and stability.

If the caretakers are unable to restore the Kumari's spirits on their own, or if she becomes actually physically ill, they send for the royal priests and astrologers, acting on the king's behalf, who do everything in their power to make amends with special *pujas* and offerings. If the Kumari can be cured or placated then disaster is averted and harmony restored. But turning the course of events is fraught with danger and sometimes even the most powerful tantric priests can be swept aside by the forces of *karma*.

Yagyaman gave an example. 'In Vikram Samvat 2036 (1979 CE),' he said, 'the Kumari – it was Anita Shakya at that time – fell ill. The priest Dharmananda Vajracharya went to Kumari Chen to do *puja*. He said he would cure the Kumari within three days. But the priest died. Eight days later his eldest son died, too. And then his wife died a month and a half afterwards. The Kumari Chen informed the palace and the king became very worried.'

Eventually, in May that year, the king announced a referendum and the Kumari was cured.

Rashmila's parents had told me a similar story. The only time their daughter had fallen ill as Kumari was in 1989-90. As communist states across Europe crumbled and pro-democracy demonstrations occupied China's Tiananmen Square, the 'Jana Andolan', or People's Movement, began to push for democracy in Nepal and violence erupted in the city. At the same time – according to her parents – Rashmila had begun to suffer violent headaches and mood swings, bursting into tears without reason. Eventually, after several months of curfews and rioting, summary arrests and imprisonments, and 300 people dead, King Birendra announced he was lifting the ban on political parties and was ready, at last, to accept the role of constitutional monarch. Nepal had become a democracy. Rashmila's headaches disappeared.

Gyanman's family had been aware of Rashmila's indisposition even before her headaches materialized.

'For three years in the run-up to democracy,' he said, 'the Kumari caretaker was worried because she could not tie up Rashmila's hair. It would come undone, no matter how she tried to tie it.' Like the Buddha's cranial mound, or *ushnisha*, the Kumari's topknot was an expression of cosmic order. 'The day the king accepted constitutional change, the caretaker gathered up Kumari's hair into a topknot in the morning and it stayed where it was.'

With the Living Goddess acting, in effect, as the nation's litmus paper, the king's advisers naturally kept a constant eye on her moods. If there was ever cause for concern, the royal priest dispatched *puja* plates from the palace and special prayers were offered as reparation.

For the king there was no ritual more important, or more weighted with personal risk, than the Kumari's blessing at Indra Jatra. It was the most public signal of his authority to rule. But no one can force the Kumari's hand. If she decided not to dip her finger in vermilion and place that crucial mark on his forehead, the king was doomed.

On 10 Jestha VS 2011 (15 September 1954), Gyanman's family had watched King Tribhuvan, Birendra's grandfather, arrive at the Kumari Chen to receive his *tika*. Crown Prince Mahendra was at his side.

'I was a small boy at the time,' remembered Gyanman. 'We saw the king enter but then we waited and waited and he didn't come out. We could see the king's shadow from here – inside the golden window on the third floor where the lion throne is. He was kneeling but the Kumari would not give him *tika*.'

Later, the caretakers told Gyanman's family what had happened. When King Tribhuvan had come before the Kumari, the Goddess had steadfastly folded her arms. The king had suggested that his son Mahendra, the crown prince, should go forward to try to encourage her. The Kumari had immediately smiled at Mahendra and unfolded her arms, ready to give him the *tika*. So Mahendra moved aside to let his father receive the blessing. But again, when Tribhuvan stepped up, the Kumari had folded her arms. This happened several times. In the end, the Kumari, looked steadily at King Tribhuvan and began to weep. The king, evidently uneasy, decided to withdraw. He offered the customary gold coin, bowed his head at the Kumari's feet and left without receiving the *tika*, instructing his son to receive it on his behalf. Six months later the forty-nine-year-old Tribhuvan died of heart failure and his son Mahendra ascended the throne.

It was no surprise that the new Kumari – and her reactions – had become the subject of intense speculation in recent months.

'The Kumari is a big subject these days,' said Yagyaman. 'Everyone wants to know how she looks, what she is doing, how she is reacting to the present situation, whether she favours the new king.

'But one thing very few people are asking is how is she being worshipped. Are we doing the right thing? Is she satisfied or dissatisfied? The Kumari has to be worshipped in conditions of utmost purity and devotion. If not, the Goddess inside her will leave and the whole country – not just the king but all the people – will be at risk.'

The oblique reference to Gyanendra brought an uneasy hiatus in the conversation. Outside Gyanman Pati's house a motorbike revved an impatient path through pedestrians. Beyond the Londonesque balcony of the old royal palace I could see lights on in the upper floor of the Kumari Chen. A string of coloured bulbs had popped to life under the eaves.

What about recently, this summer – in the weeks before the massacre, I asked; had the previous Kumari shown any signs that all was not well?

For a while there was an uncomfortable silence. I felt the gazes of the murdered king and queen boring down on me from the dresser.

'There were bad things happening inside the Kumari Chen six months ago,' said Gyanman at last, shaking his head sadly.

'The Kumari insisted on staying on another year,' Shyamman began to explain, slowly. 'The caretakers were thinking of changing her at Dasain in year 2000. The Kumari was already eleven years old and they'd found a child to replace her. But they thought there was time. No one knew such terrible things would happen. When the Kumari started showing the signs of inauspiciousness in 2001 it was already too late ...'

'There was some kind of disease on her skin, I think, something that crept up from her chest on to her face,' said Gyanman unsteadily. 'They were angry, red spots, like smallpox but not that. A rash. We didn't know what it was but it was clear the Goddess inside her was no longer happy, something was very wrong.'

'When was this?'

'Twenty-four days before the incident in the palace.'

'Are you saying,' I persisted, 'that the Kumari at the time of the massacre wasn't, somehow, legitimate?'

'It is difficult to speak of these things,' said Yagyaman, reluctantly. 'Even now there is much that we ourselves do not know, perhaps that we should not know. Some say there were powerful influences, a battle going on, you could say.'

Outside, night was falling like a shield, the daytime temperature plummeting. Walking towards the ghostly silhouette of Hanuman Dhoka, past the fearsome White Mask of Bhairab, I paused at Jagannath Temple. The erotic figures cavorting in the rafters, exorting the world to tantric practice, their limbs accentuated by the kiss of artificial light in the falling darkness had, like the carvings on the roof struts of the old royal palace itself and temples all over the valley, been an endless source of amusement to us as teenagers. But now I saw them with a different eye.

Standing in the middle of Durbar Square, between temples of Vishnu, the old royal palace and the Kumari Chen, with Taleju's gigantic temple looming in the background, I could sense the incredible power tantric practice had incarnated in the king in the eyes of his subjects, his authority radiating out from the centre like the rays of the sun.

As I headed for New Road I passed beneath the Kumari's golden window. The flicker of oil lamps and tremulous ringing of a tiny hand bell alerted me to a *puja* being conducted inside the throne room. I wondered about the tantric connection between the king and the Kumari in the present day, and what Gyanman Pati and his brothers had told me about the Kumari at the time of the royal family massacre. Had her disqualifying illness meant the Goddess had withdrawn her *shakti* from the Kumari, leaving King Birendra defenceless? Or had there been other influences at play?

Chapter 13

The Royal Astrologer

The royal astrologer lived in Patan, just south of the Bagmati. Hardly a move was made by the king or any other members of the royal family without consulting him. He advised them on auspicious dates for travel plans, diplomatic engagements, business meetings and every major personal decision in their lives. He was also a key figure in the selection process of the Kumari and determined auspicious times for all her rituals. If things went wrong, the royal astrologer was, alongside the tantric priests, first to be consulted. I hoped he would be able to shed some light on what had been going on in those fateful weeks leading up to the royal family massacre.

Patan is still often referred to by its older name – Lalitpur, City of Loveliness. Once, the two Malla cities of Lalitpur and Kathmandu would have been totally distinct but now, thanks to the continuous sprawl of buildings in between, Patan has become virtually a suburb of the capital. Its Durbar Square is barely three miles from the centre of Kathmandu.

Even now, however, Patan adheres to a gentler, kinder pace of life. Down labyrinthine backstreets, hidden courtyards echo with the sounds of hammers tapping against bronze, the rush of bellows and blowtorches, the insect whine of metal-grinders. Most of the original medieval layout survives. Elderly men in *topis* sit on resting platforms watching the world go by; women in saris wash their hair under *makara* spouts in sunken bathing-tanks; children chase each other around courtyard *chaityas*.

In Kathmandu, it was Mahendra Malla who had made his mark on the Durbar Square; here the temples and statues, pavilions and palace courtyards, devotional gongs and bells, sing the praises, first and foremost, of Siddhinarasimha Malla, Mahendra's great-grandson. Siddhinarasimha was the king who, according to legend, had recaptured the *mantra* of Taleju as it blazed across the heavens, having escaped the dying lips of his elder brother Lakshminarasimha incarcerated in the royal palace in Kathmandu. The Goddess's *mantra*, it is said, had given the young prince the power to defeat the notoriously hostile nobles of Patan and take the throne.

One of the first things Siddhinarasimha had done to secure his lineage in Patan was establish a temple to Taleju next to the royal palace, with a separate shrine for her in a courtyard he called Mul Chowk – a carbon copy of the system in the palace complexes in Bhaktapur and Kathmandu.

Siddhinarasimha's devotion to Taleju and his powers as a *siddha* were legendary. He would meditate for days on a stone platform in the palace courtyard of Sundari Chowk, sitting naked in the biting winds of winter and intensifying his austerity in summer by lighting fires all around him. And every morning the Rajarsi – Sage among Kings – as he was known, would walk across the water of the magnificent tank he had built in Taleju's honour in the palace gardens known as the Bhandarkhal, to pick lotuses for the Goddess.

While his private worship focused on his lineage Goddess, Siddhinarasimha was – like all Malla kings – conscientious in his patronage of the other gods. The stone *shikara* to Krishna at the entrance to Durbar Square was built by him; and at the far end, the magnificent Vishveshvara temple dedicated to Shiva, guarded by a pair of colossal stone elephants, was his doing too.

Siddhinarasimha, it is said, had vowed never to leave his people for the kingdom of heaven until the stone elephants of Vishveshvara temple had gone down to nearby Manidhara fountain to drink. He died, according to the chronicles, in 1710 at the grand old age of 104, his spirit living on in his beloved city, as the stone elephants, still firmly in their place, attested.

Walking through Patan's Durbar Square, meandering between temples, is far less stressful than negotiating the square in Kathmandu. Cars and motorbikes have been excluded from the area and pedestrians can take their fill of the temples without fear of being run down. On a clear day the snow peaks of Ganesh Himal power into the sky beyond the northern end. It is easy, strolling between the pagodas, to feel how a Malla city was intended to be – a bridge between heaven and earth.

The royal astrologer was up to his eyes in paperwork and consultations. His narrow house in the corner of a tiny courtyard, five minutes' walk beyond Durbar Square, was full to bursting. I joined the queue outside his door. Hill women in patterned tunics and full skirts, with heavy nose ornaments and ears dragged down with gold, squeezed up the narrow staircase; beside them, suited businessmen, sari-ed grandes dames with black handbags, and boys jangling motorbike keys. They had all come, bringing their birth-charts with them, for help with life's decisions and conundrums – what date to fix a wedding, whether to apply for a job in the Gulf, how to get a child to do better at school, what day to move house, what business to invest in, what time to set for a sacred-thread ceremony or first rice-feeding ritual, in what compass direction to start looking for a husband.

By the time I reached the front of the queue it was getting dark. The astrologer's office was a low-ceilinged room with pea-green walls, lit by a single strip-light. On one side several students in jeans – the astrologer's assistants – sat around a formica coffee table poring over heaps of scrolls, tapping at calculators, pulling battered reference books and curling papers down from pigeonholes on the wall.

The royal astrologer himself was on the other side of the room, nearest the window. He was sitting cross-legged on the floor behind a low desk, wrapped in a grey shawl with a brown woolly hat on his head, rocking from side to side like an irritable old elephant. His fingers were covered in chalk and chalky fingerprints covered his spectacles. There were birth-charts and blackboards, ink pots, exercise books and mathematical tables scattered all over his desk, and rupee notes floating about which he stuffed distractedly into a drawer as if trying to clear his mind. Behind him was a portrait of Ganesh, garlanded with Christmas tinsel, and faded photographs of himself and King Birendra with '70s sideburns.

He looked up as we sat down at last on the floor in front of him. 'Ah! British lady,' the ageing astrologer said, peering at me with interest through his spectacles. 'I was speaking to the BBC on the telephone just the other day. They wanted to know if I had any new predictions.' He flicked a hand towards the customers still waiting beyond the doorway. 'But you see what my life is like. I have no time now for catastrophes and revolutions. Every minute is taken up with the flimflam of day-to-day.'

He handed me his card – 'Prof. Dr. M.R. Joshi PhD (Urban study and planning), Royal Astrologer and Geo-Astro Consultant'.

'My family have been astrologers for thirty-two generations,' he said. 'I am eighty-two years old. I have spent seventy-six years at this desk and now I work harder than ever. I wake at 2 a.m., I see my first clients at 6 a.m. Sometimes I see my last clients at ten at night. I have no computer. All my calculations take a long time, the old way. I have barely time to sleep. It is not like in the past, when we had dozens of scribes and apprentices at our beck and call.'

He gestured with the same dismissive flick towards his assistants. 'They want to be astrologers but they don't have such good training. They have their minds filled with I don't know what. They don't know how much they have to study. They want quick answers.'

He rattled off his own education, beginning at the age of six painting almanacs under his father; then sixteen years of Sanskrit, higher mathematics, geochemistry, geophysics, geography and astro-science at university in Benares; followed by long sojourns abroad, studying at the Greenwich Observatory in London, poring over ancient charts in the Map Room of the British Museum, and then at universities in Mexico and the United States. But, like being a doctor, he said, no amount of training could beat experience.

'My father predicted the great earthquake of 1934 when I was a boy of fourteen,' he said. 'He worked it out two months before. He knew when it would happen so he told us to escape. We ran to Durbar Square. All these buildings collapsed. I rebuilt this house in clay with my own hands.'

The old astrologer's life flashed by in a series of numerical computations.

'In 1942, when I was twenty years of age, my father and I predicted the end of the Second World War – our prime minister at the time wanted to know how long it would last. In 1991 I predicted the start of the Gulf War. It took thirty-five days to calculate the time of the first attacks.'

Traditionally there were four royal astrologers who would cross-check their findings to make the most accurate predictions. Being the oldest, Mangal Raj Joshi was the most senior. Though the royal astrologers also had the country's interests to safeguard, their primary responsibility was to the king. They were invested with the vital task of drawing up horoscopes for members of the king's family. From their reading of the position of the heavens at the precise time of birth, it was the astrologers who would suggest the name of each royal child and who would inform the palace of the right moment for all the customary rites of passage. No state business, no foreign trips, meetings or receptions, no *pujas* or ceremonial duties were carried out by any members of the royal family without first consulting the astrologers. Horoscopes were drawn up, too, for important visiting dignitaries so the most auspicious days could be chosen for meetings and to give the king some indication of the characters he was dealing with.

'I have King George V's horoscope somewhere,' said Mr Joshi with a twinkle in his eye.

'What about Queen Elizabeth II and Prince Charles?' I asked, trying to steer Mr Joshi closer to the present.

'I have theirs, too,' he said.

'How did you find the details of their birth?'

'Ah, for people like the queen of England these events are always well documented. But nowadays it is easy to find out, even if someone is not famous when they are born. My students can get information from the Internet. Recently we did charts to see who would win the American presidential election. I was able to tell the king the probable outcome.'

'Were you right?'

'Fortunately,' he grinned.

He unwound a scroll that was lying on his desk. The chart, known as a *chinna* in Nepali, or *jata* in Newari, was made of shiny yellow paper, about six inches wide and two feet long, edged with decorative floral borders in red and green. It was covered in red and black letters or 'syllables' in Devanagiri script – black being the given letters of the known astrological formula; red, the added letters of that person's particular details, such as the exact time and location of birth, as recorded by the midwife; the name of the nearest shrine or temple to which they were born; their parents' star signs; number of siblings; the individual's name. This is the name the priest gives a baby at the time their *chinna* is drawn up and is often quite different from the familiar name used by friends and family. It is the official name used for all subsequent ritual purposes and *pujas*, including weddings and old-age ceremonies.

At the top of the chart was a figure of a deity in white; the bottom was divided into squares. There were wheels and geometric designs and tiny numerical figures all over it. I stared at it blankly as Mr Joshi prattled on about 'lunar mansions' and 'divisions' and 'signs in the ascendant'. It looked utterly incomprehensible.

I asked if this was what the king's birth-chart looked like. He couldn't show me that, he said – no one could see it except royal priests and astrologers; but royal birth-charts were always much more elaborate than anyone else's. The horoscopes of even the minor royals could be several metres long. In the past, royal birth-charts were truly magnificent things. Mr Joshi remembered seeing the horoscope of King Tribhuvan when he was a child. It was edged with gold and so large it had taken four men to carry it into the room.

'Nowadays, the palace is not willing to spend money on a horoscope like this,' Mr Joshi said. 'But without details – and without time to analyse – it is difficult to make accurate predictions.'

'Were you able to make any predictions about this year?' I asked.

The royal astrologer shifted uncomfortably.

'This is a very difficult year,' he said, 'very inauspicious. Everyone knew there was going to be some disaster. We knew the six days around the cusp of May/June were going to be very bad for the king. But it was complicated . . . I thought there was going to be an earthquake. I told the newspapers that.'

For decades seismologists had been warning that an earthquake in the Kathmandu Valley was long overdue. The astrologer was under considerable pressure to predict when this would be. In 2001 it seemed to have blinded him to other possibilities.

The world over, 2001 had been a year of exceptional turmoil, the astrologer explained. He cited the Gujarat earthquake that had killed 20,000 and left 600,000 people homeless in January, a spate of typhoons in Taiwan, tornadoes in the United States, floods in Bangladesh, earthquakes in El Salvador, numerous high-profile plane crashes and, of course, most recently, the terrorist attacks on the Twin Towers in New York on 11 September.

But it had also been a year of portent for King Birendra. A month or so before the massacre, Saturn had moved into Taurus – the sign it had last entered twenty-nine years ago. In the West this was known as a 'Saturn return', an astrological phenomenon occurring at twenty-seven to twenty-nine or thirty-year intervals in a person's life, coinciding with the approximate time – twenty-nine and a half years – it takes Saturn to make one orbit around the sun. According to stargazers, a 'Saturn return' has dramatic impact on a person's life, triggering a midlife crisis, perhaps, or a divorce or a volte-face in careers. It is the moment when a person crosses a major threshold, leaving behind one stage of their life and moving into the next. Birendra had been crowned on 31 January 1972, at the age of twenty-seven when Saturn was in Taurus. Twenty-nine years later, the return of Saturn into Taurus signified dramatic upheavals in the king's personal life, quite possibly jeopardizing his very position on the throne.

'What happens when there are bad planetary influences like this?' I asked. 'Is there anything to be done to avoid them?'

'The planetary positions in the heavens and their effect on human beings are like the signals we receive through a radio or TV set,' said Mr Joshi. 'We have no influence over the programmes – but,' he added with a wry smile, 'we can use the remote control to change channels.'

This was where the *dyas* came in. Worshipping a particular deity at a given time could ameliorate or even banish bad influences. It could change the course of fortune. Much of Mr Joshi's work was advising his clients on which *puja* to do, when, where and to which deity.

'Sometimes, though, the influences are too strong to change,' added Mr Joshi cautiously. Usually a family's *chinnas* are kept together in a jewellery box in the safekeeping of the eldest female member. But sometimes a horoscope is so powerful that it has to be kept in its own box, sometimes even in a separate room. If arguments break out within a family, it could be because opposing *chinnas* are kept too close together.

'What about Dipendra's horoscope?' I asked. 'What was that like?'

'I drew Prince Dipendra's horoscope myself,' he said. 'It was not bad – it was quite good, in fact. Only the raj yoga – the rulership signs – were destructive. It did not look likely he was ever going to become king.'

Another astrologer had interpreted this to mean that the prince's existence could prove destructive to his father's. Another read in it signs that were antipathetic to Dipendra's mother and had recommended, immediately after Dipendra's birth, that the baby crown prince be separated from Queen Aishwarya for a week in order to purify their relationship; but this was apparently not done.

'The birth-chart showed also complications with marriage,' said Mr Joshi. 'We advised King Birendra to delay his son's marriage until the prince was thirty-five. This seemed the safest way to proceed.'

But it was precisely this delay that seemed to have triggered Dipendra's fury. The crown prince had been determined, according to his friends, to become officially engaged to the 'love of his life' before his thirtieth birthday – 27 June 2001. His parents' refusal to grant him his wish had made him apoplectic. It was not just his age but his girlfriend that was the problem. Two years older than Dipendra, Devyani Rana was wealthy, beautiful and highly educated but she was also, according to the press, descended from the 'wrong type' of Rana: the Chandra Shamsher Ranas – the Ranas who had been responsible for keeping the Shah dynasty prisoner for generations. Her father, Pashupati Shumsher Rana, was one of the most powerful men in the country. She was also the granddaughter, on her mother's side, of an Indian maharaja: a provenance that would have provoked further opposition from Dipendra's dictatorial mother.

I wondered, though, if there hadn't been other objections to Devyani as the future queen. Had Mr Joshi seen Devyani's horoscope?

'It was not compatible with Dipendra's,' he said solemnly.

Devyani's mother, Rani Usha, however, had been ardently in favour of the match. In the 1960s she had been rejected in her own bid to marry Birendra, then the crown prince. It seemed she was determined her daughter would succeed where she had failed. Rani Usha herself went, with her husband, to consult Mr Joshi.

'I told Devyani's parents – I said to them, "No matter how many *pujas* you perform, your daughter will never marry the crown prince." They refused to listen . . .' said Mr Joshi.

I began to sense something of the power play that was supposed to have arisen between the palace and Devyani's family. Rumour had it that Devyani's mother had commissioned two priests from Gwalior to travel to Nepal to perform a tantric *puja* to remove the obstacles to the match. Apparently they had arrived at the Yak & Yeti, one of Kathmandu's top hotels, in late May where they had aroused suspicion by asking how to procure certain *puja* materials such as parrots and snakes. The *puja* in question was thought to be that of Bagalamukhi, a fearsome weapon-wielding Hindu goddess. Devyani's mother had commissioned a painting of the goddess from a renowned *citraikar* in the previous weeks, sending it back repeatedly to the artist to add more arms and weapons. Officials at Narayanhiti Palace had been alerted and Queen Aishwarya was supposed to have commissioned a counter *puja* to block their efforts. Many people claimed this exonerated the crown prince. Dipendra had clearly not been the master of his own actions. He had merely been caught in the crossfire of tantric warfare. I remembered the account one of the survivors of the massacre had given reporters, describing the crown prince bursting into the room looking like the goddess Kali wielding countless weapons.

But the king himself should have been beyond the reach of such goings-on. According to what Yagyaman had told me, the king was inviolable as long as he had the blessing of the Kumari. The power of *shakti* surged within him. No amount of *pujas*, counter-magic or worship to other deities, tantric or otherwise, could penetrate the protective forces the Living Goddess generated around the king.

But the Kumari's powers are considered to be effective only as long as she remains pure and receives proper worship. The blotches that had appeared on the Living Goddess's face twenty-four days before the massacre indicated not only that something was rotten in the state of Nepal but that the Kumari herself had somehow lost her purity. She was no longer acting as an effective conduit between Taleju and the king.

I asked Mr Joshi why they hadn't changed Kumaris when this had happened, replacing the affected incumbent with a new one. Certainly, he said, the priests always have a Kumari in reserve – a Kumari-in-waiting – in anticipation of just such a misfortune. A little Shakya girl, with the right physical criteria and whose horoscope has already been checked against the king's, shadows the real one. Living at home with her family, this little girl, providing she remains healthy and pure, refrains from eating certain polluting foods and incurs no cuts or bruises or other blemishes, can be called upon to become Kumari in the event of a calamity befalling the incumbent. When she goes to school at the age of four or five, the priests identify another candidate. Hers is not an official position, Mr Joshi said; she is merely a standby in case of emergency.

At first, when ominous signs began to appear on the Kumari's body, spreading to her face, the priests did all they could to appease the Goddess and cure the Kumari of the complaint. They appealed to the palace for the king to send special offerings but none came. The monarch, they were told, was busy. Then, about twelve days later, Mr Joshi said, the unthinkable happened. The Kumari began to bleed. Her first menstruation had arrived without warning.

'Usually the Kumari is changed well in advance of her first menses, so there is never a gap between Kumaris,' explained the astrologer. 'But in this case it took everyone by surprise.'

She has to be removed immediately, according to Newar custom, to a darkened room where she remains for twelve days while she undergoes the important Newar puberty rite of *bara tayegu*. Like *ihi*, *bara tayegu* is a rite of female empowerment involving the mock marriage of a Newar girl to a god – in this case the sun god, Surya. Its specific purpose is to eradicate the pollution traditionally associated with vaginal blood. As a result the dangers that orthodox Hindus attached to defloration, menstruation and childbirth are diffused and a Newar woman can go about her normal life much as usual during her menstrual period, cooking and eating with the rest of the family, and sleeping with her husband. The rite is especially important in the case of a Kumari, whose menstrual blood could otherwise be considered particularly dangerous.

Enthroning a substitute in a Kumari's place at short notice, however, is not a straightforward matter. It takes at least a fortnight to prepare a candidate Kumari for the powerful installation ritual. And this ritual – normally conducted on the eighth night of Dasain – has to be performed on another highly auspicious day.

The astrologer wobbled his head. 'This is a black year, as I told you; there were very few auspicious days. We were waiting for the right time to change Kumaris.'

'So, effectively,' I said slowly, as the realization dawned, 'there was no Living Goddess at the time of the massacre?'

'That is why these things came to pass,' the astrologer confirmed. 'Without the power of the Kumari, the king and all his dependants are exposed. They cannot be saved from the bad influences of the planets and the bad intentions of those who want to destroy them.'

After the massacre the priests came to Mr Joshi to check that the horoscope of the reserve Kumari, which had originally been aligned with the birth-chart of Birendra, also agreed with that of the new king, Gyanendra. Fortunately, it did. On the next auspicious day, on 10 July 2001, forty days after the massacre, a new Kumari filled the vacant throne. The ship of state had been clawed back off the rocks and set afloat again. But whether it could survive the tempestuous seas that lay ahead would remain to be seen.

'A dark period on the Earth has passed,' concluded Mr Joshi, restively adjusting his floor cushion. 'Nepal must now find peace. But the signs are still not good. There are troubles to come.'

I left the astrologer in a state of agitation, shuffling papers around his desk as though some vital document continued to elude him. A few persistent clients remained outside his door. The rest had given up and dispersed, disappearing into the night of inconstant stars.

Chapter 14

The Royal Kumari of Patan

Sri Lakshmi Kalyana Varma Samskarita Ratnakara Mahavihara is typical of the 140 or so *bahals* in Patan occupied by Shakyas and Vajracharyas. At the steps of the *bahal*, on the main road to Mangal Bazaar, a pair of large, painted stone lions with long, matted hair, pert human breasts and snarling faces brace themselves for visitors. Above the entrance, suspended in an arched stone *torana*, are the tantric forms of the five transcendent Buddhas; beneath them, on either side, a four-handed and an eight-handed form of Manjushri. Known more simply as 'Hakha Bahal', or 'Kumari Bahal', this is the courtyard of Patan's own Living Goddess.

My visit to Patan had led me to an astonishing discovery. Shortly after my meeting with the royal astrologer I had learnt that Patan, too, has a 'royal' Kumari. The practice is not, as I had presumed all these years, unique to Kathmandu. The ground on which I had been standing was beginning to shift. Kumari worship is not an isolated phenomenon. It is a practice common to all three cities in the Kathmandu Valley and older than I had previously thought. The tradition stretches back to the reign of the independent Malla kings and is intimately connected with their cult of Taleju. Each of the Malla kings had built residences for Kumaris close to their palaces, believing that worshipping their lineage goddess in the form of a *sadya kumari* – a living child – was the most powerful way to protect themselves and their kingdoms.

To Newars living in Patan their Kumari continues to be as important, if not more so, than the Kumari in Kathmandu. Yet few people outside Patan know of her existence. After defeating the Malla kings in the late eighteenth century, Prithvi Narayan Shah had made Kathmandu the capital of a unified Nepal, and Kathmandu's royal Kumari had inherited the role of protectoress of the king and focus of the nation. The other two royal Kumaris – for there is still, I had learnt, a surviving Kumari in Bhaktapur as well – had dipped below the national radar. This means, however, that the rules governing access to them are no longer so stringent. They still live in seclusion, observing the conditions of ritual purity, but there is no need for them to be so closely guarded. This could be a chance to get closer to a Living Goddess, to witness the tradition from within – inside a Kumari Chen. The Patan Kumari, I had been told, might be disposed to grant a foreigner an audience.

Hakha Bahal was bustling with activity. In one corner, on a length of rice-husk matting, young men, cross-legged, were cutting up vegetables. Mountains of gleaming radishes, mustard greens, potatoes and cauliflower towered around them. A couple of women were stitching festive sal-leaf plates together. To one side, in big bowls, were quivering mounds of buffalo meat – few Buddhists in Nepal were vegetarian. They were preparing for a wedding feast that evening for over three hundred guests. The Patan Living Goddess would be in attendance, I was told, accompanied by five Vajracharya elders in their royal crowns – the Pancha Buddha of Patan – to shower blessings of good fortune, prosperity, and the spirit of tantric union on the bride and groom.

While the Kathmandu Kumari can be selected from the communities of eighteen *bahals*, the Patan royal Kumari, I learnt, always comes from this one *bahal*. The *sangha* consists of about two hundred families; around 1000 people in all, of whom a hundred or more have received *diksha*. Another difference is that the Patan Kumari is Vajracharya – Hakha Bahal's Shakya lineage having dwindled over time to just one family.

It is likely to have been Siddhinarasimha Malla, the great seventeenth-century king of Patan, who was responsible for establishing a Living Goddess at Hakha Bahal. Since it was he who had founded the temple to Taleju and the Mul Chowk shrine in the Patan Durbar similar to the one in Hanuman Dhoka, it is highly probable that he had followed suit with Kumari worship too. He had moved Hakha Bahal here from its original location next to the palace after embarking on grand extensions to his *durbar* – including the famous Bhandarkhal gardens dedicated to Taleju.

On the side of the courtyard facing the entrance, at the foot of an imposing three-storey temple with towering pagoda roofs, is Hakha Bahal's *kvahpah dyah* – the exoteric shrine that, like Layku Bahil, contains a figure of the Buddha Akshobhya. Another fabulous pair of lions, brass this time, supported by crouching elephants and ridden by *bodhisattvas* carrying swords and tridents, stood guard – though their presence is clearly no longer a deterrent to miscreants. The entire facade of the shrine, with its archway of oil-lamps and bronze doorway with brass flags and repoussé copper *torana*, has been locked inside an unsightly iron cage to guard against theft.

Beyond the shrine, in the corner of a smaller compound, is a dilapidated building – Patan's Kumari Chen. After the magnificence of the Kumari House in Kathmandu, this small, non-descript dwelling was a disappointment. With no ornate carvings or trappings of majesty it is in an advanced state of disrepair – and clearly unoccupied.

Patan's Kumari Chen, though, is typical of the houses royal Kumaris had lived in under Malla patronage. The Living Goddess's residence in Kathmandu is, in effect, an aberration. Built by the last Malla king of Kathmandu, in desperate times when the valley was under attack from Prithvi Narayan Shah, Kathmandu's Kumari Chen is an amalgamation of palace, *bahal* and domestic house – something that had never existed before. Until then, royal Kumaris had lived in simpler, more conventional dwellings like this one, within the confines of an existing *bahal*.

Though Patan's Living Goddess has not lived here since the 1940s, the Kumari Chen continues to serve a purpose, evoking her presence in the *bahal*. Set into its exterior wall a little stone insert, carved with emblems symbolizing Kumari, is continuously worshipped, keeping her house alive.

Unlike the Kathmandu Kumari, the parents of the Patan Living Goddess continue living with her while she is in office. In the old days, after the Kumari was selected, she and her whole family would move into the Kumari Chen. If there had ever been a time when there was a special caretaker for the Patan Kumari, no one in the *bahal* could remember it.

Recently, however, families of the Patan Living Goddesses have opted to stay in the comfort of their own homes. The Kumari house is no longer a perk of office. It has been abandoned for so long, it is not even suitable for short visits.

A buckled old man sitting on one of the resting platforms at the entrance of the *bahal* offered to take me to the house of Patan's reigning Kumari. He led me a short distance down the main street, to an unobtrusive traditional building like any other, with lopsided lattice windows above a blue-shuttered shopfront. I realized I must have walked straight past it on my way to the royal astrologer. A skein of thick, black electrical cables ran across the facade and the brickwork was scarred with the paste of old advertising bills. Mounted high on the third floor, next to a small window, though, was a red tin plaque painted with white lettering: 'LIVING GODDESS', and the same in yellow Devanagari script beneath. The old man rang the buzzer and hobbled back towards Hakha Bahal.

I waited, the thrum of passing motorbikes masking any sign of a response from inside. There were loops of desiccating marigolds hanging from the lintel and auspicious symbols on the doorframe – flowers, water-pot, a watchful eye; and, just apparent beneath the street dust, three small, seated figures – Shakyamuni Buddha flanked by *bodhisattvas*.

The man who eventually opened the door – the Patan Kumari's father – welcomed me off the street with no discernible show of surprise. It was Saturday – the rest day of the Nepali working week and the usual day for worshippers. Only full Kumari Pujas require advance notice.

Though barely in his forties, Netra Raj Vajracharya's face was pitted with childhood smallpox scars. His clothes were a threadbare Saturday best and he was wearing plastic sandals, leather being taboo in a Kumari house. He smiled warmly and, without speaking, beckoned me in. Following him in silence up the dark, narrow stair-ladder, I slipped off my shoes at the entrance to a room on the first floor. By the windows some flat floor cushions had been laid out for visitors on a length of rice-mat on the beaten earth floor. A souvenir poster of Lumbini Peace Pagoda – the site of the Buddha's birthplace in southern Nepal – had been tacked to the faded, sky-blue walls and at the far end of the room a red curtain was drawn across a small doorway.

Netra Raj Vajracharya uttered some strange gutteral grunts and, signalling to me that he would be just a few moments, disappeared upstairs. The Patan Kumari's father, I realized, was deaf, the result of a childhood illness, quite possibly smallpox.

At Dasain, when the Kumari stayed in Hakha Bahal, around 400 people would come to present offerings but in her home, in an average week, she received only half a dozen or so visitors. The family had put aside three rooms in their house – a small private one in which the Kumari slept and ate; another, containing her throne, for daily and small-scale *pujas*; and a third, larger one – the one I sat in now – for post-worship feasts, large-scale *pujas* and formal receptions. As a fully initiated tantric priest himself, Netra Raj Vajracharya acted as his daughter's 'caretaker worshipper', awaking the Goddess inside her every morning and overseeing simple *pujas* from devotees.

There was a rustle on the stairs, a light jangle of anklets and suddenly a streak of red flashed past the doorway and disappeared into the adjoining room. A moment later, the Kumari's mother, a young woman in a simple *kurta suruwal* followed. There was a murmur of muted voices, the faint susurration of arrangement. The Kumari's father joined them. I could hear soft footfalls behind the curtain. Another pause and at last the Kumari's father lifted the cloth and beckoned me in.

In a tiny room, with the same sky-blue walls and earthen floor, the little Goddess was sitting bolt upright on her throne against a backrest of green and silver Nagas, their scaly heads conjoined in a crown hovering above her head.

Her eyes flashed up as she watched me enter. She was no more than six years old. Her hair was combed tightly into a bun and tied with a red ribbon on top of her head. Thick lines of colyrium exaggerated her eyes and elongated them to her temples. A clot of reddened rice from the morning's *puja* clung to the centre of her forehead. Hanging around her neck, over a scarlet jersey, was a silver amulet box – the *yantra mala* of Taleju. Her bare feet, protruding beneath a scarlet skirt of satin brocade, rested expectantly in an offering tray. She was clutching the sides of her throne like the commander of a starship; her expression, despite the freshness of her face and the adorable plumpness of her cheeks, deadly serious. I found myself smiling impulsively at her as I entered the room but – just like the Kumari in Kathmandu – the gorgeous eyes, recalling me to respectfulness, returned an uncompromising glare.

I glanced around the room. High on the wall, beside an electric clock, were paintings of the five Jina Buddhas. The Goddess's throne, auspiciously facing east, was silver-gilt, with silver staffs – symbol of power and authority – resting on either side. Here, everything was silver, compared with the gold ornaments of the Kathmandu Kumari.

Most of the Patan Kumari's jewellery – her three crowns, her *naga mala* or serpent necklace, heavy neck-chain, anklets, bracelets and armbands, apron of repoussé metal links, *narmunda mala* or necklace of severed heads, even her *drishti* fire-eye, used only for high rituals – were packed safely away with the ceremonial vestments inside a padlocked trunk next to the throne. They, too, were silver. Only the *tayo* – a hollow, lozenge-shaped amulet traditionally worn by Newar women on their wedding day – was made of gold. The trunk itself was tatooed with smudges of vermilion and sprinkled with offerings of fresh flowers and rice. So powerful were the objects inside they were considered almost deities themselves and the trunk received daily tribute for housing them, like a temple.

Uncertainly I ventured forward towards the Living Goddess's throne and, kneeling on the rice-mat, bowed my head to her tiny feet. I surrendered a hundred-rupee note into her foot-plate, a bronze tray smeared with vermilion and scattered with grains of rice and petals from this morning's *puja*, before handing her my gift of a soft toy – a lion, like the vehicle of Taleju – and a box of crayons. The little Goddess reacted with automatic reflexes, accepting the offering with barely a glimmer of interest and delicately placing them to one side.

The Kumari's father stood to one side looking on, but his daughter needed no prompting. Her timing and coordination seemed as natural as her self-assurance. Though she was no older than most children in their first year of primary school, this was a routine she had enacted a thousand times before. I thought of my daughter, the same age – her fumbling, plump little fingers still struggling to get to grips with a button, her shyness so acute that she hid behind my legs at the sight of a stranger.

The Kumari dipped her fingers into a dish at her side. As I craned forward to receive my *tika*, the cold, wet touch of vermilion paste from her fingertips sent a tiny shockwave across my forehead. Like a queen knighting her subject, she handed me some petals to place on my head and then an apple – *prasad* – which I touched to my forehead by way of thanks, before rocking back on my heels and struggling to my feet. Our ritual exchange was over.

In the days following, I looked back on this encounter and wondered why it had affected me when so little, in fact, seemed to have happened. Rather than receding in my memory the moment seemed to grow with significance. There had been the theatrical thrill of finding myself in the immediate presence of a Living Goddess, of course – something I had never expected; but the encounter had aroused subtler emotions, too – reactions that were connected not so much with anything the Living Goddess herself had done but with my part in the performance.

Finding myself on my knees for the first time since my early school days had taken me by surprise. The physical feeling of the ground beneath me, my head lower than a child's, had unexpected implications. It was a simple gesture but it had profound psychological impact. It was a surrendering of the ego, a letting go of adult assumptions of superiority and control.

To Newars this symbolic prostration also, crucially, provides a counterbalance to male dominance. This was the significance underlying the king's performance at Indra Jatra. His obeisance every year to the Kumari acknowledged, on a very public platform, his need for the Goddess's energy and inspiration, for *shakti*, in order to function. Kneeling before the small child sitting on her lion throne in Durbar Square demonstrated the inherent weakness of his position and emphasized that the source of wisdom, power and creativity in the kingdom originated in an entity far greater than the king himself. It was a ritual that overtly reaffirmed, at the highest level, the Newar belief that law and stability reposed, ultimately, in the forces of the divine feminine.

This essential message is expressed whenever someone kneels before a Living Goddess, but the practice is not just confined to the worship of established Kumaris. To Newars every little girl contains the essence of the Goddess and has the potential to be a Kumari. The practice of Kumari Puja is mirrored in every Newar household whenever there is a big event like a birth or marriage or some other important life-cycle ritual. The youngest girl in the family is made up like a Living Goddess, with a red dress, her hair in a topknot, colyrium around her eyes, fingernails painted and her feet stained with vermilion, and a red *tika* across her forehead. Everyone in the family – parents, grandparents, aunts, uncles, brothers, sisters – kneels before her to receive her blessing. It is a deliberate inversion of the orthodox Hindu custom that has women and children bowing to the feet of their husband or father every day.

To Newar Buddhists, the Goddess activated inside their children on such occasions is considered to be Vajrayogini or Vajravarahi; while in Hindu households, it is Taleju, Laxmi – goddess of wealth and prosperity, or Durga. Little girls are often worshipped as Kumaris during Dasain, on Maha Navami, the Great Ninth – the same day the official Living Goddesses in Kathmandu, Patan and Bhaktapur are being re-invested with the spirit of Taleju/Durga/Vajradevi. The correlation between the central royal Kumari and all the other little girls in the kingdom is clear.

Whatever the occasion, worshipping a little girl is one of the most powerful ways of bringing the Goddess into every home and invoking her blessings. It is also a reminder to everyone in society – but particularly men – of the expected standard of behaviour towards women and young girls. Kneeling is more than an act of reverence: it changes the person doing it. It manifests a willingness in a person to open up to a source of wisdom and experience higher than their own. It imbues a sense of humility. I had knelt at the feet of a child and in doing so I realized I had, in some way, become a child again myself. There seemed no better position from which to approach the deeper aspects of the tradition.

~

After having *darshan* of the goddess I collected myself together in the waiting room, tucking my *prasad* away carefully into my shoulder bag, ready to leave, but the Kumari's father reappeared and gestured to me, all smiles, to sit back down. His wife was already in the kitchen upstairs, fixing me a snack.

The most popular time for Saturday worshippers had come and

gone. Those who come to the Patan Living Goddess to conduct small *pujas* do so for the same reasons that worshippers visit the Kumari in Kathmandu. They could be suffering some illness, particularly bleeding problems; or they could be government officials fearing demotion; or they are people with ambitious plans who want access to the Kumari's powers of foresight; or they come to perform a Kumari Puja to obtain release from restrictions imposed on them through having participated in one of the Newar *samskara*, or life-cycle rituals.

On the floor cushions by the window, the regular street noise of Patan restored a sense of normality. My thoughts returned to the events affecting the country. I wondered if the Patan Kumari had any communication with the present king. The Kumari's father began scribbling his responses in my notebook. He wrote in a fine, looping hand – in English.

Behind the scenes, the royal palace in Kathmandu was still deeply involved in the Kumari tradition in Patan, even down to the selection process. The initial selection of candidates, Netra Raj wrote, was made by Patan's Taleju priest, a Dyah Brahmin. But once this selection was made, the Dyah Brahmin took the little girls to Kathmandu, to the house of the Shah king's personal royal priest – the Bada Guruju – for final selection. Just as in the case of the Kathmandu Kumari, a physical examination was carried out by the Bada Guruju's wife. Once the selection was over, the Patan Living Goddess-elect was taken to Narayanhiti Palace for recognition by the king.

The Kumaris of both Patan and Bhaktapur were on the government payroll. His daughter, Netra Raj said, received a monthly salary from the government of 1500 Nepali rupees (about US$15) and an educational fee of 200 rupees per month to cover private tuition – around quarter of the funding provided for the Kathmandu Kumari. But the king, himself, often supplemented this. 'King Birendra was very pious,' Netra Raj wrote. 'He often used to send offerings to the Patan Kumari. Especially if something was wrong, if the Kumari was showing signs – *puja* plates would come from the palace.'

Birendra had also provided regular contributions for *nitya puja*, but so far they had received nothing from Gyanendra. This dip in royal patronage was a serious concern for Netra Raj. The government pension on its own – a sum that had not increased for years – was no longer enough to cover the cost of *puja* materials; and the educational fee fell well short of the cost of the Kumari's school books. The Patan Kumari – just like the Kathmandu Kumari – received private tuition at home. Local offerings provided scant assistance since the average monetary donation from worshippers was only a matter of a few rupees. Ritual restrictions on the Kumari household cost time and money; and maintaining ritual purity meant that many other means of supplementing income were barred to them. Without royal subsidy, Netra Raj feared for the position of the Patan Kumari.

But it was the effect this loss of patronage was having on the spiritual well-being of the nation that seemed to concern him the most. 'These are dangerous times,' he scribbled emphatically in my notebook. 'This is "Kali Era". If there is not proper worship of Kumari in Kathmandu, in Patan, and elsewhere, we enter a time of violence and catastrophe.'

It was not just the king who was to blame. People were becoming lazy and disrespectful, he said, but there were no shortcuts where honouring the *dyas* – the gods – was concerned.

'These days the Kumari is very angry,' he wrote. 'The priests are not following the traditional regulations and Nepali devotees are offering to Kumari and other gods and goddesses without caring about *chipa-nipa*.'

Chipa-nipa is the consideration of purity and pollution. If a person has not observed the rules of purity – if they have wiped their mouth with their hand, or lifted tea to their lips without then rinsing their mouth and hand with water – then he or she is *chipa* – polluted. A devotee should only make offerings to the gods if they are in a state of ritual purity. Offerings also have to be ritually cleansed. Nowadays, though, people pay less attention to these considerations. They are thinking too much about themselves, Netra Raj said. They are distracted by modern living and always do things in a rush. But to offer in a state of pollution, he believed, is insulting to the gods.

'If people do not respect the gods and goddesses, why should they want to stay with us? That is why there is famine, violence and killing everywhere in the world.

'In my opinion, if everybody has faith in the *dyas*, then there will be good for the country and the world. I have strong faith. That is why the deities have favoured me and made my daughter Kumari.'

The little Kumari's mother came down from the kitchen with a glass of orange squash and a little tin plate of fried duck egg sprinkled with salt. She had a sharp, intelligent face and a youthfulness – she could only have been in her late twenties – that recalled me with a jolt to the tender age of her daughter. While her husband was responsible for all the ritual requirements, the Kumari's mother acted as caretaker for the Living Goddess, tending to her clothes, make-up and jewellery, and the hospitality of guests.

While his wife was serving me, the Kumari's father had produced a portfolio of watercolours from his shop downstairs. He made money on the side by selling paintings – an occupation that was not considered polluting.

As he showed me his sketches – traditional scenes of valley life, women with winnowing baskets, carpenters, bronze-casters, girls making garlands for offerings – I wondered about the little girl we had just seen, her extraordinary composure and self-control. The idea that she was drugged or hypnotized, as rumour suggested, was clearly absurd. Her reactions, her expressions, her alertness, had seemed perfectly normal. Yet, later this evening, at the wedding in Hakha Bahal, she would sit like this, quite possibly, for hours. I wondered how she managed it.

I was about to pose the question when the sound of children laughing filled the stairs. The little Kumari came running through the doorway, swiftly followed by her two brothers, and catapulted herself into her mother's lap.

'We told her you came from England,' said her mother, laughing herself. 'She wanted to take a closer look at you.'

It was as if a spell had been broken. The little Kumari settled herself, fussily arranging her red satin skirt and plonking her hands in her lap. She looked at me for a moment, a mischievous glint in her eyes. Then she craned her head to whisper in her mother's ear. This was a child I could recognize – restless, animated, spontaneous. She could have been any of the little girls who came to play with my daughter. Within moments she had run off again with her siblings.

'She seems different now,' I said. 'She's very lively.'

'Kumari Ma is different on her throne,' the Kumari's mother explained. 'When the Goddess inside her wakes up she is no longer a child.'

Fully charged with the Goddess, and empowered by *mantras* and her sacred ornaments, her mother said, the child part of her is protected, superseded; her reactions, her thoughts and feelings are no longer those of a little girl. To her worshippers – and, crucially, to the Kumari herself – she becomes something else, something greater, someone beyond normal experience. It is this deep conviction rather than intoxicating substances, she explained, that lies behind the Kumari's exemplary behaviour on the throne.

'While you're here,' the Kumari's mother said, 'would you like to have *darshan* of Dhana Kumari, too?'

Amazingly, the little girl who had just skipped out of the room was not the only Living Goddess in the house. There was another 'unofficial' Kumari whose existence, even by Living Goddess standards, was unusual. This second Kumari was fifty years old. She was Netra Raj Vajracharya's older sister, the little Kumari's aunt.

Known as Dhana – or sometimes Dharma – Kumari, she had been appointed Living Goddess in 1953, at the age of two. Over the years she had generated a strong following thanks to her special powers of divination and ability to bestow good exam results. On reaching the age of puberty, despite showing signs of physical maturity, the Kumari – according to her mother – had experienced no menstrual blood loss. There could be reasons for this – though it was a rare occurrence, she could have been born without a uterus, for example – but her condition could not be medically verified as no doctor was allowed to examine her. If a Living Goddess became ill enough to need hospital treatment, then she was, de facto, no longer a Living Goddess. But Dhana Kumari was clearly not ill. To her followers the apparent absence of menses was a sign that the Goddess did not want to leave her. Dhana Kumari had continued as official Living Goddess of Patan well into her thirties.

The little Kumari's father called up the stairs for a second time. There was a long pause and then a weighty creak spread across the floorboards above us and slowly, purposefully, footsteps descended. On the landing a large figure draped in red glided over the threshold into a separate *puja* chamber. I waited a couple of minutes before following.

Dhana Kumari had eventually been dismissed as Patan's official 'royal' Living Goddess in 1984 when a decision was made that the appointment had to return to a child. Her devotees were convinced, however, that she continued to manifest the spirit of Devi and, in typical Newar style, a compromise was reached. Dhana Kumari was allowed to remain as an adjunct. All the institutionally inherited insignia was handed down to a younger Kumari, while a separate *tayo* and other silver ornaments were provided for the old one. Dhana Kumari retained a small but devoted following – mainly of middle-aged Patan matrons – who revered her all the more because the Goddess had shown her such extraordinary favour.

Two little Kumaris had come and gone since the start of this arrangement. The one I had just met – Dhana Kumari's niece – was the third. Since Dhana Kumari's parents were now dead, her younger brother, Netra Raj, had the onerous responsibility of being priest for two Kumaris living, for the first time in the history of the tradition, under one roof. Moreover, Dhana Kumari no longer received a government pension. Small wonder Netra Raj was concerned about funding. The cost of maintaining this additional, anomalous tradition fell entirely on himself and Dhana Kumari's dwindling number of devotees.

The older Kumari was seated at the far end of a narrow *puja* room, darker than the first since it was at the back of the house and there was only a small window giving on to the inner courtyard. East, here, meant that the Kumari's throne was set facing a blank wall, with only just enough room for the priest or devotee to kneel before her. Her throne was made of wood, with four posts of polished mahogany supporting a copper-plated roof. A red cotton pelmet edged with silver hung from the canopy like the fringe on the eaves of a temple. The seat was so compact and low on the floor that the generously proportioned woman presiding on it – dressed in red satin brocade, with the same topknot and eye make-up as her niece – was crouching with her knees tucked up towards her chest, ducking her head beneath the tiny roof. It was a while before I realized the throne she was using was the little Kumari's ceremonial palanquin.

It was Crown Prince Dipendra who had eventually objected to the unusual outsize Kumari. The annual festival of Red Macchendranath – a manifestation of Avalokiteshvara, *bodhisattva* of compassion and harbinger of rain – is one of the most important events in the valley. Rooted in the towns of Bungmati and Patan, the festival involves the transfer of the god in a massive chariot six kilometres between his two homes. Both the Patan Kumari and the king of Nepal – or his representative at least – are required to witness the dramatic culmination of the festival, known as Bhoto Jatra, which takes place on the road halfway to Jawalakhel.

In the days of the Mallas, the king and the Kumari of Patan would have watched the proceedings seated side by side on a dais. Nowadays the two do not come directly into contact. They have *darshan* of each other though – the Living Goddess enthroned on a raised stage directly in front of Macchendranath's chariot; the royal family and dignitaries watching from a royal stand nearby – and it was on this occasion in 1989 that Crown Prince Dipendra, standing in for his father, took offence at the thirty-eight-year-old Goddess's ungainly arrival, carried by perspiring Jyapu bearers in her tiny palanquin, and demanded an inquiry.

A committee, headed by the royal priest in Kathmandu, the Raj Guru, conducted a physical examination of the anomalous adult Goddess and subjected both her mother and brother to intensive questioning. Apparently, the outcome of this initial inquiry was in the Kumari's favour. No evidence of any violation of the formal purity criteria was found. But the crown prince was dissatisfied and ordered a new and larger committee of inquiry to look into the matter. Dhana Kumari was eventually dismissed on the grounds that one of her ear lobes had evidently been pierced early on in her childhood, and this must have involved some loss of blood. Her mother admitted the piercing had taken place but insisted it had not caused bleeding. The Dhana Kumari's disqualification was, according to her supporters in Patan, an offence to the Goddess. To those who considered this a sacrilege of the most serious order, it was not surprising that such a terrible and bloody end had been visited upon Dipendra Shah. Everywhere I visited, it seemed, there were reasons explaining the massacre in terms of karmic forces.

There was barely a flicker of acknowledgement as I stepped forward into the gloom to present an offering of hastily scrambled rupees. The physical presence of an adult Kumari was, at first, disconcerting. While the little Living Goddess had regarded me with alert if haughty curiosity, her aunt seemed to have retreated deep within herself. She gazed steadfastly towards the floor as she performed the ritual of bestowing *prasad*, handing me more fruit, the customary pinch of marigold petals and another *tika* on top of the first without, it seemed, even seeing me.

But back in the front room Netra Raj's wife told me this trance-like state was, again, a transformation that occurred when Dhana Kumari was on the throne.

'The rest of the time she sews, cooks a little, plays with her nieces and nephews. She is a deep, thoughtful person, very gentle and quiet. She talks openly with us and other family members but she doesn't often speak in front of people she doesn't know.'

Netra Raj Vajracharya nodded, signing rapidly to his wife who articulated his words. 'Dhana Kumari goes into a very deep meditation when she feels the Goddess inside her,' he confirmed. 'She knows the Goddess has chosen her; she strongly believes this is her *dharma*.'

A few moments later we heard Dhana Kumari leave her *puja* room and slowly, methodically remount the stairs. This was the furthest she ever walked. She had been a Living Goddess for nearly half a century. In many ways Dhana Kumari's existence had become similar to that of a Trappist nun. With no external duties to perform, and no vehicle to carry her, she no longer went outside. She hadn't left the house since her official dismissal, ten years ago.

Chapter 15

A King Offends the Goddess

All was well in the valley, with the Malla kings devoutly worshipping the Goddess, and Taleju protecting them in return as a tigress guards her cubs. But there was one king Taleju favoured above them all. She took to visiting him in human form, taking upon herself her sweetest aspect, a beautiful sixteen-year-old girl, lovely as the dawn. The king would await her visitations as though his life depended on them. Every afternoon, alone in his royal apartment, while his wives and concubines were resting and his courtiers were involved in affairs of state, he would close his eyes and utter the *mantra* of Taleju and wait for his beloved protectoress to appear.

Then a warm breeze, faintly jasmine-scented, such as used to blow in the golden age of Satya Yuga, would waft through the courtyard, which would lull the guards and even the noisy parakeets into an intoxicating snooze. In their dreams, the dozing courtiers might just catch the tinkling of ankle bells as the Goddess swept past them, soft as mountain air, up the stairs to the king's apartment.

The king and Taleju, delighting in each other's company, took to playing a game of dice together, seated on silk cushions on the sal-wood floor of his private chamber. 'See, I am victorious, yet again,' he would cry with each win; and the Goddess would pick up the dice and laugh, her heart overflowing. 'You are indeed,' she would say indulgently, as she softly moved her counters. 'You are the diamond in the crown of the high Himalaya,' and, smiling to herself, she would let him win again.

Then at last, when the game was over, the king would kneel before his Goddess.

'I bow to you, Dya Bhawani, Supreme One, Most Gracious and All-Knowing. To you I owe my life, my actions, my soul.' And in return the Goddess, extending her left hand and lightly touching his forehead with the tips of her fingers, would instil him with *shakti*, saying, 'May you be fortunate, blessed king; may you be free from disease, may your heart remain pure, may you be happy; may the sun shine and the rains fall upon your crops in due season; may your treasury be full and your generosity boundless; may you rule over your people with mercy and good judgement, and may they love you just as you love me.' Then the Goddess would withdraw, well pleased, as lightly as she had come.

A day came, however, as the king and the Goddess were about to begin their game, when the king's attention lapsed. He found himself distracted for a moment by a fine needle of sunlight penetrating the lattice shutters. It played softly across the room and fell upon the Goddess's elegant fingers as they rested gently in her lap in *ksepana mudra*, the gesture of sprinkling ambrosia. As the king leant forward to pick up his dice he noticed the sunlight teasing sparkles from the jewels on the Goddess's wrist. The Goddess's skin shimmered like freshly fallen snow. He ran his eyes up her forearm to the crook of her elbow and saw that the flesh there was soft and suffused with a gentle blush like cherry blossom. Following the curve of her arm towards the rise of her breast he was overwhelmed by an imagining of what this lovely skin would feel like against his lips, how it might taste cool and fragrant like rose petals, how the very touch of it might lift his soul to the heavens. He felt the distant stirring of desire.

Suddenly the Goddess, jewels blazing, lashed out at the dice board and sent it whirling through the window. A great heat began to fill the room as she took on a terrifying form. Her body turned blue-black with rage, her face blazed red and fangs protruded from her bloody lips. In a voice that shook the sleeping household from their dreams and sent tremors through the valley she bellowed, 'How dare you entertain such thoughts about Taleju Bhavani!'

The palace shook at the sound of her voice. A terrible beam of fire blazed from the Goddess's third eye and the king shrank back.

'You are not a king! You are a mortal, a man, nothing more. Without me you are nothing, a dried fruit without seed!' she roared. 'How dare you lay your corrupted eyes on me – I, who have disclosed to you my deepest secrets, granted you my closest council, nourished you like a baby – this is the honour I receive! Your mind is weak as chaff in the wind. You are not worthy to judge the actions of others or hold the sword of fairness in your hand. I will not breathe life into such a pitiful frame. You will never see me again. I withdraw from you and your worthless kin forever.'

And so saying she tore through the palace in a thunderbolt of fury, leaving scorch marks along the walls and small fires smouldering on the stairs.

The king was beside himself with despair. 'Oh thrice-honoured Taleju Bhavani,' he wailed at the retreating blaze, 'I can no more live without you than a fish without water.' He ran, mad with hopelessness, through the courtyards and audience halls, crying aimlessly, 'Oh Goddess, I beg you, return to me. Without you, thrice-blessed one, I am useless.'

But already the sun was beginning to dim and lose its warmth, and his city was plunging into icy shadow. Horror-struck, he rushed to make reparations. He sent offerings to every shrine in the city instructing the priests to perform elaborate *ksama pujas* to elicit the Goddess's forgiveness. Sacrifices were carried out at every Goddess *pitha* outside the city walls. At Taleju's own temple 108 male buffaloes and 108 black he-goats were sacrificed and priests performed purification rites to rinse the king of his defilement. Golden doors

were made for the Goddess's temple, and gleaming new roofs, and
a new gong to summon her, and new wind-bells to delight her. And
finally the king summoned the royal priests and instructed them
to perform the most powerful of all prescriptions laid down in the
Tantras to try to bind the Goddess to him.

At last, exhausted, the remains of his energy spent, the king sank
into a deep and gloomy sleep. He did not know what else to do.
Taleju, though, had been attentive to the king's appeals and at last
her fury began to abate, just a little. And she appeared to the king
in a dream while he slept.

'Do not think that because I address you now I am not still furious,'
she said. 'Outrage boils in my breast. Know that I will never appear to
you again as I have before. Clearly the shadow of Kali Yuga advances
across the earth and the world of mortals is fast receding from the
abode of the gods.

'But I am not deaf. I have heard the prayers of your priests and of
your people, and of your brother kings. I have tasted your remorse.
I shall provide you with a way to continue worshipping me – but it
will be in such a way that this outrage can never be repeated.'

And in his sleep the king's heart rejoiced just as peacocks dance
at the sight of heavy rain-clouds.

'I shall grant you *darshan*,' the Goddess continued sternly. 'But I
will reveal myself to you in a form that will teach you wisdom and
humility. I shall inhabit the body of a living child, a girl who has not
yet bled. This *sadya* kumari must come from a caste that performs
some base and polluting occupation. Heed this with all your heart,
for it shall be your salvation and the salvation of kings to come.

'Once you have found this Kumari you must worship her with
your mind and heart and soul, and she will transform you. Be
mindful of her youth and purity. For like fire she will purify you,
like *jal* she will sustain you, and with the light of her brilliance she
will open your eyes. Know that you honour me when you honour
this child. Let this Kumari remind you of your transgression forever
and be a warning to all kings to come, who tread the earth in your
unfortunate footsteps.'

In his sleep the king whimpered in agreement. 'Go, set about your task,' the Goddess thundered. 'For this is my desire. Be thankful. Go and be a dutiful king, pious and godly as befits your position – see if you can manage it.'

With her words still ringing in his ears the king awoke and felt the sweet release of a man reprieved from sentence of death.

Chapter 16

The Royal Kumari of Bhaktapur

If Patan is a gentler pace than Kathmandu, Bhaktapur – City of Devotion – is in a slower gear still. Eight miles east of the capital it is a world apart. Here, the symbiotic flux between the city and the surrounding land remains an unbroken continuum. Farmers still leave rice out on mats in the brick-paved streets to dry in the sun. Curtains of freshly dyed yarn hang from rickety wooden balconies. Sheaths of maize cobs sprout from upstairs windows. In quiet courtyards men sit at potter's wheels and women pound grain in wooden pestles. Buffaloes and goats are tethered in backyards and chickens scratch about in piles of compost. Ducks dabble in the sludgy waters of Ganesh Pokhari.

Getting here in early 2002, however, was not a serene experience. The roads in and out of Kathmandu were punctuated with roadblocks, with vehicle searches a frequent inconvenience. With the main political parties squabbling continuously among themselves and the government providing no firm hand, the Maoists were becoming audacious. Skirmishes were being reported in the surrounding hills and the atmosphere in the valley was jittery.

Though travel outside the capital was becoming irksome it was not yet considered dangerous and I was determined to track down the third of the royal Kumaris, to complete the trinity. I also wanted to unravel the story of how the Hindu kings came to worship a Living

Goddess in the first place, and Bhaktapur, the original seat of the Malla dynasties, is where it all began.

Like Patan, Bhaktapur's Durbar Square is closed to traffic, and the heart of the city – more extensive than Patan and even more majestic – is invariably an oasis of calm. As I passed through the western city gate, the political tension, focused far away in the capital, seemed to lift. In the expansive central square with the royal palace of fifty-five windows on one side, elegant pavilions, now restaurants, on the other, and the mountainous *shikara* temple of Vatsala Durga at the far end, the air felt suddenly alive and refreshingly clear. On this fine spring day the distant snow peaks of Dorje Lakhba, rising between golden roof finials like the upstanding leaves on a Vajracharya crown, looked close enough to touch.

Originally, it is said, Bhaktapur's royal palace – the oldest and largest of the palaces in the three cities – had ninety-nine courtyards. Now only five remain, all of which – including Mul Chowk (by all accounts the most beautiful of the three royal palace Mul Chowks) – are closed to the public. In the heart of the palace complex, and also still firmly closed to visitors, is Bhaktapur's Taleju Temple, believed to contain the original *yantra* brought to the Kathmandu Valley in the waistband of the refugee prince from Simraongarh, Jagatsimha – son of Devaldevi and Harisimha.

I paused for a moment to take in the layers of history around me, the generations of Malla kings and their extravagant offerings to their tutelary goddess. Out in the square, opposite the entrance to the palace, facing the pagoda roofs of Taleju's temple rising from the centre, stands a tall column on top of which a metre-high bronze gilt statue of Bhupatindra Malla sits cross-legged, shield and sword at his side, a bronze parasol protecting him from the sun, hands together in eternal *namaskar*.

Bhupatindra had this devotional image copied from a similar column erected by the Malla king in Kathmandu. He had asked his cousin-king in Kathmandu to lend him the artisans to make it for him. But – of course – Bhupatindra could not resist making his column higher, and his cousin, outraged, had ordered his artisans to tear it down at dead of night when no one was looking.

This the artisans dutifully did but when they saw Bhupatindra's distress next morning they set to work again and repaired the shattered pillar like new, neatly earning themselves a handsome reward from both the raja of Kathmandu and the raja of Bhaktapur.

The rivalry between the Malla kings only intensified with Bhupatindra's death shortly after the turn of the eighteenth century, heralding a period of political instability in the valley that Prithvi Narayan Shah, the ambitious warlord from Gorkha, was able – with consummate skill – to turn to his advantage.

Blind to the dangers mounting against them and incapable of sustained agreement, however, the last Malla kings of the three cities continued to vie with each other, ostentatiously trumping each other's offerings to the deities of the valley.

Opposite Bhupatindra's column the spectacular gilt bronze gateway to Tripura palace, described by an early British visitor to Nepal, Percy Brown, as 'the most lovely piece of art in the whole kingdom', gleamed in the early morning sun. The 'Golden Gate' or 'Lun Dhoka' had been commissioned by Bhupatindra's son, Ranajit Malla, the last king of Bhaktapur, in 1754. In the *torana* above the doorway a three-headed representation of Taleju, framed by an arch of twisting Nagas, stands with her feet planted in warrior pose, wielding weapons in her eight arms; an allegory, it seems, of what was about to come.

It was here – fifteen years after the Golden Gate's completion – that the three Malla kings of Patan, Kathmandu and Bhaktapur staged their last stand. United in their final moments and with their loyal guards around them, they stood facing the invading forces of the Gorkha army. Their show of unity came too late.

Now, standing in front of Ranajit Malla's Golden Gate on this deceptively peaceful day, with the knowledge that Maoist forces were at this very moment massing somewhere out in the foothills around the valley rim, while the factions of Nepal's government wrangled indecisively, it was impossible not to wonder, in this land of karmic resonance, whether history was about to repeat itself.

I was late, though, and, tearing myself away from Bhaktapur's Durbar Square, I hurried east towards Tachupal Tole – the city's original central square – in the direction of the Kumari.

It had not been as easy to track down Bhaktapur's Living Goddess as it had been in Patan. Bhaktapur – unlike Patan, which is still predominantly Buddhist – is markedly Hindu in character and the Shakyas and Vajracharyas here are far less numerous.

There were several reasons for this. Shortly after Queen Devaldevi had returned from the sacked city of Simraongarh to Bhaktapur, the city of her birth, with her son Jagatsimha in 1326, the valley had suffered a devastating invasion – the only one of its kind – by the Muslim ruler of Bengal, Sultan Shams ud-din Ilyas.

The invasion itself lasted only days but the sultan's army caused the maximum amount of damage, looting and desecrating all the main temples and stupas in the valley. The four-faced linga of Shiva at Pashupati had been smashed into three pieces, the stupa at Swayambhu broken open and set alight, and all three cities in the valley badly destroyed by fire. It is likely that Bhaktapur received particular attention from the invading army as it was the most powerful city in the valley at the time. The sultan may also have targeted Bhaktapur because of its links with the Hindu rajas in the Kingdom of Tirhut and the rebellious city of Simraongarh.

In the aftermath of the invasion, Patan, Kathmandu and Bhaktapur set about restoring themselves. Under the influence of Devaldevi and the Hindu court-in-exile, Bhaktapur re-established itself with a much stronger Hindu identity. It received further Hindu impetus when, in 1354, Devaldevi orchestrated the marriage of her eight-year-old granddaughter to a dynamic nobleman from Tirhut, the man who would ultimately become one of Nepal's most powerful rulers, founder of the new dynasty of Malla kings, who introduced a new legal code and a new system of weights and measures, and who was also attributed with introducing the caste system into Nepal – Jaya Stithi Malla.

But natural catastrophe also played its part in the 'Hinduization' of Bhaktapur. The terrific earthquakes that shook the valley in 1833 and again in 1934 struck Bhaktapur particularly hard, destroying large areas of the old city, including the royal palace and the surrounding Newar Buddhist monastic complexes. The Shakyas and Vajracharyas in Bhaktapur had never – thanks to the city's predominantly agricultural economy – been as wealthy or as organized as Newar Buddhist communities in Patan and Kathmandu, and after the earthquakes many traditional *bahals* were simply not restored. The only *bahals* that were renovated and conserved were those connected with the Bhaktapur Kumari.

However, like the Patan Kumari, the Bhaktapur Living Goddess no longer resided in her official Kumari Chen. She lived with her parents somewhere in the backstreets on the other side of Tachupal Tole.

Piecing together any aspect of Nepal's history is notoriously difficult. Archaeology in the valley is still in its infancy and for the most part limited to surface inscriptions. There are reams of manuscripts – religious texts, land transfer records, dynastic genealogies (known as Vamsavalis) and private journals – spanning the centuries. Variously written in Sanskrit, Newari, Nepali and Maithili, not all of them are in the public domain and only a fraction of them have been published, and even fewer translated. Though there have been heroic attempts at making sense out of this mountain of material, it is likely to be some time before Nepal has its first complete and authoritative history book.

Conflicting oral traditions often make the historical picture even harder to piece together and this is especially true in regard to the origins of the Living Goddess tradition. Each of the three Malla cities has its own myth, claiming its own king as responsible for establishing the first Living Goddess in the valley. In Kathmandu, people claim it was the eighteenth-century ruler Jaya Prakasha, the last Malla king of the city; the people of Patan believe it was their seventeenth-century king Siddhinarasimha Malla, or his son

Shrinivasa; while in Bhaktapur, the king generally attributed with instigating the practice was Trailokya Malla, who had ruled the city over the end of the sixteenth century.

There are two texts, however – both ritual documents in private collections – that shed light on the issue. One – a copy of the Pancharaksha sacred text – records an invitation sent by the joint kings of Bhaktapur, Raya, Ratna, Ram and Ari Malla, to a Buddhist tantric priest – Jivachandra Vajracharya, son of a famous *siddha* in Kathmandu – to come to Bhaktapur to establish a *sadya kumari* at the royal palace. The officiating tantric Buddhist priest, the text explains, was to be given permanent residence in a *bahal*, Chaturbrahma Mahavihar, located close to Bhaktapur's royal palace; and special rooms were to be set aside for the Kumari in the same *bahal*. The date of the invitation is 12 October 1491. All the indications are that this is the first time the Malla kings had established a Living Goddess for their own use, and their dependence on a Buddhist tantric priest to do this for them is clear.

Another document refers to the establishment – by the next generation of kings in Bhaktapur, Jita and Prana Malla, in 1533 – of a larger, permanent Kumari Chen, located in Dipankara Bahal in the north-east of the city, together with provision for a hereditary caretaker.

This material not only pinpoints the origins of the royal Kumari tradition to Bhaktapur, it identifies the kings responsible for it – Raya, Ratna, Ram and Ari Malla, sons of Yaksha Malla and great-grandsons of the reformer Jaya Stithi Malla – and provides a solid date at the end of the fifteenth century. The story in Bhaktapur attributing the institution of Kumari worship to King Trailokya Malla is, in reality, nearly a hundred years out. The Hindu kings of the Kathmandu Valley have been worshipping Living Goddesses for far longer than is generally thought.

~

A five-minute walk from Dattatreya Temple through twisting back streets, the entrance to Pashupati Vihar in Bekha Tole identified itself with a pair of large white eyes freshly painted on old wooden gates. The pupils, half-hidden under semi-closed lids, were characteristic of the meditating Buddha and of the type that featured on the *harmikas* of Buddhist *stupas* – only, here, a pair of arched eyebrows lent them a look of distant concern.

No one knows when the Bhaktapur Kumari made the break with her traditional Kumari Chen though her hereditary caretakers continue dutifully caring for the official Kumari residence and its contents in Dipankara Bahal, and live in hope that the Living Goddess will one day return to it. The caretakers now have responsibility for the Goddess on only the most important ritual occasions. The rest of the time, the maintenance of the Kumari's purity and the overseeing of her daily worship rests with her parents.

Inside the courtyard, fading Buddhist prayer flags fluttered over a scattering of devotional *chaityas* and a large circular stone well. The Kumari's house was tucked away in a small back courtyard. In an open ground-floor portico, set against a brick wall, was an ornately carved throne, unmistakable as the throne of a Living Goddess though, at the same time, the Hindu iconography distinguishes it as very different from the Patan Kumari's. Supporting the seat, with its familiar red cushions, is a pair of snarling lions. The rest of the chair is neither gold nor silver but picked out in multicoloured paint. Ornate columns on either side support an elaborate *torana* of Durga trampling the buffalo demon, overarched by a frieze of Nagas and curling *makaras*. At the pinnacle, with wings outstretched, is Garuda, vehicle of Vishnu, the Hindu god of kings.

A young girl, introducing herself as the Kumari's sister, set down the pitcher of water she was carrying and showed me into the house. Her mother, a plump, cosy woman in a pale pink sari, a string of artificial pearls around her neck, oiled hair pinned up with a butterfly clasp, welcomed me into the Kumari's presence, in the living room upstairs, with beaming smiles.

The Living Goddess of Bhaktapur was watching TV. It was immediately apparent that here many of the Kumari's traditional restrictions had lapsed. Seven years old, Sajani Shakya was wearing not red, but a blue-and-grey uniform. Her hair was in bunches, tied with blue ribbons. She had just come home, on foot, from a busy day at school.

The Kumari leapt up when she saw me and ran to her mother's side, eyes wide with curiosity. Impatiently she gestured to her sister to turn down the volume. She wanted to hear who I was and why I had come. I presented her with a tray of felt-tip pens and a colouring book, touching them reverently to my forehead Newar-style before handing them over. She clapped her hands with joy and ran off with them into her bedroom. Compared with her sister-goddess in Patan, Sajani was an exhibitionist.

'When Sajani was a year old, I dreamt she would become Kumari,' Sajani's mother said, following her daughter's antics as she ran in and out of the room with an indulgent smile.

'When we learnt they were looking for a new Kumari, we took her to the head priest,' she told me. 'He looked at her face, turned her head this way and that – and then he looked at her palm and said, "This one will be the Goddess." She became Kumari when she was one and a half.'

The Bhaktapur Kumari is believed to manifest the traditional thirty-two physical perfections of a Living Goddess but there is no longer any formal physical identification as there is in the selection process in Patan and Kathmandu. The priest in Bhaktapur now merely intuits perfection and there is no removing of outer garments to check the child's body for scars or blemishes.

Neither is there a Vajracharya to perform the daily invocation of the Goddess. Instead, every morning Sajani's mother performed *nitya puja* herself, awaking the Goddess in her daughter before getting her ready for school.

Though she receives the same government funding as the Patan Kumari, the royal Kumari in Bhaktapur is now, in many ways, merely a part-time role and Sajani only usually wore red, with her hair in a topknot, when she was involved in larger rituals and seated on the colourful throne on the ground floor. The rest of the time she received devotees on a simple *asan* on the first floor, next to the living room. Like the Patan Kumari, she had a small, mainly Newar, following who would come to the house with offerings, usually on Saturdays.

Sajani flew back into the room and catapulted herself on to a chair next to her mother. She looked me up and down, wide-eyed, intrigued. 'Have you come to worship me?' she asked.

The sound of her voice took me aback. Direct conversation with outsiders was obviously another taboo that had fallen away. I asked Sajani if she would mind answering some questions. What it was like to be a Goddess, for example?

'Since I was a baby I always wanted to be a Goddess,' she said, with a playful wobble of her head.

'What happens when people come to worship you?' I asked.

'Devotees sprinkle water on my feet. Then they put *tika* on my feet and flowers and rice. And they give me chocolate and fruit and things like that.'

'Does your mother tell you what you need to do?'

'Nobody had to teach me,' said Sajani adamantly, a look of sudden intensity on her face. 'I am a Goddess. I know everything.'

'From the moment she became Kumari, she knew how to behave,' her mother confirmed. 'Even when she was little and I was busy, she knew what to do and would often receive devotees on her own.'

'Do you ever get annoyed having to do these things?' I asked Sajani.

'Sometimes I don't feel like going on my throne when Ma asks me,' Sajani admitted, with a mock frown directed at her mother. 'I've got to get up so early. It's so warm inside and so cold outside. But when I'm on my throne I feel warm again. I feel power coming from somewhere.'

'Do you feel the Goddess inside you?'

'I feel the Goddess's power when I put on my third eye,' she nodded firmly, her face sober again. 'And when I go to Taleju Temple at Dasain, I get shivers in there. I feel *shakti* there, too.'

By far the biggest event for the Bhaktapur Kumari is Dasain. Mirroring the rituals conducted simultaneously in the other two Malla cities, Dasain is the moment when the Hindu population of Bhaktapur, normally casual in their regard to the Buddhist child Goddess living in their midst, are recalled to her presence as the incarnation of Taleju, protectoress of their former kings and emanation of Durga. Then, Sajani's mother described, barely able to contain her pride, her daughter would be dressed in the full insignia of a royal Kumari including *tayo*, *naga mala* and *yantra mala* – items of empowerment that, for the rest of the year, are kept under lock and key in a strong room in Taleju Temple, inside the old royal palace complex.

'The ninth day of Dasain is my most important day,' Sajani said enthusiastically. 'That is when Goddess Durga kills all her enemies and bad people. Durga is very powerful, like Kali,' she added, helpfully, for my benefit. 'Taleju, Durga and Kali – they are the same.'

'What happens on the ninth day?' I asked.

Sajani swung her legs matter-of-factly under her chair. 'I get up early. I drink tea and eat sweets and biscuits. Ma helps me get dressed into my Kumari clothes and she puts on my third eye. Then everyone worships me. The priest of Taleju comes to our house and he carries me to Taleju Temple, to the *agam* in Mul Chowk, inside the royal palace.'

'Only the priests can go inside Mul Chowk with Kumari,' her mother added. 'They take Dya Maiju to an upstairs room for tantric worship. The necklace they give her is the one worn by Goddess Taleju.'

'I sit with buffalo heads all around me,' said Sajani proudly. 'But I'm not frightened of the *agam*. That's why I'm a Goddess.' Then she checked herself. Suddenly she looked very serious and flashed me a warning look. 'But I'm not allowed to tell you what happens in the temple during Dasain, OK?'

Even her mother was not allowed to know what went on.

'When the Kumari comes out of the temple her face changes – her eyes are brighter and her face looks fuller,' her mother continued. 'Many people wait outside the entrance to Mul Chowk for *prasad* from the Goddess. The Kumari gives the people flowers. Whoever gets the first flower from Kumari, his greatest wish will be fulfilled.'

Sajani was listening intently, taking her mother's account of her supernatural powers in her stride.

'Long ago, at Dasain,' Sajani's mother continued, 'the Kumari used to give a flower – a blue lotus – to the Malla king. This is the flower that gave the king *shakti*, that filled him with power. Once, the Kumari gave this flower to Prithvi Narayan Shah when he was staying in Bhaktapur. It gave him the power to conquer the city.'

The story of Prithvi Narayan receiving *prasad* from the Kumari is recounted in the chronicles. The Gorkha prince is known to have come to Bhaktapur as a young man, in NS 859 (1739 CE), and to have stayed in the palace as guest of the king of Bhaktapur. He came as a special envoy to establish the special bond of '*mit*', a sacred friendship, between his father, the king of Gorkha, and Ranajit Malla, the last king of Bhaktapur.

The Malla kings often made pacts and alliances between themselves and hill states outside the valley – there were more than sixty hill states in the outlying regions – in order to improve their trading and economic power and gain the upper hand over their cousin kings. Generally, though, they were careful to protect their combined interests and ensure that any alliance with an outside raja did not threaten the status quo of their three kingdoms.

But an alliance was exactly what the house of Gorkha was after, to drive a wedge between the Malla kings. According to Prithvi Narayan Shah's autobiographical account, the Dibya Upadesh – a compilation of oral counsels delivered by the Shah king towards

the end of his life – his ambition to conquer the Valley of Nepal
stemmed from a moment when he was a fourteen-year-old
boy. Returning from his marriage to the daughter of the raja of
Makwanpur – a kingdom to the south of the valley – he had stood
on the valley rim and looked upon the Malla cities for the very
first time. Disguising himself under a poor man's raincover made
of bamboo and plantain leaves – so as not to be recognized and
taken prisoner as a spy – the Gorkha prince had climbed to the
top of Chandragiri ridge with two astrologers from his entourage.
Looking upon the broad sweep of the valley before him he had – in
his own words – asked his companions, 'Which is Nepal?' To which
they had replied, indicating the Malla cities in turn, 'Sire, that is
Bhaktapur, that is Patan, and there lies Kathmandu.'

It was then, according to Prithvi Narayan Shah, that 'the
thought came to me that I might be lord of them all'. His
excitement did not escape the two astrologers with him at the
time. 'Sire,' they exclaimed, 'your heart is melting with desire.'
'How did you know my innermost thoughts?' he asked them.
'At the moment your gaze rested on Nepal,' they answered, 'you
stroked your moustache and so in your heart you longed to be
king of Nepal, it seemed to us.'

The moment is immortalized in a bronze statue of the Gorkha
conqueror, extravagantly moustached, standing in front of
the western gate of Singha Durbar, the parliament building in
Kathmandu, one finger raised in the air signifying his vision for one
nation under one flag.

The question that plagued Prithvi Narayan Shah from the outset
was how to achieve his ambition. The Valley of Nepal was renowned
for being impregnable. Before embarking on his campaign to conquer
it, it was vital he learn about the Malla kingdoms, the secret of their
power and success, from the inside.

The bond of *mit* is an alliance akin to the bond of blood brothers.
Close Newar friends, both male and female, still enter into it today,
regarding it as a lifelong vow of love and loyalty. When King Ranajit

Malla of Bhaktapur accepted the king of Gorkha as his *mit bhai* he was entering into an alliance that he considered unbreakable. He would have welcomed the king of Gorkha's proxy, Prithvi Narayan, into Tripura Palace as his own son.

It is easy to imagine the delightful, appreciative guest the young prince Prithvi Narayan Shah would have made, all the while veiling his distaste – as he later confessed in the Dibya Upadesh – for the 'softness', the 'empty pomp and pleasure' of the Malla way of life; the conspicuous lack of military training and conditioning; the courtly preoccupation with music and the arts; even the ubiquitous bathing tanks and ponds of standing water – so offensive to him after the rigorous icy streams he was used to in the mountains.

'This three-citied Nepal is a cold stone,' he said in his counsels. 'It is great only in intrigue. With one who drinks water from cisterns, there is no wisdom; nor is there courage. There is only intrigue.'

The peaceful sophistication of Bhaktapur, its low city walls minimally defended, must have confirmed in Prithvi Narayan's mind the role Goddess Taleju played in protecting the cities in the valley and invigorating the Malla kings. He would have noted the importance Ranajit Malla placed on his daily prayers and offerings at Taleju Temple, his belief in the empowering nature of her *prasad*, the fierce competition between the Malla kings for Taleju's attention and, most conspicuous of all, Ranajit Malla's personal worship of the Living Goddess.

The story of the blue lotus given by the royal Bhaktapur Kumari to the visiting imposter Prithvi Narayan Shah is very similar to the story about how, in recent times, the Kathmandu Kumari had bestowed her *tika* on Crown Prince Mahendra the year his father King Tribhuvan died. If Prithvi Narayan Shah had, indeed, received this powerful symbol from the Living Goddess when he was staying in Bhaktapur, he would have noticed the troubled reactions of the court and King Ranajit himself. It might have been this occurrence that ultimately inspired his coup – a stroke of genius – thirty years later, when he timed his attack on Kathmandu to coincide with the festival of Kumari Jatra and dramatically usurped King Jaya Prakasha Malla's blessing from the Living Goddess of Kathmandu.

Sajani had grown tired and slipped off her chair to go and play with her toys in her bedroom, leaving me to talk with her mother.

'Early in the morning, on the day of Navami,' Sajani's mother said, describing Dasain, 'before Dya Maiju herself comes to the royal palace, the tantric priest of Mul Chowk must worship nine other little Kumaris.

'They are the "Gana Kumaris",' she explained. 'They are like the main Kumari but temporary ones – they are Living Goddesses only for the length of the festival.'

These temporary 'Gana' – or 'group' – Kumaris, she said, are emanations of the Goddess that come into force during Durga's victory over the agents of darkness. Like the royal Kumari, the Gana Kumaris are selected from Bhaktapur's Shakya and Vajracharya community. They are traditionally of different ages, ranging from the youngest – two years old (the age when it is believed a child becomes fully conscious and sensitive) – to the oldest who, at eleven, is still prepubescent. They are chosen in a way similar to the royal Kumari, with the priests checking for auspicious signs, ensuring they have no obvious blemishes or scars. Most importantly they cannot have undergone *ihi* – the mock marriage ritual to the bel fruit. Like the royal Kumari they also have to avoid pollution of all kinds but since they are Kumaris for such a short period this is no particular hardship. For this reason, Sajani's mother told us, many families want their daughters to be a Gana Kumari and preference is always given to those who have not yet had the chance. Originally the youngest Kumari would be worshipped on the first day of Dasain, with the next Kumari added to the worship on each subsequent day. But this cumulative worship has fallen by the wayside. Now all nine Gana Kumaris are worshipped together on the ninth day of Dasain.

The Gana Kumaris are accompanied by two boys – or *kumaras* – similarly chosen, from the same caste, and similarly purified, who embody the gods Ganesh and Bhairab. The boy gods are present principally in an attendant capacity, as guardians – equivalent to the two boys embodying Ganesh and Bhairab who attend the Kathmandu Kumari at the festival of Indra Jatra. All eleven children wear red, their hair tied up on their heads, with red *tikas* emblazoned on their foreheads, third eyes, and adorned with gold and silver ornaments kept specifically for them in the strong room of Taleju Temple.

'The Gana Kumaris represent the Navadurga – the nine aspects of Durga,' Sajani's mother said. 'This is how most people see them.'

But the Gana Kumaris have another role – a purpose more specific to the Newar system and one that was crucial to reaffirming the king's power over his kingdom. This role is connected with the protective boundaries of the city. The Gana Kumaris are identified by name as the Astamatrika, the eight Mother Goddesses whose *pithas* encircle the city in a protective ring, together with Tripurasundari, the fierce emanation of Durga central to the Bhaktapur pantheon. At Dasain these wild, terrifying protectoresses, normally confined to their bloody *pithas* in polluted ground outside the city walls, enter the sacred centre of the city in the living bodies of children, the purest of human forms. It is a concept charged with tantric inversions of purity and pollution, and immensely powerful. It is as if Durga, the Supreme Goddess, is gathering in all her emanations once again, drawing all her cohorts back to their source.

While the royal Kumari is the focal point, the central receptor, it is her relationship with the Gana Kumaris that, every year, connects her with the boundaries of the city – like the hub of a wheel or the turning point of a *chakra*.

Each Malla capital has its own group of Gana Kumaris and exactly the same performance is carried out at Dasain in all three cities. On the climactic day of Navami, the Gana Kumaris come together in the central *agam* of Mul Chowk and each royal

Kumari – in Bhaktapur, Patan and Kathmandu – becomes the apotheosis of nine goddesses merged into one, supercharged with the forces of destruction, creation and preservation. Revivified by this spectacular collection of energy, the central Living Goddess, in turn, re-dispenses power to her cohorts so they can return to their stations on the boundary of the city at the end of Dasain, replenished and renewed, armed and dangerous, ready to defend the kingdom from all its enemies. This is, surely, another aspect of Kumari worship that would not have been lost on Prithvi Narayan Shah.

The image of these nine Kumaris as one made a strong impression and later, as the pattern took root in my mind, further layers of symbolism began to emerge.

The sacred play of numbers and patterns within the Newar way of thinking was gradually becoming more familiar to me. It is the frame behind every notion – the bones that give form to all their spiritual concepts. It is different from the everyday, linear processes I was used to; closer, I imagined, to the way scientists or mathematicians might see things.

There is, clearly, particular relevance in the geometrical shapes that spring to life at Dasain. The triangular connection between Kumari, Taleju and the king is key. Together with the Gana Kumaris forming a circle around them, this is a design that expresses the essence of the Goddess herself.

The Goddess is synonymous with the shape of a triangle – the shape, or *yantra*, through which her abstract, essential form expresses itself. It is the symbol used by devotees in meditation to identify themselves with the Goddess and in the Kathmandu Valley the downward-pointing triangle appears anywhere the universal Goddess is invoked. It is carved on temples and *toranas*, depicted in meditational paintings and on the tools of ritual, drawn in vermilion or white powder on the floor during *pujas*.

In most depictions of the Goddess's *yantra* there is a single dot, or *bindu*, in the centre; and the triangle itself is often encapsulated in a protective circle or an eight-petalled lotus. The *yantra* is, in a sense, the Goddess's genetic code; and the dot contained within it the quintessential seed of existence. Once you recognize the significance of this shape it is all-pervasive, replicating itself everywhere you look, like a multiplying cell. Any triangular hole in a pavement or brick wall, any suggestive cleft in a rock or the trunk of a tree, is acknowledged as an expression of the Goddess, its *yoni*-shape accentuated by smears of vermilion, sometimes encircled with paint, so that passers-by can, almost subconsciously, reach out and touch it and bless themselves with it.

At a metaphysical level – the level recognized by the royal tantric priests and articulated in their meditations – the king, Kumari and Taleju form a triangle that is a reflection of the three *gunas*. The *gunas* are the fundamental aspects of reality manifested by Prakriti – the Goddess who is the creative origin of all matter and energy. Originating in desire (*iccha*), action (*kriya*) and knowing (*gnana*), each has an associated colour – dark blue or black; red; and white. The king represents the *guna* known as *tamas* – the descending quality or inertia; the Kumari, *rajas* – the kinetic quality; and Taleju, *sattva* – the ascending quality. Implicit in this relationship is the notion that, without the kinetic quality of the Kumari, the king would remain impotent and inert – incapable of connecting with transcendent divinity.

At this deeply symbolic level, the Gana Kumaris, like the circle of Astamatrika around the city, form a protective ring or eight-petalled lotus around the central triangle. They relate to the eight *tattvas* or principles of matter – the five elements of earth, water, fire, air, ether, plus mind (*manas*), intellect (*buddhi*) and ego (*ahamkara*) – that are generated by Prakriti, the cosmic female creative energy, at the next grosser, phenomenal stage of existence.

In this sense, the coming together of the Gana Kumaris inside the royal palace in the secret *agam* next to Taleju's temple on the night of Navami represents the reintegration of the gross principles of matter back within the sacred triangle, into the fundamental equilibrium of the *gunas*. It is energy returning to its source. The dark rituals of Dasain mark the moment of involution when the Goddess reabsorbs the forces of nature back within herself, reaching that point of primal resolution, of non-duality, of union with Purusha, the male principle of cosmic consciousness, before her compulsive creative urge begins the explosive process of generation once again.

This is believed to be a supremely powerful moment and not without risk for the little Kumaris involved. Everything is done to ensure the rituals are followed to the letter. Above all, it is crucial that the Gana Kumaris do not have *darshan* of the main, central – or 'mul' – Kumari. As Living Goddesses they are, temporarily at least, emanations of the permanent one; their spirits, in essence, part of her. If they see her before the energetic exchange of Dasain is over, their spirits could be pulled back into her, into their source, and the children themselves could die.

The Goddess's *yantra* manifests itself on many levels during Dasain but her triangular nature expresses itself in all sorts of other connective patterns and relationships. It seemed, for example – as I travelled between the three royal cities – that the royal Kumaris of Kathmandu, Patan and Bhaktapur formed a triangular power-base of their own.

It is clear from the assiduous patronage of all three royal Kumaris by the ensuing Shah dynasty – and, indeed, their autocratic Rana regents – that the stability of the kingdom of Nepal continued to be regarded as being, in some fundamental way, dependent on the continued triple worship of the Malla royal Goddesses. The recognition of this triangle has persisted even into the modern era of elected government with stipends allocated from government funds to maintain all three Living Goddess traditions, even though few people outside the Newar communities in Patan and Bhaktapur know about the existence of these other two 'royal' Kumaris.

It is interesting, too, that despite – or perhaps because of – the popular clamour for democracy and removal of power from the monarchy, kings Tribhuvan, Mahendra and Birendra had continued their personal patronage of all three Living Goddesses. Whether or not they recognized their reduced power as resulting from some egregious fault of their own – or some oversight committed by their ancestors, as legends such as Gorakhnath's prophecy portrayed – they seem to have acknowledged that their survival as kings rested on the continued worship of the three royal Goddesses. Break this sacred bond and they risked losing kingship altogether.

~

Before leaving Sajani to the secular demands of her homework, I asked her mother about the Kumari's present relationship with the royal palace in Kathmandu. There was an echo of the sentiments of both Rashmila, the ex-Kumari of Kathmandu, and the Patan Kumari in her response; an expression of deep connection with the previous king.

'Last year, before the royal family massacre,' Sajani's mother told us, 'when Dya Maiju was taken to Taleju Temple during Dasain, on the night of Navami, she cried and cried. She had never cried before. The priests were very worried. They suspected something bad would happen to a visiting head of state or a high-ranking government official. Then one week before the massacre she started to cry again.'

Her voice trailed away. The Living Goddess had grown restless with her toys and turned up the volume on the TV. News of another Maoist attack on a police station in the Terai was swiftly switched to cartoons. The Kumari's mother struggled to raise her voice above the noise.

'King Birendra often sent *puja* things here,' she said. 'Sometimes we did not know why he did it. He was a very pious man.' There was another pause before she added sadly, a concerned furrow pinching her brow, 'But the new king has sent nothing yet. This is not good for our country.'

~

On an auspicious day in July 2002 King Gyanendra moved from his mansion in Maharajgunj into Narayanhiti Palace at the top of Durbar Marg, the royal priests having done all they could to purify the bloodstains and exorcise the lurking ghosts of his family. But the atmosphere remained tense. A year into his reign Gyanendra was still an unknown quantity. No one knew where the new monarch's allegiances lay, what his motives were; whether he had the best interests of the country at heart, or – as many suspected – merely his own. Most people assumed, even a year on, that he had been responsible, in some way, for the royal family massacre; or that his son, Paras, had been behind it.

However, the country, post-massacre, was patently in crisis. Nepal desperately needed leadership and many – even some committed to democracy – felt that the king might be the only person who could restore a sense of unity to Nepal. Nepalis were used to living in the shade of the royal parasol and King Birendra's calm, avuncular presence and the long tradition he represented had provided a feeling of protection and stability. Few people, now, had confidence in the alternatives.

Over the past decade, Nepal's political leaders had shown themselves poor figureheads, unable or unwilling to take a stand against the Maoists, lazy and nepotistic once in office, obsessed with infighting and mud-slinging and prone to corruption. There had been as many as ten governments in Nepal since democracy had been restored in 1991, with fragile coalitions see-sawing between two main contenders, Sher Bahadur Deuba and Girija Prasad Koirala, both scions of the Nepali Congress, the largest political party. Koirala, brother of two previous prime ministers, was now seventy-seven years old and had been prime minister five times; Deuba, twenty years his junior, was in his second term as prime minister and had, since May, been ruling by decree. Earlier in the year, as fighting escalated between Maoists and government forces in the hill districts, Deuba had called for a renewal of the state of emergency and dissolved parliament. The move had resulted in a dramatic split of the Congress Party. Fresh elections had been called – scheduled for November 2002 – and Deuba, heading a separate Congress Party faction, had assumed leadership of the interim government.

The Maoists, meanwhile, were taking advantage of the political confusion and making serious in-roads into the valley. Most businesses – hotels and travel companies included – were now paying them protection money. Defiant factories and offices had been targeted with small, home-made pressure-cooker bombs. Though the bombs were rarely fatal, the impact was considerable. Telecommunication facilities were being specially targeted and, now and again, burnt-out vehicles smouldered by the sides of the roads.

As the year progressed the Maoists introduced 'hanging bombs' – explosive devices left dangling from power cables, usually alongside garish banners of Maoist slogans. They rarely caused casualties, either, but occasionally the devices were less easy to spot and in July 2002 a bomb blast rocked the prime minister's offices, injuring eight people.

Intense clashes between government forces and the rebels continued to rage in the hills and even, on occasion, around villages inside the valley. In September, in response to the worsening security situation, Deuba's interim government was given a 'full mandate' to postpone the November elections indefinitely.

Then suddenly, on 4 October 2002 – a little over a year after Gyanendra had inherited the throne – everything changed. The king sprang into life. Accusing the cabinet of incompetence, Gyanendra sacked the prime minister, installing another former prime minister – the pro-monarchist Lokendra Bahadur Chand – as his puppet, and appointing thirteen other royalist-leaning cronies as ministers of the cabinet. It was the first time since 1990 that the king had had direct control.

The political parties responded by staging major protest rallies in Kathmandu and journalists both at home and abroad railed against this most undemocratic of 'coups'. But among orthodox Hindus – affluent non-Newar Bahuns and Chettris – and the foreign diplomatic community in Kathmandu in particular, feelings were more ambiguous. Many hoped that Gyanendra's intervention would at least provide some sense of direction, that some invisible hand would steer the recalcitrant monarch, the world's last Hindu king, recalling him to his *dharma*.

Perhaps, some people argued, being a kingdom was Nepal's natural state of being. And anyway, this state of emergency was only a temporary measure. The king had vowed his allegiance to the constitution and promised to return his powers to parliament once the crisis was over. In the meantime the army, whose generals were ardent royalists and had, on occasion, appeared reluctant to rally to the cry of the prime minister, would surely, with this turn of events, receive the impetus they needed to eliminate the Maoists once and for all.

But visiting the 'royal' Living Goddesses of Patan and Bhaktapur had impressed upon me a different perspective. In the *bahals* and courtyards of traditional Newars, at least, there was a growing conviction that the monarchy was losing its moorings, that a gap was widening between the king and the gods.

PART THREE

Chapter 17

An Empty Throne

One particular aspect of Kumari worship continued to puzzle me after my visit to Bhaktapur. The Malla kings had clearly regarded the practice of worshipping living children as empowering – perhaps crucial, even, to their survival. But why, if the Goddess these children were believed to incarnate was categorically Hindu, did the Kumaris themselves have to be Buddhist? Why couldn't the girls be Bahun or Chettri, from families attached to the kings' own court? Wouldn't it be more appropriate for a Hindu king if the Kumaris were Hindu, at the very least?

A key aspect of Kumari worship appears to have been its strong tantric overtones. All the variations of the royal Kumari myth emphasized Taleju's insistence, after the king's misdemeanour, that from then on he should worship his lineage Goddess in the form of a girl from a 'polluted' caste. This inversion of taboo was, in a tantric sense, especially empowering. It was a symbolic act echoing the tantric rules that exhorted a person of high caste to have relations with someone of a lower caste or an untouchable, or even a corpse or an animal of the most polluting kind, like a dog.

In strict Hindu terms the Shakyas were considered to practise a polluting occupation. As goldsmiths, they made a living recovering gold from worn-out images – in Hindu eyes, a glorified form of scavenging. The process of bronze casting also involved smelting base metals – an occupation that, in India, had long been work designated to untouchables. For someone of the king's stature to prostrate himself before a female child of a 'polluted' caste would, in the Hindu interpretation, be especially empowering. The Malla kings were even said, on occasion, to have received a *tika* of a Kumari's first menstrual blood – the most empowering substance in the world.

But why, I wondered, did the king not worship an untouchable Hindu child? It was perhaps, understandable, that the chosen Kumari was a Newar. There would have been considerable political advantages to this. Bowing his head to a Newar child would have pandered to the sensibilities of the Newar population and kept the indigenous people of the valley on side. But why not select a Newar Hindu Kumari – a girl from the Newar butcher caste, for example? Surely a Hindu king worshipping a female, non-Parbatiya child from a caste practising a polluting occupation would have been effective enough, without her having to be Buddhist as well? Why risk alienating his own Hindu following and offending the powerful Brahmin priests and Hindu courtiers?

This paradox seemed to lie at the very heart of the tradition. It offered vital clues to the origins of the Living Goddess.

For some time I had been hearing intriguing stories of a Living Goddess whose residence was barely ten minutes' walk from Durbar Square – a separate Kumari, sponsored not by the king but by the Buddhists of Kathmandu. I hoped that here I would find the answers I was looking for.

Mu Bahal was a dilapidated courtyard tucked away down a narrow side street off the frenetic hub of Indra Chowk. It was one of the eighteen Maha Viharas of Kathmandu. Once it would have been a *bahal* of great beauty, small but exquisite. Now, though, its Naga-scale roof tiles have been replaced by sheets of corrugated iron and concrete additions have created an extra storey around the residential sides of the quadrangle. The entrance to the courtyard, at the end of the alley, is an archway beneath a long, elegant fivefold window with telling, faded red curtains. This whole side of the *bahal*, a two-storey elevation in its original form, is in a dangerous state of collapse. One end of it is, already, little more than a pile of rubble.

Laxmi Vajracharya, a woman in her late fifties in a red-and-orange sari, her black hair tied neatly in a bun, was waiting inside the courtyard. She showed me to a doorway and up a dark staircase into a tiny dark room, barely nine feet by seven feet. Inside, taking up almost the entire volume of the room and raised on a brick plinth, was a low red-upholstered seat – a Kumari throne. Dark pillars supported an elaborate wooden canopy over the top of it. On either side of the throne, a pair of small stone lions, beguilingly smiling and wearing fresh marigold garlands, had recently received *tikas*. On the clay floor in front of the *asan*, a *sukunda* lamp had been lit and beside it sat a brass drinking-cup in the form of a skull with three tiny projecting Goddess heads. On the seat of the throne was a scattering of rice and marigolds and, this being 'sugar-cane day', a stick of freshly cut cane.

A toothless old man with white hair, in checked shirt and glasses, and a bandage on one leg, was sitting on the far side of the *asan*, squeezed on to the floor by a small open lattice window. Laxmi Vajracharya and her husband, Shaubagya Ratna Vajracharya, were the *palas* – the god guardians – for a Living Goddess who no longer existed.

The last Kumari of Mu Bahal, Shaubagya's niece, had retired in 1972. There had been two Kumari thrones at Mu Bahal, the couple told me – a secret one for tantric *pujas*; and this one, for public worship. When, after two decades of neglect, the Kumari's throne room – the long chamber over the *bahal* entrance – had begun to collapse, Shaubagya and his sons had moved the public throne to this tiny room for safety. The esoteric throne was still in the *agam*. It could not be moved until there was somewhere tantrically sanctified for it to go. It sat there, inside the deteriorating building, in danger of being crushed at any minute.

Meanwhile, Shaubagya Ratna's family took it in turns to worship the public throne, performing *nitya puja* to its invisible occupant and receiving non-initiates who came to present offerings. The family lived in hope that one day a Living Goddess would be reinstalled in Mu Bahal. In the meantime, worshipping the throne kept the Goddess's presence alive.

'We feel the spirit of the Kumari is still here,' said Laxmi. 'Often you can smell resin incense – the scent of *gungu* – around the place. Sometimes our sons hear the sound of her footsteps going up and down the stairs.'

She pointed to a tiny chink in the wall, up near the ceiling.

'We keep this *nasa dya* hole open so the Goddess can come and go when she pleases, even when the room is locked. It was bigger before but we put a stone in it to stop the rats. Once we blocked it up completely and my daughter got sick because the Kumari could not get through. So now we leave just a little space. It is enough.'

Mu Bahal is, according to oral tradition, the oldest *bahal* in Kathmandu. The word 'mu' or 'mul' means 'main', in the sense of being the 'principal' or 'original' one – like the Mul Chowk in Hanuman Dhoka or Bhaktapur Palace.

The Kumari of Mu Bahal is also believed by Vajracharyas to be the oldest in Kathmandu – and more important than the royal adjunct in Durbar Square, or the royal Kumaris in Patan and Bhaktapur. According to Laxmi and Shaubagya Ratna, the priority of the 'Mul Kumari' – and her superior power – is borne out by the fact that, up until recently, if the royal Kumari in Durbar Square fell ill her caretakers would send offerings to the Mu Bahal Kumari to cure her.

'The Mu Bahal Kumari was here already, long before a Raj Kumari was established in Kathmandu, Patan or even in Bhaktapur. She was here even before there was a city in

Kathmandu,' said the old man. 'Our ancestors were told by
Guhyeshvari how to find her.'

Guhyeshvari is the 'Hidden' or 'Secret' Goddess at the heart of
the Buddhist creation myth of the Valley of Nepal.

'Our *sangha* came originally from Pashupati area, from Pim Bahal,'
he explained. 'There was a famous Vajracharya there who was the
god-guardian of Pashupati and a very powerful *siddha*. He used to
worship Guhyeshvari at her *pitha* at Pashupati. Guhyeshvari told
him to come here, to establish a *bahal*.'

Kathmandu was still forest in those days, Shaubagya Ratna
said, and when the legendary Vajracharya arrived here he found
an enormous tree. Sitting in the tree was a Kumari. He begged
the Kumari's permission to cut down the tree and she agreed.
Mu Bahal, the old man said, was built out of the timber from that
single tree. The Kumari had taken up residence inside the *bahal*
and from that day on the Vajracharya community of Kathmandu
had worshipped her.

'We were blessed to have the Goddess living with us,' said
Shaubagya Ratna. 'She brought joy and happiness to everyone in
our community.'

For Vajracharyas, Mu Bahal Kumari was the most perfect living
form of Vajradevi, the Buddhist manifestation of the divine feminine,
the one they would call on when they wanted to perform any
ceremony involving tantric worship. The Mu Bahal Kumari had
played a key role in all the important Vajrayana Buddhist *pujas*. She
could also be called upon to attend private rituals inside people's
houses. She had always been busy, Laxmi said.

The Mu Bahal Kumari had observed all the usual Living
Goddess restrictions. She had had to take special care not to
become impure and could eat neither garlic nor onions. She
had to avoid contact with leather and other impure substances.
Whenever rituals required her attendance outside the *bahal*, she
had been carried in a *khat* – a palanquin – or in her father's arms.
Though she had lived with her parents in Mu Bahal, and could

play in the courtyard with other children, she could not go out of the compound except to meet her ritual obligations. She had always been dressed in red, with her hair in a topknot, and for *pujas* she had worn a third eye, a crown with five upstanding leaves, or '*mukuta*', and a *naga mala*, as well as other empowering ornaments and jewellery. She was dismissed if she fell ill or experienced any significant blood loss or, ultimately, when she had her first period.

I asked how the Mu Bahal Kumari had been selected.

'The Kumari candidates would be checked for any signs of imperfection,' Laxmi told us, 'then they were brought to the Kumari throne room above the entrance to the *bahal* and the Kumari would be chosen by casting lots.'

The seniormost Vajracharya – the 'Chakreshvar' – would place small rolls of paper in a ritual bowl. His wife would hand one out to each candidate. The girl who took the paper with a *vajra* drawn on it became the next Kumari. The changeover could be made on any auspicious day. The newly selected girl would be seated beside the outgoing Kumari on her throne. One by one, the senior Vajracharyas would transfer the various items of jewellery and other insignia from one girl to the other.

It seemed far simpler than the process involved in identifying a royal Kumari. There were no bloody sacrifices or midnight rites of passage such as featured on the dark night of Dasain with the installation of Taleju. This was an intrinsically Buddhist process. And – significantly – there was no mention of the king.

'Why was there no replacement for Mu Bahal Kumari when the last one left, in 1972?' I asked.

Shaubagya Ratna shook his head sadly. 'The old people who know about Kumari worship have died,' he said simply, 'and the young people don't care.'

'There were not many girls of the right age in Mu Bahal when the last Kumari was dismissed,' his wife elaborated. 'And the ones that there were came from families that had intermarried. Nowadays there are not so many families with a pure lineage.'

But there were other considerations, too. The restrictions on a Kumari's family were demanding, especially in the modern day, and donations were on the wane. Without the kind of government and palace sponsorship the royal Kumaris received, maintaining a Kumari somewhere like Mu Bahal was an increasingly expensive proposition. No one these days wanted their daughter to miss out on an education but the cost of private tuition was daunting. Then there was Mu Bahal itself, in its sadly neglected state.

'I wanted my granddaughter to be Kumari but we would have had to move back here,' said Laxmi. 'Our family has a new house now – across the river.'

There was no doubting the couple's regret and the Kumari continued to haunt their dreams. Sometimes the Living Goddess visited members of the family in waking moments, too.

'A month ago my son was struck by a powerful feeling that the Kumari was remembering him,' said Laxmi. 'She was calling him. He came straight here on his motorbike with offerings.'

Five years after the last Mu Bahal Kumari had left, there had been an unseemly wrangle over who was to safeguard all the Living Goddess's paraphernalia. Shaubagya Ratna and his wife had taken the public throne; while the family of Shaubagya's father's first wife had taken the crown and other ornaments, and worshipped these things separately in their house.

For certain *pujas*, though, the Kumari's things were reunited, the crown placed on the seat of the public throne. Occasionally, when an important Kumari Puja was needed, Shaubagya's brother would return the crown and other ornaments to the *agam* – a dangerous proposition given the state of the building – and place them on the seat of the tantric throne for worship. The reconnection was powerful but, still – Laxmi said – it was not the same as worshipping an actual Living Goddess.

'The *dya* is with us when her ornaments are placed on the throne but her presence is not as strong as when there is a *sadya* Kumari on the throne. That is a wonderful thing. The people can see there is a

Goddess among them. The effect is very powerful. It brings people closer to God.

'In Newar Buddhism every big *puja* concludes with Kumari worship. It makes the *puja* complete. It fulfils the person performing it. Without a *sadya* Kumari, we can perform these things but there is not the same feeling of fulfilment, of completion in your heart.'

The division of the Kumari's accoutrements – and the ruptures it had caused within Shaubagya's family – seemed symptomatic of the collapsing infrastructure of the *sangha* of Mu Bahal itself; its buildings, and the traditional frameworks of patronage and sponsorship.

Time was getting on and Laxmi said she had to get back to their house in Chamati to look after her grandchildren. Before we left, locking the empty throne behind us, I asked if Laxmi could tell me about the tradition of the Mu Bahal Kumari curing the royal Kumari if she fell ill.

Laxmi remembered the last time the caretakers from the Kumari Chen had come to Mu Bahal with offerings. Laxmi herself had taken the healing water from Mu Bahal to cure the royal Kumari.

'There is a big silver mask, a mask of the Kumari's face,' she explained. 'It was always kept in the *agam*. We would draw pure water from a well near here and it would be poured over the Kumari mask, flowing down onto a special stone *mandala* underneath. When water has been empowered in this way it is called "*yachin lah*". The healing water was stored carefully in a copper water-pot. Every day people would come to take this water to be made well.'

'Only water from here can cure the royal Kumari,' Shaubagya repeated vehemently. 'No doctor can do it.'

'What happens now if the royal Kumari gets sick?' I asked.

Shaubagya shrugged. 'I don't know what they do. They don't come here.'

He didn't know where the silver mask was now. Perhaps his brother's family had it. Recently, even the well where they used to

draw pure spring water – water that came directly from the sacred
Himalaya – had dried up. The lid on it had been padlocked. Now the
only water available for *nitya puja* was municipal tap water.

I asked Shaubagya if he knew anything about the ailment that
was said to have disqualified the royal Kumari the previous summer.

'The people at the Kumari Chen did not tell us anything,' he said.
'They do not communicate with us any more.' He stretched out his
bandaged leg, rubbing it to relieve the pressure.

He was adamant about one thing. 'If there had still been a Kumari
here at Mu Bahal,' he said, 'she would have made the Raj Kumari
well. The Mul Kumari would have cured her little sister. Who knows
– the royal massacre might not have happened. Everything would
be different today if we had the Mu Bahal Kumari.'

~

The Mu Bahal Kumari threw the doors of the Kumari tradition
wide open. It proved that the Living Goddesses of the Kathmandu
Valley were rooted not in Hindu palaces but deep in Newar Buddhist
practice. Far from being a phenomenon exclusive to kings, Living
Goddess worship is clearly something the Newars had originally
practised themselves, for their own benefit. Royal Kumari worship
is essentially the veneer on a much older tradition.

I began to dig into the history of Goddess worship, increasingly
conscious as I did so that, while the tradition continues in parts of
India and is clearly vibrant in Nepal, it has entirely vanished from
my own culture. We had lost our Mother Goddesses long ago, with
the burning of witches and the crushing of Cybele's temple under
the mighty edifice of St Peter's Basilica in Rome. The closer I came
to understanding the survival of the Goddess in Nepal, the more
I became uncomfortably aware of her absence in my own culture
and the entrenched androcentricity of almost every aspect of life
into which I had been born.

In the Indian subcontinent, the roots of virgin worship can be
traced back to pre-Vedic times, tapping into ancient primeval fertility

rites and Mother Goddess cults of the kind that had predominated in places like Mohenjo-daro and Harappa in the third millennium BCE. But the moment the 'Kumari', the aspect of the Goddess with which I was concerned, came into being seems to have been towards the late Vedic period.

While male gods tend to be conceived of as single deities with separate identities, the concept of Devi had evolved in the Indian tradition, as in many other traditions in the world, as an all-pervasive figure – the universal Mother. Her different aspects, from nurturing child-bearer to warrior-saviour to aged crone, from fierce protectoress to compassionate healer, impulsive destroyer to fount of wisdom, are all manifestations of the same creative and regenerative force.

By the late Vedic period an aspect of Devi that began receiving particular attention was her virgin form – the Kumari, the beautiful young, pre-menstrual, unmarried maiden. The word 'Kumari' is listed in the Mahabharata and other early texts as an epithet of Durga. This virgin aspect of Devi is also included in the class of eight Mother Goddesses – the Astamatrika – arising around this time as the sexual partners of leading male deities, and who together took on a protective role as the guardians of the eight directions. Many Hindu cities had been founded on the principles of sacred space – just like the Malla cities of the Kathmandu Valley – with the king at the centre, the castes radiating out from him in hierarchical priority, and the Astamatrika ranged outside the city walls, protecting civilization from the forces of chaos and destruction.

The paradox of the Kumari's combined chastity and sexuality is mirrored in her partnership with Kumara, the eternally young, bachelor son of Shiva. Kumara, himself chaste and virginal, is often also known as *Skanda* – the 'spurt of semen' – or Kartikeya, the god of war. His sexual ambivalence is particularly significant to Newar Hindus. Kumara is the god to whom prepubescent high-caste Newar Hindu girls believe themselves safely married during their *ihi* ceremony.

Despite the obvious antiquity of the virgin goddess Kumari, and prominent references to Kumari Puja in the literary texts, there seem to have been few temples – at least few that survive in India today – that were specifically dedicated to her worship, with one conspicuous exception. At the beginning of the Christian era, around 60 CE, a Greek sea captain had reported a flourishing cult of virgin goddess worship at the Kanya Kumari Temple on the southernmost tip of India though it is not clear from his account if the Goddess was being worshipped in the form of a living girl.

The earliest clear reference to Kumari worship through a living human being appeared in an eighth-century CE Indian Buddhist text. The text, known as the *Manjushrimulakalpa*, or 'Garland of Manjushri', describes the ritual of using a *kumari*, a premenstrual girl, to spin thread for making a *'patah'*, or cloth, on which images of the Buddha could be painted. The text is emphatic about the girl's purity in terms of being both free from sin and free from polluting substances like menstrual blood – attributes that, in a sense, rendered her semi-divine. The Kumari's role in this kind of ritual was only temporary, however – and brief. Once the canvas was finished and consecrated, the girl would return home and resume normal life.

By the end of the tenth century, according to the literature of the *Kalachakra*, both Kumaris and kumaras – young boys – were performing in Hindu and Buddhist rituals as agents for divination. The practice was clearly already well established by the time the *Kalachakra* was in circulation in Southeast Asia. In ritual context, these texts imply, a child of either sex was believed capable of providing an open channel to the divine and could be invested with the powers of prophecy. There are references to a Kumari seeing, for example, the image of *pratisena* – an 'Opposing Army' – reflected in a mirror, an indication that Kumaris were being used by kings for battle intelligence, as psychic spies. The texts generally indicate a preference for young girls, especially in the longer rituals. This is presumably because girls tend to be more placid and better behaved, and more interested in ritual performance at a younger age.

By the tenth and eleventh centuries the preference for Kumaris over *kumaras* in rituals of divination was boosted by a growing interest in Goddess worship and tantric possession – key aspects of the subversive religions that had become popular in places on the periphery of the subcontinent, like Kashmir, Assam, Bengal, Tamil Nadu and Nepal.

The first-known text recording actual tantric Buddhist worship of a Kumari is the *Samvarodaya Tantra*, an eleventh-century text that seems to have been composed in Nepal. It refers to Kumaris, dressed as Goddesses, being invited to sit in the centre of a *mandala*, where they are worshipped as 'Vajradevis' – goddesses in the flesh.

A couple of centuries later – but probably no later than the thirteenth century – a Buddhist master based in Nepal called Jagaddarpana wrote a vast digest of tantric ritual called the *Kriyasamuccaya*, or 'Compendium of Ritual'. Here, the account of a Kumari ritual is more detailed and instantly recognizable as a forerunner of the practice that has endured in the Kathmandu Valley in the present day. The text describes in detail how Kumaris should be dressed in red, their foreheads painted with vermilion and colyrium applied to their eyes; that their feet should be washed and they should be offered pure water to sip; that sacred jewellery should be placed around their necks; and how the officiating Buddhist priest should, through meditation and the utterance of *mantras*, transform the Kumaris into divine beings. It urges worship of the Kumaris with offerings of the taboo substances of alcohol and meat, stating that the sponsor of such a ritual – who must, crucially, have deep and genuine faith in tantric Buddhism – will thereby receive considerable material blessings, or boons, from the girls in their possessed state.

This tantric form of Kumari worship found a natural home in the Kathmandu Valley where it was bolstered by Himalayan shamanic traditions of spirit possession and the inherently matrifocal society of the Newars; but in India, as Buddhism began to wane and finally, under Muslim occupation, to wither away completely, Kumari worship survived only in those peripheral areas where Hindu Tantra continued to persist.

Today, Kumari Puja is still practised in Bengal where, during the five-day festival of Durga Puja, Brahmins worship the prepubescent girls of the household as living forms of Durga; and at the Kamakhya temple in Assam – site of a spring whose ferrous water was said to be the Goddess's menstrual blood – where special Kumari ceremonies are still held in which little girls incarnate the Goddess and are worshipped – but only for the duration of an hour or so.

Whether Hindus in India ever established a system of regular long-term or 'permanent' Kumaris such as the Newars came to favour in Nepal is almost impossible to ascertain. The underground nature of Tantra, with its taboo practices and transgressive belief in the power of the female, means its history has been very difficult to trace. There have, however, been records of individual Living Goddesses in India as recently as the early twentieth century.

It seems likely that in India any attempt to establish a permanent institution of Living Goddesses would have met, sooner or later, with opposition from the predominantly orthodox Hindu, Muslim or Christian establishment, and been either undermined or openly prohibited. In the Kathmandu Valley, however, there was no such bias; conditions prevailed that allowed Living Goddesses to flourish.

By the time the Mallas arrived in the valley from the neighbouring Hindu kingdom of Tirhut – in present-day Terai in southern Nepal – Kumari worship was clearly a central part of the Newar belief system. The complex, dangerous process of installing a Goddess inside a human child had become the preserve of the Newar Buddhist professionals – categorized, eventually, under the caste system imposed on them by the Hindu kings, as the priestly caste of Shakyas and Vajracharyas; and Kumari worship in its tantric form – the form that was thought to confer the invincible powers of a *siddha* on a worshipper – was confined, in all but exceptional circumstances, to Newars born into tantric Buddhist monasteries.

Quite when Hindu kings began to worship Buddhist Kumaris in the Kathmandu Valley is impossible to tell, though late chronicles assert that Shivadeva I, a king who ruled in the valley from 590 to 604 CE, placed four Kumaris at the crossroads of Navatol – present-day Deopatan – when he established that city.

Wright's Chronicle also tells of a king, Gunakamadeva, in the tenth century CE, attaining enormous wealth and conquering vast tracts of land – 'the four quarters of the world' according to the narrator of the chronicle – through worshipping a Kumari living in Patan.

Whichever king was responsible for creating the precedent, it seems likely to have happened at a time of crisis. Hard-pressed and with his own gods failing to deliver, the Hindu king would have found himself compelled to approach the Buddhist priests and ask them to allow him to consult a Kumari – perhaps one whose powers were particularly famous at the time. Such were the king's rewards for this imaginative departure that subsequent kings, finding themselves in a similar tight spot, followed suit and a tradition was born. The king would have been able to justify his devotion to a Buddhist child in Hindu tantric terms, as being especially empowering. In this light the Shakyas' occupation as goldsmiths could be usefully interpreted as 'polluting', when – in fact – they were a highly respected and privileged tier of the community and Malla kings often took Shakyas as their secondary wives.

From the Newar side, tantric initiation was never normally given to non-Newars, let alone non-Buddhists, but the Vajracharyas would have been prepared, if circumstances were favourable, to make an exception in the case of a king. The king would, himself, already have been a practising *tantrika* – but from the Hindu side. In return for being allowed into the inner Buddhist sanctum, the king could offer protection and patronage, something that Buddhist monastic institutions everywhere, not just in Nepal, were always eager to secure.

As Kumari worship became not only customary but essential for the Hindu kings, the Mallas must inevitably have begun to look for a way to establish permanent Kumaris exclusively for their own use, whose services they could call upon at short notice as the need arose. But this step would have been highly controversial in the Newar Buddhist community and would have been likely to do more than ruffle the feathers of the tantric Buddhist preceptors keen to protect their innermost teachings from the abuse of the powerful.

According to the colophon on the Pancharaksha text referring to the establishment of the first permanent royal Kumari in Bhaktapur, the tantric master exhorted to the task by the Malla kings was a certain Jivachandra Vajracharya. Jivachandra was the son of a very famous *siddha* in Kathmandu called Suratvajra – a Vajracharya from Takshe Bahal who had also been strongly influential at Mu Bahal. Suratvajra was a servant of Guhyeshvari and endowed, according to legend, with staggering magical powers. The fact that his son, Jivachandra, did not return to Kathmandu after establishing the royal Kumari in Bhaktapur but was granted a permanent residence at Chaturbrahma Mahavihar, next to the royal palace – where his descendants live to this day – suggests either that Jivachandra had been cut off by his *sangha* in Kathmandu for having carried out this audacious commission, or that he was required to stay at close hand to guard against any problems arising from this new practice.

The installation of a high Hindu tantric deity inside a Buddhist Kumari marked an ingenious effort on the part of the Malla kings to convert the Buddhist practice and bring it further into their own sphere of influence. Once the tradition of Newar Kumari worship had been successfully manipulated in order to accommodate their own lineage deity the Malla kings might have been tempted to 'Hinduize' the practice even further. The Gana Kumaris, the masked dance of the Navadurga and the mass sacrifice at Dasain, for example, all seemed to be late Malla additions.

But the rule of precedent is a powerful thing. A popular story in the valley relates how an orthodox king in Bhaktapur, having taken exception to having to bow to a Shakya Kumari, selected a Brahmin girl to take her place. When the priests brought the girl to Taleju Temple at Dasain for the mass buffalo sacrifice, however, she became afraid and cried. This was reported to the Malla king who immediately re-established a Shakya Kumari and worshipped her thereafter without complaint.

It is this deeply superstitious respect for tradition that explains why even the Shah kings, far more orthodox than their Malla predecessors and less tolerant of Buddhism in general, nevertheless enthusiastically continued the practice when they took over the valley. Just like the Mallas, it seems the Shah kings were quite simply in awe of the Newar institution of Kumari worship; they fell under its spell, convinced it was capable of conferring upon them incredible gifts, insights and powers as well as dreadful retribution should they break with the tradition. They added their own embellishments to the Hindu repertoire instigated by the Mallas that were appropriate to the worship of their adopted Hindu lineage deity, Taleju, but the core practice remained true to the original Newar template and continued to be managed by tantric Buddhist priests. Any deviation, any oversight, any omission in this formula, however unintentional, would – it was believed – rob the kings of their privileged access to the power of the Goddess and deprive them of their ability to rule over the Valley of Nepal.

The king's dependence on the Living Goddess for his survival was clearly still a strongly held conviction, not only at the palace itself, but among the people of the valley. The central Kumari in Kathmandu's Durbar Square quite possibly held the key to the future of the monarchy.

But the Mu Bahal Kumari pointed to a much broader, deeper tradition, and it is highly probable that Living Goddesses – unconnected with royal patronage – had once been numerous in the valley. As the Maoist presence intensified around the valley, I set out to see if I could find any more forgotten Kumaris.

I was spurred on by an optimistic thought. I had only been three decades late for the Mu Bahal Kumari. Perhaps, in some other hidden *bahal* down a quiet back street or in an unobtrusive village or town in the valley – somewhere less affected by the pace of change – I would find other 'non-royal' Living Goddesses still presiding on their thrones.

Chapter 18

Living Goddesses under Siege

My search for other Living Goddesses in the Kathmandu Valley had an urgency to it. Time was running out for many of the Newar traditions but now there were even more pressing reasons for haste. The political situation had taken a nosedive since the king had sacked the government. Police roadblocks and sandbag sentry posts had sprung up at all the main traffic intersections in and around the valley but, despite the national state of emergency, the Maoist presence in the foothills was looming larger and blockades were a regular occurrence.

Excursions now had to be planned with one eye on news reports of Maoist mobilizations, another on petrol supplies. Almost all Kathmandu's petrol and diesel came by tanker from India along a single highway. It was ludicrously easy for the Maoists to block this artery, restricting the flow of lifeblood into the capital. Queues of stationary cars and motorbikes stretching for miles from closed garage forecourts had become a regular sight, with drivers taking it in shifts, sleeping in the back seat, as they waited – sometimes for days – for a few precious litres of fuel.

So far, supplies of food and other vital commodities were holding out but the inhabitants of Kathmandu had been uncomfortably reminded of their geographical vulnerability. Prithvi Narayan Shah's devastating blockade two and a half centuries ago had been buried deep in the valley's subconscious. It was something the Gorkha conqueror himself and his Shah descendants had been keen to eradicate from history. But now, with the Maoists banging the same drum, the atavistic memory came back to life.

Consulting ritual texts connected to Nepal's sacred places for references to Living Goddess worship and sometimes just acting on a hunch, I set off on excursions into the valley. Sometimes my searches were fruitless. In the Vajrayogini temple in the beautiful village of Pharping, twenty kilometres south of Kathmandu, a black-and-white photograph of a Kumari was pinned to a wall next to the shrine. She was wearing a magnificent old-fashioned tunic dress and heavy brocade. It looked as though the picture had been taken in the 1950s but no one at the temple could remember the event and it was not clear if the Kumari was from Pharping itself or had come for a specific occasion from somewhere else.

Often, where there was strong evidence of a Kumari tradition, I found I had arrived just too late. In Deopatan, on the outskirts of Kathmandu, I interviewed the last Kumari of Cha Bahil, a beautiful young Shakya woman, twenty-four years old, now working as a nurse in the Teaching Hospital in Sinamangal. It was another poignant encounter, similar to my visit to Mu Bahal.

'We have no Kumari now and it is as though we have lost our guardian,' the mother of Cha Bahil's last Living Goddess told me. 'Everyone here feels it.'

The same pattern of pressures – rising costs, dwindling funds, the onerous responsibility of purity restrictions and caring for a Living Goddess, the modern nine-to-five six-days-a-week work ethic squeezing the life out of ritual – meant there had been no candidates coming forward for selection when Cha Bahil's last Kumari had retired in 1994. It was clear to me now just how the provision of government funding and palace offerings underpinned the existence of the three 'royal' Kumaris.

In Bungamati, a quiet medieval village perched on a spur of land overlooking the Bagmati, not far from Kathmandu – home to Red

Macchendranath, the God of Compassion – I had better luck. An old priest told me they still had a Kumari, but she no longer lived in the village. Breaking a fundamental taboo she had moved across the river to Patan where she lived with her parents and went to school. Her father was a gold dealer with a shop there. Now she only came back to Bungamati for rituals. Her term was nearly up, the old priest said regretfully, and, with so many of the younger Vajracharyas leaving Bungamati in search of work, he was worried about her replacement.

Losing their Living Goddess, he said – the prospect almost too sad to contemplate – would be like losing a parent. The Bungamati Kumari, he explained, was like the god Macchendranath's mother. When the two of them were together the god's face changed. It became redder. One of the most joyful moments in the festival calendar, he said, was when Red Macchendranath returned to Bungamati after months away on his chariot ride around Patan, and the Kumari, waiting for him at the temple, welcomed him home.

In all the communities with a Kumari tradition, whether still clinging on or just recently lapsed, it was clear the locals felt more connected to their own Kumari than the central Living Goddess in Kathmandu. Unique myths bound these goddesses to their locality and made them deeply relevant to their own community. Invariably, too, these communities interpreted the current political situation as arising, at least in part, from their own failures to sustain their Kumari, and on diminishing respect for the Goddess among younger generations and the public at large.

~

In February 2003, four months after Gyanendra seized power and following intense talks with government, the Maoists declared a ceasefire. The state of emergency seemed to be over. The Maoists had declared their willingness to take part in general elections and other ostracized political parties were demanding a place at the table in the peace negotiations. The world now looked to Gyanendra to step back as he had promised and allow the normal process of government to resume.

To almost universal consternation, however, the king refused to concede, insisting the threat remained. He would retain his emergency powers – he declared – until he personally deemed the situation safe enough to hand back control to the government. When this would be was anybody's guess.

Days turned to weeks and then months. Political tension in the valley began to mount as the dry season drew on. The city's water supply, stretched to its limits at the best of times, began to dwindle. It was as if the nation's thirst for a political resolution was manifesting itself in the seasonal drought.

In the midst of this unproductive impasse a fourth Living Goddess on the government payroll unexpectedly came to light. This new Kumari was a good four hours' drive from Kathmandu, outside the valley, at the hill-fort of Nuwakot. The discovery was highly intriguing, especially given the current security situation. The fact that this Living Goddess was still receiving government funds indicated she was, like the three royal Kumaris in the valley, considered to be fundamental to the stability of Nepal.

~

Climbing through the queen's forest on Nagarjun Hill, towards the pass on the north-west corner of the valley rim, the refreshing dawn breeze seemed to lift the spirits of the driver I had engaged for the trip. He had been searching all night for enough petrol to get to Nuwakot and had been worried about Maoist roadblocks and impromptu tariffs. As we passed water-lorries – decommissioned petrol tankers – pulled in tight against the banks, filling up with trickles from struggling rivulets, though, he broke into light-hearted song. It was early March 2003 and the monsoons were still many weeks away. Seasonal 'load-shedding' – power cuts aimed at regulating the hydroelectricity supply from Nepal's shrinking reservoirs – had been adding to the capital's woes. Some days the electricity was cut off for more than ten hours at a time. It felt good to be getting away from Kathmandu, if only for the day.

Nuwakot perched like an eyrie on a knife edge jutting out over the Tadi river a few miles from the confluence with the great Trisuli river, the old border between Nepal and the hill-state of Gorkha. High on its rocky ridge the fort had stood sentinel over the trade route to Tibet, guarding the north-western approaches to the Kathmandu Valley for well over a millennium. This was the Malla stronghold that had resisted Prithvi Narayan Shah's father in 1736 and that Prithvi Narayan Shah had singled out as his first objective in his campaign.

But Nuwakot had been a hard nut for the Shah conqueror to crack. In 1742, the year of his father's death, Prithvi Narayan had launched an attack on the fortress of Nuwakot and been soundly repulsed.

Swallowing the bitter pill of a second defeat, Prithvi Narayan Shah had retired to his *durbar* in Gorkha to cogitate on the lessons of his failure. Never again would Prithvi Narayan's military strategy be anything but meticulously planned and executed with consummate patience and timing.

Borrowing heavily from the Gorkha treasury, he recruited mercenaries from the Khasas and Magars in the outlying hill-states, promising them a share in the spoils of victory and a right to hold lands in return for their loyalty. At the same time, he requested his father's *mit-bhai* and erstwhile host, Ranajit Malla, the king of Bhaktapur, to send spies into the courts of Patan and Kathmandu, to gather any information that could be of advantage to him, particularly concerning feuds or squabbles arising between the kings and their courtiers. This Ranajit Malla seemed only too pleased to do. Using Ranajit's information, Prithvi Narayan dispatched his own spies into the valley to start fomenting dissent.

Then, having made his dedications to Gorakhnath, the lineage deity of Gorkha, the ambitious new Shah king embarked on a pilgrimage to Benares in India, ostensibly to present offerings to Shiva but also, crucially, to buy arms. Travelling by turns in a splendid palanquin and on a sturdy Tibetan horse, his Khas bodyguard dressed in blue, red and green, and flying the yellow battle standard of Gorkha embroidered with the figure of Hanuman, Prithvi Narayan Shah stopped en route to visit the military establishments of the British East India Company to acquaint himself with the latest in western military hardware and training. He made an alliance with a powerful raja in the region, Abhiman Singh (Singh's daughter became Prithvi Narayan's second wife), who helped him acquire a number of firelocks from the British gunsmiths of Lucknow and Cawnpore; and on his way back from Benares he met with other Indian rajas, including those of Sirmoun and Jajarkot, who sold him quality steel for his soldiers' *khukuris*.

Back at home Prithvi Narayan Shah entered into treaties with the western hill states of the Chaubisi Rajya, even making his peace with the kingdom of Lamjung, an age-old enemy of Gorkha. Then he set about raising an army, conscripting every Gorkhali between the age of sixteen and thirty, employing the Hindustani experts he had brought with him from his travels to train them in the use of guns.

But there was another aspect of Prithvi Narayan Shah's preparation over which he now took particular care. His extended stay in Bhaktapur as guest of Ranajit Malla had impressed upon him the efficacy of the Malla kings' tantric worship of Taleju. Convinced his failure at Nuwakot was in no small part due to the protective powers of the Goddess, he decided to try and generate those powers for himself – to fight fire with fire.

Before launching the third Gorkha attack on Nuwakot, Prithvi Narayan Shah made a special detour to Sallyan Kot, a hill-fort in Dhading, to worship at the temple of Tripurasundari, a goddess from whom his illustrious forebear Ram Shah was said to have received *siddhi*. There, according to Prithvi Narayan's own account in the *Dibya Upadesh*, he received an apparition that fulfilled his desires.

Arriving in Sallyan Kot, Prithvi Narayan inquired of the headman if he could have *darshan* of the Devi but, being told that only priests were allowed into the temple, the determined Gorkha king waited morning and evening outside the gate, reading, worshipping and praying. One night – Prithvi Narayan related – he had a dream:

> A seven- or eight-year-old girl came to me, bearing a sword in either hand. She covered her head with a pale rose-coloured cloth and came close to me ... she placed the swords in my hands. Then she took from her bosom a small object shaped like the 'arasi' and placed it on my lips, saying: 'This you must swallow. Then, whatever you wish for, you will receive' ... so saying, she took steps and vanished.

When Prithvi Narayan awoke he summoned the astrologers and priests of Sallyan Kot and told them about his dream. They informed him he had indeed been blessed with *darshan* of the Devi. By way of thanks Prithvi Narayan presented the Goddess with offerings of 'incense, lights, flags and a feast', and for her permanent worship established an annual fund for the temple of 'seven buffaloes and seven goats and the income from Borlang Ghat and the ridge near the ghat'.

But this was not all. Shortly after this apparition he received another transmission, this time from the Bhairabi at the temple of Indrayani at Betravati Beni, another powerful goddess he had gone to worship. The Bhairabi of Indrayani – Prithvi Narayan related – supplied him with the exact time for his attack on Nuwakot, an auspicious moment which happened to coincide with the last day of Indra Jatra in Kathmandu. The commander of the fortress, Jayant Rana, had taken leave to join King Jaya Prakasha Malla in the festivities in Kathmandu, leaving his inexperienced son in charge. The Trisuli river was in spate and the Gorkha threat to Nuwakot – the commander assumed – was negligible.

This time Prithvi Narayan Shah had been careful to conceal the advance of his soldiers, disguising them as farmers setting off to dig irrigation channels on the eastern border of Gorkha. Reaching the great Trisuli river, close to Nuwakot, and pressing the nervous local boatmen into service on pain of death, the Gorkha king launched his soldiers into the torrential monsoon-swollen waters. Smashed about in leaky boats they managed to cross under cover of darkness – a feat, it seemed, made possible by the divine powers recently invested in their king – and took the fortress by complete surprise. Nuwakot fell to Prithvi Narayan Shah on 26 September 1744. He had done what hill-states around the valley had tried but failed to do for centuries. He had penetrated the mythical energy shield of the Malla kingdoms.

~

Our car ground to a halt at the entrance to the village. Down one side, in classical Newar style, with red brick, carved roof-struts and ornate triple-windows, were the palaces of the Malla kings of Patan, Kathmandu and Bhaktapur. Unlike the Gorkha conqueror, the Mallas had disdained life in the hills, preferring the sophistication of the valley even during the hot summer months. Their palaces here had been rarely visited.

But on the other side of the street, several storeys taller than its Malla neighbours, was the awesome seven-storey edifice of Prithvi Narayan Shah. Clean, linear, unadorned, the Shah's *durbar* – built after he had completed his conquest of Nepal – commanded the ridge with Shogun muscularity. Its scale and towering perpendicular walls were reminiscent of a modern high-rise; to the Newars who built it, over two hundred years ago, it must have seemed an outrageous affront to their cultural sensibilities.

Even now, the audacious statement of self-confidence and ambition presented by the palace of Prithvi Narayan Shah's dreams was stunning. It was this tower that the Gorkha conqueror, shunning the 'softness' of the valley, had made the operational headquarters of his new kingdom, and where he had spent his very last days. It was here that he had dictated the *Dibya Upadesh* to his courtiers in December 1774 before succumbing to a fever in January 1775. His body had been taken down to the holy confluence of the Tadi and Trisuli for cremation.

The Nuwakot Kumari was surprisingly easy to find. It was still early and she had not yet left for school. Her house was a medieval earth-and-timber cottage perched precipitously at the far end of the village, opposite the temple to Bhairab. Her parents, who were also the temple guardians, were astonished at my arrival. They ushered me into a tiny room, sending the youngest children excitedly to summon the rest of the family.

The Nuwakot Living Goddess was in class 5. The eight-year-old sat shyly on the opposite bed in her school uniform, sandwiched between her mother and grandmother, both of whom had been Kumaris before her. It was instantly apparent that this Living Goddess was different to the other 'royal' Kumaris. Her family name was Dangol. She was not Shakya or Vajracharya but Jyapu – from the Newar farmer caste. Her 'royal' status originated not with the tradition of the Malla kings but with the Shah imposter.

'Our family is originally from the town of Kirtipur in the Kathmandu Valley,' explained the Kumari's grandmother. 'Prithvi Narayan Shah granted us the privilege of providing a Kumari for Nuwakot. He brought our family here.'

The Nuwakot Kumari is symbiotically related to the temple of Bhairab, in the same way as the Kathmandu, Bhaktapur and Patan Kumaris receive *shakti* from the temples of Taleju. The temple of Bhairab in Nuwakot is an ancient locus of tantric worship not simply of Bhairab but of his powerful female consort, Bhairabi – Durga, in her passionate form. Prithvi Narayan Shah had carried an image of Nuwakot Bhairabi – or Nuwakot Bhagavati as he called her – in his pocket when he finally conquered Kathmandu.

After Prithvi Narayan Shah had finally become king of the Valley of Nepal, more than twenty-five years after the capture of Nuwakot, he established a shrine for Nuwakot Bhagavati in front of the big gong in Kathmandu Durbar Square; and another inside the palace of Hanuman Dhoka. Subsequent generations of Shah kings – and, indeed, ensuing Rana oligarchs – continued to regard the Bhairabi of Nuwakot as crucial to their survival in the valley.

To Prithvi Narayan Shah's mind – and the mind of all those around him – he could only govern effectively from Nuwakot once he had established a Living Goddess here. However, a Shakya or Vajracharya Kumari would not have been an option. It had been hard enough for Malla kings to gain access to Vajrayana Buddhism, but a newcomer, an orthodox Hindu raja from a barbarous hill state, would have been beyond the pale as far as Newar Buddhists were concerned.

Newar Jyapus, being predominantly Hindu and middle – rather than high – caste, would have been more accessible to the Shah king. The fact that Nuwakot Kumari's family came from Kirtipur, too, was significant. Kirtipur was the Newar town in the west of the valley that had withstood two gruelling sieges by Prithvi Narayan Shah. It had fallen, eventually, on the Gorkha army's third attempt. Newar tradition insisted the town had not surrendered but had been betrayed by a handful of collaborators. The punishment meted out by the Gorkha conqueror on the stubborn citizens of Kirtipur after its fall had been barbaric. Perhaps this 'reward' of Kumariship had been given to a family who had thrown in their lot with the besieging Gorkhas.

Whatever the circumstances of her origin, it is clear the Nuwakot Kumari is still, in the present day, considered vital in terms of the stability of Nepal. The current government continues to pay her 1500 rupees a month – the same as the Patan and Bhaktapur Kumaris – though the duties and purity conditions at Nuwakot are clearly far less onerous.

Apart from being forbidden to eat chicken during the fortnight of Dasain, or to cross the river, the Living Goddess of Nuwakot can behave much like all the other children in the village. She would be dismissed, her parents said, on first menstruation. If possible another Kumari would be chosen from this family; but if there are no girls of the right age, one would be selected from other Jyapus in the village.

It is at Dasain, as ever, that the Nuwakot Kumari comes to life. In a mirror image of rites conducted simultaneously at the old royal palaces in Kathmandu, Patan and Bhaktapur, a team of ten ritual officials from Hanuman Dhoka arrive in Nuwakot the day before the start of Dasain. The group, including six women *kalash*-bearers and *mangalini* – women singers of auspicious songs – sow the sacred shoots of barley in a secret room on the fourth floor of the Nuwakot Durbar and conduct a special *puja* at the temple of Bhairabi.

On the night of Navami, the Nuwakot Kumari – who is confined to her house from the start of Dasain – is taken to the Shah's *durbar*. In the secret room on the fourth floor she is dressed in the scarlet garments and tantric ornaments the women have brought with them from Hanuman Dhoka. Seated on her *asan*, the priest tantrically empowers her and worships her as the embodiment of Durga/Taleju. In this way, the strategic fortress of Nuwakot is revivified and reconnected with the energy centred in the Valley of Nepal. In recent years this reinforcement of the boundaries of Nepal Mandala has come to seem more vital than ever.

~

As 2003 wore on, the situation in the valley showed no signs of improving. The three-way political stalemate between King Gyanendra, the government and the Maoist rebels persisted through the month of March and the sense of impending crisis was compounded by dire astrological readings. The forthcoming year – Vikram Samvat 2060 – beginning in April, was forecast to be a highly inauspicious 'sunna sal', or 'zero year', and as the final month of vs 2059 drew to a close, the streets of Patan, Bhaktapur and Kathmandu and other Newar towns and villages filled with marriage processions as couples rushed to tie the knot before malign influences took over.

Local Living Goddess traditions, meanwhile, continued to come to light. As I became more adept at looking for signs and finding the right people to ask, the list continued to grow. It seems likely that every major Newar town in the valley once had its own Living Goddess. But, now, in the more populous cities a bewildering number of 'neighbourhood' Kumaris – offshoots of the mainstream Buddhist tradition – also emerged.

These lesser-known Kumaris – in neighbourhoods like Kilagel and Thahity in Kathmandu, Mikha Bahal in Patan, and Wane Laeku in Bhaktapur – seem to have sprung up at some point in the late Malla period in response to a growing desire among non-Buddhist communities to have their own Living Goddess. One surviving tradition – in the Tebuk neighbourhood of Bhaktapur – has the unique distinction of worshipping a baby Kumari who has not yet been weaned. These local Kumaris are almost always chosen from the Shakya or Vajracharya community even if they are worshipped by other castes like Jyapus or Pradhans; and invariably their worship is conducted under the auspices of Vajracharya priests.

The more local Kumaris I encountered, both surviving and recently lapsed, the clearer it became that the royal Kumari in Kathmandu, because of her national importance and the tight protective cordon still in place around her, is the one who has retained the purest and strongest identity. Here, too, are both Hindu and Buddhist traditions of Living Goddess worship rolled into one, their exoteric and esoteric practices combined, at their most vibrant and complete.

Chapter 19

The Living Goddess in the Supreme Court

In late May 2003, mountaineers from around the world led by Sir Edmund Hillary and Norgay Tenzing gathered in Kathmandu to mark the fiftieth anniversary of the first ascent of Mt Everest – known in Nepal as 'Sagarmatha', Head of the Sky. Frustrated by the continuing stalemate and the king's refusal to restore the powers of the elected government, Nepal's political leaders took advantage of the international media frenzy to stage a demonstration in front of parliament – the old Rana palace of Singha Durbar.

The riot police responded with a heavy hand. In the ensuing clash, the upper-house lawmaker was knocked unconscious, the former health minister fractured his elbow and the former minister for foreign affairs was seriously wounded. Only the four-times former prime minster, G.P. Koirala, now seventy-eight years old, was left alone by the police, sitting on in protest under the scorching sun.

A day after presenting Sir Edmund Hillary with honorary Nepali citizenship, Lokendra Bahadur Chand, the 'King's Prime Minister', resigned. The gesture proved conspicuously ineffectual. Chand was immediately replaced by Surya Bahadur Thapa – another prime minister hand-picked by the king.

The monsoons arrived at last, bringing water into the valley and relief for the farmers but no tonic for the stranded political situation. The king, Maoists and the government refused to move from their entrenched positions in the peace negotiations. In August, as the rains withdrew, and with no end to the triangular deadlock in sight, the Maoists decided they had had enough. They pulled out of the peace talks and called a three-day strike. The seven-month truce was over. Newspapers ran daily stories of villagers murdered and beaten, property destroyed, children abducted for military training. As the violence escalated, however, it was clearly not only the Maoists with blood on their hands. Amnesty International and other human rights monitors claimed violations by the security forces were also on the increase, with widespread use of extrajudicial executions, disappearances, torture, death in custody, arbitrary detention and villagers forced to sign false witness statements.

The 'military crack-down' funded largely by foreign powers and orchestrated by the king, was, in effect, fuelling the blaze. New rifles and explosives provided for the Nepali armed forces by the US and UK had been falling into Maoist hands, either sold by corrupt and poorly paid government soldiers or seized in raids from vulnerable and remote police outposts. Now both sides were better equipped to kill each other and any civilian who happened in their way.

As the guerrilla conflict closed in upon the valley, speculation mounted. No one seemed to know – or was prepared to admit – who or where the Maoists really were. Just before the ceasefire in January, the chief of the Nepali Armed Police Force had been murdered right in the centre of Kathmandu, along with his wife and bodyguard. The murder marked a turning point for those living in the valley cocoon. Cadres in camouflage ranting over loudhailers in remote training camps in the mountains, intimidating impoverished villagers and ambushing police posts in the distant hills and down in the Terai, were one thing; but a targeted assassination in the streets of the capital suggested there were now Maoist sympathizers inside the valley providing the rebels with support.

The atmosphere in the valley was becoming increasingly paranoid. Police began conducting arbitrary house-to-house searches in Kathmandu in the middle of the night, banging their batons on metal gates, sending all the dogs in the neighbourhood into a frenzy. Restrictions were imposed on motorbikes – this being one of the Maoists' preferred methods of transport. It was now forbidden for anyone in the valley to ride pillion. The endearing sight of an entire family balanced on a single motorbike vanished overnight. Visors of helmets had to be worn lifted in order to show the biker's face, and pollution masks were banned.

Meanwhile the Maoists had taken to declaring nationwide *bandhs*, bringing the country to a standstill for up to three days at a time. People who defied the *bandh* risked their lives or those of their families; offices and factories that stayed open might be ransacked or set on fire; taxi drivers were threatened with having their hands chopped off if they so much as touched a steering wheel.

But there was a silver lining. With cars, motorbikes, trucks and buses banned from the roads, *bandh* days revived the opportunities for pilgrimage. Newars used the enforced holiday to visit temples out in the valley countryside; walking became joyful again, the art of *pradakshina* a devotion in itself, as ancient and spiritually reviving as the hills. With no exhaust fumes and with none of the valley's brick kilns and cement factories in operation, pollution levels plummeted, the air cleared, and breathtaking vistas of the Himalaya sprang back into view. On *bandh* days, despite the Maoist threat, everyone breathed more easily.

By the time the festival of Indra Jatra hove into sight in September 2003 the security situation in the valley was clearly in crisis. A week before the festival, Maoists rebels tied a Nepali journalist to a post as though they were tethering a goat for sacrifice and publicly cut his throat. Then, the day before the Kumari and her attendant gods, Ganesh and Bhairab, were due to be pulled around Kathmandu in their chariots, five small bombs went off in the city, killing a twelve-year-old boy and wounding several others.

Madhav Kumar Nepal, the general secretary of the Communist Party of Nepal – an unlikely champion of religious freedom – made a public statement, urging both the Maoists and opposition parties to refrain from violence for the duration of Indra Jatra, Dasain and Tihar. 'How can people celebrate festivals under such terror?' he demanded. In an attempt to calm the situation down, all sides agreed to postpone their demonstrations until the festival season was over.

As international television crews took up their positions outside the Kumari Chen, waiting for the Goddess and her attendant gods to emerge, the atmosphere among the crowds thronging the temples in Durbar Square was hushed and tense. The army was out in force. No one knew if the Maoists would keep their word or would – like the Gorkha conqueror – use this key moment as an opportunity to attack. At the backfiring of a motorbike, a number of spectators fell off the temple steps in fright. Police batons crushed them back into place.

In the grip of such uncertainty, people were hungry for omens and the progress of the Kumari's *jatra* was being watched more closely than ever. As the cavalcade of gleaming Jaguars and 4x4s swept into the square, spectators craned for a view of the dignitaries and foreign diplomats taking up their place on Hanuman Dhoka's royal balcony. All eyes were on the lookout for the king. Rumours had already begun circulating. According to some reports Gyanendra was not even in the country. The queen, who was still suffering from bullets she had received in the massacre, had flown to London for medical attention and the king had accompanied her. According to the latest news, the royal couple, on their way back to Nepal, were still in transit in Dubai.

No king in living memory had missed the first day of Kumari Jatra. As the minutes ticked by and Gyanendra failed to appear the mood in the crowd grew restive. If the king didn't show, what effect would this have on the nation; and who would offer the Kumari the gold coins in his place?

A murmur of amazement went up from the crowd as Crown Prince Paras stepped forward on to the royal balcony. As the Living Goddess in all her splendour, wearing her tiered golden crown, garlands and jewelled amulets heaped around her neck, and her all-seeing third eye, was led out along the white cloth to her chariot, Ganesh and Bhairab preceding her, the triumphant blast of the military band seemed to mock the mood of the assembled throng. The Kumari was lifted high on to her chariot. Her priests, ritual attendants and male caretakers followed, clustering around her like bees protecting their queen. Gangs of Jyapus heaved on the ropes and slowly, haltingly, the three chariots began to move, the Kumari's mobile temple drawing up beside the palace to receive the royal offering.

As Paras handed his offering of gold coins to the royal priest to present to the Kumari the crowd reeled back as if from a mighty slap. That such a man – in the eyes of many, a murderer – should approach the Goddess in this way, assuming the place of the king, was nothing short of an outrage.

Perhaps the palace had hoped that Paras's appearance at such a high-profile event would increase his popularity and prepare the nation for his future role as monarch; but if so, it had underestimated the strength of popular feeling against him and overlooked the terrible portent – in the eyes of the Newars, at least – of insulting the Goddess by breaking with tradition.

Preceded by the chariots of the gods, the Kumari's rath moved off at last towards the lower boundary of the city, forcing its way through the crowds as a mass of devotees surged forward to throw petals and rice. Few people managed to have *darshan* of the little goddess, however. Slumped far back on her cushions in the shadowy recess of her moving temple, the Kumari seemed reluctant to show her face. As the procession made its way through the streets of Kathmandu, dark clouds scudded overhead, stubbornly refusing to release Indra's blessing of rain.

Despite his failure to appear for the first day of the Kumari's *jatra* Gyanendra was taking no chances when it came to receiving his *tika*. Everyone remembered what had happened when Gyanendra's father, King Mahendra, had failed to present himself for the Kumari's blessing in 1971. He had died on a hunting trip in the Terai four months later.

King Birendra, too, had received a rebuke from the Goddess just a few years earlier when, in 1997, he had disappeared to London for a week in the middle of Indra Jatra. He had attended the first day of the Kumari's *jatra* but missed the second and third days of the festival. Though Birendra had returned in time to receive his *tika* on the last day, the Goddess had clearly not been impressed by his absence in the interim. Shortly after the festival was over Birendra had suffered a near-fatal heart attack.

Gyanendra's plane touched down on the second day of the chariot procession and, several days later, after the Kumari's third and final tour of the city, the king presented himself at the Kumari Chen for his blessing. After the spectacle of the first days of the festival, the final day of Kumari Jatra was always a more muted affair. There were inevitably fewer spectators gathered late that evening to see the return of the Kumari and her two accompanying gods to the Kumari Chen for their rendezvous with the monarch, fewer people to witness the moment in the darkness when a young man attending Ganesh stumbled as he lifted the boy out of his chariot, dropping him to the ground.

Reports in the papers the following day were full of reassurances. The king had received his blessing from the Kumari inside her throne room with no hitches. But the Newar community was racked with worry. The incident with Ganesh was an ominous portent: the support on which the gods had relied for centuries was giving way.

On the night of 20 March 2004, three weeks before the end of the inauspicious 'sunna sal' year of Vikram Samvat 2060, a remote police post in the town of Beni in west-central Nepal came under attack from the Maoists. Twenty-two policemen were killed; thirty-four were taken captive; eighteen were injured. In the ensuing struggle for the town the Nepalese army lost thirteen men; the Maoists several dozen. It was the biggest battle of Nepal's eight-year war to date.

Even when the unlucky year of vs 2060 was over Newars continued to watch for omens like farmers watching the clouds. As people rushed to secure the blessings of deities and household gods over the Nepali New Year in April 2004, rituals were conducted with more than the usual care.

When the chariot of Red Macchendranath came crashing down mid-jatra in June 2004, it seemed as if the sky had fallen. Just like the Kumari Jatra in Kathmandu, the passage of Red Macchendranath's spectacular sixty-five-foot chariot through the streets of Patan had been an augur of fortune for centuries. Its safe passage spread the god's compassionate blessings throughout the valley; but if its wheels got stuck in a rut, or if the red paint on the god's face began flaking away, it predicted disaster.

In the past, broken shafts and axles had presaged earthquakes and regicide. In 1741 – the year Jaya Prakasha Malla had been exiled from Kathmandu by a coup masterminded by his queen and her lover – the oscillating tower on top of the chariot had toppled over twice. But it was rare for the *rath* to tip over completely. In recent times the chariot had turned over twice – once, in the run-up to the violent democracy demonstrations that had plunged the country into chaos in 1991; and again, in 2001, just weeks before the royal family massacre.

In 2004 the crowds that gathered for Red Macchendranath's jatra were larger than ever, its cumbersome progress willed on by a mass of celebrants. News that Red Macchendranath's chariot had fallen passed like an electric surge through the valley. I heard about the incident within minutes from a friend who had been standing with her family just feet away from the chariot as it fell. Six people had been seriously injured. The god himself had been picked out of the debris and installed unceremoniously in a resting-*pati* nearby.

A few weeks later, in June 2004, there was another alarm. The statue of Bhimsen, patron deity of commerce, in Dolakha, began to 'sweat', drops of condensation appearing on the god's face just as they had in the run-up to the royal family massacre. Devotees, risking the excursion towards Maoist-held territory in the east, thronged to the shrine beyond the valley rim.

Tension was ratcheting. The Maoists were now conspicuous, their flags appearing on bamboo poles in villages, the red of the hammer and sickle clashing ominously with the pacific emerald green of the valley paddies. In August the Maoists imposed a week-long blockade, the most ambitious yet. Container lorries, tankers and trucks carrying livestock and vegetables from India and the Terai backed up in long, constipated tracts along the three main arterial routes snaking into the valley over the mountains. Twenty thousand businessmen and travel trade officials in Kathmandu responded with a peace rally, marching through the streets with placards: 'We want PEACE – withdraw the blockade'.

But this time the Maoists could not be moved. They responded with a small bomb, planted in the Soaltee Crown Plaza, a five-star hotel in the capital owned by the king. In September three more explosions caused a fire at Pashupati Spinning Mills. There were further bomb blasts in Birgunj at the Zonal Labour Office, the offices of the Guthi Sansthan and the regional office of the Nepal Oil Corporation.

In December there was another week-long blockade. Nepal, the 'yam between stones' as Prithvi Narayan Shah had once described it, was being crushed, not between the might of China and India as the Gorkha conqueror had forewarned, but between Maoists and the monarchy – opposing forces within Nepal itself. As the prospects of peace seemed to vanish into the thin mountain air, Nepalis braced themselves for the disaster the gods were predicting.

They did not have long to wait. On 1 February 2005, barely

a week after giving assurances to the visiting UN Human High Commissioner, Louise Arbour, that he would do everything in his power to restore full democratic processes as soon as possible, the king declared a state of emergency and cut off all contact with the outside world. The government was dismissed; the prime minister was placed under house arrest; and his deputy detained by the police. Free speech and freedom of the press, the right to assemble peacefully and the right to privacy, all were suspended. Armoured cars began patrolling the streets of Kathmandu, the airport was closed, telephone lines were cut, Internet servers and mobile phones blocked; independent Nepali and foreign media were shut down; and military personnel installed in national TV and press offices to censor the news.

Gyanendra's proclamation was followed almost immediately with a sham celebration intended to show he had widespread support. Nepal's fifty-fifth Democracy Day was marked on 18 February by the king receiving a military salute in front of bands of flag-waving schoolchildren bussed in for the occasion. Giant billboards bearing the king's portrait and the slogan 'Beginning of Nepal's New Era' lined the route from the royal palace to Tundikhel parade ground. Public transport was banned to prevent awkward demonstrations.

The performance fooled no one. Governments across the world registered official protests and the international press railed against the coup. Within Nepal, though, open dissent was impossible. Journalists, previously targeted by the Maoists, were now being singled out for punishment by the military. Editors were placed under house arrest and anyone who defied the news blackout was thrown into prison. There were echoes of the 'Jana Andolan', the 'People's Movement' of 1990, as familiar public figures began to disappear if they criticized the king.

Try as he might, the king could not lock down every means of communication with the outside world. Internet connections at embassies and diplomatic missions were unblockable, as were satellite telephones. Soon, news of arrests, beatings and abductions began filtering out of the country. The Hong Kong-based Asian Centre for Human Rights claimed that extrajudicial killings by Nepal's security forces had risen 'exponentially' to an average of eight a day. Later, Human Rights Watch in New York would label Nepal the world leader in 'disappearances', with more journalists detained in 2005 than in any other country.

The communications blackout remained in place for almost a week, long enough for the king to consolidate his position and sweep key opponents out of the way. On 8 February – a day alarmingly punctuated by minor earthquake tremors – local and international telephone lines, email and Internet connections were restored, though mobile phones, which were less easy to monitor, remained blocked. The country, reeling and disorientated, began to stagger to its feet and adjust to the strange new order.

Amid this chaos, the nation's attention was diverted by an extraordinary human rights case filed on 6 May 2005 in the Supreme Court. It was filed by Pundevi Maharjan, a young human rights lawyer, and was levelled – amazingly, given the atrocities raging elsewhere in the country – at the Living Goddess.

Though the case was aimed principally at the royal Kumari in Durbar Square, the advocate asserted there were eleven other Kumaris 'living in similar circumstances' elsewhere in the valley and that all of them should be 'liberated'. 'Chanira is a prisoner,' Pundevi proclaimed to news reporters, pointedly referring to the royal Kumari by the name of her birth rather than the honorific title of 'Dya Maiju', Mother Goddess. 'I want to give her equality, freedom.'

Attacks on the Kumari had been escalating in recent years. One of the most vociferous opponents was Bidya Bandari, a central committee member of the CPN-UML (Communist Party of Nepal-Unified Marxist Leninist) and chairperson of the All-Nepal Women's Association (ANWA) who, in September 2002, had made headlines in the Nepali press calling for the outright abolition of the Kumari tradition. Under pressure from colleagues in both the CPN-UML and the ANWA she had initially been forced to retract some of her more extravagant allegations – such as her claim that the husbands of ex-Kumaris invariably died 'with their heads burst out' – but she continued periodically to rekindle the Kumari debate in the Nepali media.

International journalists had picked up on the controversy. In January 2003 the UK's *Mirror* Magazine ran a piece 'From Goddess to Girl Next Door', and *Marie-Claire*, a similar story, 'From Divine to Dumped?' in August 2004.

To Nepalis, impassioned views from both sides of the Kumari debate had become a regular feature of the news of the past few years. What made this latest assault on the Kumari tradition so striking – apart from the fact that it had been taken to the highest level in the land – was that it had been launched by a Newar. Editors of the Nepali press, bound by the post-royal coup strictures on political reporting and, finding themselves at last with a public interest story they could cover without censorship, encouraged the debate, with both sides heatedly pressing their case in leaders and letters pages. Before long the Supreme Court case against Nepal's Living Goddess was grabbing headlines in leading papers in Europe and Asia.

By the time I caught up with Pundevi Maharjan in December 2005, the advocate had become something of a celebrity. Not all the attention had been welcome – there had been threats posted against her on the Internet, even from members of her own caste – and she was highly cautious about giving an interview. We met in the quiet upstairs room of Café Mitra, an old Newar house with wooden shutters and low ceilings, on a back street in Thamel.

Wearing a traditional *kurta suruwal* and looking considerably younger than her twenty-nine years, Pundevi Maharjan was pretty, fresh-faced and soft-spoken, and at first seemed almost shy. She admitted she had been surprised by the adverse reaction to her petition. Not only had the royal palace itself recently called for the case to be dropped but, at the other end of the political spectrum, Mukti Pradhan, a former central committee member of the Maoist party, had also denounced it.

'I expected more support when I started,' she said, 'but it seems people have misunderstood what I am trying to do and they have come out against me.'

She sounded hurt rather than indignant but was clearly more determined than ever to win her case. Tradition and superstition should not be given priority when a child's welfare was at stake, she insisted.

'When a child is small they cannot have knowledge about what will happen to them,' she said. 'They have no choice. That is why there is a need for the law to protect them. The time has come to modernize our traditions – to bring them in line with universal standards of human rights.'

Two reports recently published by the UN – one by the Committee on the Elimination of Discrimination against Women (CEDAW) in January 2004; the other by the Committee on the Rights of the Child (CRC), on 3 June 2005 – underpinned Pundevi's case. The CEDAW report criticized the culture of gender inequality in the country – citing domestic violence, trafficking in women and girls, prostitution, female illiteracy, deep-rooted patriarchal attitudes, underage marriage, negative female stereotypes, lack of family planning and general absence of women in leadership roles. The CRC report focused on child poverty and exploitation, identifying street children, refugees, the Dalit community, orphans and children belonging to indigenous or ethnic minority groups in Nepal as being particularly vulnerable.

Both reports called for the abolition of specific 'harmful traditional practices' such as *badi* – the ethnic practice of prostitution among young girls of 'untouchable' caste; *kamlari* – indentured slavery; *chaupadi* – the isolation of women in mud huts during menstruation; and *deuki* – the dedication of girls to a Hindu temple, commonly used as a smokescreen for prostitution.

All these are practices found almost exclusively in the remote, impoverished regions of western Nepal. However, also mentioned on the list was *kumari pratha*, the practice of 'having a girl child as a living goddess'.

Pundevi was adamant that, even though the people who practised Kumari worship were comparatively affluent and well-educated Newars like herself, *kumari pratha* is a tradition like all the others – mired in ignorance and superstition, and 'causing extreme insecurity, health hazards and cruelty to girl children'.

'In western Nepal, in the *deuki* tradition,' said Pundevi, 'a rich family can buy a girl from a poor family and offer her to the gods for fulfilment of their wishes. It is like offering a goat without sacrificing it. The girls have to stay in the temple. They are supposed to work in the service of the god but they go into prostitution in order to survive.

'What makes the Kumari tradition different? Where children are concerned there must be a rule – one rule – to protect them. You cannot discriminate and say in this case it is wrong to deprive a child of their freedom and human rights; but in this case we must turn a blind eye. You can't give children to god like an offering.'

Pundevi's conviction was heartfelt. Her generation had grown up during a time of transformation. TV had only arrived in Nepal in 1985; yet fifteen years later the Kathmandu Valley had cable, satellite, FM radio and full Internet access. Now, like young the world over, the new generation in Kathmandu are texting each other on mobile phones and posting themselves on YouTube and Facebook. In February, in response to the state of emergency, they had launched 'United We Blog' – one of the web's most influential blog sites.

The young in the Kathmandu Valley – especially the affluent, educated young, like Pundevi – feel the disparity between the haves and have-nots of their generation more keenly than their predecessors and many are galvanized by a growing sense of injustice and social responsibility. To many of them, tradition stands in the way of progress and global integration. The Kumari is an all too conspicuous example of ancient practices mired in the superstitions of the past.

But even to those who are less hostile to the tradition, the Kumaris are an uncomfortable presence. Living Goddesses exist nowhere else in the world and the practice is extremely difficult to explain to outsiders. The Kumari tradition simply doesn't square with the views of the outside world.

There were other internal influences at play behind the Supreme Court case, too. Simmering caste tensions were finding expression in the rising democracy and human rights movements, and some lower- and middle-caste Newars considered Pundevi Maharjan's petition a timely attack on the closed world of the high-caste tantric specialists.

Then there was the question of the Kumari's relationship with the king. Pundevi's case, coming so quickly after Gyanendra's autocratic coup, had garnered particular support from those who viewed the Living Goddess as inextricably linked with the monarchy. For them, an attack on the royal Kumari represented an attack on a despotic king.

Many of Pundevi's specific allegations about the tradition – child cruelty, coercion, intimate physical examinations by priests and terrifying initiation rites – however, seemed still to be rooted in rumour. In interviews with the press Pundevi had described the royal Kumari as a child captive 'pacing to and fro' in the Kumari Chen, and 'forced' to give darshan. The Kumari, she claimed, was deprived of family life, an education, medical attention and adequate food. She was adamant that Kumaris were 'never properly rehabilitated after their term expires', describing ex-Kumaris as 'destitute' and 'pathetic'.

Pundevi herself, though, had not solicited the views of any ex-Kumaris or their families, or interviewed any of the priests or caretakers involved in the tradition prior to bringing the case. Though she had cited eleven other 'permanent' Living Goddesses in

the valley in her writ (I had found eight) she was unable to provide
their names or the towns in which they lived.

She need not have looked far to become better informed. In an
effort to shed light on the circumstances of a Kumari's life and to try
and dispel some of the rumours once and for all, ex-Kumari Rashmila
Shakya had just published her memoirs. Her book, *From Goddess to
Mortal: The True-Life Story of a Former Royal Kumari*, is dedicated 'to
my two families: the family of Jujubhai Shakya of Kumari Chen,
who raised me as a goddess, and my original family, who taught me
how to relate to the world as a human being'.

In it Rashmila describes her time at the Kumari Chen in meticulous
detail and refutes most of Pundevi's allegations – including the
persistent story about the Kumari being forced to spend a night
in a room surrounded by severed goat and buffalo heads during
the festival of Dasain in order to prove her courage. While there
is certainly a big sacrifice in Mul Chowk on the night of Kalaratri,
Rashmila explained, the Kumari is never present for it. She is led
through the courtyard when the sacrifice is over, so she sees none of
the violence, and there are no men dressed as ghouls howling in the
shadows trying to terrify her. She is never, then or at any other time,
locked in a room by herself. There are, indeed, goats and buffalo
heads lying around the shrine but they are part of the ceremony to
honour the Goddess. The *puja* conducted on the night of Kalaratri
is in no sense a test of her courage. It is solemn and secret, Rashmila
maintained, but it is never frightening.

To Rashmila, her period as a Kumari had not only been
exceptionally happy, it had given her experiences that had enriched
her life. Though her book did not shy away from describing the
trauma of leaving the Kumari Chen and adapting to the outside
world, she stated she had 'absolutely no regrets about being
Kumari'.

But the clearest testament to Rashmila's claims was Rashmila
herself. I had continued to meet with her over the years and
had watched the timid teenager who had barely uttered a word

when I first met her in 1997 grow into a confident and successful young woman. Now twenty-four years old, she was studying for a BA in information technology. She was still soft-spoken – Rashmila would never be garrulous – but she had become sociable and articulate, with an easy, radiant smile. There was still an air of ethereal serenity about her but this was married with an inner strength – 'stubbornness' her sisters called it, a combination of the wisdom and self-belief that had helped her through her difficult transition.

The only criticism Rashmila had of the Kumari tradition was on the subject of education. During her time as Living Goddess a teacher had come to the Kumari Chen every day to give her an hour's lesson in Nepali and maths. However, if devotees arrived, Rashmila's lessons were interrupted and often days would go by without her being able to get to her books. Inevitably she had struggled when she left the Kumari Chen and entered school. Though twelve years old she had to start in Class 2, sitting on a bench next to her six-year-old sister. She had found English – in which she had received no teaching at all – particularly difficult. It took an enormous amount of effort and extra tuition at home to catch up with a class that was only a year or two junior, and eventually to pass her secondary examinations, the School Leaving Certificate.

Rashmila had not been the first ex-Kumari to pass her exams. Nani Maya Shakya, who had been Kumari from 1961 to 1972, had completed her SLC and opened a pharmacy; and Harsha Laxmi Shakya, Kumari from 1955 to 1961, had become a nurse. Rashmila, though, was the first ex-Kumari to enter higher education. At Amrit Science College, however, she had discovered the competition was fierce and her lack of experience and grounding in her subjects had continued to be a handicap. To secure a place at a non-fee-paying university or to get a scholarship at a private one Rashmila needed to attain marks of 80–90 per cent in all the subjects she had taken for her higher secondary examinations, the Intermediate Science

Certificate. In the end she had managed only 48 per cent overall – a Second Division grade – and though she had managed to pass the additional university entrance exam she had been nowhere near the top twenty-four students selected to go on to study architectural engineering.

The failure had been a severe blow but Rashmila's sisters had encouraged her to take a computer course while she considered her next step, and she had discovered an aptitude for it. Now in her first year of studying for her Bachelor's in Information Technology, Rashmila felt that the doors to higher education had finally opened for her.

But she was keen to ensure that subsequent Kumaris did not suffer the same difficulties. Thanks largely to the insistence of Rashmila and her family, and the parents of Rashmila's successor, Amita Shakya, there had been considerable improvement in the education of reigning Kumaris. Lessons are now conducted six days a week between 11 a.m. and 3 p.m. and are not interrupted by worshippers or demands for *darshan* from tourists in the courtyard. When Amita was dismissed in 2001 she went straight into the class for her age at school, and was taught by teachers who already knew her, so – according to Amita's parents – her adjustment had been comparatively easy.

Rashmila felt, however, that there was also a need to modernize the Kumari pension and to target it towards education. In the past, education had not been an important issue, for Kumaris or anyone else. Only fifty years ago, most Nepalis – men and women – had been illiterate. The Kumari pension had originally been intended to provide money for a woman who, it was assumed, would never be desirous of earning her own living. Rashmila received 3000 rupees a month – about $40 – which was enough to pay for food and clothing but not to provide private tuition or fund a place at a private university.

'I would much rather have been given a scholarship for school and university so I could earn my own living than receive a cash handout for life,' Rashmila told me. 'It would cost the government less in the long run, too.'

The question remained as to why UN reports had included the Kumari tradition alongside the most brutal examples of child abuse and sex discrimination in the country when evidence existed suggesting that, far from constituting child abuse, the tradition actively protected and championed the rights of women and children; and that ex-Kumaris themselves supported the practice. Sloppy research must be partly to blame. Like most journalists it seems the UN reporters had also been persuaded by the prevailing rumours and had failed to examine the tradition closely, including the Newar beliefs and intentions behind it. But then, perhaps the answer is simpler than that. Perhaps no one, let alone at the UN, can conceive of a tradition anywhere in the world where a little girl is genuinely worshipped as a Goddess.

The festival of Indra Jatra, conducted that year under a heavy armed presence, was a more muted affair than usual. The Kumari fell asleep in her chariot on the first day. Kiran Citraikar, the royal photographer – descended from the long hereditary line of royal portraitists – had never, he told me, seen the Living Goddess actually fall asleep during the opening procession before. Cameras flashed and bands played, the masked Lakhe leapt and cavorted, but the Kumari lolled back in her throne completely oblivious. When a jolt from the chariot wheels eventually jarred her awake she scowled at the crowds and shuffled angrily on her seat.

On the following two days of the jatra she was more animated – far too animated according to her caretakers – smiling and pulling faces and acting the clown. No one had known such indecorous behaviour in a Living Goddess. Most worrying of all, though, was the Kumari's restlessness. Her crown – the magnificent golden *matuu* weighing close to one kilo, its jewel-encrusted bands widening upwards from her temples like a fan – seemed to be causing her particular problems. She was constantly shifting it about on her head or trying to support it with both hands;

repeatedly summoning her caretakers to adjust it. To spectators, seeing the Living Goddess's impatience and her crown in danger of slipping were the most alarming signs of all.

~

As the summer of 2005 drew to a close I believed I had tracked down most – if not all – the remaining Living Goddesses in the Kathmandu Valley. During the course of my explorations, however, I had become increasingly aware of one vital aspect, central to the Kumari tradition, linking them all, that I had not yet addressed. As the streets – post Indra Jatra – filled once more with students throwing rocks against riot shields, and battered blue police vans screeched back and forth from the prison next to the old armoury of Kot, I applied myself to the pivotal enigma of Guhyeshvari, 'Mistress of the Secret', 'She Who Must Remain Hidden' – from whose *pitha*, according to both Hindus and Buddhists, flows the female energy that pervades the valley. Guhyeshvari is the fount of creative power, quite simply, the source of everything.

Chapter 20

Sati's Yoni Falls to Earth

Of all the gods and *bodhisattvas* who delighted in visiting the Valley of Nepal, none took more pleasure in its boundless beauty than the wild god Shiva who, shunning the society of his fellow gods, often descended from his home on the summit of Mt Kailash to run in the forests known as Mrigasthali on the banks of the Bagmati. Taking the guise of an amorous stag, he would gambol and leap with the animals, playing with them and copulating with them whenever the desire came upon him. In this form the gods called him Pashupatinath – Lord of the Beasts.

But in time even Shiva, reclusive though he was, began to long for a wife. Over the ages the hero Daksha Prajapati and his wife Virani had produced 330 million daughters, and now all these daughters were married to all the other gods, *yakshas*, *gandharvas*, *nagas* and *rakshashas*; and Shiva, seeing how blissful and complete these couples had become, realized this was how it was meant to be – that without his own *shakti* he was like a bird with no wings.

Only one of Daksha's daughters, the youngest and most beautiful of them all, called Sati, was not yet married and it was this daughter whom Shiva now greatly desired to have as his wife. Daksha, however, was reluctant to surrender his last remaining daughter in marriage to a god like Shiva, looking as he did like a filthy old *yogin* with matted dreadlocks, his body covered with ashes, who spent his time fornicating with animals or sitting all day smoking ganja and eating *yasa* and datura and other intoxicants in the cremation ground. So when Shiva, carrying his trident and dressed in a stinking leopard skin, came to beg Sati's hand in marriage, Daksha wrinkled his nose in distaste and turned him away.

But the great god Vishnu, seeing Shiva's desire and knowing how unbalanced the world would become if he did not find a wife, intervened, tricking Daksha into believing that it was he, Vishnu, who wanted to marry his daughter.

When Daksha discovered that Shiva had taken Vishnu's place in the wedding ceremony at the last minute, he levelled unspeakable curses at Vishnu for his deception. Nonetheless, the marriage rites had been completed and Daksha had no alternative but to acquiesce. So Sati left her father's palace in all her wedding finery to go with her husband in his animal skins and ashes to their home on Mt Kailash.

When the inhabitants of Kailash – Nandi the bull, Bhringi the dwarf and the hosts of other attendants – saw the divine couple arriving they were overjoyed and scattered flowers upon the road to welcome them. And when Sati – who had been expecting a smoky hovel full of dust and spiders – saw Shiva's shining palace with its halls of marble and gold, its walls and floors set with jewels, every chamber full of riches, and a kitchen with never-ending supplies of fragrant dishes, she was utterly astonished.

Then Nandi, Bhringi and all the ghosts and spirits bowed at the feet of Shiva Mahadeva and joined their hands in praise, exhorting the great lord to show his true form to his blessed wife.

So, sitting in the central courtyard of the palace, on a part of the ground that had been cleansed with the dung of a wish-granting cow, Shiva held Sati in his lap and, as his yogic form began to fall away from him, he revealed himself in his true nature to his wife. He was the most beautiful being Sati had ever seen. His skin was flawless and clear and glowed like burnished gold, except at his throat where the skin was blue. In his hair, bound up with rudra beads, within a golden crown that blazed like the sun, he wore a crescent moon and from his face, which was unspeakably handsome, his three lotus-shaped kohl-rimmed eyes gazed ecstatically upon her. There were garlands of snakes hissing around his neck – but they were peaceful and did not bite. In his left hand he held a dazzling trident; in his right he beat a soft and thrilling rhythm with a *damaru* drum. An impish smile played about his lips.

As she took *darshan* of her husband, Sati was overwhelmed with love.

So Shiva Mahadeva and Sati Devi took their combined form as Shiva-Shakti and, feasting on fruits and nectars, spent their days and nights in ecstatic love-making, and ruled together peacefully in Kailash.

Unbeknownst to the couple, Sati's father had decided to hold a horse sacrifice – the greatest of all sacrifices, to which he had invited the 330 million gods and their wives, all the *yakshas, gandharvas, kinnaras, rakshasas, nagas,* sages and the guardians of the ten directions – everyone except Sati and her husband.

While Sati and Shiva lay in each other's arms in their bedchamber, all the other gods were arriving at the pavilion erected by Daksha at the site of the sacrifice. *Apsaras* danced and *gandharvas* sang, and Brahma, Vishnu, Indra, Narada and other *rishis* seated themselves in front of the fire-pit to recite the Vedas and Puranas. Grains, butter, honey, vermilion and cloth were offered and burned on the fire. The 330 million gods performed the sixteen-offerings *puja* while devotees and pilgrims offered up other donations – hundreds of thousands of horses, elephants, the nine gems and other precious stones. All the gods heaped praise upon Daksha, flattering him and telling him what a noble host he was and how great his feast.

All except for one – Dadhici Rishi – who decided to speak the truth. 'O Daksha!' he cried. 'If you really want to hear how great your sacrifice is, I will tell you. It is like jewellery adorning a body that has no life. It is a splendid house that is uninhabited. It is like a person who has riches, land and possessions, but no children. I don't see your daughter Sati Devi eating. Does your mind have a heart? Have you lost your wisdom? This feast without Shiva and Sati is like a funeral; this sacrifice of yours, a cremation.'

So saying, Dadhici Rishi stormed out and some of the other gods followed him. Soon news of the argument reached Mt Kailash.

When Sati heard that her father was holding a feast for all the gods except for herself and her husband she immediately began readying herself to go down to remonstrate with him. Desperate not to let his wife come to any harm Shiva tried to stop her but Sati became very angry, showing her husband an aspect of herself she had never shown before.

'O Swami!' she cried. 'A woman does not need an invitation to visit her parents' home, her husband's home, her best friend's home, her teacher's home or her priest's home. Do not – I warn you – try to keep me from going.'

But Shiva replied, 'O my dear Sati! The rule of etiquette you mention is indeed true. But since your father is a man of exceedingly bad manners and because he doesn't know any better, if you go there, you'll be humiliated – indeed so greatly will you be humiliated, it will be like a death,' and he refused to let her leave.

Whereupon Sati became even more angry and turned black as pitch, swelling to a tremendous size. She grew long, fang-like teeth and her hair stood on end. In one left hand she held a sword, in the other left hand a demon's head dripping with blood; while in her right hands she displayed the wish-granting and fear-dispelling mudras, vara and abhaya. Around her neck was a garland of severed heads and her tongue flicked 'culu, culu', while her mouth gurgled with blood. In her hair was a crescent moon and she sat on a corpse, laughing.

Shiva was utterly terrified seeing Sati like this but whichever way he turned he was unable to avoid the sight. Then Sati changed from her appearance as Kali to a blue form – Ugra Tara – immense in size and draped with snakes, wrapped in an elephant skin, holding a skull cup. And Shiva again was so frightened he tried to run away. But Sati took another form, the red form of Rajarajeshvari; and then another, the splendid shining form of Bhuvaneshvari; and another, Bhairavi; and all the while Shiva was trembling with fear. But the next apparition was even more terrifying. As Chinnamasta she stood on a three-cornered lion throne, wearing a Naga around her neck, holding a bloody sword in her right hand, and in her left, her own severed head emitting three great fountains of blood.

Seeing this terrible emanation Shiva closed his eyes. But even with his eyes closed Sati appeared before him again, this time in the form of Dhumavati, a mad old widow riding in a chariot, her two slack breasts throbbing as she breathed; and then she changed again, to Bagalamukhi, emanating a brilliant shimmering halo of light; and then to Matangi, blue-black in colour, carrying a flayed skin, a noose and an elephant goad.

By now Shiva was quaking with fear and Sati, realizing her husband was close to fainting, revealed herself to him in her tenth and most beautiful form, Mahalakshmi, full of passion and desire. Golden-coloured and seated on a lotus throne with four four-tusked elephants libating her with *amrita* from gem-studded vases, she emitted an aura of such gentleness and compassion that Shiva, still quaking with fright, was reassured and dared to address her: 'O beautiful one!' he said. 'Who are you? I've never seen you before. Why have you appeared to me? Have you seen my beloved Sati Devi? Where has she gone? Please tell me the truth.'

And Sati replied, 'O Mahadeva! Why are you afraid to see me? Why did you try to run away from me? Let me remind you of your origins for I am the supreme force of creation, Parama Prakriti, born of Adishakti Mahamaya. Long ago, before it was possible to have birth from wombs, you three – Brahma, Vishnu and Shiva – were created by me. When you three were in that watery place called Jalamaya, wondering why you were there, it was I who taught you to do *tapas* and meditation and who gave you your powers.'

And realizing the absolute truth of this Shiva was overjoyed and, thinking to make this precious knowledge secret, he converted it all into tantra and *mantra*.

Then the Goddess resumed her form as Sati Devi and embraced her husband. But as soon as she remembered her father's insult she abandoned her golden figure and changed again into her Kali form; and when Shiva saw her like this again he said, 'O my dearest Sati! Go wherever you want to go!' and he summoned his bull Nandi to bring the chariot and Sati left for the place where her father, Daksha Prajapati, was holding his sacrifice.

As soon as Daksha saw his daughter Sati arriving, black as pitch, he became angry and immediately began denouncing Shiva to his daughter's face: 'See, see! In such a beautiful place as this, with Vishnu and all my other guests, how could I possibly have sent you and your husband an invitation to this sacrifice? It is because you have been living with Shiva that you have degenerated so much. Look at you! Shameless! See how dark your face is! *Chi, chi*! I can't bear to look at it. No one can change the fate that is written on the forehead. You have become just like Shiva and he is the very image of sin!'

The sages and Brahmins hearing these insults cried loudly, covering their ears and walked out of the sacrifice. And Sati grew angrier and angrier.

'Oh father!' she cried. 'What benefit do you get from insulting my husband like this? What kind of corrupt sacrifice are you performing? Without Shiva this sacrifice will not bear fruit. If you want to be virtuous, invite Sri Mahadeva right now. Only then will your sacrifice be a success.'

But her father answered, 'How could I possibly invite your shameful, naked, ugly husband into a gathering such as this? No matter what you say, I won't have him at my *yajna*!'

Sati swelled with fury. Stamping her feet, gnashing her teeth – '*katatata!*' – and shaking her fists, her eyes blazing red, she cried, 'You ignorant fool! Until I abandon this body which I received from you, I'll never be rid of this curse!' Then, circling the *yajna* three times and crying the name 'Shiva! Shiva! Shiva!' she hurled herself on to the fire, abandoning her life. And so her soul fled her body, taking refuge in the womb of Queen Menaka far away in the Himalaya.

A great wind began to blow. The sky became dark with cloud and a storm of dust engulfed the guests. Nandi the bull flew back to Mount Kailash and, with tears streaming down his muzzle, reported to Shiva all that had happened. Shiva closed his eyes as he listened to the dreadful words of his faithful servant and when he opened them again all hell broke loose. Emitting a beam of fire from his third eye, gnashing his teeth with rage, letting out a lion's roar, he untied one of the strands of hair from his topknot, whipped it through the air and dashed it to the ground. Ghosts, spirits, ghouls and the god of fever came dancing from the ground and together with the host of *bhutas* and *pretas* Shiva rushed from Kailash over to the place where Daksha had been holding his sacrifice. Vultures and hawks assumed a *mandala* formation in the sky over the *yajna*. Jackals howled and vomited blood.

Seeing the fallen body of his beloved Sati lying in the fire-pit, Shiva lifted her out and placed her on his lap. Gazing into her face, he embraced her as tears streamed from his third eye. 'O Praneshvari! O my life-breath!' he cried, beating his chest. 'Wherever you have gone, invite me there too! Kailash is deserted and there is no one there to protect us!'

Howling with anguish he shouldered the charred body of his wife and went from village to village, country to country, wailing 'O Sati, Sati!' and because her corpse was resting on Shiva's shoulders it did not decompose but remained as though merely in sleep.

All over the world he went in his agony, dancing a terrible dance of destruction. The earth could not bear his burden and the fourteen planes of existence began to tremble and shake. All Nature shuddered with Shiva's sorrow. Volcanoes erupted, storms and floods engulfed the land, harvests failed and the gods themselves quaked in fear.

At last Vishnu, the Great Preserver, foreseeing the annihilation of mankind and the whole of the world unless Sati's corpse could somehow be removed from Shiva's shoulders, dispatched some flies to lay their eggs in Sati's body. So, one by one, and unbeknownst to Shiva in his madness, bits of Sati's body began to decay and fall away. Only when the last piece had slipped from his back did Shiva notice that the weight of his beloved wife had been lifted from him and, resigned at last to his loss, he retired to Mt Kailash, his abode in the Himalayan snow peaks, to lose himself in meditation.

In all, fifty parts of Sati's body dropped to the ground and where each fell became a *shakti pitha*. Her tongue fell in Kashmir, her hair in Benares, her left eye in Paurabandhana, her nose in Purnagiri, her right cheek in Amrataka, her anus in Trisrotaka, her naval in Kamarashtra, her left rib in Devikota, her left ear in Gokarna, her stomach in Kolapura, her right thigh in Elapura, her lungs in Jayantipura.

And in the very centre of the Valley of Nepal fell the secret part of the Devi's body – her vagina, entrance to her womb. The site where Sati's *yoni* fell was the most precious *pitha* of all, the *pitha* of Guhyeshvari – 'Mistress of the Secret', 'She Who Must Remain Hidden' – and here the 330 million gods, *yakshas*, *gandharvas*, *kinnaras*, *daityas* and *danavas* came to worship. Therefore, in this world, whatever person takes *darshan* of this *pitha* will have all their sins eliminated and they will attain liberation.

Chapter 21

The Hidden Goddess

At first glance Pashupati seems an unlikely spot for the source of primordial female power. Located at a *tirtha*, a holy crossroads at the confluence of three rivers, to the east of Kathmandu, Pashupati is the site of Nepal's most important Hindu temple, renowned throughout the subcontinent as sacred to Shiva. It has been a place of pilgrimage and worship for over 1500 years. Scores of *lingas* – stone phalluses representative of the god – line the streets down to the Bagmati where funeral pyres smoke day and night on the cremation ghats. Stone shrines house yet more Shira *lingas*; while on a hill overlooking the site, a crazy array of gigantic boulders stand nakedly priapic, thrusting up at jaunty angles from the skyline. Legend claims there are 100,000 *lingas* around the site of Pashupati.

Most revered of all is the *linga* enshrined inside the magnificent Golden Temple on the banks of the Bagmati. Three feet tall, of black stone, with four faces carved on its shaft, the *chaturmukha linga* is considered so sacred only Hindus and certain Newar Buddhists can set eyes on it. It is housed inside a two-tiered pagoda twenty-four metres tall, with copper roofs, and bronze-gilt and silver doors, protected by high walls. In its inner sanctum, enclosed by a silver-plated fence, is the *linga* itself, usually shielded from sight – even from the worshippers who file by with offerings – by a solid silver sheath. Only a handful of specialist Brahmin priests from southern India are permitted to touch it. The throbbing energy it contains is believed to make the *linga* so 'hot' with sexual fire it has to be cooled constantly with libations. The whole site of Pashupati, it seems, is dedicated to honouring this arresting totem of masculine energy.

But beyond the stalls selling marigolds and necklaces of dried *rudra* beads and the funeral pyres dispensing their acrid smoke, over the bridge on the other side of the Bagmati, past the ashrams with half-naked *sadhus* and *linga babas* sitting cross-legged by their tridents, a gentle incline between an avenue of stone *lingas* leads around a sparsely wooded hill towards another temple enclosure. This is the site of Guhyeshvari's *pitha*, the place where Sati's *yoni* fell to earth; where, in Buddhist legend, the lotus seed that was tossed into the lake by Vipashvin Buddha took root. This is the notional source of the Goddess's *shakti*, the place that identifies the whole of the Kathmandu Valley, Pashupati included, as sacred to the Goddess. I imagined Newars regarded it like some great Charybdian sink-hole, only in reverse, a swirling vortex discharging female energy from the unfathomable depths of its being.

A set of high walls had been raised around the site in 1654 by one of the valley's most illustrious kings, Pratap Malla. The story of Pratap Malla's discovery, or re-discovery, of the Hidden Goddess is a cautionary tale directed at the excesses of masculine power.

Pratap Malla's reign had not begun well. His father was Laxminarasimha, the hapless mad king imprisoned by ambitious nobles who prevented him from passing on the *mantra* of Taleju to his son. Deprived of the Goddess's guiding wisdom, Pratap Malla's early life was mired in weakness and corruption. According to the chronicles, he had indulged in 'all manner of perversion and games of debauchery': 'seduction became his cup of want', 'his life's ambition the conquest of 100,000 concubines'. Having 'corrupted the chastity of three thousand women' Pratap Malla took for himself a girl who had not yet arrived at puberty and so 'forceful was his lust' that the young girl died.

After the girl's death, however, Pratap Malla was overcome with fear. In penance he came to Pashupati where he remained for three months erecting devotional *lingas* to Shiva by the thousands, modelling them out of clay with his own hands. He performed a *kotihoma* – a lavish fire sacrifice – and the magnificent rite of *tuladana* – an offering of silver, precious stones, gold and pearls equal to his own weight – that he dedicated to Shiva's temple; and to this extravagant gift he added a hundred horses. He even ordered the erection of *lingas* at intervals of a pace along the road all the way from Pashupati to Hanuman Dhoka as a reminder of his vow to overcome his lustful desires. Yet for all this apologetic organ-raising, Pratap Malla had remained haunted by his crimes.

He had surrounded himself with famous gurus in the hope that they might provide him with the means to redeem himself. One particular priest, a Brahmin called Narasimha Thakur, had become a follower of the *Mahakala Samhita*, a Hindu tantric text concerning the esoteric form of the Goddess known as Guhyakali – another name for Guhyeshvari, the Hidden Goddess. While the guru was meditating on this text he had received an insight – that the *pitha* of Guhyeshvari was lying neglected in a forest near the site of Pashupati and was in danger of becoming lost to the world. The priest communicated this intelligence to the king, telling Pratap Malla how to go about uncovering the *pitha* so it could be properly venerated again.

With the auspicious help of a sword-bearer and an oilman, Pratap Malla located the *pitha* in dense undergrowth, in the middle of the grove of trees known as Sleshmantak, on the hill overlooking Pashupati. Covering the *pitha* was the triangular yoni-shaped stone slab – the same stone that the *bodhisattva* Manjushri had placed upon it after he had drained the valley in the Golden Age; only, the tiny hole in the centre through which the waters of Guhyeshvari had issued forth for millennia had become blocked and the waters had begun to turn back on themselves, retreating underground in broiling confusion.

Summoning his subjects to the spot, Pratap Malla had commanded them to lift up the stone and start digging a tank. As the people dug, a great trembling and shaking was felt beneath the ground and the water began appearing in the hole, and beneath it raged the glow of a mighty subaqueous fire. In order to prevent the fire and water rushing up out of the hole, the Brahmin told the king to instruct his subjects to place iron beams over it in the shape of the *yantra*, and to place a cover on top of this in the form of an eight-petalled lotus made of stone. And in the centre of the lotus, as per the Brahmin's instructions, the king placed a *kalash*, or sacred water-pot. Finally Pratap Malla built a temple over the *pitha*, in front of which he erected devotional pillars – one surmounted by a lion and the other by a statue of a man, and surrounded the entire precinct with high walls.

The restoration of Guhyeshvari's *pitha* and the safe, auspicious flowing of her waters once again is commemorated in a poem composed by Pratap Malla himself and inscribed in stone inside the temple.

Dear mother, beloved Kali, I will not abandon you and honour another deity.
　　I do not honour, nor do I bow to others.
There is no truth among the lordly gods, the son of Nanda and the rest.
　　Nor do I speak to them of my troubles.

I praise you, great fierce one, seated on top of the five great pretas,
　　in the middle of the great pitha,
Which is a lovely place, a bower dense with rites like vines.
　　Make your glances fall on me!

Pratap Malla also extolled the Goddess in verses he inscribed in the courtyards of Hanuman Dhoka, and on the plinths of Jagannath and Taleju temples. He wrote thousands of hymns, eulogizing her in all her forms, as 'The Primal One', 'Composed of Bliss', 'Transcendent', 'Made of Pure Thought', 'The Queen of Breath',

'Treasure of Victory', 'Mother of Speech', 'Sea of Compassion', 'Whose Own Self Consists of Ultimate Truth'. Under the instructions of another guru, Lambakarna Bhatta, he built another temple to Taleju inside his palace – the rooftop Degutale, on the corner of Karnel Chowk, facing Durbar Square; and in front of this, he raised a devotional pillar bearing a gilt image of himself, his two queens and his sons, kneeling, their hands together in eternal prayer.

He had gone to extraordinary lengths to equip himself with tantric knowledge, taking as one of his gurus a famous Vajracharya called Jamana who initiated him into the secrets of Vajrayana in a shrine up at the great *stupa* of Swayambhu, site of the Buddhist origin myth of the valley. Subsequently, in 1688, the chronicles describe how Pratap Malla was able to use these powers to relieve the valley of a terrible drought. He ventured into a chamber deep underground and, using the rainmaking tantra written in the blood of the Chobar Naga that the *siddha* Shantikara Acharya – the first Vajracharya initiated by Manjushri – had stored there centuries before, he exerted his power over the Nagas, forcing them to release the rains.

Pratap Malla had attributed his powers as a *siddha* primarily, though, to his special veneration of the 'Hidden Goddess'. He called himself 'Lord of Guhyeshvari'. His fortunes had, indeed, seemed to rise spectacularly following his discovery of Guhyeshvari's *pitha*. He had reclaimed territories from the Tibetans; defeated Dambara Shah, the king of Gorkha, taking the king's elephant as his prize; and, having captured several fortresses belonging to his cousin-king in Patan and compelled his other cousin-king in Bhaktapur to offer him an elephant in tribute, ensured that Kathmandu became – for a time – the most powerful of the three kingdoms in the valley. Fundamental to Pratap Malla's story, though, was the notion that his greatest achievement had been to bring the Goddess within reach of his people again so that the whole valley could receive her blessings.

Like the Golden Temple, the enclosure of Guhyeshvari is, for reasons of purity, barred to foreigners. The only glimpse I could get of it was from the top of Sleshmantak hill. From there, I could just about see the large courtyard inside the precinct walls where the Temple of Guhyeshvari – a square, single-storey building with silver-plated doors, gilt-latticed windows, and an open, silver-plated canopy supporting a silver finial over an open roof – stood surrounded by devotional pillars. Inside this temple, somewhere at its heart and still unimaginable, is the watery hole of Guhyeshvari's *pitha*.

I had resigned myself to the fact that the Hidden Goddess would remain beyond my sight until an encounter with one of the most powerful tantric priests in the valley – the closest, on the Hindu side, to the royal Kumari – presented me with a remarkable opportunity.

I was back in Gyanman Pati Vajracharya's sitting room overlooking Durbar Square. This time I had come to meet Uddhav Karmacharya, the Hindu priest of the Living Goddess, who was now sitting opposite me, cross-legged on the floor, with a look of guarded amusement on his face. The two Newars had been friends since school and the priest was clearly at home in the Buddhist household in Layku Bahil. Though currently dressed in a well-cut jacket and an open western shirt, Uddhav was familiar as the figure I had seen at Indra Jatra, wearing a long white *kurta*, riding in the chariot with the Living Goddess.

I had also encountered him several times early in the morning arriving at the Kumari Chen to perform *nitya puja* for the Kumari in her royal throne room. Again dressed in white, he had been hurrying across Durbar Square from the direction of Taleju Temple, holding his bare hands out in front of him like a surgeon scrubbed up for theatre. Bystanders at the entrance of the Kumari Chen had stood urgently aside to let him pass. Anyone touching his body or crossing his path would defile him, deactivating the Goddess's *shakti*.

I had been keen to meet the royal Hindu priest for some time.

My investigations had taken a wide sweep in recent months as I searched for evidence of Living Goddess worship across the length and breadth of the valley. Now it was time to return to base, to the vibrant tradition in the very heart of Kathmandu, to peer into the esoteric world surrounding the central Kumari. Uddhav Karmacharya was as close as anyone could get to Hindu tantric worship of the Kumari. I felt privileged to be given a chance to speak to him and hoped this was because he trusted my intentions but it was clear from the outset that this would not be a straightforward encounter.

The Karmacharya was an intimidating figure. Tall for a Newar, with a dashing moustache and an unusual, almost Roman, nose, he sat with his back effortlessly elevated, chest broad, an easy balance to his shoulders, hands relaxed in his lap – the classic pose of a man practised in long hours of meditation. He opened the conversation with a stern blast of admonition. It is always difficult for outsiders to understand the Living Goddess, he said, transfixing me with dark eyes. What made me think I was different? Instead of writing about the Kumari, I should be meditating on her. This is the only way to understand. The Kumari is not something that should appear casually in print. Just as her name should not be used to advertise – like Kumari Laundry; or used in a store for selling gold. How did I, someone who was born not in Nepal, the land of the gods, but in the self-ruled world, expect to be able to experience these things when I did not follow the *niyams* or observe the rules of purity? These were considerable obstacles in my path.

His tone took me by surprise and I wondered why he had agreed to see me at all. I hoped I was not there simply for a dressing-down.

Uddhav had taken on the powerful role of acting Taleju priest in his early twenties. Both his father and his uncle were Taleju priests but, since both were of an advanced age, they now participated in only a few of the most important temple functions. Uddhav's was a full-time job requiring a young man's energy and focus.

The caste Uddhav came from – the Karmacharyas – are the

Newar *tantrikas* who traditionally control the highest Hindu *mantras* and initiations. They had dominated the political/religious life of fifteenth- to eighteenth-century Kathmandu, enjoying a position that became, in effect, closer to the king than his own high-status Brahmin chaplain.

In recent times the Karmacharyas' great rivals, the Newar Rajopadhyaya Brahmins, had managed to negotiate a greater role for themselves in both the Vedic and tantric religious life of the kingdom and had become the priests closest to the present royal family; but control of the cult of the great royal goddess Taleju, the enduring heart of political power in the valley, remains in the hands of the Karmacharyas. Much like a secret service agent with top security clearance to handle codes and classified documents, Uddhav Karmacharya safeguarded *mantras* and tantric scriptures that no other person, not even the king, could access without his help. He presided over the festival of Kumari Jatra and the blessing of the *tika*, as well as the midnight rituals in the courtyard of Mul Chowk during Dasain. From the Hindu side, Uddhav Karmacharya was holder of the deepest secrets of Kumari worship.

Eventually, though, once Uddhav had set the tone, instilling due reverence into the conversation, he began to soften. Beyond the windows, the diurnal jangling of bicycle bells dislocated us from the outside world as the Karmacharya began to expound on the esoteric teachings of Living Goddess worship. He began by explaining the fundamental relationship between Taleju and the Kumari, and the inner realizations of the Kumari *bhakta*, or devotee.

'The goddess Taleju is one of the most secret things in *dharma* – religious lore,' he said. 'She cannot be seen in the same way other deities in the valley can be seen. There is no image of her for people to bow to and worship. Taleju is formless. It's just our conceit, our ego, that says she has to have eight hands or sixteen hands, ten heads or so many eyes. This is just interpretation; it is the creation of the artist. We have to see beyond this image, to the ultimate reality of Taleju; to *sunyata* – emptiness, non-duality.

'But it is difficult to have that single-hearted concentration, the self-discipline and purity of heart necessary to reach this point. The reality of the Goddess is so powerful that to envisage her, to experience her, you must be specially prepared, through training and tantric initiation. That is not possible for everyone.

'So Taleju reveals herself in Kumari. Kumari is the *murti*, the human image, the Goddess takes in order that everyone, even the uninitiated, can see her. We all need to do worship – you need it, I need it. It is necessary for all human beings. So Kumari is a form we can all see and touch, while Taleju herself cannot be touched.

'The name Taleju can be related to the Sanskrit word *"tula"*, the word for "scales". In one hand Taleju holds a sword, which is Kumari, the form of the Goddess that is visible to everyone. The sword represents the nation. Kumari is the one who looks after the nation.

'In the other hand Taleju holds a *kalash*, a water-pot. This represents Guhyeshvari.'

Here was the Goddess in her trisul form again, expressing the three points of her *yantra*, the three essential aspects of her nature: Kumari – Taleju – Guhyeshvari. The Goddess Without, the Goddess Beyond, and the Goddess Within. Taleju, the highest, purest aspect of the Goddess, associated with *sattva*, the ascendant quality, pure white and brilliant; the Kumari, in blood red, with *rajas*, the quality of action, or rising energy; and Guhyeshvari – the site where Sati's rotting flesh fell – charged with *tamas*, dark and black, the power of destruction and decay.

'Every year there is a *jatra* for Guhyeshvari from Taleju Temple to Pashupati,' the priest said. 'This is when the *shakti* of Taleju is pulled down to Guhyeshvari's *pitha*.' On this rare occasion, he explained, people can have *darshan* of the Hidden Goddess out in the open, without having to enter her temple.

The *jatra* had been established three hundred or so years ago by Jagajjaya Malla, father of Jaya Prakasha Malla, the last king of Kathmandu. According to the chronicles Jagajjaya Malla had, like his forebear Pratap Malla, assumed the throne under highly inauspicious circumstances. His predecessor, King Bhaskara Malla, had died of a terrible disease that had swept the valley, taking thousands of lives, including Kathmandu's royal Kumari. The plague was believed to have been caused by the Goddess who was angry with the king for having altered the date of Dasain for his own convenience.

Since Bhaskara Malla had no sons, Jagajjaya, a male relative of Bhaskara's daughter, was invited to take the throne. Jagajjaya would have been fully aware of his vulnerable position. Like Pratap Malla sixty years before him, Jagajjaya Malla had not received the *mantra* of Taleju by direct transmission and had none of the other auspicious credentials usually required of the king. Jagajjaya's *jatra* in honour of Guhyeshvari must have been, at least in part, an attempt to hotwire himself to the powers of the Secret Goddess – just as Pratap Malla had done – and secure his throne.

At Jagajjaya's instigation an image – a '*pratima*', Uddhav called it – of the Hidden Goddess was worshipped in Taleju's inner sanctum in Mul Chowk in Hanuman Dhoka. Once a year, on the ninth day of the dark fortnight of Margh, this image was brought out from Taleju temple and carried on a palanquin to Pashupati where it lay all night on the site of the original *pitha*, revivifying connections, exchanging energies. After a night of intense tantric worship, the *pratima* of Guhyeshvari returned to its place in Taleju's shrine.

To Uddhav Karmacharya this image of Guhyeshvari was not simply a copy, or even a mirror image, of the original. It was one and the same, another portal through which to gain access to the Inner Goddess. Jagajjaya had, through tantric means, cloned the original. Mahendra Malla had done a similar thing when he replicated Taleju's *yantra* in order to worship it in Kathmandu; and Siddhinarasimha Malla, king of Patan, had replicated it again, when – as the chronicles describe – he surreptitiously 'stole' Taleju's *yantra* from Kathmandu and established it in his own city. Just as these *yantras* of Taleju in

Kathmandu and Patan were considered in every way as powerful as the original in Bhaktapur, so the *pratima* of Guhyeshvari established by Jagajjaya in Kathmandu was clearly, to the tantric priests who safeguarded it, equivalent in every way to the manifestation of Guhyeshvari at Pashupati.

'But how is it possible to take Guhyeshvari on a *jatra*?' I asked Uddhav, wondering how something that was considered, in essence, a hole – the Goddess's *yoni*, the yawning source of everything – could be carried through the streets on a palanquin.

'Come and you will see,' he said.

I was amazed at the turn my meeting with the tantric priest had taken. What had begun with rebukes had ended with an open invitation. It seemed Uddhav Karmacharya was, despite his guardedness – like a lion at the temple gate – faced with the same dilemma with which all other keepers of esoteric practices in Kathmandu are now having to contend. In the hope of demonstrating the value of what he was charged with protecting Uddhav had chosen to open a window on to his world for me – just a chink.

I left Gyanman Pati's house with Uddhav Karmacharya's unexpected gift in my notebook: the exact time, astrologically calculated, just days from now – on the ninth day of the dark half of Marga – when the procession of the Goddess's *yoni* would begin.

My meeting with Uddhav Karmacharya, affecting as it was, had made an even deeper impression in my subconscious. That night the tantric priest reappeared in my dreams – in the guise of a rickshaw manager. I was sitting next to him, in the back of one of his rickshaws in Durbar Square, vainly attempting to explain to him where I wanted to go. We didn't seem to have a driver. 'You should have told me you wanted to see the Kumari,' he said simply. 'She's right here.'

I looked across at the rickshaw next to us and was amazed to see the Living Goddess sitting inside. As I looked at her, she burst into flames. Hovering in mid-air, in the spot where her head had been, was a stone plaque, a Licchavi-style stele, engraved with an image of the Goddess wielding a sword, severing a woman's head from her body. The woman's head was mine.

With a sting of recognition I felt two contradictory forces wrestling with each other within the realms of sleep. The dream seemed to be willing me deeper while my waking self struggled to break free. Alarming though it seemed, I recognized that the image being offered to me was a gift – my decapitation was not death, but liberation. Yet even as I felt the siren-like pull of the beyond, I found another part of myself – the worldly, security-seeking part – battling for consciousness.

I woke with a start. In the unearthly half-light of dawn I lay awake, pondering the obstacles of the ego. My dream seemed to be confronting me with the opposing forces of the rational and irrational. The closer my investigations came to the phenomenon of the Living Goddess, the more challenged I felt. Uddhav had drawn a line in the sand. Cross it, he suggested, and I would understand. I would move from the world of observation to the world of experience. But from that side I would no longer be willing, or able, to put into words what it was I had come to understand.

~

Sitting on the steps of Kakeshvar pagoda in the late afternoon sun, facing the entrance to Taleju Temple, I was surprised to see no crowds gathered for the *jatra* and for a moment wondered whether I had mistaken the time. Above me loomed Taleju's towering pagoda roofs, casting a protective shadow over the courtyards of Hanuman Dhoka. Directly opposite, Jaya Prakasha Malla gazed out across the square from his miniature pavilion on the top of the Lion Gate.

Inheriting the throne of Kathmandu had been just as precarious for Jaya Prakasha Malla as it had been for his father, the instigator of the *jatra*. Jagajjaya had died – according to the chronicles – in a state of anxiety and dread, after the first Gorkha attack on the strategic fortress of Nuwakot. The fortress had stood firm but some of the outlying lands had been captured. Grief-stricken by the unexpected deaths of his eldest and youngest sons and troubled by his courtiers' preference for Jaya Prakasha's younger brother, Rajya Prakasha, Jagajjaya had nevertheless handed on the baton to his second son. On 20 January 1736, the day before Jagajjaya died, a doe had wandered into Durbar Square – a troubling sign.

Jaya Prakasha Malla had been enthroned in haste, even before the thirteen days of mourning were over, by a courtier loyal to his father. Like Pratap Malla and his own father, Jaya Prakasha had not been born in Mohan Chowk in Hanuman Dhoka – the auspicious birthplace for any prospective king – and opposing factions in the court were bent on enthroning his younger brother Rajya Prakasha, who had.

In an effort to cleanse his court of these viperous connivances, Jaya Prakasha discharged all those he considered untrustworthy – from the Khasia, Jaisi, Bhandel and Rajlawat tribes – from Hanuman Dhoka, and expelled his younger brother Rajya Prakasha from the city. Rajya Prakasha fled to Patan where he was taken in by the childless king of Patan, Vishnu Malla, and adopted as his heir.

In response, the Khasa officials in Kathmandu took Jaya Prakasha's remaining thirteen-year-old brother Narendra and declared him king over the towns of Sankhu, Changu, Gokarna, Nandigram and Deopatan. Jaya Prakasha retaliated and deposed Narendra, who took refuge with Ranajit Malla, king of Bhaktapur.

Within months of his succession, Jaya Prakasha Malla, the new king of Kathmandu, had become enmeshed in the triangular antagonism of the three kingdoms and was battling to hold on to his throne. He embraced Guhyeshvari's *jatra* as a vital opportunity to empower himself.

A hefty wooden palanquin, painted red and yellow and three-storeyed like a miniature temple-pagoda, sat on the ground between the guardian lions at the gate. It looked decidedly worse for wear, the brunt of numerous outings only superficially rectified. In an attempt to correct the wonkiness of the structure, corners and joints had been inelegantly reinforced with metal brackets. Several Rakamis, assistants of Taleju Temple, were unceremoniously hammering the *jhallar* – a red valance edged with silver – on to the wooden roof-eaves with a stone.

As the appointed hour drew near Khadgi musicians – members of the butcher caste – emerged through the lion gate and began thumping a thunderous beat on their drums. The tempo crescendoed as a rival band could be heard approaching Hanuman Dhoka down New Road. These were Jyapus arriving by bus from Pashupati to accompany Guhyeshvari from Taleju Temple all the way to her *pitha*. They had brought with them members of the 'Pashupati Creative Boys' Club', a band of teenagers in sneakers, imitation designer jeans and an array of European football shirts who had volunteered to carry the Goddess on her *khat*. They were, one and all, auspiciously drunk.

As the two bands competed exultantly with each other, circling the palanquin, clashing symbols, beating drums and dancing about in a frenzy, Guhyeshvari was brought out of Taleju's shrine in the Mul courtyard of Hanuman Dhoka, and carried across the temple precinct and out through the gate. Inside, hidden from view, Uddhav Karmacharya had completed *pujas* that would protect the *pratima* for its seven-kilometre journey down to Pashupati and back again.

In the thirteen days since meeting Uddhav I had puzzled over the form Guhyeshvari would take for her procession. I had no idea what to expect and it took me a while to identify her. The *pratima* had been laid on a square red paten, rather like a Middle Eastern tea tray, with a metal stand on four legs over the top of it supporting an honorific silver finial, echoing the canopy over Guhyeshvari's temple. The shape on the tray was, at first, hard to make out but beneath the rich coating of blood-red paint and a tight garland of marigolds were bulbous mounds of what looked like an inverted jelly mould. This was the exact same image, made in silver, of the eight-petalled stone lotus Pratap Malla had placed as a cap over the watery hole of Guhyeshvari's *pitha*. In the centre was a small silver water-pot or *kalash*, almost totally obscured by a crown of red poinsettias.

As the image began to take root in my mind it seemed there could indeed be no more triumphant a symbol of an omnipotent Goddess than this. The water-pot in the lotus echoed the sexual tension of a *linga* lodged inside a *yoni* yet the water-pot was, like the lotus flower it rested in, incontrovertibly female. It was the primordial womb, the pot of plenty; both productive vacuum and inexhaustible cornucopia. This was sex, conception, the very force of creation, expressed in purest feminine form. And hidden at the centre of the image, implicit and invisible, where the *kalash* touched the heart of the lotus, covering the opening of the sacred hole, was the inner secret of the Goddess, the yawning of universal insubstantiality, the great inner beyond – the cosmic reality that lay beyond the illusion of this existence – Adishakti Mahamaya.

With great reverence Guhyeshvari was installed inside her palanquin where she was honoured with flowers, vermilion and rice, white and red radish, sugar cane, curd, soya bean, lapche fruit and bread. The Khadgi god-keepers fussed about with final adjustments, wedging in the precious occupant as securely as they could. On the back of the palanquin was hung a painted cloth depicting the womb-shaped *kalash*.

Finally they slotted enormous bamboo poles into the hoops beneath the palanquin, securing them with string, and with a triumphant roar the Pashupati Creative Boys' Club took up their posts with the poles on their shoulders, half a dozen or so in front, another half dozen behind, and set off at break-neck speed, the mobile temple swaying crazily from side to side as it careered off into the maelstrom of Makhan Tol.

A sword wrapped in yellow cloth symbolizing the attendance of King Jagajjaya Malla, father of Jaya Prakasha Malla and founder of the *jatra*, was carried along by a specially appointed sword-bearer: the hand of history, as ever, clasped in the hands of the present.

I had to run to keep up. As the palanquin charged ahead,

pedestrians were squeezed out of the way, cyclists swept aside, the wing-mirrors of motorbikes and cars snapped back, and all the while the Jyapu band joyously clashed cymbals and beat drums and the bearers laughed even as the sweat began cascading down their faces, their teammates cheering 'Victory to Guhyeshvari' and punching the air as they ran alongside.

This was no *bandh* day and the traffic along Kathmandu's narrow market streets was congested. The bearers might have had an easier time of it had they taken the wider New Road from Durbar Square but for a *jatra* this was inconceivable. We were following in the slipstream of ancient processions. The surface of the city may have changed – New Road had been bulldozed through the rubble of the 1934 earthquake – but the direction of a *jatra* did not. It travelled an invisible plane, recalling ghost processions, tracing ghost roads and passing ghost buildings. In the minds of the people participating in the *jatra* the landscape of the Mallas was as real as the world in the present day.

The palanquin ploughed on, bobbing above the heads of the market-goers who paused, curious, respectfully touching their foreheads or reaching out for *prasad*. A few older pedestrians, recognizing the *dya* with a cry of joy, stretched in a hand to make contact with the *yoni*. Coins and flowers flew into the palanquin; flowers flew back out again; and so the sacred vehicle sped on, showering blessings as it went.

The road through Siphal, Navalitole, Dahutole and Pancutole undulated crazily, dipping down to the river and rising up the other side, challenging even the sturdiest of legs as they struggled on beneath the increasing weight of the *khat*. As the bearers tired they swapped, one by one, with members of their team jogging alongside. Occasionally, misjudging the changeover, the palanquin came crashing to the ground and the bearers took a break as attendants poked their heads inside the *khat* to check on the precious occupant.

Finally, as dusk fell, the ancient boundary of Deopatan hove into view and the Pashupati Creative Boys' Club, on home turf at last, sent up a cheer. They had carried their extraordinary load over seven kilometres in under an hour. Descending through the trees to the banks of the Bagmati, just north of Pashupati, on the Guhyeshvari side of Sleshmantak hill, flagging energy soared. With renewed spirits the bearers laid down the *khat* and took off their shoes to make the crossing.

The bend in the river – a 90-degree dogleg winding around Sleshmantak hill back down to Pashupati – was a diversion created by Jaya Prakasha Malla in honour of Guhyeshvari, redirecting the Bagmati so it flowed 'within an arrow's flight' of her *pitha*. As I followed the musicians, crossing by the drier if less auspicious route of the bridge, it seemed to be pulling me closer to the core of tantric philosophy in the valley and the power struggle upon which the fortunes of the last Malla king of Kathmandu had spun.

Alone of the three Malla kings, Jaya Prakasha had understood the threat posed by Prithvi Narayan Shah. As the king of Gorkha began his twenty-year siege of the valley, conquering, one by one, smaller outlying hill-kingdoms, squeezing the ancient trade routes, Jaya Prakasha Malla was spurred into action. He began recruiting professional mercenaries from India into his army and performing special *pujas* to Taleju and the royal Kumari in order to increase his strength. In Nepal Samvat 872 (1743 CE), the year snow fell in Kathmandu – a rare and inauspicious occurrence – Jaya Prakasha presented the Living Goddess with a garland of gold coins and pipal leaves weighing 21 *tolas* (about 245 g).

The following year, however, the fortress of Nuwakot fell to Prithvi Narayan Shah and Jaya Prakasha Malla's attempt to recapture it ended in disaster. The Goddess seemed to be turning away from him. Exasperated by the defeat, Jaya Prakasha put the commander of his army, Kasiram Thapa, and several of his colleagues to death. It was a deeply unpopular move. In protest, several other Thapa commanders defected to the Gorkha side, handing over forts on the north-east of the valley to Prithvi Narayan Shah. Kasiram Thapa's brother took office under Ranajit Malla as the commander of Bhaktapur, rather than remain in Jaya Prakasha's service.

Shortly afterwards, the Pradhans – powerful Newar nobles
– took advantage of the political unrest to attack the king of
Patan, gouging out his eyes. Though there had been no love lost
between Jaya Prakasha Malla and his younger half-brother, he was
outraged by this assault. He invited the Pradhans and their wives
to Kathmandu but instead of entertaining them on their arrival
he imprisoned them, and for several days forced them to beg for
a handful of beaten rice from every shop in the city before letting
them go.

Smarting from their public humiliation the Pradhans threw in
their lot with a disaffected and ambitious minister called Taudhik,
brother of one of the commanders who had been put to death with
Kasiram Thapa and who had himself been expelled from the court
of Kathmandu by Jaya Prakasha. Taudhik had become the lover
of Jaya Prakasha's wife, Dayavati, and – with the support of the
Pradhans – persuaded the queen to depose Jaya Prakasha, putting
his son, the Crown Prince Jyoti Prakasha, who was then only nine
years old, on the throne in his place.

The plotters chose the day of Maha Navami during Dasain as
their moment to pounce, knowing the king would be distracted
with festival obligations. Jaya Prakasha was forced to flee the city.
He wandered from town to town in the valley desperately seeking
refuge but found none willing to take him in. At last he found himself
at the temple of Guhyeshvari, where, taking as his guru one of
Guhyeshvari's devotees, a powerful *siddha*, he spent two and a half
years learning the arts of *shakti* tantra.

One day – the chronicles relate – a Shakya man, whose
daughter had recently been made Kumari, came to the temple
of Guhyeshvari to make offerings at the *pitha*. Seeing the exiled
raja sitting inside the shrine the noble Shakya was moved to tears.
He entered into conversation with the king, telling him about his
daughter, and Jaya Prakasha asked the Shakya if he would allow
him to worship her.

The Shakya brought his daughter out at dead of night, hidden under a sheet, to Narayanhiti, on the outskirts of the city of Kathmandu. Here the exiled king offered the Kumari a *dakshina* of 150 mohari rupees and, in return, the Kumari gave Jaya Prakasha a flower from the garland she was wearing on her head, assuring him that in four days the throne of Kathmandu would be his once more.

Jaya Prakasha returned to Guhyeshvari *pitha* to give thanks to the Goddess and, taking up the sacred water-pot and dipping it into the water, caught a fish. Jaya Prakasha's guru was deeply impressed by this miraculous *prasad* and, seeing it as a sign, entrusted to him the sword of Guhyeshvari. Grasping the Goddess's fabled weapon in his right hand, Jaya Prakasha Malla rode like the wind for Kathmandu. Beside him an invisible army, sent by the Goddess, cut down all those who stood in his way.

On 1 May 1750 Jaya Prakasha Malla entered Hanuman Dhoka via the auspicious route of the Lion Gate entrance to Taleju Temple and the courtyard of Mul Chowk, to find his treacherous queen Dayavati sitting in her chamber in Mohan Chowk clutching the young prince Jyoti Prakasha to her lap. Jaya Prakasha swept up his son in his arms, covering him in kisses. Then he put all the conspirators to death, including his wife's lover, the Brahmin, Dhanajuju, son of the raj guru; and imprisoned his treacherous queen in the same windowless room in Lakshmipur Chowk where Pratap Malla's father had died.

Turning the course of the Bagmati so that it ran close to Guhyeshvari's *pitha* had been Jaya Prakasha Malla's extravagant gesture of thanks to the Goddess for his restoration. He also built a special *ghat* on the river in front of her temple, with resting-houses for pilgrims, and assigned lands to cover the cost of a daily *arati* at Guhyeshvari's *pitha* and for keeping a lamp burning there continuously every year during the Navaratris of Chaitra Dasain and Dasain.

Once again, it seemed, Guhyeshvari had worked her magic. Within the year Jaya Prakasha Malla had recaptured the fortress of Nuwakot that had been eight years in the hands of Gorkha, and vital provisions once again began to flow into the valley.

To his cousin-kings, too, Jaya Prakasha's remarkable reversal of fortune was, without doubt, the work of Guhyeshvari. Yet, even now, rather than appreciating their common benefit, they continued to compete with him for the Goddess's favour. Ranajit Malla, king of Bhaktapur, dispatched men to steal the water-pot made of gold and gems that Jaya Prakasha had dedicated to Guhyeshvari's *pitha*. Scarcely had the thieves laid hands on the *kalash*, however, than they were struck blind and forced to throw it away and make their escape. Six months later Guhyeshvari's *kalash* was found and restored to its rightful place over the Goddess's *yoni*.

The band of musicians, revived by the sight of Guhyeshvari's Temple and playing fit to bust, ushered in an entourage that had swelled in size as the procession neared its destination. The *khat*, with a few more knocks and dents to commemorate the kamikaze journey, was laid reverently at the foot of the temple steps. The bearers, wiping the sweat from their brows, posed in front of it for photographs, laughing and leaning into each other with thumbs up for their friends' digital cameras. As the final preparations were made for the Goddess's reception up at the temple and the sides of three sacrificed buffaloes were carried in up the steps, a drummer played and people began to dance. In the glow of sunset the colours of the gateway leapt around the entrance, playing on the water-pot in the lotus in the central *torana* above.

As night drew on, the auspicious moment arrived. The *khat* was lifted aloft and passed inside. It was carried up the steps and out of sight into the temple compound where it would circumambulate the *pitha* three times before coming to rest.

Inside Guhyeshvari's inner sanctum Uddhav's father and uncle, having purified and prepared themselves for three days, were waiting to receive the visiting *pratima*. The water-pot and silver lotus that normally covered the *pitha* had been removed to a storeroom and the watery hole was waiting for its double image from Taleju Temple. Just as at Kalaratri during Dasain, the Karmacharya priests of Taleju and Guhyeshvari would begin the secret *gupta puja* at midnight – the most auspicious time for awakening tantric goddesses. Together the priests would reconnect the Goddess Beyond and the Goddess Within, celebrating the energetic bond between the two, meditating on the origin of all things, dissolving physical being in union with the divine, perpetuating the worship that King Jagajjaya Malla had pulled into being two centuries ago. The next morning the *pratimas* of Guhyeshvari would be exchanged once again and the Taleju Temple image would be lifted back on to her palanquin for the journey home.

As I wandered back towards Kathmandu along the route she would take the following day, around the side of the hill, down towards the cremation *ghats* of Pashupati, I pondered on the role of the divine feminine in the history of the subcontinent, on her ability to continue subverting and transforming received doctrine, bending powerful kings, and even the gods themselves, to her sway. Above me, a sparse, litter-strewn wood was all that remained of Mrigasthali, the mythical forest where Shiva as Pashupatinath, Lord of the Beasts, once ran wild with leopards and deer.

Shiva's own craving to enter feminine form is told in a story from the Puranas describing how the mythical King Ila, on a hunting trip, had happened upon a grove where he found the god Shiva making love with his wife. The king was astounded to see that Shiva had taken the form of a woman in order to please his beloved. Everything in the woods, even the trees, had become female, and as he approached the divine couple, King Ila, too, was turned into a woman. Shiva just laughed, and told King Ila he could ask for any boon he liked – anything, except masculinity.

Here, it seems, is the root of the survival of Goddess worship – in stories that chart the dominance and sublimation, the ebb and flow, of the divine feminine. Like so many myths related in Nepal they revel in the subversion of stereotypes and demonstrate how the Goddess herself, in her myriad, ubiquitous forms, keeps religion fluid, breaking boundaries and preventing ideas from solidifying into dogma. The Goddess's realm is indefinable, her playground the unfathomed expanses of the unconscious, seat of wild and transgressive notions. Throughout valley history she has defied those elements of human nature that tended towards hegemony and control, and orthodox, reductive ways of thinking – aspects that are more associated with masculinity and the patriarchal religions. It is these certainties that the Goddess continues to break down.

I continued down between the avenues of *lingas*, observing how each *linga* rises from its own vulva-shaped plinth, carved with an encircling channel and a pronounced lip from which the *linga's* milky libations can flow. Even where there is no visible *yoni*, where large boulders thrust straight up from the ground, the presence of the *yoni* is implicit. The *yoni* is the earth itself. Without the *yoni*, and the *linga's* desire to be rooted there, the *linga* is lifeless.

A little way off the path a knot of people had gathered. There were gasps coming from a late-evening group of tourists and encouraging jeers from a gaggle of Nepali boys. One of Pashupati's resident *sadhus*, a naked ash-covered Naga Baba, was hanging bricks from his penis. As I drew closer the *sadhu* released the sling of bricks and, as deftly as stretching dough around a rolling pin, wound his penis around a stick and passed it through his legs. Holding the stick at hip height behind him with both hands, he nodded to an assistant who adroitly hopped up, like a bird on to its perch. Incredibly, even with another man's weight supported on his coiled *linga*, the Naga Baba was still smiling.

The forces of the divine feminine are at work even behind displays of machismo like this. By using the *linga* in this way, by destroying the erectile tissue and the *linga's* sensitivity, the Linga Baba was directing his sexual energy within, converting semen into *shakti*, forcing the seed back to its source. Through force of will he could raise the creative energy of the *kundalini*, lying dormant in coils like a snake at the base of his spine, up through his body, piercing the *chakras* one by one, until it breaks through the top of his skull, opening the legendary thousand-petalled lotus of the *sahasrara chakra* and flooding his whole being with indescribable bliss. In this way he was transforming his propensity for physical

arousal into a spiritual awakening; converting his own desire to
have sex and procreate into a rocket-fuelled charge to reach the
source of creation itself. This is mind over matter – the impulse
at the heart of tantra.

It is also, for the *shakti tantrika*, the relationship that is implicit
between Shiva and the Hidden Goddess. Tomorrow, before making
her riotous journey back to Kathmandu, the *pratima* of Guhyeshvari
from Taleju Temple would enter the Golden Temple of Pashupati.
She would circumambulate the *chaturmukha linga* three times,
revivifying it with *shakti*, raising the god's kundalini.

Guhyeshvari's visit signifies the hidden worship of the Shiva *linga*.
Unknown to most worshippers, every night at midnight the tantric
priests of Pashupati perform a secret *puja* in the Golden Temple,
constructing a Sri Yantra made of sandalpaste mixed with saffron
on the upper face of the *chaturmukha linga*. The *yantra* honours
the Goddess as the epitome of the gods: the four faces of the *linga*
– Shiva, Surya, Vishnu and the Buddha – combined. A handful of
this paste was taken every day as prasad to the king, who received
it reciting the name of Pashupatinath in a female form – *Om
Pashupatinatha Raja Rajeshvari Bhattarika*.

The hidden worship of Guhyeshvari is a perfect paradigm of
religious life in the valley, where what is happening out in the
open is so often at odds with – or at least a remove from – what
is happening concurrently, out of sight, or just around the corner.
On ceremonial occasions and before embarking on an important
journey, the king would come in full view of the public to the Golden
Temple to worship Pashupati but as he made his offerings to Shiva
it was the worship of the Goddess he kept in his mind. This was
his *sadhana* – his permanent realization – as a *shakti tantrika*: that
whenever and wherever he worshipped, he was, above and beyond
all, worshipping the Goddess; and at Pashupati he was, first and
foremost, worshipping Guhyeshvari. In the words of the eighth-
century *Nishisancara Tantra* 'I seek Pashupati, the Lord of Beasts,
the god seated in Nepal, united with the Hidden Goddess'.

Before heading back up the streets of old Deopatan to the ring road, I paused by the *ghats* of the Brahmins and nobility where centuries of Nepali kings had been cremated, their queens and concubines sacrificing themselves on the funeral pyre like the goddess Sati – until the practice was outlawed in 1920. Kings like Jaya Prakasha Malla had come here to die, lying with the waters of the Bagmati trickling over their feet as they passed away, their souls guaranteed immediate release from the cycle of rebirth. This is where, not so long ago, the bodies of King Birendra, Queen Aishwarya, King Dipendra and eight other members of the royal family had been consumed by flames.

As I looked down into the treacly Bagmati, its meagre pre-monsoon waters clogged with plastic bags and rotting offerings, the river seemed to be struggling to release these traumatic events into the disembodiment of history. I thought of Gyanendra and wondered whether he, too, had been receiving the Goddess's blessings from the tip of Shiva's *linga* over the past few dramatic weeks; whether like Pratap Malla, and Jaya Prakasha, the last Malla king of Kathmandu, he might even, secretly, have been seeking empowerment at Guhyeshvari's *pitha*.

From one of the ghats a pyre was billowing smoke, charred human limbs jutting out between lumps of wood – a signal reminder of the fundamental precept of Hindu tantra: that Shiva without *shakti* is 'shava' – a corpse.

Chapter 22

The Circle of Bliss

After venturing into the Hindu mysteries of Guhyeshvari and meeting the chief Hindu priest of the Kumari, I knew I needed to balance the books, to explore the tantric worship of the Kumari from the Buddhist side. I needed to meet Uddhav Karmacharya's Buddhist counterpart – the royal Buddhist priest.

Owing to the royal patronage of the Kathmandu Kumari and the increasing influence of orthodox Hinduism in the valley over the years, the Hindu aspects of the tradition, especially the theatrical pageants of Indra Jatra and the bloodthirsty dramas of Dasain, have tended to dominate the stage in recent years, while the older, Buddhist practice has withdrawn into the shadows. When Nepalis talk of the Goddess embodied by the royal Kumari, they generally speak of Durga or Taleju, rarely Vajradevi or Vajravarahi. But Vajrayana is fundamental to the very existence of the Living Goddess. Kumari worship continues to depend, root and branch, on the participation of the Newar Buddhist community and the cooperation of the Vajracharyas.

The royal Buddhist priest himself was now too frail to conduct *nitya puja* at the Kumari Chen every morning so his son, Manjushri, acted for him. We were on familiar terms by now and would exchange pleasantries when we encountered each other at the Kumari Chen. Manjushri would enter the courtyard at the same time every morning, on his way to work, motorbike helmet under one arm, plastic bag containing *puja* materials in the other. He was hesitant about discussing his role, however. Unlike the Newar Hindu priest, the charismatic Uddhav Karmacharya, he seemed nervous about talking to outsiders. He didn't have the authority to speak about these things on his own, he said. Then, one day, he offered to take me to his father.

It was nine in the morning – late by Nepali standards – and Puspa Ratna Vajracharya was still in his bed. Only four days earlier the venerable royal Buddhist priest, or Raj Gubhaju, had celebrated his *bura janko* – the Newar life-cycle ritual marking his attainment of the age of seventy-seven years, seven months and seven days, having seen 950 full moons in his lifetime. The family house in Maru Bahi where Puspa Ratna had been born – an old Buddhist courtyard just beyond the pavilion of Kasthamandap – was festooned with paper flags and the five auspicious leaves – mango, bamboo, banyan, pipal and cane. Strings of fairy lights were hanging from the top floor. In the street outside, tied with red ribbons, were the two palanquins that had carried Puspa Ratna and his wife on their triumphant *jatra* of the neighbourhood.

Newars believe the old-age ceremony confers almost godly status on a person but in Puspa Ratna's case this achievement seemed superfluous. He was already renowned for his accomplishments as a *siddha* – an enlightened state he was believed to have reached over a lifetime of tantric practice. His supernatural powers were widely recognized in the Newar community who came to him for healing or to ask for help with the removal of some obstacle in the way of personal happiness or success.

Puspa Ratna – 'Flower Jewel' – Vajracharya had been Raj Gubhaju for twenty-three years, having inherited the role on the death of his father, Ratna Man Vajracharya, in 1982. The title dates back to the time of the Malla kings when the Raj Gubhaju acted as chief priest for the kingdom of Kathmandu. The Shah dynasty had subsequently enlisted their own Parbatiya 'Raj Guru' for religious performances at court but the hereditary position of the Buddhist Royal Priest retains deep spiritual force among the Newars and its duties are still wide-ranging. The Raj Gubhaju conducts some of the most important rituals in the valley such as the lime-washing worship of Swayambhu *stupa*, temple renovations, *pujas* at Pratappur and Anantapur, and the twelve-yearly worships of Bhimsen, Bijeshvari and Vajrayogini at Sankhu and Pharping.

One of the Raj Gubhaju's most important roles is as senior member of the 'Pancha Buddha' – the five Vajracharyas who officiate at Kumari Jatra and other ceremonies involving the Living Goddess. The 'Pancha Buddha' attend these occasions as living personifications of the Five Transcendent, or Meditational, Buddhas. Dressed in their full regalia, leading the Kumari's chariot through the city, they cut exotic figures, with their gilt-copper *chaitya*-shaped helmets embossed with bejewelled images of the Pancha Jina Buddha and carrying *vajra*-bells in their left hands; each robed in a different colour – red, blue, green, yellow and white – according to the colours manifested by the Buddhas. As Raj Gubhaju, Puspa Ratna was responsible for selecting the other four members of the Pancha Buddha. He himself wore white, the colour of the central Buddha, Vairochana.

Despite their position at the front of the procession, however, most non-Newar spectators at Indra Jatra are unaware of the significance of the Pancha Buddha. Many people have no idea who they are, Indra Jatra being fundamentally a Hindu celebration, a state ritual. Newar Buddhists, while playing their role in it, have never tried to dominate the machinery of state. These acclaimed tantric Buddhist priests simply merge into the general pageantry.

The Raj Gubhaju's primary responsibility, however – and the role to which he devoted the best part of his attention – was as *dya pala*, 'deity guardian', of the Kumari Chen. All regular Buddhist rituals connected with the Living Goddess were conducted by him.

The old royal priest's son, Manjushri Vajracharya, showed me into a small shadowy room where his father was sitting on an unmade bed. On the wall above the bed was a painting of Swayambhu *stupa* surrounded by the nine planets, with the Pancha Buddha seated on lotuses hovering above it.

At first, the sight of the Raj Gubhaju in an old Adidas tracksuit, a stained brown blanket pulled over his head, took me aback. I wondered if the venerable sage was still suffering the effects of his old-age celebration. The shaving of his head and piercing of his ears, the bumpy *jatra* in a palanquin, followed by an elaborate fire sacrifice, auspicious sips of rice wine and a feast of seventy-seven different dishes must have taken their toll. Eight hundred people had attended the occasion – friends, neighbours, office associates, other Vajracharya priests and four generations of Puspa Ratna's family – every single one of them bowing before him in turn, ritually washing themselves in the water from his foot-plate, presenting offerings and receiving *prasad*. It must have been tiring, even for a Vajra Master accustomed to conducting rituals for days at a time. Puspa Ratna's face, covered in liver spots and white stubble, looked washed out. His large, beaked nose, unusual for a Newar, gave him the air of a ruffled eagle.

But there was more than simply a day or two's overexertion behind the old priest's pallor. Puspa Ratna's health was failing and the old man's lack of concern for outward appearances indicated a withdrawal from the world of the senses. As Newars pass the milestones of their *bura jankos* (the next at the age of eighty-four years, four months and four days, when they have witnessed a thousand full moons; followed by the grandest of all, at the age of ninety-nine years, nine months, and nine days, after 1200 full moons), their status rises in the eyes of the community to a rank comparable to gods or royalty, and society accords them the privilege of relinquishing material responsibility. Gradually, approaching closer and closer to divinity, they begin to disentangle themselves from ordinary life in preparation for death.

The old priest peered at me through rheumy eyes as I entered the room, made my salutations and sat down on a chair by the bed.

Manjushri sent for some tea. I began by asking the old Vajracharya what the Kumari stood for, in Buddhist eyes.

'The Goddess gives us different forms of herself, according to our ability to see,' Puspa Ratna began to explain in a husky voice. 'In each *yuga* it is different.'

In Satya Yuga, the Golden Age, he said, she had appeared fiery in colour, as Vajrayogini, the supreme deity of the tantric Buddhist pantheon – the female essence of all Buddhas. In Treta Yuga she had manifested herself as Vasundhara, goddess of the earth and the harvest, and was yellow. In Dwapara Yuga she had appeared as Mahalaxmi, goddess of wealth and good fortune, orange in colour.

'Now, in Kali Yuga, she appears to us as Kumari – and she is red.'

It is our own limitations that cause the Goddess to manifest in this way, he said, echoing the sentiments of his Hindu counterpart. In this age of Kali, the era of disintegration and violence, the Kumari – the Goddess as a human being – is the image we are most able, in our reduced circumstances, to see. Perhaps it is also the one we now most need to see. But, Puspa Ratna said, it is becoming increasingly difficult to establish the Goddess inside a living child. He drew his blanket closer about him, silver lozenge-shaped rings on the fourth fingers of both hands – decorations from his old-age ceremony – catching the light as it began to filter in through the window.

'It requires the power of Vajrayana to do the Goddess's bidding, to pull her into human form,' the old priest said. 'But these days the conditions make it very difficult for a Vajracharya to do the practice to acquire these powers. There are many obstacles in the way of getting *siddhi*.'

Modern life, with all the preoccupations of making money and no time for the lengthy process of training and meditation, is one of the problems, he said. But there is also the question of peace and quiet. The valley has become a very noisy place in recent years, full of roads and traffic, loud music and electric light at all hours. Not only is this distracting to the mind, it puts actual physical barriers in the way of *pradakshina*, meditational pilgrimage – one of the crucial ways a Vajracharya acquires tantric knowledge.

'For a Vajracharya, one of the most important ways of acquiring *siddhi*,' the old man said, 'is the practice we call "Pitha Sewa" – Serving the Power-Places. These are the twenty-four *pithas* represented by the *chakras* of Chakrasamvara Mandala.'

Newar Buddhists – Puspa Ratna explained – consider the Kathmandu Valley to correspond to a sacred design of three protective circles, or '*chakras*'. Each *chakra* is formed by eight power-places. These are the *pithas* of the Astamatrika, the Mother Goddesses – twenty-four in all. The first *chakra* rings the perimeter of the city. The second forms a ring inside the valley. The third, in the foothills, encircles the valley itself.

'A Vajracharya must do Pitha Sewa at least once in his lifetime,' said Puspa Ratna.

Usually a group of Vajracharyas from the main *bahals* of Kathmandu make this pilgrimage together. Over the course of a year they visit one shrine every half of the lunar month, performing special *pujas* and visualizations to each of the twenty-four goddesses of Chakrasamvara Mandala in turn.

The *mandala* is a concept fundamental to Newar Buddhism. Like the *yantra*, the *mandala* is a geometric form delineating sacred space and embodying divinity; but over time, and under Mahayana Buddhist influence, it has developed infinitely greater detail and become a highly complex meditational tool. The most obvious forms of *mandala* are in sacred paintings, or *paubhas*. The intricate, brightly coloured designs are displayed in the shop windows of Thamel or Patan and are often bought by tourists for their beauty alone.

The paintings, though, are not merely pictorial images on a flat canvas, as most non-Buddhists see them. In the eye of the meditational practitioner, the *mandala* – like the *yantra* – is beyond two-dimensional, beyond even three-dimensional; it is infinitely expansive and representative of boundless states of being.

The multidimensional nature of the *mandala*, and the way it resonates in the Newar mind on many different levels at once, is reflected in Newar architecture. Everywhere in the Kathmandu Valley, temples, *stupas*, *bahals* and votive *chaityas*, water fountains and public bathing tanks – and the Kumari Chen itself – have been built as *mandalas*. Like the *mandalas* in paintings, these constructions are geometrically perfect, usually square, with entrances in the four directions. Doorways, garlanded and surmounted by elaborate *toranas*, correspond with the bejewelled entrances leading into the divine palace on painted *mandalas*. Carved mouldings and cornices running around the walls of a building or the rim of a bathing tank denote the protective *raksha chakras*.

The centre of the *mandala*, where the principal deity resides, is key. In Buddhist *bahals* it is usually pinpointed by a *chaitya* in the middle of the courtyard, representing Swayambhu, while in Hindu courtyards it is commonly a Shiva *linga*. In artificial ponds and bathing tanks – like Nag Pokhari, next to Narayanhiti Palace – the mandalic centre point is marked by a golden snake's head, the king of the Nagas, rising through the water.

All Newars – even regular householders and non-initiates – are aware of these *mandalas* as they go about their daily life. Even if, as lay people, they remain largely ignorant of the esoteric visualizations and meditations practised by the tantric adepts, they nonetheless rely on the religious professionals to activate the *mandalas'* powers on their behalf. Regular tantric worship of *mandalas* is believed not only to empower the practitioner but to bestow blessings and protection on the wider community, generating a state of happiness and prosperity on all the people who live in or use them.

On a larger scale, the city itself is considered to be a *mandala*, with the divine palace at the centre, encircled by the *raksha chakra* of the city walls, and beyond them the *smasana* – the wild and dangerous regions of the dead where the butchers' yards and cremation *ghats* are located, the realms of fear and illusion.

However, the practice of Pitha Sewa the old priest was describing expands the concept of the *mandala* even further – to the valley itself.

'Chakrasamvara *mandala* is the *"Maha Mandala"* – the Great Mandala of the Valley of Nepal,' the old priest explained, 'but it is also the *mandala* here, the *mandala* of the body.' His hand hovered lightly for a moment over his chest.

I concentrated hard as I prepared to follow the old priest into the realms of tantric psychology. The teachings of Chakrasamvara, he said, are the esoteric visualizations that had, according to Newar tradition, been revealed to the great *bodhisattva* Manjushri by Guhyeshvari at the beginning of historical time when Manjushri drained the lake and made it habitable for human beings. They are the teachings that Manjushri had, in turn, transmitted to Shantikar Acharya, the first Vajracharya of Newar Buddhism. They are at the heart of the secret worship carried out by tantric Buddhists every day in every *agam* in the valley. These are the teachings behind the worship of the Living Goddess herself. They relate the Goddess with the Valley of Kathmandu and every initiated Vajracharya, man and woman, who lives within it.

The pilgrimage of the Vajracharya around the three rings of Astamatrika in the valley manifests the fundamental principles of Newar Buddhism. The three geographical circles in the valley correspond with the three nerve centres or 'plexuses' located in the human body and identified with the 'Three Bodies' of the Buddha. This physical and meditational pilgrimage brings the Vajracharya to the realization of how the world is mirrored in his own body, of how mastery of the self is to be achieved by conscious control of the body and how this control culminates in the resolution of individual existence and the attainment of *nirvana*. In effect, the old priest summarized, the practice of Pitha Sewa awakes in the Vajracharya the awareness that his own body is a *mandala*.

'The Vajracharya's way outside, his visit to the twenty-four *pithas* in the valley,' Puspa Ratna said, 'is a way to find the Buddha within himself; it is a way to acquire *siddhi*. One who has performed this Pitha Sewa, who has got *siddhi*, can do it again without physically moving; he can project himself to these places through his own will.'

Puspa Ratna was twelve or thirteen years old when he did Pitha Sewa under the auspices of his father. They went on foot, taking special precautions to purify themselves and being careful not to touch anybody. They stayed one night at every *pitha* and practised tantra there throughout the night.

'Nowadays it is very difficult to do Pitha Sewa,' said Puspa Ratna. 'There is so much traffic. It is difficult to walk and there are so many people it is impossible not to touch someone. People have built houses near the *pithas* – even right next to the cremation grounds – so now there is noise and electric light everywhere. For *siddhi* it has to be dark, and quiet.'

When Puspa Ratna completed his Pitha Sewa as a boy in the 1940s, part of the city walls would still have been standing, and most – if not all – of the *pithas* would have been located in cremation grounds away from any other dwelling and auspiciously close to sources of flowing water. There would have been gigantic shadowy trees – cedars, jacarandas, pipals and plane trees – no tall modern buildings, few roads and no vehicles other than the occasional ox-cart. It was easy to imagine how frightening the atmosphere of these *pithas* would have been in Puspa Ratna's day, especially at night. I remembered vividly my visit to some of them with Laxminath during the blood sacrifices of Dasain, with haunting echoes of cannibalism and the suggestive presence of all manner of ghosts.

And this is, at least partly, the intention. In order to acquire the powers of *siddhi*, the *tantrika* first has to overcome his or her fears of pain, disease and death. He has to pass, literally and metaphorically, through the terrifying realms of the cremation grounds before he can enter the temple of divinity, the sacred inner space delineated by the *raksha chakras*. This Vajracharya practice is normally carried out in a small group but the most powerful Pitha

Sewa of all is conducted by a Vajra Master and his wife braving these challenges alone.

But now other obstacles stood in the Vajracharya's way. Several of the *pithas* in the inner circle – the Circle of Thought – ringing the city itself had, in recent years, become difficult to access. One had been enclosed within the heavily fortified grounds of Narayanhiti Palace; another, close to Army Headquarters, had been isolated six months earlier, the public road barricaded with sandbags manned by sentries with bullet-proof vests and pistols. The *pithas* of the middle circle out in the countryside – the Circle of Speech – and the outer circle – the Circle of the Body – in the foothills around the valley, were also under siege. Swathes of new buildings – extravagant houses with Disney World turrets and Doric pillars – were springing up in the rice fields around them, and everywhere traditional farmland seemed to be passing into non-Newar hands, restricting access to sacred sites.

Back in his bedroom Puspa Ratna had closed his eyes. The squeals and shouts of little boys returning from the waterspout at Maru Hiti filled the courtyard.

'Have you done Pitha Sewa?' I asked Manjushri, filling the silence.

'Not yet,' the younger priest answered, 'but I hope to – soon … sometime.'

Puspa Ratna opened his eyes again. 'He must go with a group of Vajracharyas,' he said, looking gravely across at Manjushri. 'But these days there are not so many Vajracharyas who can go.'

It was difficult to find a group of initiated Buddhist priests with the time, or inclination, to perform such a lengthy *pradakshina*, he said, harder still to find a Vajracharya with the knowledge to lead them.

'I am instructing my son,' the old priest went on, his face clouding, 'but he has come to his path late and I am old. He is not an expert. He has much to learn and there is little time left for me to pass on the teachings.'

Manjushri had received his Monastic Ordination or *bare chuyegu* in 1970 when he was eight years old; followed, in the same week, by *achah lueyegu* – the Vajracharya Initiation. The Vajracharya Initiation had inducted Manjushri into some preliminary priestly practice and he had learnt further Vajracharya ritual worship from his father and grandfather over the years; but he had only received *diksha* – full tantric initiation, qualifying him for entry into the *agam* – twenty-eight years later, in 1998.

'I have been preoccupied,' Manjushri admitted sheepishly, 'with running my business.' Manjushri was an administrator at the pharmaceutical Royal Drug Company Ltd.

Only now was Manjushri coming to terms with the complex worship of Chakrasamvara Mandala. Every day, as he conducted the morning rituals at the Kumari Chen in his father's place, after awakening the images of the Pancha Buddha in the ground floor shrine, he would disappear upstairs to activate the deities in the tantric Buddhist *agam* beneath the Kumari's throne room. Though he would not refer to them by name, the deities in the *agam*, as I now understood it, were Chakrasamvara and Vajravarahi – the deities at the heart of the *mandala* – the same deities that are worshipped in most of the *bahals* in the valley, and in most Buddhist household *agams*; that empowered initiates like Gyanman Vajracharya and his brothers, and all the other Shakyas and Vajracharyas who had taken *diksha*. Locked in a dissolving state of sexual climax, their erotic palpitating dance conjuring up an aura of burning flames, this is an image intended only ever to be seen by initiates. Since the 1960s, though, these exquisite figures – most of them stolen – have been making their way on to the art market and replicas are now sold openly in galleries and tourist shops. To Manjushri, the people that buy them see only the surface beauty of the figures; they do not have the eyes to see the transformative power that lies within.

As Manjushri described for me the stages of his *puja*, the hierarchy of the levels of worship was striking: the Five Transcendent Buddhas in the *kvapah dyah* on the ground floor rising up into the state of bliss generated from Chakrasamvara's union with the goddess Vajravarahi in the *agam* on the first floor; Vajravarahi, in turn – the supreme deity, 'mother' of the Transcendent Buddhas – rising to manifest herself as the Living Goddess in her throne room on the third.

'Vajravarahi is the *"sambhoga kaya"* – the bliss-body of the fully enlightened Buddha,' Puspa Ratna said, 'and the Kumari is the *"nirmana kaya"* – the transformation body of Vajravarahi.'

I asked Puspa Ratna if the Kumari ever enters the Buddhist *agam* at the Kumari Chen, to be directly invoked with the spirit of Vajravarahi; as she does when she enters the Singhasan to be invoked with the spirit of Taleju by the Hindu priest.

'Normally, the Raj Gubhaju performs daily worship of the tantric deities on his own. He has the power to do this. The Kumari need not be present,' the old priest said. 'But on the tenth day of the dark half of every month we perform a special *puja* called Dishi Puja. That is when the Kumari enters the *agam*.'

Dishi Puja – also known as Dashami Puja or Tenth Day Puja – is performed on the tenth day of the dark fortnight of each lunar month by senior-most members of every *bahal*. It commemorates the day that the *bodhisattva* Manjushri received the teachings of Chakrasamvara from Guhyeshvari. It is a *puja* of particular significance at the Kumari Chen. Twice a year – on the 10th of Marga in winter and on the 10th of Jestha in summer – Dishi Puja is commemorated with a 'great vermilion worship' involving all the Pancha Buddha and lasting all day.

Puspa Ratna was careful not to enter into details but from his general description, Dishi Puja, like all other *pujas* conducted in the *agam*, involved powerful visualizations. Using *mantras* and *mudras* the royal Vajracharya, seated in front of the little Kumari on her *agam* throne, the goddess Vajravarahi activated within her, would begin to ignite the inner heat of Vajravarahi within himself. As the purifying fire of the Goddess destroyed the impurities of his inner body, giving rise to the generation of cosmic energy and the experience of *mahasukha* – all-consuming bliss – the tantric *siddha* would become one with the divinity inside the Kumari. The priest and the Kumari – Puspa Ratna indicated – become interchangeable. The tantric priest becomes the Goddess herself.

'When we perform these *pujas* we have to generate great devotion in our heart-mind. We repeat to ourselves over and over again – "may this benefit all living beings". We have to have the feeling that the Goddess is actually our own self,' Puspa Ratna explained. 'All the time we are doing these visualizations we are keeping the feeling, the motivation, let us be like the Goddess so that – like her – we can work for the welfare of others.' The practice, he said, generates in the practitioner a feeling of *maitritva bhavana* – all-encompassing kindness and goodwill towards all sentient beings; the limitless, unconditional love of the universal mother.

To the royal Buddhist priest the Kumari is, herself, a *mandala*; she is the blueprint of divinity manifested in human form; the archetype that shows the way, opening the route to enlightenment, to the powers of *siddhi*, inside the practitioner's own body. At the same time, worshipping the Kumari as the Goddess Vajravarahi activates the powers of Chakrasamvara Mandala, keeping the wheels of protective energy turning around the city of Kathmandu and the valley itself, showering the Goddess's blessings on all its inhabitants.

While I had been refreshed by a continuous supply of tea and biscuits, Puspa Ratna had not touched a thing. He had not yet performed morning worship of the deities in the household *agam* and until he had completed this *puja* nothing would pass his lips. I left the old man in peace so he could reunite himself with Chakrasamvara and Vajravarahi.

As I walked back through the city streets I was overwhelmed by a sense of loss. How much knowledge would die with Puspa Ratna before he had a chance to transmit it to his son? All over the city, throughout the valley, the same process is affecting the transmission of Vajrayana – a younger generation too busy and distracted, too caught up in the wheels of commerce and the demands of earning a living, to concentrate on the disciplines of inner revelation.

A few generations ago there had been many hundreds of full-time Vajracharya priests in Kathmandu. Now there are only about a hundred and fifty, and they are hard-pressed to make a living. Fifty years ago a Buddhist priest might have expected 2500 households as his customers; now he has only five or six. There are fewer demands for the services of Buddhist priests now and payments have not increased over time. It is virtually impossible to be a priest with services to the community as your only source of income – which means no time for studying sacred texts and practices, or acquiring the intense meditational focus and self-discipline that Vajrayana demands. Who knows what flowers and jewels of the *dharma* could be dying with the loss of *siddhas* like Puspa Ratna, I thought, and whether there will be Vajracharya priests in future generations who believe they have the power to pull the Goddess into a living child.

Chapter 23

The Fall of the Shah Dynasty

Eight months after Gyanendra seized power the tide began to turn against him. As always in Nepal the decisive moment – the traditional time for engaging in battle – came at the end of monsoon with passable roads, crops in the ground and a chance for communities to regroup. Suddenly, it seemed, after the better part of a year on the back foot, the nation was of one mind and ready for action. In September 2005 the Maoists announced another ceasefire. Now, whatever people's political affiliations, be they Maoist, United-Marxist-Leninist (UML), Nepali Congress or any of the other myriad political factions springing up in the country, the biggest obstacle in everyone's path was the king.

The king himself, though, clearly entertained no thoughts of reversal. During the fortnight of Dasain in October 2005, Gyanendra performed overtly public *pujas* at all the major power-places of the Kathmandu Valley, including the Astamatrika *pithas* around the capital and the *pitha* of Guhyeshvari. And he kept a close eye on the stars. In November the royal astrologers advised Gyanendra to leave the country for a couple of weeks. Mars was in the ascendant and the aggressive planetary influence did not bode well for the monarch at home.

To the protesters and political activists in the country, though, the king's departure could not have been more fortuitous. Some even dared hope that Gyanendra was preparing his exit – rumour had it he was looking at properties where he could live in exile on the east coast of Africa. In the king's absence, the Maoist rebels and seven main political parties seized the chance to sign an accord. 'It is our understanding,' their agreement read, 'that unless the autocratic rule is ended and full democracy is restored, there will be no peace or progress in the country.'

By December, however, the king had returned to Narayanhiti Palace, clearly undeterred. But the mood on the streets remained determined. Once again, armoured personnel carriers mounted with machine guns were ordered into the capital and leaders of the main political parties were placed under house arrest. By January 2006 the demonstrations had swelled to tens of thousands. The king blocked Internet and telephone communications again and extended the curfew in all the major towns and cities. The central Durbar Squares of Patan, Bhaktapur and Kathmandu – traditional foci of political agitation – were locked down, armed police stationed on the steps of the pagoda temples.

But this time the demonstrators would not be deflected. National strikes were called, endorsed, now, universally by the political leaders. The People's Movement, the Jana Andolan of 1990, was springing back to life. Seventeen years on, the democratic movement had broadened its base, the risks and the rewards no longer restricted to the affluent classes of Kathmandu. The hunger for self-government, the thirst for peace, had been gnawing at the country's core.

In an effort to recover his footing and regain international support King Gyanendra announced municipal elections. Now, though, the Nepali political parties refused to be fobbed off with a vote they knew could be nothing more than a 'fig leaf for Gyanendra's autocratic rule'. Only the restoration of full democracy would satisfy the people.

The king scheduled the elections – the first in the country for seven years – for February 2006 but the seven main political parties called for a national boycott and the Maoists, characteristically, promised to maim anyone taking part. Gyanendra responded by ordering security forces to 'shoot to kill' anyone trying to disrupt the elections and this, in the south-western district of Dang, they did – opening fire on 150 protesters who were trying to prevent people voting, killing one person and seriously injuring several others.

Turnout – perhaps unsurprisingly – was less than 20 per cent. In more than half the seats voting had to be postponed or cancelled because 600 candidates had decided not to stand, some of them judiciously slipping away to go on pilgrimage to India. In the eastern town of Dhankuta, just hours before polls opened, the Maoists launched a major assault, bombing government buildings and destroying the local bank. Across the country the remaining candidates were rounded up by police and forced to stay inside heavily guarded compounds 'for their own protection'.

Though the elections were only for mayors and local councils, this was the battleground upon which the king had staked his flag and, whether the low turnout was the result of a genuine boycott or fear of reprisals by Maoists and the heavy-handed security forces, the farcical outcome was another blow to the king's credibility. Yet still Gyanendra refused to yield.

Throughout the turbulence Newars continued their religious celebrations, honouring the deities and steering their *jatras* through the trouble spots like ships ploughing through stormy seas. Now, more than ever, the ritual calendar had to be kept on course, the *dyas* persuaded, cajoled, beseeched, to remain on side. Despite the peace-seeking objectives of the festivals, though, violence now often spilled into them.

In March 2006 a heavy police presence inflamed the followers of the three-day annual *jatra* of White Macchendranath around the streets of old Kathmandu. The procession broke out repeatedly into riots, the crowds beaten by police cracking down on their backs and heads with batons and long bamboo staves. On the final day, as the *jatra* reached its climax in Lagan Tol, with the Living Goddess watching, tempers reached boiling point. In the vortex of violent scuffles and counter-charges, the chariot of White Macchendranath was prevented from completing its customary three honorific revolutions of the shrine of the god's mother. The God of Compassion was carried back to his temple – many Newars believed – in a state of grief. Preventing a son from honouring his mother was, they declared, a telling sign of the times.

Violent demonstrations continued in the capital and on 6 April 2006 the coalition of the seven main political parties, backed by the Maoists, declared another national strike. The king responded by arresting over twenty lawyers, doctors and writers for defying the curfew. They included the former Justice at the Supreme Court, the former Speaker of the House of Representatives; Padma Ratna Tuladhar, a senior human rights leader; and Kanak Mani Dixit, one of Nepal's most distinguished journalists and editor of the *Himalayan Times*.

The group of twenty-four – the 'Chaubises' as they called themselves – were taken to Duwakot Armed Police Force Barracks in a sand dune of the Manohara plains together with forty or more political activists from the UML and Congress parties who had been snatched at dawn from their homes. Clearly the king had hoped that extricating these key dissidents from the scene would remove much of the driving force of the protests, but the consequence was the reverse. Imprisonment gave the activists the chance to formulate ideas and consolidate strategies. Their messages were smuggled out of the detention centre by visiting sympathizers and then posted online. The Chaubise blog site became a noticeboard for some of the strongest voices of the rebellion, calling for non-violence and single-minded determination on the part of the protesters; restraint and understanding on the part of the armed forces; and nothing but complete surrender of sovereignty on the part of the king. The long-awaited awakening of civil society had begun.

On 14 March the Maoists imposed an indefinite blockade on the Kathmandu Valley and all other major towns in Nepal. Across the country, roads fell quiet. Within days of the strike being called, with no trucks arriving in the valley, fuel and food began running low in Kathmandu. A week into the blockade the price of those vegetables that were still available rose fivefold; the cost of eggs, chicken and mutton doubled. Petrol was rationed. For months the country's electricity supply had been subject to dry season 'load-shedding' with power-cuts lasting up to eight hours at a time. Now, supplies of drinking water, normally supplemented by the tankers filling up at mountain streams, began to dwindle. Queues of people lined up at old wells and spigots – any that were still functioning – for a few precious litres of cooking water. But the intensifying hardships only strengthened universal resolve. No one wanted to endure these conditions again. Action had to be decisive. The monsoon season would begin again in a month or so. It was now or never.

As tension mounted, monks, priests and lamas began to pray. *Sadhus* vowed not to speak another word until freedom of speech was restored. Political leaders sought to ratchet up the pressure on the king still further by appealing to the people to stop paying taxes, customs duties, interest on loans from state banks, as well as electricity, telephone and water bills from the state-run utilities. Street sweepers and refuse collectors joined the strike. Soon the streets were filled with mountains of putrefying rubbish – an embarrassment to the proud citizens of Kathmandu yet also a true reflection, many felt, of the rotten state of the nation. As bands of demonstrators took to the streets, braving the rubber bullets and baton charges of the security forces, the protest spread to the diaspora. The 1.6 million Nepalis working abroad were urged to stop sending money home, staunching the flow of income – an estimated US$1.2 billion a year – that helped keep the country's economy afloat.

Throughout Kathmandu shops were shuttered, roads deserted, people were confined to their houses and tourists to their hotels. The valley entered an eerie twilight of anticipation. Tyres burned in the streets of Thamel and the markets of the old city as the valley geared up for the biggest demonstration so far. In order to give the mass protest legitimacy the Maoists announced they would stay out of the picture and declared a unilateral ceasefire within the valley.

On Thursday, 20 April 2006, 100,000 people defied the king's shoot-to-kill policy to march on the capital demanding 'loktantra' – the newly coined term for total democracy. They came from the fields and terraces, trekking along village paths, and rallied at six main intersections around the Ring Road, the boundary of the curfew zone.

Several of the protests met with violence. One of worst clashes was at Kalanki, where police fired tear gas at the demonstration as it tried to advance towards the centre of Kathmandu; when that failed, they opened fire with live rounds. Sixty-six people were wounded and three men were killed. A Nepali television station, prevented from relaying film footage of the shootings, showed photographs of bloody bodies being dragged from the scene.

What outraged people even more than the images of murdered civilians, however, were actions taken by the armed forces later in the day. In an effort to hide the fatalities from the press, police in riot gear stormed the hospital where the bodies of the three dead protesters were being held and snatched them away for a summary cremation without any of the customary funerary rites. As news of the desecration spread, portraits of Gyanendra and his wife were hurled out of office windows; straw effigies of the king were set on fire; furious protesters shouted 'Cut off the heads of Gyanendra and his son'.

Two weeks into the uprising, with the demonstrations stronger than ever, the armed police began to show signs of exhaustion and weakening resolve. They had held the protesters – their own people

– at bay, preventing them from penetrating the curfew zone and reaching the palace, but it was clear they would not hold out for much longer. Their allegiance to the king was waning.

On Friday, 21 April, in an attempt to diffuse the explosive situation, a sour-faced Gyanendra appeared on television with a conciliatory statement: 'The Nepalese people have chosen that democracy is a way of life. We return the sovereign power of the country to the countrymen.'

The statement was met with suspicion in the country. The king claimed to be backing down – but was he, really? Gyanendra offered a return to multiparty democracy under a constitutional monarchy – but for the time being, he insisted, power would remain in his hands until such time as elections could be held and a prime minister appointed.

Gyanendra's statement was welcomed with tentative optimism abroad but in Nepal there was no longer the will or the patience for compromise. The day after the king's statement, 100,000 protesters again defied the curfew and took to the streets. This time the police officers, backed by the Royal Nepal Army, for the most part stood by and let them pass through the heavily fortified Ring Road into the city centre. Only at the gates of Narayanhiti Palace were the protesters kept at bay. By mid-afternoon, the seven-party coalition formally rejected the king's offer, vowing to continue the agitation and Prachanda, the Maoist chairman, pronounced the king's statement 'an insult' to the people.

What King Gyanendra had asked the political parties to do, according to the Chaubises, was to set up yet another government with 'executive power' but without legislative authority. This was a far cry from the 'total democracy' that Nepal's 26 million citizens were calling for.

For three days after the king's attempt at conciliation the demonstrations – hundreds of thousands strong – persisted, with the seven-party coalition planning to bring a mass protest of two million people into Kathmandu on 25 April. At last, close to midnight on Monday, 24 April 2006, Gyanendra finally gave in. There was nowhere left for him to turn. The people were calling for his blood at the palace gates and several generals had signalled their reluctance to lead the army against civilians in the capital. In his final televised address, Gyanendra agreed unequivocally to step down as the chief executive of the nation and restore the elected parliament. It was the move the seven-party coalition had been waiting for. The absolute rule of the monarchy was over.

What had happened in those few weeks of civil disobedience in Nepal was nothing short of a miracle. Most unexpected of all had been the almost total reversal of traditional respect for the monarchy in a matter of five years, since the death of King Birendra. No international observer had believed the views of the Nepalis towards their king could change so dramatically in such a short time. As one student protester put it, 'My grandfather viewed the king as a god; my father thought the king stood between god and the devil; I believe the king is the devil. That's the generation gap.'

Two days after King Gyanendra's surrender the Maoists lifted the crippling three-week blockade of roads into the valley and fresh food and fuel once again began arriving in the capital. People took to the streets as protest marches morphed into celebration rallies. The Chaubises and other political agitators were released. On 28 April 2006, parliament convened in the government palace of Singh Durbar for the first time in four years. Girija Prasad Koirala, eighty-four years old and prime minister for the fifth time, was too ill to attend his swearing-in ceremony but in a letter presented to parliament he signalled momentous changes in Nepali politics including, in due course, the drafting of a new constitution by an elected assembly; and, crucially, he offered the hand of political inclusion to his erstwhile enemies, the Maoists.

The reinstated House of Representatives was swift to begin the dismantling of the trappings and privileges of monarchy. By mid-May the 'Government of Nepal' was no longer 'His Majesty's', and the Nepal army and Nepal airlines no longer officially 'royal'. Orders were given for the reprinting of Nepal's currency, starting with the 500-rupee note, on which the portrait of the king was to be replaced by a picture of Sagarmatha – Mt Everest. The first line of the national anthem – 'May glory crown you, courageous Sovereign' – was changed. The king, formerly Supreme Commander of the army, was to sever his links with the military completely. The Privy Council, the powerful advisory body thought to have urged the king to take direct power in 2005, was dissolved. The Raj Parishad, the branch of government that liased with the palace, was shuttered, its files tossed out on to the street. Most significantly, parliament assumed the right to make and change laws regarding the royal succession, the reviled Crown Prince Paras being a worrisome problem yet to be addressed. Meanwhile the king, whose conspicuous wealth and extravagance had mocked the poverty of a nation, was to be subject to tax and his spending controlled.

To all outward appearances the king had been reduced to little more than a figurehead but as the festival of Indra Jatra approached in September many in Kathmandu began to worry that Gyanendra might yet try to manipulate the event to stage a comeback. The ageing prime minister, G.P. Koirala, had himself voiced his reluctance to abolish the monarchy entirely during the current 'sensitive period'.

No one was taking the reinstated democracy for granted. History had a tendency to repeat itself in Nepal and kings an uncanny way of resurrecting themselves. Fearful of a royal rebound, members of the Newa Mukti Morcha (NMM) – the Maoist-affiliated Newar National Liberation Front – appealed to the Newar community and everyone involved in Indra Jatra to boycott the event.

Over the past decade, a growing number of young Newars had begun supporting the Maoists. The unlikely alliance stemmed from a number of shared grievances – loss of indigenous language and autonomy, all of which were historically associated with the Shah monarchy. But land, too, was a burning issue. Following Prithvi

Narayan Shah's conquest of the valley, generations of Shah kings and their Rana regents had taken land from the Newars. Land reform was also a key demand of the Maoists.

There were similarities, too, in ideology. Newar culture, heavily influenced by Buddhism, was still essentially egalitarian in nature even though it had, back in the fourteenth century, been persuaded to accept the Hindu caste system. Even the secret practices of Tantra – which had, over time, become the prerogative of the high priestly castes – were still, in principle, open to any Newar equal to the task of acquiring them.

In attitudes to women, too, there was a striking correlation. The Newars had been resisting patriarchal, misogynistic influences for centuries. But in the remotest regions of Nepal, where no such cultural feminism existed, impoverished, browbeaten, disenfranchised women had found a voice in the Maoists. An estimated 30 per cent of Maoist cadres were women.

On the political platform, at least, Maoist leaders seemed to display an almost Newar ability to walk the political tightrope. 'We are not dogmatic communists,' declared the Maoist leader, Prachanda, in 2006, 'and we are prepared to change and debate our beliefs with anybody.' The Maoists, now, had even signalled their willingness to enter into democratic elections and embrace capitalism.

As preparations for Indra Jatra 2006 were under way, the Maoist-affiliated Newar National Liberation Front unfurled their flags. It was time to remove the Kumari's *tika* from the brow of Gyanendra – they declared, to put a full stop to the Shah dynasty.

But how, was the question. Not even young, Maoist-leaning Newars believed they could force the hand of the Living Goddess. Yet if Gyanendra received her blessing this year, what would it mean for the democratic process, for the hard-fought people's revolution? Despite the extraordinary anti-monarchist feeling manifested in the April uprising there was genuine concern that a single mark made by a child's finger might yet reverse the course of events. Once

again, all eyes were on the forthcoming festival of Indra Jatra and
the actions of the Kumari.

~

The Supreme Court case against the Living Goddess tradition had
rumbled on throughout 2005. It had continued through the long,
impotent months of the king's autocratic rule, gathering participants
and respondents like tumbleweed and blowing directionless this way
and that. At last, on 10 February 2006, as democracy demonstrations
burst on to the streets, the Supreme Court launched an official
inquiry, charging the Ministry of Culture, Tourism and Civil Aviation
with the task of compiling a report into the Kumari tradition and
examining the human-rights implications.

In response, a teacher of culture at Tribhuvan University, Professor
Dr Chunda Bajracharya, filed a counter-case at the Supreme Court,
demanding the preservation of the Kumari tradition. 'Any verdict
impeding continuation of the tradition will violate people's religious
and cultural rights,' she declared.

There was now a compelling subtext to the Kumari investigation.
Coming at such a critical juncture in Nepal's history, the report
would have to clarify, once and for all, the relationship between
the Living Goddess and the king; and what would happen to the
Kumari tradition if, as people had begun to suspect, the monarchy
was to be abolished.

But by the time Indra Jatra came about in September 2006, not
only was there no sign of a report, an investigating committee had
yet to be appointed. Doubt about the future of the royal Kumari
was compounded by the confusion surrounding the position of the
king himself. Gyanendra had been stripped of his powers but he
was still living in Narayanhiti Palace with his wife, with the crown
prince waiting in the wings. He was still enjoying the privileges of
a royal head of state; still performing *pujas* at power-places in the
valley. It was far from clear whether Gyanendra's ambitions had
been decisively thwarted, or – as many suspected – he was, even
now, plotting to regain his power.

On the afternoon of 6 September 2006 – the first day of Kumari Jatra – cadres from the Newar National Liberation Front massed along New Road and Dharmapath distributing leaflets.

'This is a black day!' the leaflets proclaimed. '238 years ago today the Shah king usurped our festival, attacked our country, depriving us of our land, ethnicity, culture and autonomy. Newars became powerless from this day. The Shah dynasty has celebrated Indra Jatra not as a festival belonging to the Newars but in order to flatter themselves. So we call to all people who love the Newar culture, to musicians, dance groups and all those involved in the Kumari Jatra to prevent Gyanendra Shah from participating in the chariot procession of our worshipful Kumari and prevent him from receiving *tika* from Mother Kumari.'

As the king and queen's cavalcade advanced down New Road the Maoist-affiliated Newar youths began shouting anti-monarchist slogans and waving black flags as though attempting to shoo the royal couple away from Durbar Square. Five thousand armed police intervened, caning protesters with bamboo batons and sending three of them to hospital. The royal cortege swept on regardless up to the front of Hanuman Dhoka.

It was a paltry gathering that assembled on the balcony of the old royal palace and an alert, watchful crowd facing them from the steps of the pagoda temples. In an effort to play down the political significance of the occasion none of the usual cabinet ministers and high-ranking government officials attended; and only four ambassadors – from Norway, North Korea, Egypt and Denmark – appeared alongside the king and queen to witness the procession of the Kumari's chariot. Crown Prince Paras was also, wisely, kept away.

Six days later, on the last day of the *jatra*, despite the protests, the king's car drew up outside the Kumari Chen under armed escort and Gyanendra ducked his head beneath the entrance *torana*, mounted the stairs to the Kumari's lion throne room and received his *tika*.

Critics of the Kumari tradition were quick to claim that the fact that the Kumari had given her blessing to the despised Gyanendra, when his authoritarian powers had just been stripped away from him by the will of the people, was proof that the two institutions – King and Kumari – were symbiotically conjoined, that they depended inexorably on each other for survival. The recent *tika* blessing, they argued, demonstrated that the Living Goddess did not, after all, defend the interests of the people or the country, but was an outmoded construct ripe for abolition, like the monarchy itself.

Most non-Newars, however – especially critics of the tradition – were unaware of the historical evolution of Kumari worship: that it not only pre-dated the Shah kings but probably the Malla dynasties, too, and was once a far broader practice involving Living Goddesses all over the valley; and that the Buddhist Living Goddess of Sikhanmu Bahal in Durbar Square was already long established when the last Malla king, Jaya Prakasha, took the unprecedented step of building a separate Kumari Chen for her. The 'royal' Kumari had existed long before royal patronage. To Newars it was inconceivable that the king's demise would also be hers. No one could put an end to a Goddess.

But then how would Newars explain this latest blessing? Why had the Kumari given her *tika* – her empowerment – to a king who so patently had his own, rather than the country's, interests at heart? Why had she not simply withheld her blessing, as she had in the year when King Tribhuvan died? I was keen to know how the caretakers viewed her latest endorsement and asked Jujubhai Shakya if he could spare me a moment at the Kumari Chen.

The official caretaker, Gyan Devi, now in her late sixties, rarely appeared outside the domain of the Kumari's house but her husband, Jujubhai, their sons, Mahendra and Gautam, and daughter, Durga, now regularly engaged me in conversation. Over the years, as I came and went, following the Kumari's *jatras* or studying the iconography of the *toranas* and roof struts in the little courtyard, a feeling of trust had developed between us, and though I would never be able to enter the Kumari Chen itself, the caretakers had begun to open up and we had made friends. One day, shortly after Indra Jatra, I sat with Jujubhai in the shade of the eastern *pati* over a glass of tea, watching groups of tourists come and go.

Jujubhai and Gyan Devi had tended five Kumaris during the reigns of Birendra and Gyanendra. Gyan Devi's mother-in-law had served six Kumaris and known kings Tribhuvan and Mahendra. I began by asking him who, of the last four Shah monarchs – Tribhuvan, Mahendra, Birendra and Gyanendra – had been the most devoted in his worship of the Kumari.

'Birendra Sarkar – King Birendra,' Jujubhai answered without hesitation. 'He used to come here with his father, King Mahendra, as a young man. In Vikram Samvat 2023 (1966 CE), he persuaded his father to organize the restoration of the paintings in the Kumari's throne room – and he replaced the Kumari's throne, which was in bad shape, with a new one.

'When Birendra became king, he was even more a Kumari *bhakta*. One year – on the last day of Kumari Jatra in 2042 Vikram Samvat (1985 CE) – there was a big mix-up with timings when the *rath* got stuck in a big hole in the road and King Birendra had to wait over an hour here at the Kumari Chen for the Kumari to arrive.

'But the king was very relaxed. None of us men were here – we were all on the chariot – so my wife and Durga, our daughter, showed him around the house. That's when he saw that certain repairs were badly needed. So later, he ordered the restoration of the whole roof of the house, and the *rath* as well.

'Finally, after seeing the house and hearing the *rath* had been released from the hole and was approaching Hanuman Dhoka, Birendra Sarkar said, "Let's go and watch it arriving." So out he walked – into Durbar Square, into the crowd. And when people tried to part the crowds in front of him, he said, "No need, let them be. I'll just walk behind like everyone else." He escorted the Kumari back to the house and then sat in on all the preparation *pujas* with the Kumari, Ganesh and Bhairab, before going into the lion throne room to get his *tika*.'

And Gyanendra, I asked.

Jujubhai's face clouded. 'We have not received so many offerings from the palace in recent times,' he said. 'There is one problem we have been very eager to address but the palace will not help.'

Over the recent years, he explained, they had been hearing sounds from a storeroom on the first floor like the lid of a big box or a trunk slamming shut. But when they went inside the room everything was as it should be and all the trunks were locked.

The Kumari household took these omens very seriously. In the week before King Tribhuvan fled to India in 1950 to organize seizing his throne back from the Ranas, the caretakers had heard the sound of the storeroom bolt sliding back – even though the door remained locked. And in 1972, just before King Mahendra died, they had found seven dead snakes in as many days at the threshold of Kumari's bedroom.

'When we first heard the noise we made a formal plea to the palace but when the royal representatives came to check on it, they said it was just rats. We have continued to inform them that it's still going on but they do nothing.

'We need to offer the *shanta puja* – a *puja* of pacification. We would do it at our own expense if we could but the caretakers can't do it alone. It's not just the money. The royal astrologer has to be instructed to find out what is causing the noise – then a *shanta puja*, *homa* and *chema puja* have to be done. Many people are involved. But the noise is still happening. So far nothing has been done.'

'But if the palace is so disrespectful towards the Kumari Chen, and it is obvious the people do not want Gyanendra as their king any more, how is he allowed to come and receive *tika* from Kumari?' I asked.

'As caretakers we cannot stop anyone from entering the Kumari

Chen to seek to worship Kumari – unless it is on purity grounds.
Sometimes worshippers are self-seeking; they come with the wrong
intent. But how can we know this? Only Kumari Ma knows if
worshippers are genuine.

'If Kumari Ma gives *tika* to Gyanendra it may not be that he is the
strongest Kumari *bhakta*. But perhaps he is not the least deserving.
He knows what is required for proper worship of the Goddess. How
can a prime minister, who has never before worshipped Kumari Ma,
know what to do? His lack of experience may be very dangerous for
the country. He may anger the Goddess without knowing it. And
his worship is not something he does on just one occasion, in one
year, when he receives *tika*. He must worship the Kumari constantly,
every day of every week, of every year, with all his mind, and with
a pure heart. This is something he should remain aware of in all his
waking hours, through all his life.'

Jujubhai seemed to be expressing a dilemma that was now
suddenly confronting not only the Kumari caretakers, but the
entire Kumari tradition. Even if Gyanendra had proved himself
to be a corrupt and irresponsible king – and there had, after all,
been many such kings in Nepal's past – at least he belonged to a
system that was fully integrated with the Kumari tradition. Even
if Gyanendra himself was no true Kumari devotee, the institution
of the Hindu monarchy recognized the importance of the Kumari
and the belief system to which she belonged. A king, moreover,
was for life – time enough for the Goddess's influence to prevail,
to show him the error of his ways perhaps – as in the case of
Pratap Malla. But a prime minister's term of office would only be
a matter of years. If the prime minister was not already a Kumari
devotee or a *shakti tantrika* himself, this was scarcely time for him
to become one. Devotion to the Goddess was a state of mind, a
way of life. Ritual practice had to be repeated, over and again,
with sincerity, not just every year but every day if it was to instil
rightmindedness and sound judgement in a leader. And what if a
Maoist or a Christian or a Muslim were to be elected prime minister
one day? What then?

A day or so later, Jujubhai's daughter Durga spoke to me of broader concerns. Soft-spoken, demurely elegant in a yellow sari, Durga Shakya was in her late forties and unmarried. She had known seven royal Kumaris. She was born in 1958 when Harsha Laxmi was royal Kumari and had grown up alongside Living Goddess Nani Maya Shakya, subsequently her best friend. After Nani Maya came Sunina, then Anita, Rashmila, Amita, and now the reigning Kumari, Preeti. The present Kumari – Durga said – behaved very differently from the others.

'She is extremely frank,' said Durga, 'she chatters away at top speed. She doesn't keep anything in her *"man"*, her "heart-mind"; she keeps nothing to herself.

'None of the others I have known talked so much, especially not when they were on the *asan*. Others have smiled; some may even have laughed when they were sitting on the throne; but talking is very unusual. Sometimes Kumari Ma even pulls faces and acts the clown – you've seen her do it – even when she is wearing the crown at Indra Jatra.'

Durga spoke gently and with affection. There was no criticism in her observations. To her, the behaviour of the little Kumaris was beyond censure. It was the expression of the Goddess. A Kumari could be advised as to what might be appropriate behaviour, but she could never be told off or prevented from doing what she wanted. The present Kumari's reactions, Durga felt, were quite possibly a reflection of the current atmosphere of antagonism.

'In our Hindu *dharma* and Buddha *dharma* we believe we have to respect Kumari Ma with both *shraddha* – inner, invisible faith – and *bhakti* – the kind of devotion, or service, that is visible to others. One has to worship Kumari Ma with a completely true and faithful heart. Then the effect is an orderly and peaceful society with regard for human life.

'But what is happening these days is that people who have no *shraddha* or *bhakti* are spreading false rumours and speaking ill of the Kumari. There is an atmosphere in Kathmandu, in the country, of insult and contempt for Kumari Ma. That may be why she is so restless. In a society that doesn't respect Kumari Ma, there will be more war, more quarrels. Peace will not last if there is not *maitritva bhavana* – the feeling of deep friendship, of loving kindness towards everyone – that comes from worshipping Kumari Ma, if we do not remain under her *sharan* – her care and protection. Kumari Ma teaches us that we are all mothers in our hearts. The hope for our country – for every country in the world – is that we care for each other with this same universal devotion.'

~

On 22 November 2006 the Maoist leader Prachanda signed a peace deal with the acting prime minister, G.P. Koirala, in the Nepal parliament, ending the Maoist insurgency and paving the way for the former rebels to join the government. The relief in the capital was palpable. During the past ten years of fighting, 13,000 people in the country – most of them civilians – had been killed; scores of children had been recruited to fight; hundreds of people had disappeared never to be seen again. At last, it seemed, there was an end to the bloodletting and the healing process would be allowed to begin. Within minutes of the signing, the people of Kathmandu were lining the streets, lighting candles and scattering flowers on the road, paving the way for the cavalcade of the prime minister and other signatories of the peace deal.

The agreement with the Maoists seemed, at first, to have given fresh impetus to the coalition government's sluggish efforts to tackle the issue of the king. A special assembly was planned for the following year to decide on the future of the monarchy, with the Maoists pressing strongly for abolition. Meanwhile, a government commission named Gyanendra and 201 government officials and members of the security forces as responsible for the killing of protesters during the demonstrations, and declared its intention to bring them to trial.

But the government, never an incisive instrument in Nepal, and now a coalition of seven disparate and ill-disciplined political parties with an eighty-four year-old prime minister at the helm, was proving singularly ineffective at moving in any direction at all. As autumn faded into winter and with no progress on the question of the king, people in the valley began to grow agitated once again. On 16 February Gyanendra's motorcade was pelted with stones by crowds chanting anti-monarchist slogans as the king made his way to the Golden Temple at Pashupati to celebrate Shiva Ratri.

The following weeks were electrifyingly tense as the capital was overwhelmed by demonstrations, both Maoist and anti-Maoist. Incredibly, though, the political turmoil failed to derail the peace process and on 1 April 2007 the Maoists joined the interim government – making it a coalition of eight political parties. The Nepali Congress leader Girija Prasad Koirala retained the post of prime minister, and Maoists were appointed to five out of the seventeen positions in the cabinet. Maoists were now responsible for the ministeries of Information and Communication, Local Development, Physical Planning and Works, Forest and Soil Conservation, and Women, Children and Social Welfare.

The coalition was hanging by a thread, though. Until national elections were held no interim government could sustain the faith of the nation. The mood in the country, ravaged by sectarian fighting, was desperate for the stability of a legitimized parliament but the holy grail of democratic elections was proving frustratingly difficult to grasp. A date of 20 June was set for the Constituent Assembly polls, only to be cancelled less than two weeks later as being 'too soon', the chief election commissioner citing a number of 'technical processes' that had yet to be completed. The commission needed 'more time to prepare', he said, before elections could be held. The coalition government would have to hang on until after the monsoon, September at the very earliest.

In this atmosphere of intense political uncertainty the capital began preparing for September's Indra Jatra, an event that this year – 2007 – happened to coincide with the 250th birthday of the Kumari

Chen. As the end of the Shah dynasty hove into view the anniversary of the founding of the royal Kumari's residence by the last Malla king in 1757 presented itself to the Newars of Kathmandu like a gift. To them the moment was more than an architectural milestone. It was a stroke of synchronicity, the fortuitous folding of history, the ripening of *karma* – the very fabric of the Nepali story. Here, it seemed, was an opportunity for the Newar community to reclaim their tradition, to restore to its original platform the practice that had been usurped by the Shah conqueror 238 years before.

Chapter 24

A House for the Living Goddess

Around midday on Saturday, 15 September 2007 Babu Ratna
Maharjan, a young Newar from Patan, drove his motorbike down
New Road in central Kathmandu with his colleague Bhim Tamang
riding pillion, a rucksack on his back. Parking near the intersection
with Dharma Path, the two young men walked together past the
tourist police ticketing kiosk and up the pedestrianized area of Ganga
Path towards the Lion Gate of Basantpur, the eastern approach to
Kathmandu's Durbar Square. Babu, the older of the two, had taken
charge of the rucksack. What it contained was, to their minds – and
to those of the small group of people who had come to meet them
– more awesome and, once it had been fully primed, more dynamic
than any bomb.

The two young men were welcomed at the entrance to Basantpur
Square by Jujubhai Shakya, husband of the Kumari's caretaker, who
had walked the short distance from the Kumari Chen barefoot.
With Jujubhai were his eldest son Mahendra, and Mahendra's wife,
Kamaltara Shakya – next in line to inherit the position of Kumari
caretaker; two of the Pancha Buddha – one in blue robes, one in
green; and a group of Newar women, known as the Lady Jaycees,
decked out in gorgeous red saris, red fingernails and their finest
gold jewellery.

As Babu opened the rucksack, an explosion of drums and clashing symbols was unleashed by a band of Jyapu musicians. Bowing his head Jujubhai Shakya received into his hands the object the two young men had been assiduously working on for the past two months.

The young men, both bronze-casters, had begun work in their smithy in Jom Bahal in Patan on 7 July in the middle of the *jatra* of Red Macchendranath. They had started on a day of special auspiciousness – the day the tunic belonging to the God of Compassion had been exhibited to the crowds; the day the Living Goddess of Patan had left her house on one of her rare outings to witness the viewing.

The craftsmen were confident the joyful meeting of the two deities had, indeed, cast blessings on their enterprise. The casting had gone perfectly – there had been no mishaps or accidents; the furnace had been brought up to a high and steady blaze; no one had been scalded during the hazardous process of smelting, or pouring the liquid metal into the moulds; the excellent quality of the bronze had withstood the repeated tappings of the repoussé hammers; and the image itself, once it had been polished and finished to the finest detail, had received the hundred grams of pure gold like a second skin.

This all boded well for the installation ceremony and, if all continued in the same vein, the Mulacharya – the royal Buddhist priest, Puspa Ratna's son Manjushri Ratna Vajracharya – who had already entered into a deep meditation at the Kumari Chen in preparation – would have no problem pulling the Goddess into the image.

The Kumari Chen had never had a bronze *pataka* before though many temples in the valley have them, the long metal ribbons hanging down their roofs to the windows on the second floor. Some temples have several *patakas*, the metal now blackened with age, links rusted and curling – offerings made by wealthy patrons many centuries ago.

When Jaya Prakasha Malla had dedicated the Kumari Chen in

1757, a customary *pataka* made of white cloth had fluttered down from the roof finials like a ladder – an invitation to sky deities like Indra, king of Heaven, to come and visit. It had represented the finishing touch, a banner proclaiming the occupancy of the building by the deity.

Most temples are consecrated with a cloth *pataka*. A bronze *pataka* is usually donated in later years, well after the establishment of a temple, as an extra offering of beautification. Sometimes the donor is simply a pious layperson wishing to gain merit for himself and his family; often it is given by a wealthy Newar merchant in thanks to a deity for securing him lucrative trade and safe journeys to and from Tibet.

On many temple *patakas* the broad end plaque is blank, a simple trefoil with bronze oak leaves hanging from it on tiny links so they rustle gently in the wind. But the *pataka* for the Kumari Chen follows the tradition of the great temples like Akash Bhairab where the deity of the temple is featured in the centre of the end plaque, a repoussé bronze-gilt figure in relief. A *pataka* of this kind is also, in a sense, a nameplate – like an entrance *torana* – identifying a deity and projecting it into the outside world.

As Jujubhai lifted the plaque – a plate of bronze 21 inches wide by 21 inches high – out of Babu's rucksack into the bright September sun a flash of light lit up the faces of everyone standing around, craning to see. In the centre the golden goddess Ugrachanda – the same image that danced the death of the buffalo demon in the *torana* above the entrance to the Kumari Chen – unfurled her eighteen arms, weapons at the ready. The craftsmanship was exquisite; each tiny detail on the figure, only nine inches tall, was perfect, from the faint smile playing about the Goddess's lips, down to the submissive eyes of the severed buffalo head at her feet.

Like a visiting dignitary on the threshold of a palace the newly arrived deity was honoured on the spot, between the pair of sentinel lions recently installed at the entrance to Basantpur Square. The ladies in red saris came forward with vermilion, rice, yoghurt and marigolds, anointing the *pataka* with its first offerings. Then the procession made off, Kamaltara Shakya leading the way through Basantpur Square, along the stuccoed southern elevation of Hanuman Dhoka, drawing the Goddess towards the Kumari Chen with a long, iron key – like a mother-in-law welcoming her son's bride to her new home.

~

The valley was already suffering considerable hardships from the Gorkha blockade when Jaya Prakasha Malla conceived of a unique residence for the royal Kumari in Kathmandu, right next to his palace. Though he had managed to recapture the fortress of Nuwakot from the Gorkhas after reclaiming his throne, the forts of Naldum and Mahadev Pokhari to the north-east had fallen to Prithvi Narayan Shah; and in the west, the wooded ridge of Lamidanda was now occupied by Gorkha forces, depriving the city of Patan of its primary source of fuel and timber. The king of Patan, Rajya Prakasha – half-brother of Jaya Prakasha – being weak and blind, had been powerless to resist. Trade routes into the valley were now so constrained, according to the chronicles, that even salt had become scarce and 'for lack of yarn the looms of weavers had fallen idle'.

Pressures had been mounting on the king of Kathmandu. His army, comprised mainly of Indian mercenaries, far from home and with no prospect of acquiring land or booty, was growing restive. After years of economic blockade the royal treasury in Kathmandu was empty and the beleaguered raja had already been forced to commit sacrilege, removing golden finials from temple rooftops and melting them down in order to pay his troops.

There were spies everywhere in the city and the wider valley – disgruntled courtiers, ambitious nobles, hard-pressed merchants – willing to surrender information to the Gorkha commander in the hope of furthering their own aims. Even the king of Bhaktapur, Ranajit Malla, was still openly communicating with Prithvi Narayan

Shah, unable or unwilling to believe that the son of his *mit-bhai* – the prince he had entertained in Tripura Palace as his own son – could be capable of hostile acts against him.

Of the three Malla kings it was still only Jaya Prakasha who was prepared to counter the Gorkha threat. For Jaya Prakasha, building the Kumari Chen was not simply an act of devotion to the Goddess and an attempt to empower himself – just as he had empowered himself at the *pitha* of Guhyeshvari before regaining his throne – it was a means of raising a protective shield around the entire valley. He was building a *mandala*, a representation of the valley in microcosm, right in the heart of Kathmandu. Here, he and his priests could worship the Goddess in the manifestation that was believed to bring the most immediate results – her living form. They would generate the Goddess's protective energy within the Kumari on her throne inside the Kumari Chen just as they would summon the powers of a deity at the centre of a *mandala*. With the Gorkha army closing in around the foothills it had become dangerous for the king and his priests to perform tantric *pujas* at the more remote Goddess *pithas* in the outer valley and temples like those of the Vajrayogini at Sankhu and Pharping. The mandalic construction of the Kumari Chen provided a way to continue worshipping these power-places without actually going there, like a Catholic might follow the Stations of the Cross inside a church.

Before building could begin on the extraordinary new residence for the Kumari, the existing residential courtyard on the site adjoining Sikhanmu Bahal had to be demolished and its inhabitants resettled elsewhere. Gyanman Pati's lineage was moved across Durbar Square to Layku Bahil and by way of further recompense the *sangha* was given another piece of land at Jamal, north of Ranipokhari.

Traditionally, the erection of any building in the valley was a sacred process, every stage accompanied by astrological readings and *pujas*. With the building of the Kumari Chen, however, the levels of care would have been particularly meticulous. Everything had to be perfect – from the alignment of the building to the carving of *toranas* and wood-struts to the placing of every brick and nail, auspiciousness confirmed every step of the way. This had to be a building that the Goddess herself would find worthy and desirable; but it also had to safeguard her living form and the efficacy of the *pujas* to be conducted inside it. To Jaya Prakasha Malla the future of his kingdom and the safety of Kathmandu lay in the precision of every detail.

After initial consultations with the royal astrologers and the appropriate forgiveness *pujas*, the existing building on the corner of Basantpur and Durbar Square was demolished, the site cleared and the royal priest began the consecration of the ground by the ritual of casting the cords: twisting together the five threads – white, yellow, red, green and blue / black – into one cord and calling the five Transcendent Buddhas down from the sky to reside in it. Having drawn out the root cords, the direction cords and the side cords, casting them in a clockwise direction from spike to spike, the priest stood in the south-western corner of the ground facing the north-east and, with a *bali* offering, dismissed the cord of wisdom with the *mantra* of dismissal 'Om ah hum. Vajra! Muh' and returned it to the hearts of the Tathagatas in the sky.

On the second lunar day of the dark fortnight of the month of Phalgun in the year NS 877 (27 March 1757), small golden images of a fish, a turtle, an elephant, a horse and a lotus were placed in the consecrated building ground and the foundation stone laid over them. The Vajracharya priest performed a *kalash puja*, forgiveness was sought from the Nagas in their underground kingdom for the disturbance and work on the Kumari residence began.

Tree fellers and carpenters were dispatched into the foothills to look for suitable timber, setting out under armed guard since these areas were now under the eye of the enemy. The brick kilns in the valley were fired up for the preparation of tens of thousands of new bricks, the smell of baking clay alerting the 330 million gods dwelling in heaven to the magnificent undertaking.

The house itself was measured in a square around an internal square courtyard and aligned so that the four entrances in the centre of each side faced the cardinal directions. The main entrance, on to Durbar Square, faced north, towards the Himalaya, abode of the Gods.

The Newar craftsmen worked to the prescription of the Vastu Shastra. Each facet of the house was created in the image of the gods. The *dyas* were believed not only to inhabit the building – they were the building; the building itself, the universe in microcosm. The foundation supporting the house was the Serpent King, Sesha; the main pillars, Shiva; and the capitals of the pillars, Parvati. The sleepers on top of the walls were the Eight Bhairavas; the ceiling joists the Eight Mother Goddesses. The threshold was the *vetala*; the right-hand side of the doorframe, the lioness-faced *dakini* Simhavaktra; and the left-hand side, the tigress-faced *dakini* Vyaghravaktra. The lintel was Chandamaharoshana; the two door-leaves, Shiva-Shakti. The key to unlatch the door was Ganesha; the bolt, Karmalekha; the peg in the latch, Kameshvara; the latch-chain, Vidhata; the socket for the latch, Dharmalakshmi; the lock, Sthiralakshmi. The stairs were the Seven Sages; the trapdoors over the stairs, Jaya and Vijaya.

The ridge of the roof was Vajrasattva; the ridge-pole, Vairochana. The rafters were the sixty-four Yoginis. The struts supporting the eaves were the wings of Garuda. The beam supporting the rafters was a Naga raja; the roof space divided into the twenty-eight lunar mansions and the twelve signs of the zodiac. The laths laid over the rafters under the tiles were clouds; the mud mortar, the sky; and the bricks, the stars. The sleepers under the left-hand doorjamb were Chandra, the moon; and those under the right-hand jamb, Surya, the sun.

The building was erected on three levels like a Newar house – the ground floor, the underworld; the middle story, the world of mortals; the top story, heaven; and the roof, the *chatra*, the divine parasol protecting the whole.

On the northern facade facing Durbar Square, on the third and heavenly level, where the throne room of the Kumari was to be, an ornate *nyapa jhyal* – a carved casement window with five sections – was constructed. The central window, through which the Living Goddess – and she alone – would look, was made of repoussé bronze gilt and framed by the goddesses Jaya and Vijaya, attendants of Durga.

Fourteen other windows, made of wood and intricately carved, graced the north-facing elevation, each with elaborate *toranas* of the Goddess in her different aspects, including a pair of beautiful peacock windows and circular windows intertwined with Nagas; a window depicting the sun, and a window depicting the moon; and, to the right of the doorway, a window with the *yantra* of Guhyeshvari embossed upon a lattice screen.

Above the main entrance the central *torana* displayed the Goddess in warrior aspect as Ugrachanda, an eighteen-armed emanation of the demon-slaying Durga unique to Nepal and championed in the late Malla period as the ultimate destroyer of enemies. The doorway itself was beaded with tiny carvings of human skulls and decorated with carved fringes and fabric patterns like the garments of a bride, for the building was also regarded, in a sense, as the clothing for the Goddess.

But perhaps the most unusual attribute of the new Kumari Chen was delivered by the deities depicted in the window *toranas* on the inside of the building, ranged around the four sides of the courtyard. On each of the three levels, eight *toranas* depicted the Astamatrika – the eight protective Mother Goddesses; only, here, their customary attributes had been combined with their fiercest aspects to produce a circle of sixteen-armed Mahamatrikas – a circle of Great Mothers to help the Malla king of Kathmandu resist the invader.

In less than six lunar months all three floors, stairways, the roofs and all the doorways, windows, pillars and resting-platforms had been finished. On the fifth day of the dark fortnight of Shrawan

(21 September 1757) the recessed interior courtyard was paved and a *yajna mandala*, a burnt offering hearth, was sunk into the floor of the courtyard so that a magnificent *homa* sacrifice could be performed to bless the building, its future occupant and its donor. The sacred fire was lit and the ritual of ten thousand oblations, including costly ornaments, jewels, grains, herbs, flowers, incense and alcohol were consigned to the mouth of Agni blazing inside the pit.

~

The *homa* conducted outside the Kumari Chen 250 years later was not such a lavish affair but it was, nevertheless, a rare and extravagant occurrence. An excited crowd had gathered to greet the arrival of the *pataka* procession and to watch the fire sacrifice by which the Goddess would be installed inside the devotional banner.

A large area of the pavement in front of the stone lions, in the main thoroughfare of Durbar Square, had been purified with a smearing of cow dung mixed with red soil. In the middle of this 'sacrificial land' a *yajna kunda* firepit had been constructed out of twenty-four clay bricks and a fire lit inside it to receive the offerings. The end plaque of the *pataka* bearing the image of the Goddess was welcomed into the sanctified area and propped up on some bricks, facing west. Opposite, the Pancha Buddha sat cross-legged in a row and facing east, wearing their robes of five colours and their bronze Vajracharya crowns. The Raj Gubhaju, Manjushri, dressed in white as the Buddha Vairochana, sat in the middle, with his wife, embodying Vairochani, on his left. An assistant Vajracharya – the Mahanguruju – sat separately with his wife, facing north, to perform the *pataka bhavana puja*.

Even eighteen months ago an event as momentous as this would have required the permission of the palace, the Department of Archaeology and any number of official bodies but – with the king now stripped of his powers and the interim coalition government at a loss as to how to manage delicate matters like Kumari patronage –

the Newar community was, temporarily, a law unto itself. Without a ratified parliament there was no clear authority to consult; no labyrinthine palace or government departments to be negotiated; no wheels of bureaucracy to be oiled. Permission for the dedication of a *pataka* and all the other events planned for the anniversary celebrations of the Kumari Chen lay entirely at the feet of the Living Goddess.

Earlier in the year, on 2 April 2007, the 250th Kumari Anniversary Committee had sponsored a special *ksama* or 'permission' *puja* in the throne room at the front of the Kumari Chen. Seated on her lion throne the Kumari had eyed the supplicants cautiously as they presented their offerings and begged permission for the dedication of the *pataka*, requesting her also to accept the organization of the anniversary committee. Jujubhai Shakya had lit incense sticks and pine-tree powder, and burnt *bdellium* in a fire pot in front of the throne. At first the smoke had made the Kumari cough and she had wafted her hands about in irritation. But to the relief of all assembled the Kumari had accepted *sagun*, biting into her duck egg and dried fish, and sipping three times from a silver skull cup filled with rice spirit. With her right hand she had planted a *tika* on the foreheads of every member of the 250th anniversary committee, empowering them all. From that moment the celebrations took flight.

A number of local Newars had come forward expressing their eagerness to make offerings to the Kumari. One family – of six brothers and sisters – commissioned a huge new silver-plated Kumari palanquin in memory of their parents, and funded the restoration and re-gilding of the Kumari's lion throne. Another devotee had sponsored repairs to the three massive chariots of Kumari, Ganesh and Bhairab, replacing – among other things – the bronze necks of peacocks, jutting out from the sides of the Kumari *rath*, battered and twisted from years of being pulled on by enthusiastic devotees.

The Kumari Chen itself had been restored and beautified in preparation for the celebrations. The clay roof tiles had been weeded. Missing elements of the golden roof finials had been replaced and the elegant set of three-bells-over-lotuses had been polished until it gleamed out across Durbar Square as brightly as it had quarter of a millennium ago. Another donor had commissioned 108 new wind-bells for the eaves. The Kumari window facing on to the square had been repaired: the goddesses Jaya and Vijaya on either side danced with new arms, wielding golden swords and discs that had been missing for decades; layers of corrosive pigeon guano had been scraped away from the repoussé work, the elaborate lattice-work window and its surrounds cleaned and regilded and protected from further avian desecration by a fortress of tiny golden pins.

Inside the Kumari courtyard a pair of new mud-plaster friezes had been set into the walls on either side of the ground floor Pancha Buddha shrine. Painted by a renowned Newar artist from Bhaktapur, they depicted the auspicious symbols of the *astamangala* – parasol, two fishes, conch, victory banner, endless knot, *kalash*, lotus and fly whisk – hovering in the sky over the green hills of the Kathmandu Valley against the distant snow peaks of the Himalaya.

In the corner of the courtyard a derelict storeroom had been freshly painted, a leaking water pipe repaired and a clay stove installed in readiness for the preparation of massive celebratory feasts.

The current political vacuum had one downside, however. In the absence of effective local policing, audacious art theft was on the rise. In the past months two original window *toranas* from the exterior of the Kumari Chen had been stolen, wrenched from their mounts in the middle of the night. The desecration had appalled the local community but there was little they or the Kumari household could do to track down stolen artefacts, let alone bring perpetrators to justice, while the country was in chaos. Sponsors would need to be found to pay for replacements. There were photographs, taken by tourists and art historians over the years, from which to make copies – but unfortunately not in time for the anniversary celebrations.

Meanwhile, across the country frustration was mounting as constituent elections were, once again, postponed – this time to November. At a meeting of the Revolutionary People's Council on 4 September, the Maoists decided to take law enforcement into their own hands and reinstate their kangaroo courts.

A few days later the Maoist-affiliated All Nepal Peasants Association declared their intention to resume confiscating land from large landowners, violating an agreement to return all properties and lands seized by the Maoists during the period of insurgency.

As clashes continued between all the various factions in the countryside, the death toll continuing to rise every day, it seemed to many political observers that the ground gained since the peace accord ten months ago was in danger of slipping away entirely. At the very moment Jujubhai, the Pancha Buddha and the Lady Jaycees had been welcoming the arrival of the *pataka* in Basantpur Square, the prime minister, G.P. Koirala, had been receiving the Maoist chairman, Prachanda, and his deputy, Baburam Bhattarai, at his official residence to hold 'serious discussions' on the escalating political crisis. The Maoists were now pressing to declare the country a republic before the November polls and insisting upon a proportional representation system of elections – both issues on which the Nepali Congress was refusing to give way.

But the mood in Durbar Square as the Kumari anniversary celebrations began was anything but gloomy. There was a growing conviction among Newars that, if the people of Kathmandu came together to worship the Living Goddess at this moment, it could be a turning point.

Friends and family of the Kumari and her caretakers squeezed together for the bird's-eye view from the top floor windows of the Kumari Chen as the complex rituals of the *homa* began beneath them – first the *sinha puja* of red powder and the *devatahuti* offering of thirty-two different grains to summon the deity; then the *sahasrahuti* offering of a thousand oblations, followed by the *samkalpa*, or 'solemn vow' of the donor; and the *purnahuti* offerings of medicinal plants to the fire.

In past centuries – perhaps even at the *homa* for the inauguration of the Kumari Chen 250 years ago – the tantric priests would have dedicated themselves to the fire, leaping into the flames where, it was believed, they were transformed for a split second into rays of light, before returning again, purified and unharmed, on the other side. Kings, too, were known to have performed this *mamsahuti homa*. Perhaps Jaya Prakasha himself, as sponsor, had flown into the heart of the fire, lighting himself up like a great lamp, dissolving into the void and returning, after a moment's obliteration, back into the world, on the other side of the flames.

Today such feats of dissolution and transformation are accomplished in the mind. With his *ghanta* in one hand and *vajra* in the other, Manjushri Vajracharya recited the sacred texts laid out on the ground before him, his mind in deep meditative focus while his wife beside him directed the participants, and the other Pancha Buddha followed the beads of the *japa mala*, their hands hiding the secret *mudras* under their robes. Somewhere, in the midst of the *mantras* and *mudras* and the drawing of *mandalas* and the elaborate correlation and juxtaposition of ritual objects like pieces moved around a divine chessboard, the gods and *bodhisattvas* were called to bear witness, the *shakti* of the Goddess was pulled from the ether and Ugrachanda – or Vajradevi in the Buddhist mind – was installed inside her new image at the end of the *pataka*.

After nearly two hours under the blazing sun, the performance concluded and the participants – the family of the Kumari caretakers, the donor and the members of the committee and various subcommittees of the Kumari anniversary celebrations – were ritually bound together by means of five-coloured threads wrapped around their hands. The symbolic donation of a bed to the officiating priest was made and the remaining grains were offered to the fire in a final *shesahuti*.

The craftsmen Babu Ratna Maharjan and Bhim Tamang, their

hands purified and empowered by a *shilpakar hasta puja*, mounted
the roof of the Kumari Chen carrying the links of the *pataka*
in their backpack. The crowd watched nervously from below,
tension mounting, as the two men clung with their toes to the
roof-tiles and, after worshipping the finials, began to connect
the twenty-two bronze links together, each one embossed with
a flower or one of the *astamangala*, hanging them from the stem
of the lotus under the central bell. At last the *pataka* was in place,
twenty feet of gleaming bronze running down the steep slope of
the roof, the unfinished end dangling expectantly just above the
Kumari's golden window.

Babu Ratna reappeared through the entrance of the Kumari Chen
and, with the end plaque cradled carefully under his arm, climbed
the bamboo scaffolding on the front of the house to the Kumari's
window. As he connected the final piece, the auspicious music of the
mangaldhun struck up, and the crowd – Newars and other Nepalis,
tourists, press photographers – broke into applause. Kites sailed
around the sky. From up on the roof, Babu Ratna and Bhim Tamang
threw down handfuls of rice pastries like manna from heaven and
the spectators rushed about, laughing, hands outstretched, to field
them. A man next to me leapt into the air and caught a piece of
pastry as it fell. He broke it in half and handed me a piece. Sharing
its blessings doubled the auspiciousness, he said.

The *pataka* offering was the opening event in a whole range of
dedications scheduled over the coming fifteen days. Suddenly, it
seemed, every corner of the old city was erupting in acts of Kumari
devotion. Only metres away from the *homa* another performance
was taking place. On the raised platform in front of the temple to
Narayan, opposite the big, yellow garage doors where the Kumari
chariot was kept, where the Malla kings used to be crowned and
where the royal Kumari had given her blessing to the Shah conqueror
on that fateful day in 1768 CE, another tantric priest – Badri Ratna
Vajracharya – was conducting a spectacular *kanya puja*.

The *kanya puja*, or virgin girl worship, had been sponsored by the locality of Maru Tol. Throughout the morning 320 little girls from Maru Tol had been arriving in Durbar Square. They came on foot, holding their older siblings' hands, or squeezed between their parents on a motorbike. Some were barely two years old. All of them were dressed as Kumaris in a dazzling array of pink and scarlet, with traditional red velvet slippers or baby pink cowgirl boots, painted fingernails, pearls and gold, bright lipstick and gleaming, kohl-painted eyes.

The 320 little Kumaris, the Goddess invoked in them by the tantric priest, sat in long rows inside a huge tent erected in front of Hanuman Dhoka while well-wishers lined up to present them with offerings of sweets and small denominations of rupees. I joined the queue. Simply presenting a token to each one, bowing and repeating *namaste* hundreds of times over, took almost an hour. It was an exhausting process in itself but as I paused briefly before each child – most of them by now gorged on sweets and dozing in the heat – it seemed this, in a way, was the intention. To a Newar, proper worship requires stamina, the repetition of ritual invoking a sense of perspective, a glimpse of infinity. These little girls were just a tiny fraction of all the little girls in the city, in the valley, in the country, in the world, at this moment; a generation in time, one link in the *pataka* stretching from generations past to generations to come. This was a reminder of the universality of Devi, the preciousness of every single one.

While the Kumari household watched the comings and goings in Durbar Square through the windows of the Kumari Chen, the Kumari herself remained at the back of the house for the duration of the entire *kanya puja*. As the permanent embodiment of Devi, her presence is so powerful it is believed she can endanger the 320 little girls if their eyes meet. Like the Gana Kumaris and Navadurga at Dasain, the *shakti* of the temporary Kumaris could be reabsorbed by the central Living Goddess if they came into contact, like drops of mercury returning to their source.

~

In May 1757, while Jaya Prakasha Malla was engaged in building the Kumari Chen, Prithvi Narayan Shah launched his most audacious attack on the valley so far. The Gorkha conqueror had set his sights on the town of Kirtipur, just five kilometres to the south-west of Kathmandu, and only two kilometres from the city of Patan. Kirtipur was perched on a hill, three hundred feet above the plain. If the Gorkha king could capture the town he would secure a fortress within the valley where he could station his army and from there launch his offensive on the Malla capitals.

The people of Kirtipur resisted fiercely and were – this time – able to defend themselves. Hearing of the attack, Jaya Prakasha Malla sent out his army to set upon the Gorkhas as they retreated. In the ensuing rout Jaya Prakasha's Indian sepoys succeeded in slaughtering a considerable number of Gorkha soldiers, including Prithvi Narayan Shah's senior commander and adviser, Kalu Pande. It was a crucial victory and one the king of Kathmandu would doubtless have attributed to his ongoing project in honour of the Kumari.

~

Three days after the inauguration of the *pataka*, on 18 September 2007, it seemed the country was heading for another reversal. The Maoists suddenly announced they were pulling out of the government. Thousands of Maoist supporters assembled on Tundikhel parade ground waving red flags as their leaders declared their intention to launch a 'people's movement' to press for their demands – principally the proclamation of a republic before constituent assembly elections and a fully proportional system of election. Once again the country faced a nationwide strike. Coverage in the press suggested the five-month coalition was over, the November polls in jeopardy, the entire peace process on the rocks.

But the very next day, after concerted pressure from international diplomats and UN representatives, and with the will of the people of Kathmandu manifestly set towards a peaceful solution, the leaders of the eight main parties – including Prachanda – agreed to continue the unity of the alliance and resolve the crisis through dialogue. Despite the scramble for political advantage and sporadic outbursts of violence, somehow the fragile peace process remained on track. To many Newars it was evident a crisis had been averted by the upsurge in Kumari devotion.

Chapter 25

A New Era

As the first day of Indra Jatra approached, speculation mounted about who would be taking the king's place in the festival. Most people presumed the role would now fall to the prime minister – though the image of a career politician centre stage in Durbar Square was hard to imagine. There were also rumours that the ageing Girija Prasad Koirala was ill and might not even be fit enough to attend. Gyanendra himself was not unequivocally out of the picture. People were saying he had been secretly empowering himself with tantric *pujas* and was planning to arrive in a carriage pulled by white horses – the mounts of Taleju. Others were convinced the Maoists would attempt to sabotage the event, preventing anyone at all from receiving the Kumari's *tika*.

At 8 a.m. on the day before the opening Kumari Jatra, members of the Newari-speaking Women's Association arrived in Durbar Square with a spectacular honour for the Kumari Chen. Gigantic nets, unrolled from protective sheets of plastic, were slowly hoisted up the front of the building. The nets were exquisite; delicate cotton threads knotted together and strung with individual grains of puffed rice. Once the sections were in place, framed spaces carefully matched over the windows, they were stitched together to form one piece. The *tayamala* measured eighteen by nine metres and covered the entire facade of the Kumari Chen, from the eaves of the roof to the top of the doorway entrance, in a hanging shower of tens of thousands of little snow-white puffs. The last time a building in Kathmandu had received such a tribute was on the first day of Kumari Jatra in 1999 when the trading community of Asan Tol had honoured the Temple of Annapurna, Goddess of Bounty – one of the landmarks on the route of the *jatra*.

The *tayamala* had taken hundreds of women months to put together, from rice donated by women from all over the valley. In total, eight *muris* – about 750 kilos – of special long grain *tayashiva* rice had been puffed in domestic kitchens over an intense heat in earthen pots. The puffed rice had been winnowed, the husks discarded. Fifty women had collected up the puffed rice in big baskets and distributed handfuls on to their friends for sewing. In the monsoon evenings that summer, while their families watched TV after the evening meal and the children were bent over their homework, the women had strung the rice on to long cotton threads with needles, knotting each delicate white 'flower' in its place. The threads were collected in the big community room above the temple of Akash Bhairab where they were woven into large sections; each section rolled in plastic and hung from the rafters to protect it from rats and mice.

In the early morning sunlight the magnificent *tayamala* shimmered over the facade of the Kumari Chen like the net veil over the face of a bride. In a matter of a few short weeks the threads would fall apart, dissolving with the rain and sun, the rice carried off by birds, its blessings scattered over Kathmandu with the winds; but the women knew their communal act of creation would endure, threading their present lives and future incarnations with jewels of merit.

~

For two years following the completion of the Kumari Chen and the installation of the first royal Kumari inside it, fortune seemed to smile on Jaya Prakasha Malla. It was not so kind to the king of Patan. On the evening following the procession of Macchendranath in Nepal Samvat 880 (1760 CE), King Visvajit Malla was murdered by two sons of a prominent official, at the very door of Taleju's shrine. Visvajit's wife had cried out desperately for help from a window in the palace but no one had come to her husband's aid. The distraught *rani* uttered a curse against the people of Patan – that their voice might also be ignored in time of need.

Following the king's murder the people of Patan appealed to Jaya Prakasha Malla for his protection and for two years he ruled as king of both Kathmandu and Patan.

But then, according to the chronicles, dreadful portents began to manifest themselves in the valley. In Dolakha the stone face of Bhimsen began to sweat and cracks began to appear in the great *stupa* of Swayambhu. At midnight on 21 Asadha NS 879 (1 July 1759), the peak of Shivapuri on the northern valley rim fell to the Gorkhali forces; and six months later the new hill fort of Palanchok was captured, and then the fort at Kabre.

As the menace of Prithvi Narayan Shah drew ever closer, with his kingdom unravelling at the edges and the city of Patan, too, eventually slipping from his grasp, Jaya Prakasha redoubled his efforts to bind the Goddess to him. No doubt he would have known about the tantric *pujas* being conducted by the Gorkha raja at power-places of the Goddess outside the valley – it would certainly have been in Prithvi Narayan Shah's interests to spread word of his empowerments – and the beleaguered Malla king would now have felt himself engaged in a tantric battle of wills.

In desperation – and plundering the treasuries of Pashupati in order to fund it – Jaya Prakasha renovated the spectacular Lion Gate at the entrance to Taleju Temple in Kathmandu, mounting a little figure of himself in a pavilion on the top; and on 19 April 1760, in front of the gate, performed a magnificent fire sacrifice of 100,000 oblations – more lavish even than the inauguration *homa* for the Kumari Chen itself – which took a full nine days to complete.

But, with the Gorkha army making inroads into the valley, he knew he needed to do more to fortify Kathmandu itself. He devised a *jatra*, in which the Living Goddess would be pulled around the periphery of the capital in a massive *rath* – like the chariot of Macchendranath – reinforcing the protection of the city walls and binding the people of Kathmandu together. On the thirteenth day of the waxing moon of Jestha – 27 May 1760 – the Kumari was brought out from her new residence to Hanuman Dhoka to receive the king's offering of a splendid *rath*. Four months later, the Kumari *jatra* was incorporated into the existing festival of Indra Jatra – a festival celebrating the rule of the king – and for the very first time the royal Kumari was pulled through the streets of the city in her golden chariot.

~

Tuesday, 25 September 2007, the first day of Kumari Jatra, seemed a day more than usually fraught with conflict and drama. On Tundikhel parade ground a visiting *yogi* from India was conducting a massive pre-dawn yoga class for 30,000 people. The home minister had already attempted to cancel the camp, fearing the *yogi*'s presence would encourage Hindu fanatics and boost support for the king but such was the outcry from the *yogi*'s devotees that the prime minister, fearing further unrest, had changed his mind and given permission for the classes to go ahead.

The Nepal Mountaineering Association had also chosen this day to launch their campaign to prevent nudity on Mt Everest, following the first case of a streaker on the summit of the sacred mountain.

In Kapilvastu, the Buddha's home province, meanwhile, riots had broken out, triggered by the assassination nine days earlier of a prominent political figure who had headed an anti-Maoist vigilante group. Though the Maoists had denied his murder, Mohit Khan's supporters held them responsible and the riots would eventually claim the lives of more than sixty people.

In the capital the Special Representative of the UN Secretary General in Nepal, Ian Martin, was meeting the CPN-UML General Secretary Madhav Kumar Nepal, urging him to seek unity among the eight coalition parties and hold the polls on time.

Elsewhere in the city, the prime minister and leader of the Nepali Congress party, Girija Prasad Koirala, and the former prime minister Deuba, leader of the Nepali Congress (Democratic) Party, were holding a press conference announcing the healing of the vertical split that had divided their party back in May 2002 following the row over Deuba's decision to dissolve the House of Representatives. The reunified Nepali Congress party had also, it appeared, at last agreed that Nepal should, in principle, become a republic – thereby resolving one of the most contentious obstacles in dialogue with the Maoists.

It was a move that, though broadly welcomed in political circles, failed to dispel demonstrations against the prime minister later in the day as he drove in cavalcade into Durbar Square to take the king's place at the opening of Kumari Jatra for the very first time.

There was a profound sense of distrust in the capital, now, towards politicians of any persuasion – but most of all for Nepal's ageing political leaders who had failed for decades to deliver meaningful democracy or to forge ahead with the economic development the country so desperately needed.

But the demonstrations against the prime minister at Indra Jatra were more than simply a question of political protest. The most conservative elements in the Newar community considered the participation in Indra Jatra of anyone other than the king far too radical a departure from tradition.

Crowds crammed on to every inch of the temple steps as the gleaming 4x4s swept up, past the three temple chariots bedecked in flowers waiting expectantly outside the Kumari Chen, and came to a halt in front of the west-facing facade of Hanuman Dhoka.

In the Lion Throne Room at the front of the Kumari Chen, removed from the rowdy scenes outside, Uddhav Karmacharya, dressed in white, was entering the final stages of the *vishesh puja* to the three deities, Kumari, Ganesh and Bhairab. The Living Goddess was installed on her *asan* – two golden lions lifting an upturned lotus, a golden peacock displaying between them. In the flickering light from two standing butter-oil lamps she sat in *yantra mudra*, her legs forming a triangle with the soles of her feet pressing together, mirroring the *yantra* carved into the wooden seat beneath her, under the flat red cushion. Beside her throne stood two swords wrapped in red cloth. Seven hooded Nagas with jewels hanging from their mouths spread their protective canopy over the Living Goddess's head. Above the Nagas, under the throne's golden finial, a *chhyepu* chomped its snaking tails in a timeless act of regeneration.

Preparations for the day had followed the course that had begun at the Kumari Chen two and a half centuries ago. The Goddess had woken as usual, of her own accord, shortly after 7 a.m., lifting her head from her red pillow, tossing aside the red bedclothes and lowering her bare feet, with toes stained vermilion, to the red painted floor. Within moments of calling out, a compliant throb of footfalls had announced the familiar appearance of her elder 'sister' Durga, drawing aside the red door-curtain and bowing *namaste*.

After a brief ablution in her private washing area on the roof, using her pink soap, red towel, pink toothpaste and red toothbrush, and mains water that had been purified with holy water from the Ganga and libations of cows' milk, the Kumari had run back downstairs for a simple make-up, to be ready for the stream of devotees coming for *darshan* on the first day of Indra Jatra.

The caretaker had retouched the Kumari's eyes, sliding open the lid of a tiny, silver goose-shaped compact, releasing the subtle scent of colyrium into the room. There were modern products the caretaker could use but it was unwise to innovate with aspects as crucial as the Goddess's eyes, especially on a day like this. She used a special blend of lamp-black containing camphor and musk with traces of clove and fenugreek. The Kumari had kept her eyes closed as the brush trailed her eyelids, then opened them again so her caretaker could draw underneath and, then, in two sweeping curves, continue the thick black lines to her temples.

Then, with her right thumb the caretaker had placed a *tika* on the little Goddess's forehead, between her eyebrows. No man, not even a tantric priest, could do this. The Kumari's *tika* could be bestowed upon her only by the touch of a woman.

Shortly afterwards the Raj Gubhaju, Manjushri Vajracharya, had completed his morning worship of the Buddhas in the *kvahpah dya* and performed *nitya puja* in the *agam*; Uddhav Karmacharya had conducted his parallel installation *puja* with the Kumari in the Lion Throne Room; and, after a cup of tea and biscuits, the Kumari was ready to receive her devotees in the public throne room on the southern side of the courtyard.

Then the special order of the day had begun. At around 11 a.m. the Pancha Buddha priests had begun a two-hour worship, one of the most powerful invocations in their repertoire, evoking the tantric Buddhist Goddess in the body of the Kumari. It was one of the occasions when the Kumari herself needed to be present in the *agam*. It had been followed by a feast for the Buddhist priests, the caretakers and the Kumari inside the *agam* itself, the Kumari, naturally, eating first.

When the feast was finished, at around 2 p.m., the Kumari had returned from the *agam* to her bedroom to get dressed for her *jatra*. Gyan Devi, Durga and Kamaltara were all there to attend her. They had combed out her hair, piling it up again and binding it with red *sachika* thread into a tight knot over a knob of sandalwood on top of her head so as to prevent the *shakti* of the Goddess escaping through the cranial opening.

Careful not to stand disrespectfully in front of her, the caretakers had knelt on the floor to either side of the Kumari as they worked. Next to them was a tray with cloths and cotton wool, oils and powders, pots and brushes. The Kumari sat on a low red seat while her face was smoothed with mustard oil, then lightly exfoliated with a paste of fine rice and barley powder mixed with drops of pure water in her caretaker's left hand. The water came from the well in Basantpur Square, the pail lowered deep into the realms of the Nagas, where it flowed with the chill of the Himalayan glaciers.

After rubbing the kolan mixture on the Goddess's skin, over her forehead and cheeks, chin and neck, gently scuffing off any traces of yesterday's make-up, Durga had removed the paste with a cloth that she placed in a separate bowl. Later the caretaker would dispose of the cloth in a compost ditch in the back courtyard where no one could accidentally walk on it and endanger themselves. Residues of the body, especially those of a Goddess, are considered to be dangerous and volatile. There is life in death, product in waste. Ganesh himself is said to have been created from dead skin cells saved from his mother's ablutions.

The first make-up to be applied was the '*tago sinha*', the big red *tika* covering the whole of the Kumari's forehead. Durga used her fingers for this, dipping them into the thick red paint and smearing it carefully on the Kumari's skin; then, rinsing her fingers, she drew a yellow borderline around it. Like a three-pointed *yantra*, solid red, two corners at the temples and a point dipping down between the eyes, the power of the *tika* expanded beyond boundaries, its saffron outline like the halo of light around the sun and the moon.

Then came the *drishti* – the lozenge-shaped eye with its black wax pupil lying blindly on a pad of velvet on the tray. Carefully moulding sacred *talas* resin into the back of the *drishti* the caretaker pressed it firmly into the centre of the Kumari's forehead. As the fire-eye took its place the skin contracted slightly under the resin, as though drawing it in.

The room filled with a heady scent as the caretakers lit incense for the ritual of dressing. Carefully the Kumari had lowered her new festival robe of scarlet silk over her head, lifting her arms as the gold-embroidered apron was tied over it around her waist. The *yantra mala* was placed around the Living Goddess's neck. The square gold amulet box set with the *navaratna*, the nine auspicious gems, represented a *mandala* of the universe; a ruby in the centre,

the others flying out around it in the petals of a lotus-flower worked
in gold repoussage. The *yantra* evoked the presence of Taleju. Like
a comet travelling through time it spun through worlds, conjuring
creation from the origins of the Goddess in the formless void,
entering the dark time of Lanka and waking Lord Rama to his
dashing rescue; spinning in flight from Simraongarh tucked inside
the waistband of Prince Jagatsimha; landing at last in the *mandala*
of Nepal to rest here, against the Kumari's beating heart. Sealed
inside the *yantra mala*, it was said, was the secret *mantra* of Taleju
written on red cloth.

The Kumari's other ornaments were loaded on top: the *sikha* – a
chain of large, solid gold links; the *singli mala* – a long string of small
gold coins with a heart-shaped pendant containing a single betel-
nut leaf; the golden *tayo* of a bride – a hollow, six-sided, almond-
shaped pendant with the sun and the moon clasped together and
a hood of nine golden Nagas suspended from a neckband of red
cloth ornamented with twelve gold plaques of peacocks; a *suta*,
or ceremonial collar of padded velvet and gold thread; and on top
of them all, a garland of fragrant white ginger flowers. A pair of
wide gold cuffs, segmented into nine horizontal bands set with the
navaratna, was clipped around her wrists. On the little fingers of
both hands she wore simple gold rings – adjustable in size so as to
accommodate a Kumari's growing fingers – and around her ankles,
adjustable tinkling-bell *gareghalas* of high carat gold.

Only when her escorts Ganesh and Bhairab had arrived at the
house, signalling the time for the *vishesh puja*, did she put on her
crown – a golden gem-encrusted multi-tiered shield widening like
a fan as it rose from her head. The *jatra matuu* was heavy and took
three people to fix in place. Once it was on, the Kumari walked
carefully and steadily as though balancing the order of the universe
on her head, which, in a sense, she did. The base band of the crown,
resting above her forehead on a red velvet support, was emblazoned
with another set of *navaratna*, starting from the left with a ruby for
the sun; followed by a pearl for the moon; a diamond for Venus;

an emerald for Mercury; a cat's eye for the descending node of the moon; topaz for Jupiter; sapphire for Saturn; zircon for the ascending node of the moon; and coral for Mars; each stone acting as a receptor into which the corresponding astral deity had been summoned. The *navaratna* transmitted the cosmic energy of the nine celestial bodies and, arranged in this specific order, are believed to provide powerful protection against misfortunes and calamities. Rising up from the *navaratna* were five further golden bands encrusted with yet more gems and edged with rows of pearls fanning out like an expanding galaxy of planets and stars. From the sides of the crown issued cascades of red tassels, the top exploding in fresh blossoms of red hibiscus.

Wearing their own simple crowns, the two gods Ganesh and Bhairab had accompanied the Kumari into the Singhasan. It was here that she received her final adornment – the thick gold naga mala, the king of the Nagas, encrusted with rubies and emeralds, the end of his tail coiled around his head, his hood raised as though about to strike, his watchful eyes two glittering diamonds. This is the most powerful ornament of all, according to ex-Kumari Rashmila; it had given her a surging, energetic sensation of heat whenever it was placed around her neck. From the moment the Naga Raj closed his coils around her, she had never felt like talking or smiling. She had entered another dimension.

In the shadowy Singhasan, the Lion Throne Room, the light from the oil lamps flickering against the blood-red ceiling and red-painted floors, the air suffused with incense, pinewood powder and bdellium, the atmosphere was highly charged. The noise of the waiting crowds, and the bands and dancers entertaining them, rose in waves through the lattice windows as the priest conjured the divine forces into play.

On the walls around the room the paintings of the Mahamatrika, commissioned by Jaya Prakasha Malla 250 years ago, danced their eternal rhythms, conjuring up forces to conquer the demons of this world and the next. For their performance in the Singhasan of the Kumari Chen the eight Mother Goddesses manifested themselves with sixteen arms. They had lions by their sides and were decapitating black buffaloes with their bloody swords. Accompanying them was elephant-headed Ganesh, Master of Beginnings, Fulfiller of Desires, Bestower of Success; and at the other end, Bhairab, with fangs and bulging eyes, his vehicle, a dog, beside him. On the north wall, to the right of the five-bay window looking out on to Durbar Square, was a portrait of King Jaya Prakasha Malla himself, standing with his hands pressed devoutly in prayer.

Opposite him, on the southern wall, nearest the throne, was the monumental figure of Taleju Bhavani. Flames blazed from her body. Her four heads, crowned and bejewelled, faces burning brilliant red, turned towards the four directions, each with three all-seeing eyes; a fifth, with face pure-white and three eyes blazing, raised itself above the rest. Above her, swept with flames of glory, hovered a golden temple-pinnacle, crown of transcendence.

From Taleju's shoulders hung a necklace heavy with human skulls. Ten arms, heavily braceletted, ranged about her body in angry motion. With a right arm she plunged her trident into the chest of a demon kneeling in human form by her left foot; with a left she held his severed head by the hair. In her other hands on her right she held a skull-bowl, *chakra*, bronze mirror and sword. Her left hands brandished a shield, scroll and conch shell, and another made the sign of the *chakra*. From her bejewelled girdle swung a set of dancer's bells; her feet, with bell anklets, beat ecstatic rhythms upon her double-lotus pedestal.

At the Goddess's feet, to the left of the vanquished demon, was another image of Jaya Prakasha kneeling, his hands in prayer, large jewels in his ears and around his neck, a yak tail quivering at the front of his emerald crown. On the other side, next to the Goddess's lion mount, knelt Jaya Prakasha's queen and two sons.

~

Uddhav Karmacharya gently replaces the hand bell on the floor. The area in front of the Kumari's throne has been sanctified with a smearing of cow dung and red clay and a sprinkling of holy water. The *sukunda* is lit, its flickering light dispelling all but the assembled implements and bronze vessels and the priest's hands as they recreate the time-honoured rituals and flutter through the sacred *mudras*. The priest pours pure water from a conch shell, like a mother river flowing over the Goddess's red-stained feet resting on their silver plate. He scatters rice – the gift of abundance, food of the gods – then, shaking a drum in his left hand, begins a low mumbling of *mantras*, the fingers of his right hand tracing a string of beads beneath his robe. The vibrations of their cosmic dance begin. He takes a red hibiscus flower from the worship-plate, tears its petals to pieces and presents them to the Goddess as if to himself.

The priest is consumed in his actions, opening himself as a conduit to divinity. He offers the Kumari a peeled duck egg and watches carefully as she takes a bite. The egg is followed by dried fish – the male component, the primordial swimmer – sperm meeting ovum. Receiving the silver skull-bowl in her hands, the Goddess takes a sip of rice wine, holding out the cup to be refilled. She sips again and for a third time it is filled and she drinks.

As the priest shakes the hand-drum and rings the bell, his wrists flashing in tandem, the *puja* crescendos to a climax. Then he bows, touching his forehead to the tiny feet resting among the sacred debris of rice and water and petals and vermilion. The Living Goddess is ready.

~

The tall figure of Girija Prasad Koirala, head and shoulders above his entourage of medalled dignitaries, stood awkwardly smiling on the royal balcony as first Ganesh, then Bhairab, resplendent in their red robes and crowns, were led out of the western exit of the Kumari Chen through Sikhanmu Bahal and along the white runners to their waiting chariots. The crowds heaved forward, straining for *darshan*, and were beaten back by police with staves.

As the bands blasted out a triumphal welcome, first Bhairab, then Ganesh emerged, a *ninicha* – a female attendant from Taleju temple – on either side of them holding their hands. The Kumari emerged last, the tiered *navaratna* crown towering on her head. Jujubhai, Mahendra and Gautam Shakya followed. The male caretakers were wearing traditional tunics tied with eight strings representing the Astamatrika, their five pleats signifying the Pancha Buddha. Jujubhai in a colourful *dhaka* cap was a smiling oasis of calm, directing the careful installation of the Kumari in her chariot. Uddhav Karmacharya, all in white, climbed up beside her, along with other ritual attendants from Taleju Temple and members of the caretaker's family. In front of the chariot, out of sight of the Kumari, the ritual butchers sacrificed a goat, its blood jetting from the jugular over the axles and wheels to ensure a safe journey.

Having already danced a welcome to the *dyas* in the Kumari courtyard, Manjushri Ratna Vajracharya and the other Pancha Buddha in their brightly coloured robes and Vajracharya crowns took up their places at the front of the procession, ready to dance the Shodash Lashya, the Dance of the Sixteen Mudras, to ward off evil spirits at every crossroads along the route. Jyapu bearers took up their position at the ropes. The military bandsmen in medieval black tunics with white cross-belts and turbans struck up a triumphant, galvanizing tune on drum and fife. Slowly Ganesh, the Remover of Obstacles, and Bhairab, the Protector, moved off in their chariots. All eyes were on the Kumari chariot as the Jyapu bearers heaved. Nothing happened. The band played on. Men clustered at the front wheels of the chariot were shaking their heads and gesticulating. Something was wrong. For the first time in the history of the *jatra*, the main brake on the Kumari's chariot had broken. 'No wonder this country is going downhill so fast,' quipped a tourist beside me in the crowd.

For two hours the band played their refrain over and over again while on the main platform the dancers repeated their steps in the sun and the three deities sat stranded in their chariots, attendants fanning their faces. At ground level the red demon Lakhe and Indra's elephant charged about in their heavy masks valiantly entertaining the crowds with dancing pranks and clashing symbols. By the time the brake had been mended and the chariots were able to move off at last, the prime minister was nowhere to be seen. The ageing politician had retired from the balcony to sit down inside the palace. His aides had rushed to alert him but the critical moment had passed. The Kumari's chariot had pulled alongside the palace side window for the customary offering of *namaste* and coins but finding no one waiting there had continued on its way. The procession stopped again as soon as Koirala reappeared but it was already halfway across Durbar Square. Realizing there was nothing to be done the chariots set off again in the direction of Pyaphal Tole. As Koirala stood there staring vacantly after them having missed his moment, it looked to all the world as though the Kumari had turned her back on Nepal's prime minister.

~

For two years following Jaya Prakasha Malla's inauguration of the first Kumari Jatra the Gorkha threat seemed to have been held at bay.

But then, in 1762, Prithvi Narayan Shah began making gains again, this time to the south of the valley. In the summer he stormed the fortress of Makwanpur, the capital of his own brother-in-law, capturing 700 muskets and seven of the raja's elephants. Two months later Sindhuli and Hariharpur fell; and by January 1763, the town of Parewa Danda was also in the Gorkha king's hands. An attempt by the powerful nawab of Bengal, Mir Kasim, to come to the aid of his friend, the raja of Makwanpur, was roundly repulsed by the Gorkha warriors.

With all the southern approaches to the Valley of Nepal now under his control and the outlying kingdoms intimidated into submission, Prithvi Narayan Shah moved around to the east, capturing the Newar trading centre of Dhulikhel on the eastern rim of the valley – only thirty-two kilometres from Kathmandu – on 23 October 1763.

All seven passes into the valley were now in Prithvi Narayan Shah's hands. After a campaign of nearly twenty years the noose was finally set and the Gorkha conqueror began to draw it tight, squeezing the very life-blood from the arteries of Nepal. Anyone who attempted to violate the blockade was killed – apart from 'unkillable' Brahmins, who were thrown into prison. Soon the trees along the roads into the valley were laden with a pitiful harvest – the bodies of men, women and children hanged by the Gorkhas for possessing even the smallest quantity of cotton. Meanwhile, 2000 Brahmins in the service of Prithvi Narayan Shah were roaming freely around the valley, fomenting dissent among the population against the Malla kings.

Back in Kathmandu, personal tragedy was adding to the woes of the Malla king. His beloved son, Jyoti Prakasha, twenty-six years old, had succumbed to smallpox on 27 April 1763. His body was burned at Pashupati and his wife committed *sati* over his corpse.

Jaya Prakasha Malla must have begun to wonder whether, despite all his devotions, he had grievously offended the Goddess – by putting to death his wife's lover, perhaps, who, though treacherous, had been a Brahmin and was therefore *avadhya*, non-killable; or by plundering the treasury of Pashupatinath and other temples to pay his mercenaries; or whether, since he was not of the illustrious solar dynasty of Nanyadeva like the Malla kings before him, there was yet more he needed to do to secure Taleju's protection. Perhaps he began to wonder whether destiny was simply turning against him, bringing to fruition the sins and omissions of his ancestors, awakening the threats and curses of murdered kings and thwarted queens; or perhaps now he began to intuit that the Gorkha king had indeed cracked the code of Nepal Mandala, turning the powers of the Goddess against him, just as he had once turned the course of the Bagmati in her honour – that the Gorkha king was, quite literally, stealing his thunder.

After two years acting as king of Patan, beset by troubles in his own city, Jaya Prakasha Malla was forced to release the City of Loveliness from his grip and focus his mind on Kathmandu. The opening was pounced on by Prithvi Narayan Shah who swiftly immobilized the wavering kingdom of Patan by installing his brother Dalmardana on the throne; and, with the western approaches to the valley secure, on 16 September 1764, he launched his second attack on the strategic town of Kirtipur. Once again, though, the Newar inhabitants fiercely resisted, throwing down the Gorkha ladders and raining arrows from the battlements, sending the Gorkha army into retreat.

Encouraged by Kirtipur's success, Jaya Prakasha Malla seized the moment to try and free the fort of Naldum in the north-east of the valley. The fort was well within his grasp when his troops committed a terrible blunder. Mistaking the Gorkha relief party as an addition to their own numbers, they allowed the enemy to move inside their lines. It was virtually an act of suicide.

All Jaya Prakasha Malla's attempts to secure the valley, it seemed, were doomed. By the time Prithvi Narayan Shah launched his third attempt to capture Kirtipur, laying siege to the town in October 1765, the die was cast. Sources differ as to how the town of Kirtipur fell – whether it surrendered or was captured – but by the time the gates were opened, six months later, Prithvi Narayan Shah was in no mood for mercy. The Gorkha king ordered his troops to put to death all the town's leaders and to cut off the noses and lips of every remaining inhabitant, including infants old enough to stand. The only ones spared were the players of wind instruments. The total weight of lips and noses, collected together in baskets after amputation, came to 17 dharnis – about 80 pounds.

Shocked by the fate of Kirtipur, the inhabitants of Patan ousted Dalmardana Shah from their city and restored the throne to Visvajit's heir, Tejnarasimha Malla. Ranajit Malla of Bhaktapur, too, saw the light. Realizing that his ally, the son of his *mit-bhai* and former guest at his palace, had nothing but total dominion of the valley on his mind, and that the conquest of Bhaktapur was, and always had been, Prithvi Narayan Shah's aim, Ranajit sent forces to the aid of Kirtipur; but they arrived too late to prevent its fall.

Meanwhile, in Kathmandu, the people were already half-starved and reduced to rags. With no money left in his treasuries Jaya Prakasha Malla had to devalue his coins to the pitiful rate of thirty-six mohars to one Shah rupee. The sepoys he had recruited from the Terai were restless, unpaid and on the verge of revolt. An attempt to supplement his troops with Nagas – a lawless band of *sannyasins* from Bengal and Bihar – had failed when Prithvi Narayan Shah cut them off before they could enter the valley. In desperation Jaya Prakasha appealed for help to the only other effective fighting force he could think of – the British. It was a profoundly unpopular move among the inhabitants in the valley, despite their desperation. The British were already stealing trade from the Newars and Jaya Prakasha's readiness to make allies of the beef-eating impious Phirangis from across the Black Water seemed to many of his subjects an act of treachery worse than surrendering to the Gorkhas.

The British needed no encouragement. Eager to extend their sovereignty into the Himalaya and break through a trade route into China, they dispatched an expedition of 2400 men under the command of Captain Kinloch on 26 August 1767 to break Prithvi Narayan Shah's blockade. Their eagerness propelled them into disaster. Setting off with scant provisions in the middle of the monsoon – mosquito season – the English soldiers and their Indian sepoys were laid low with malaria before they even reached the foothills. The rains swelled the rivers, cutting off supply routes and washing away bridges as fast as they could build them.

When at last Captain Kinloch and his exhausted, weakened soldiers reached Hariharpur on the outskirts of Nepal, the Gorkhas were waiting. Rarely had the British soldiers encountered such a ferocious, disciplined enemy or such a terrifying battery of weapons – guns, *khukuris*, bows and arrows, daggers, slingshots, rocks hurled from great heights, even balls of rash-inducing nettles and clay bombs that exploded on impact releasing battalions of angry wasps. One day the British would recruit these warriors as mercenaries for themselves, but for now they were at their mercy. Of the 2400 men Kinloch led into the hills, barely 800 returned with him to the plains.

~

On Wednesday, 26 September 2007, the day after the opening Kumari Jatra, a very different procession, the first of its kind, passed through Durbar Square. It had been conceived in the spirit of the 250th celebrations to honour the service of all those who had served as Living Goddesses. Eight women, dressed in beautiful saris, were escorted one by one, out through the entrance of the Kumari Chen into Durbar Square. Durga Shakya, the Kumari caretaker's daughter, purified the way, sprinkling libations of holy water; and five young girls – the Pancha Kanya – in traditional dress, their bare feet stained vermilion, with tinkling anklets, tossing flowers and puffed rice in their path, danced a welcome in front of them to the tune of flutes.

Walking in order of age, the oldest eighty years old, the youngest nineteen, with a female attendant holding them on either side and a retinue of bearers following them with offering plates, the women by-passed the usual entrance into Hanuman Dhoka, taking the auspicious route into the royal palace through the Lion Gate past Taleju's Temple. From the temple compound they filed through into the palace courtyard of Mul Chowk where they had all once, as children, celebrated the black night of Kalaratri, walking barefoot through the arena of sacrifice to the shrine of Taleju. As they emerged into the broad central courtyard of Nasal Chowk and mounted a dais where eight chairs were waiting, the audience of Nepali and foreign dignitaries, the great and the good of Kathmandu, and friends and families of the Kumaris, seated in rows in front of them, broke into applause.

It was the first time the former royal Kumaris had been seen in public together. The venue, too, was momentous. In the political vacuum the 250th Kumari Anniversary Committee had simply assumed jurisdiction, reclaiming the venue of the old royal palace and placing the Living Goddess tradition centre stage. We sat, the audience, where Pratap Malla had once danced, possessed by the spirit of Vishnu; where queens and concubines had whispered to their lovers, and courtiers plotted the overthrow of kings; where all the rajas of the Shah dynasty had been crowned – Gyanendra, twice. And here we were, being recalled to the fundamentals. Stripping away the ambitions of men, the wars and the wrestling for worldly power, wrong intention masquerading as right, all the manifold illusions of the world, was Adishakti Mahamaya, the Supreme Power of the Goddess.

After the vice president of the Committee for the Celebration of the 250th Anniversary of Sri Kumari Chariot Festival had given his welcome, members of the committee ascended the dais for the honorific ritual of washing the ex-Kumaris' feet. The Gurujuko Paltan struck up auspicious music, the Pancha Kanya danced in the wings and devotees from the audience lined up to garland the ex-Kumaris with *khatas* and present them, one by one, with shawls, bolts of silk, fruit and bread. Jujubhai Shakya offered them eggs and fish – the cosmic male and female principles together; the vice president recited a 'letter of felicitations', read out in English for the benefit of foreigners, and presented a copy to each Kumari, bowing his forehead to their feet. A special 'letter of merit' was presented to the principal caretaker, Gyan Devi Shakya.

Gyan Devi's son, Gautam Shakya, offered each ex-Kumari a small bronze etching of the Kumari Chen; and Durga Shakya gave each a necklace of pearls. Between them, the caretaking family had known generations of Kumaris. They had loved them like their own, guided them – one after the other – through their first days as Living Goddess, coached and worshipped them, held their hands through processions, watched them grow, and finally delivered them back to the outside world.

The treasurer of the Anniversary Committee presented each ex-Kumari, as well as Gyan Devi Shakya, with a coin of a quarter *tola* of gold, stamped with an impression of Mother Kumari. Later on, coins would be offered to the Kumari and her fellow deities Ganesh and Bhairab.

Finally the ex-Kumaris were presented with *samay baji* and betel nut, and a thin strip of red cloth – a *kokha* – was placed around their necks.

Laden with offerings, the ex-Kumaris sat mutely accepting of their honours like queens upon their thrones. Most of their faces were by now familiar to me. At the end of the row on the far left was the oldest surviving ex-Kumari, Dilkumari Shakya, twice married, now a tiny, bowed figure barely four feet tall; and next to her, Nani Shobha Shakya from Om Bahal, who was seventy-five and a grandmother of six. Both had been Kumaris in the 1950s, during the reign of King Tribhuvan. Then came Harsha Lakshmi Shakya from Nag Bahal, fifty-six, Kumari in the reign of King Mahendra, the first to pass her School Leaving Certificate, now a Senior Nurse at Bhaktapur Hospital, and married with two sons; and Nani Maya Shakya, forty-nine – Kumari for eleven years, who ran a pharmacy in Bag Bazaar and had just become a grandmother. Then Sunina Shakya, forty-three, whom I had recently met at the Kumari Chen, also a nurse in Bhaktapur, and the first Kumari in the reign of King Birendra; and her successor, the soft-spoken Anita Shakya, thirty-seven, the Living Goddess I had first seen at the window of the Kumari Chen when I was a teenager living on Basantpur Square. Next to her was the familiar figure of the lovely Rashmila, now twenty-six; and at the end, the youngest, Amita, now nineteen and studying commerce in Grade XII at school – the Kumari who had presided during the royal family massacre and whose afflictions had, in the eyes of those closest to the Kumari tradition, opened the door to the forces of *karma* and changed the course of history.

Scanning their faces, assembled together in public for the very first time, it seemed fortuitous that there were eight of them, as though the Astamatrika themselves had materialized in our midst, like the Gana Kumaris at Dasain. The row of goddesses in front of us spanned a lifetime, every stage of womanhood revered.

After the presentations were over, Rashmila Shakya carefully laid aside her gifts, stood up and approached the microphone. Her hair curled for the occasion, she looked calm, serene, and more beautiful than ever. Only months earlier she had passed her MA in Information Technology, the first Kumari to gain a university degree. There was no sign of nerves as she unfolded a paper and began to read aloud to the audience in Newari:

Mayan jahgu jvajalapa! Salutations to all with love!

Nepal is famous throughout the world as the land of the great mountain Sagarmatha. She is famous as the birthplace of Buddha and Sita, the heroine of the Ramayana. She is famous also as the country of festivals and rituals. Among these rituals is the Kumari tradition. This tradition is one of the most important to us in Nepal. The honouring of the Kumari is a way in which people can awaken themselves, to find the source of wisdom and compassion, the components that bring peace into our lives.

Nowadays there is a lot of noise about the human rights of the Kumari. People say she is treated unjustly and harshly. I can tell you this is not my experience.

I am not saying that some aspects should not be modernized to keep pace with life in the present day. But I stand here before you, as an ex-Kumari, to commend to everyone in Nepal not to look back on our history and judge it only in the light of today, by modern assumptions. We ought not to condemn indiscriminately that which we know to be fundamental to the well-being – to the liveliness, the good perceptions – of everyone in our culture. If we have a small scratch on our hand, we should not cut off our hand in order to make it better. Instead, we should heal the scratch for the good of our hand.

I have dedicated eight years of my life as a Goddess to serve and protect our nation. I did this not with any care for what my nation could give me in return. It is my deepest honour to have been able to serve my country and its people in this way.

On behalf of myself and all the other ex-Kumaris here today I would like to thank you all for remembering and honouring us. This is a wonderful occasion. May it be auspicious and may it bring peace to our beautiful country Nepal. Blessings on all of you from the depths of my heart.

~

As the end of the month of Bhadra – mid-September – 1768 approached, Prithvi Narayan Shah prepared to launch his attack on Kathmandu. He moved his troops up to the village of Thamel, a musket's shot away from the northern walls of the city. There was no military response from the Malla king. Jaya Prakasha was engrossed in the festival of Indra Jatra, his attention on the Kumari's imminent chariot procession. The Gorkha king's time had come. In the evening of Sunday, 25 September 1768, at a time precisely determined by Prithvi Narayan Shah's astrologer, a thousand Gorkha warriors stormed the city.

At that moment Jaya Prakasha was riding his horse alongside the Kumari's chariot through the locality of Kohiti in the southernmost part of the capital. Prithvi Narayan Shah entered the city through the western gate of Naradevi. The south-western gates of the city were thrown open by treacherous ministers from Jaya Prakasha's court; and at the eastern gates the Gorkha troops encountered little resistance from Nagarkoti soldiers who simply turned and fled. The inhabitants inside the city, intoxicated by the copious *prasad* of rice beer spouting from the mouth of White Bhairab in Durbar Square, put up no resistance.

When news reached Jaya Prakasha Malla that the enemy had entered the city he galloped back to Hanuman Dhoka, where,

with a band of loyal guardsmen, he fought the Gorkhas for an
hour or more.

At last, though, unable to resist any further and in a final desperate
effort to prevent his protecting deity from falling into his enemy's
hands, the Malla king issued orders to his men to mine the courtyard
of Taleju Temple and scatter her steps with gunpowder. Then,
with two hundred loyal Nagarkoti sepoys, he turned and fled,
escaping through the southern gates of the city, never to set foot in
Kathmandu again.

Prithvi Narayan Shah entered Hanuman Dhoka at eleven *ghadi*
past night – about 10.30 p.m. – and, having penetrated his enemy's
durbar, ordered his *sardar*, Tularam Pande, to fire a victory salute.
The salute fired a spark on to the gunpowder scattered by Jaya
Prakasha's men, killing Tularam Pande and several soldiers. But
Jaya Prakasha's final desperate attempt to defend his city was but a
trifling inconvenience for the conqueror.

Prithvi Narayan Shah's timing was perfect. When the Kumari's
procession returned to Durbar Square, the Living Goddess,
alighting from her chariot, took up her throne on the dais outside
the Kumari Chen ready to give her blessing to the king. The Gorkha
king simply stepped up in Jaya Prakasha Malla's place to receive
it. Before the stunned inhabitants, Prithvi Narayan Shah bent his
forehead to the Living Goddess's feet, and she, calmly dipping her
finger into the *tika* plate at her side, pressed her blood-red blessing
to his forehead.

~

At 9.15 p.m. on 30 September 2007, Girija Prasad Koirala, prime
minister of Nepal, entered the Kumari Chen to receive the Kumari's
tika. The prime minister ducked his head through the doorway and
entered the building to jeers and whistles from the crowd. Earlier in
the week, following his attendance on the first day of the festival he
had given a jaunty announcement to the press. 'I, as prime minister,
have observed Indra Jatra,' he told the *Rising Nepal*, 'breaking the

tradition of the kings. This has erased a chapter in our history. It is a victory of the people.'

Now, though, as he climbed the staircase to the second floor and entered the Singhasan, it was clear some of the people, at least, considered his actions the deepest sacrilege. Chants of 'Girija, don't kill tradition', 'Down with the flesh-eating Bahun', rose up to greet him through the golden window where the plaque of the gleaming new *pataka* dangled like a Naga head about to strike.

In 2007 regime change was nowhere near as clear-cut as Prithvi Narayan Shah's coup 239 years earlier is said to have been. The prime minister had left Durbar Square, posing briefly to reveal the red mark on his forehead to the cameras, believing the fate of the country was now sealed. But, after most of the crowds had gone home, two cars drew up outside the Kumari Chen. Rows of soldiers in plain clothes appeared out of nowhere, linking arms and making a protective cordon up to the lions at the entrance. Out of the first car stepped the king. He slipped swiftly through the entrance and made his way up to the Singhasan.

~

Within days of entering Kathmandu, Prithvi Narayan Shah put to death all the remaining courtiers loyal to the Malla king and secured his possession of the city.

Less than two weeks later, the city of Patan surrendered. The Gorkha conqueror led a triumphal procession into Patan's Durbar Square and then unleashed his soldiers on the town. The powerful, untrustworthy nobles of Patan were tortured to death in an imaginative variety of gory ways, their wives and daughters forced to marry men of lower caste. The most beautiful houses in the City of Loveliness were looted and set ablaze. Within days the streets of Patan were deserted. Only one Malla city remained.

Jaya Prakasha and his relative the king of Patan had, themselves, fled for sanctuary to Bhaktapur – the city where their dynasties had originated and where, united in purpose for the first and last time, the three Malla kings now braced themselves for a final stand against the conqueror.

Prithvi Narayan Shah took his time. For eight months he annexed villages in the surrounding area, encouraging them to plunder Bhaktapur's crops. Then, on 10 November 1769, again at a time dictated by his astrologer, Prithvi Narayan attacked.

Though the Malla contingent, fighting in the streets of the city and energetically led by Jaya Prakasha, resisted the Gorkhas for much of the following day they were forced, eventually, to fall back on the defences of Tripura Palace. By 11 November the three Malla kings were surrounded. Gorkha troops rained down arrows and gunfire on the palace compound from surrounding rooftops, picking off the terrified civilians crammed into the courtyard of Mul Chowk. Several of Ranajit Malla's soldiers, taking reconnaissance from the Palace of Fifty-Five Windows, were shot dead. The kings fell back on the building of Hiti Chowk but the Gorkha artillery fire reached here, too, killing two servants who were shielding the aged Ranajit Malla from the gunfire.

On 12 November, having risen before dawn to perform *nitya puja* at Taleju Temple, Ranajit Malla retreated with his cousin-kings to the redoubt of Chaukot, a building taller and easier to defend than others in the palace; but as Jaya Prakasha was climbing the stairs he received a bullet in the leg and had to be carried to the upper storey. With their commander wounded and unable to fight, confusion broke out among the Malla troops. Defecting nobles from Ranajit Malla's court were providing the Shah commanders with information about the layout of the palace and before long the golden gate that Ranajit Malla had dedicated to Taleju only fifteen years before was broken open. With tears falling down his cheeks the king of Bhaktapur ordered Hemnaran, his faithful guard, to remove his white turban and wave it in surrender.

The battle for Bhaktapur had lasted barely two days. Fifty Gorkha soldiers had been killed but on the Malla side more than 1700 soldiers and civilians had lost their lives. Five hundred and one houses had been reduced to ashes.

Prithvi Narayan Shah went himself to Tripura Palace to meet with the three kings who had been imprisoned in separate rooms in Mul Chowk. According to the chronicles, the king of Patan 'sat engaged in the worship of God and would not speak', so Prithvi Narayan Shah had him sent to Kathmandu, to be kept in confinement in Lakshmipur – the same tower in which Pratap Malla's father, the mad king Lakshminarasimha, had languished, and where, eventually, Tejnarsimha also died.

Jaya Prakasha Malla continued to show spirit despite the severity of his wound, rebuking the Gorkha king for mocking him in his misery and warning the conqueror against trusting those treacherous factions in his court that had played such a pivotal part in his own downfall. He had fought to the bitter end but, to all accounts, seemed resigned, now, to his destiny.

Impressed and somewhat chastened by the Malla king's words, Prithvi Narayan Shah asked what he could do for him. Jaya Prakasha requested to be carried to Arya Ghat at Pashupati 'where he would obtain salvation' and Prithvi Narayan ordered his own bearers to take him. Hours later, with his feet in the waters of the Bagmati, the last Malla king of Kathmandu died – his soul, according to some, absorbed into the southern face of the four-faced *linga* of Pashupati; according to others, awaiting reincarnation as Prithvi Narayan Shah's own grandson.

Prithvi Narayan Shah then went to pay his respects to his former host and friend, his father's *mit-bhai*, and found the incarcerated king of the City of Devotion 'even now displaying great patience, attending to his religious observances'. He waited until Ranajit Malla had finished, then embraced him and entreated him to remain in Bhaktapur, to rule there on his behalf. The last king of Bhaktapur, however, remained Malla to the last. 'You have obtained sovereignty over my kingdom by the favour of the gods,' he is said to have replied. 'I ask only that I be allowed to journey to Benares to spend my last days there.'

Providing Ranajit Malla with expenses and attendants for the journey, Prithvi Narayan Shah gave him leave to go. As the old king reached the top of Chandagiri pass on the southern rim of the valley, the chronicles relate, he paused one last time to look upon the Valley of Nepal and, 'with tears in his eyes, bade farewell to Taleju, Pashupati and Guhyeshvari forever'.

~

News of Gyanendra's appearance at the Kumari Chen that night, and the *tika* the Kumari had manifestly bestowed on him, sent shockwaves through the capital. Rumour had it there had been significant differences in the way the two supplicants had approached the Living Goddess. While the prime minister had spent a cursory ten minutes inside the Kumari Chen, offering the Living Goddess a few crumpled hundred rupee notes, the king had stayed a dutiful hour and given her a gold *asarfi* coin. In response, the Kumari had apparently given the first *tika* to Koirala with the utmost reluctance, having played the vermilion rice in her fingers for agonizing minutes before planting it on his forehead. But most significantly of all, the Kumari was said to have given the *tika* to the prime minister with her right hand, reserving her tantrically empowered left hand for the king.

While Kumari caretakers and tantric priests were beset with misgivings about having granted access to the Kumari to Koirala – someone not tantrically initiated, not a Kumari devotee, and not of the king's lineage – Nepal's politicians were more concerned about the king's performance at the Kumari Chen and his unauthorized military escort. The coalition government took immediate steps to quash any further ambitions on the king's part. Within a week the army personnel deputed to the palace had been cut by half and the King's Household Cavalry had been brought under the direct control of the Chief of the Army. If there had been any government officials still in doubt about the wisdom of removing the king as nominal head of state, they were no longer. The Kumari's continued blessing of the king that year had, ironically, hastened Nepal's transformation into a republic.

~

On my last morning in Nepal I paid a final visit, by special invitation, to the Kumari Chen. My husband and children, who had flown in for the 250th celebrations, came with me.

It was early as we crossed Basantpur Square, past the closed shutters of our old flat. The familiar little courtyard was bristling with activity – preparations for a *puja* that had been carefully guarded from outsiders and the press. The ground-floor shrine was open, the Transcendent Buddhas, and the tantric deities in the *agam* above them, already awoken by Manjushri. Rows of butter-wick lamps were fluttering on the railings of the courtyard *chaitya* and, around the edge of the raised *mandala*, the overhanging jasmine was greeting the rising sun with a heady release of scent. On the east side of the courtyard, under the portico, flat red cushions had been laid out on an area of ground freshly purified with a terracotta wash of cow dung.

Soon a queue of women were gathering at the entrance, plastic bags and *puja* plates in hand – old Jyapu women, flowers in their hair, their ears heavy with gold, and stately matrons in gold hair nets wearing their dazzling red-and-gold wedding saris.

The sound of wooden flutes and drums in Durbar Square heralded the arrival of a troupe of Newar dancers twirling bamboo poles. Levelling the bamboos to the horizontal the men entered the courtyard like jousters, then raised the poles again, flags and yaktails whirling dervishly as they spun and twirled, orbiting the *chaitya*, tossing the six-metre lengths of bamboo to the heavens, stirring up the Goddesses assembled in the *toranas* and dancing on the roof struts, before exiting the courtyard and carrying the flute music back across Durbar Square.

At some point, unnoticed by us in all the excitement, the Living Goddess herself had descended to the ground and, seated upon the red cushions under the eastern portico, was receiving her devotees, accepting offerings and dispensing *prasad*. Some of the women were carrying their own little Kumaris, all dressed in red, for her blessing. For us, seeing the Kumari this close, in the protected courtyard of the Kumari Chen, was an unprecedented gift. This was an intimate moment of exchange, an audience I had never, in all the years I had been pursuing the Living Goddess, expected to share.

Occasionally young men in sunglasses and jeans, pausing on their way to work, motorbike helmets under one arm, joined the line. A man dressed in a full skirt, his long hair tied in a topknot, entered the courtyard to pay his respects. He was a tantric dancer who, dancing the part of a Goddess, had taken on her persona. Like all tantric dancers, including the famous Navadurga of Bhaktapur, he rigorously observed the *niyams* in order to retain the Goddess's *shakti* within him, and – though he could be married – would be identified as female for the whole of his life.

The stream of devotees swirled around the courtyard, touching their foreheads to the feet of the Kumari, circumambulating the *chaitya*, tossing rice over their heads, and exiting past us, generating a river of *maitritva bhavana*, the essence of *shakti* dissolving sense of self in an outpouring of limitless motherly love.

When the tide of devotees had begun to ebb at last, Jujubhai and Durga beckoned to us to come forward. We joined the line and one by one, in turn, my daughter, myself, my husband, and my son, bowed down to the Living Goddess.

Acknowledgements

This book could not have been written without Kashinath Tamot and I owe Ian Alsop a huge debt for introducing us. When I first approached Kashinath, one of Nepal's leading scholars of Newar culture, to help me with research, back in 2003, I suggested a time-frame of six months. Little did either of us imagine we would be trawling for Living Goddesses together for the next nine years. The richness of the subject was thrilling for us both and it has been nothing but a delight to have shared the main part of this journey with him. Many of the findings expressed in this book are new and entirely a result of his painstaking searches through archive material – much of it not yet fully documented or translated from Sanskrit, Newari and Nepali into English. On several occasions he was able to examine original texts and inscriptions in private collections that had not yet been recorded, and has consequently produced a number of papers and articles in Newari and Nepali from his findings. His knowledge, curiosity and boundless energy, as well as his ability to gain the trust of our informants, have been a joy but I would like to thank him, above all, for his companionship on so many of my adventures around the valley and for fielding an incessant stream of emails over the years with such extraordinary patience and generosity of spirit. My files are bulging with reams of notes, descriptions, translations and transcriptions made by him over the years. His endurance has been astonishing but I'm sure he'll be as relieved as I am to see this book finally in print.

My Living Goddess journey began, though, long before I was fully aware of it and I would like to acknowledge the inspiration of my parents who were among the first tourists to visit Nepal when the borders were opened in the 1950s. Their stories, and my father's pen and ink drawings covering the walls of their bedroom in London, filled me with childhood longings and a determination, one day, to see the *stupas* and pagoda temples of the Kathmandu Valley and the legendary child goddess for myself.

I am eternally grateful to my three school friends – Emma Mahony, Somerset Charrington and Charlie Burrell – for making this dream a reality. Renting a flat with them in Freak Street, Kathmandu, in our gap year in 1983, just yards away from the Living Goddess's house, lit the touchpaper.

I am deeply indebted to Cheryl and Willie Bickett, then Colonel of the British Gurkhas, whose invitation to stay with them in Kathmandu in 1997 provided me with the chance to pick up the threads; and in particular to Laxminath Shrestha, Cheryl's Nepali teacher, for his guidance during Dasain and for introducing me to the ex-Kumari Rashmila Shakya.

The idea for a book came in 2001 after the massacre of the Nepali royal family. With the country suddenly in turmoil I found myself, unexpectedly, with the openings I needed to take my investigations further. Faced with uncertainty and the very real threat of a Maoist takeover, as well as mounting attacks from anti-monarchists and human rights activists, the traditional guardians of the Living Goddess tradition were beginning to feel that continued secrecy could be their downfall. If they did not attempt to show the world the value, at least, of the esoteric knowledge they had been protecting for centuries, these wisdoms could be in danger of disappearing altogether.

I am deeply honoured to have been given the chance to talk with many learned tantric priests – among them the late Puspa Ratna Vajracharya, Manjushri Vajracharya, Yagya Man Pati Vajracharya, Netra Raj Vajracharya and Uddhav Karmacharya. I hope I have honoured the trust they placed in me by speaking about the esoteric side of Kumari worship. I would like to emphasize, however, that on no occasion did they, or any of my other informants, reveal to me any of the secrets that, according to the prescriptions of Tantra, can only be transmitted in conditions of initiation under the personal guidance of a guru. Neither did I ask them to. They told me only as much as I needed to know in order to understand the fundamentals of the tradition and to address some of the persistent fallacies that have grown up around the Living Goddess over the past few decades. Any misunderstandings, errors or misinterpretations that have crept into the book as I wove these conversations into narrative are entirely my own.

In particular I would like to thank the Kumari caretakers – Gyan Devi Shakya and her husband, Jujubhai, sons, Mahendra and Gautam, and especially her eldest daughter, Durga – for their generosity and kindness. The role of the Kumari caretaking family is often overlooked but their religious knowledge, devotion, self-sacrifice and love for their charges is quite extraordinary. A life of ritual, especially at the helm of a tradition as deep and as prominent as that of Kathmandu's royal Kumari, is exceptionally demanding and I am constantly amazed at how they manage to fulfil all their duties and remain consistently welcoming to the stream of devotees and tourists who pass through their doors. I owe them a huge debt of thanks for sparing the time to talk to me on so many occasions and for including me in the wonderful 250th Sri Kumari Anniversary celebrations in 2007 and subsequent rituals at the Kumari Chen.

I would like to offer my deepest thanks to all the ex-Kumaris of Kathmandu I have met over the years. I'm aware that many of them have had unfortunate experiences with photographers and journalists and I am doubly grateful, therefore, that they were kind enough to give me the benefit of the doubt. In particular I would like to thank Anita Shakya, the first Kumari I ever saw, and Rashmila Shakya, the first I ever met, for a number of wonderful conversations. I would also like to thank the former Kumaris of Patan – Samita Vajracharya, Chanira Vajracharya, Chandrashila Vajracharya – and reigning Patan Kumaris, Unika Vajracharya and Dhana Kumari; Urmila Shakya, ex-Kumari of Cha Bahil; Sajani Shakya, ex-Kumari of Bhaktapur; and the reigning Kumaris of Bungamati, Kilagel, Tokha and Nuwakot – and all their families for receiving me.

I also include the Kumaras – the young boys who embody the gods Ganesh and Bhairab, and who keep special purity observances throughout their everyday life in order to escort the Kumaris on the big festival occasions. Again, their role is often overlooked. In particular I would like to thank Kapil Ratna Shakya (Ganesh) and his family for their hospitality and for describing their part in the Kumari festivals. I wish there had been room in this book to include these, and other, remarkable aspects of the tradition.

I owe an immeasurable debt of gratitude to Professor Michael Allen, whose book *The Cult of Kumari – Virgin Worship in Nepal*, first published in 1975 – the result of several years' anthropological study in the Kathmandu Valley and now in its third edition – remains the seminal work on the subject to this day. Often during my Kumari travels I found myself following in Michael's tracks and meeting people, now in their fifties, who remembered the kind, twinkling-eyed Irish anthropologist who brought them clothes and pencils when they were children. I am grateful for his enormous generosity in sharing his information, for delightful discussions in his garden in Sydney, Australia, and for reading not one, but two, drafts of the book. Above all I would like to thank him for his unstinting encouragement and enthusiasm along the way, and for his infectious creative energy – a manifestation of *shakti* if ever there was one.

I am hugely endebted, too, to Professor Alexander von Rospatt and Iain Sinclair for sparing the time amid the heavy demands of academia to read drafts of the manuscript and provide me with such thoughtful and incisive notes. Their gift, like Michael Allen's, is in the true Newar spirit of giving, without – since I am not an academic – any expectation of a return favour, and their support and scholarship have been invaluable, though I must emphasize that any errors that may have crept in over the course of subsequent rewrites are my responsibility.

One of the joys of writing this book has been the people I have met along the way and I will be forever grateful to the Kumari for leading me to Ellen Coon. Her deep understanding of Newar ritual has been an inspiration. Her own research, as a Fulbright scholar, into the *'dyamas'* – Newar women who act as mediums for the deities – in many ways elucidated my own and listening to her talk sparked off fizzing chain reactions of thought. Staying with her and her wonderful husband, the historian and Sanskritist Ted Riccardi, in their house in Chhauni during my last years of research was like rocket fuel and I loved every minute. Having children almost the same age was an added boon and I thank Miranda and Nicky for being such fun and for entertaining my own on several visits. I am particularly grateful for Ellen's sensitive assistance for several key interviews, and to her research assistant, Rajani Maharjan, for helping transcribe and translate the recordings.

I met Ellen's great friend and *mitini* Anjana Shakya back in 2001 and I would like to thank her for setting me on the right track at the very start of the book. Being not only related to several ex-Kumaris in Kathmandu but also one of Nepal's most acclaimed human rights activists with special interest in the protection of women and children, she was particularly well-placed to unravel the knot of human rights allegations that have entangled the Kumari tradition over recent years. I am grateful to her for her insights and for delicious feasts on many occasions including Mha Puja; but I would also like to pay tribute to the extraordinary work she continues to do in Nepal, and for her courage during the uprisings of 2005 in Kathmandu when she fearlessly entered the fray, talked sense into a contingent of jittery riot police and quite possibly prevented a massacre.

I am enormously grateful to Prem Basnyet for introductions in the early stages of the book. Prem directed a fictional feature about the Kumari, the first colour film in Nepal, in 1976 and kindly shared his connections with me – among them the caretaker's husband, Jujubhai Shakya, and Gyanman Pati Vajracharya and his delightful family in Layku Bahil, who in turn introduced me to the royal Hindu tantric priest Uddhav Karmacharya.

A special thank you, too, to Professor Mukunda Aryal and Dina Bangdel for other help with introductions, for enjoyable excursions around the valley and for shedding valuable light, from their own different perspectives, on the Living Goddess tradition. As Dina once described to me, the Living Goddess is like a diamond with many facets: she appears in many different ways to many different people. Gathering in all these perspectives enriched my understanding of the Kumari and took me in directions I could never have imagined.

For further enlightenment I would like to thank other luminaries: renowned painter of sacred *paubhas* in Bhaktapur, Madhu Krishna Chitrakar; royal astrologers Keshar Mangal Joshi and the late Professor Mangal Raj Joshi; the late Fr. John Locke, Ramesh Prasad Pandey, Dr Rama Pandey Poudel and Siddhi Bahadur Ranjitkar.

Nijiros Shrestha was of great assistance, describing the interior rooms of the Kumari Chen that, as a foreigner, I couldn't see for myself, as well as researching into the Kumari's costume and jewellery, and other aspects that needed a woman's touch. I am most grateful to her, too, for allowing me to witness her niece Annie Shrestha's *bara tayegu* ceremony – a beautiful and empowering ritual for young Newar girls on the cusp of puberty. I was struck, not for the first time, by how impoverished western culture seems by comparison and wish my own daughter could have had a similar affirmation of her inner strength and beauty at the same stage in life.

Similar thoughts occurred to me when I witnessed, thanks to the late Man Kumari Shakya and her family in Oku Bahal, Patan, a Newar *bura janko* – a beautiful old-age ceremony for a person reaching the landmark seventy-seven years, seven months and seven days.

I am hugely grateful to a number of friends in Kathmandu – Emma and Will Cave, Camilla and Luca Corona, Rabindra and Mendira Puri in Bhaktapur, and Shova Shakya and her wonderful family in Guji Bahal, Patan – for having me to stay, for helping me with all sorts of logistics, and for putting up with obsessive conversation about Kumaris. I'd also like to thank Mrs Ambika Shrestha and the staff at Dwarika's Hotel for their hospitality over the years. There can be no nicer place to be holed up for the duration of a *bandh.*

For additional support, help and encouragement of all kinds in Nepal I would like to thank Diwakar Acharya, Ian and Lois Alsop, Ian Baker, Tom Bell, Lisa Choegyal, Kiran Man Chitrakar, Bidur Dangol, Kanak Mani Dixit, Keith and Meryl Dowman, Carroll Dunham, Annamaria Forgione, Bibi Funyal, Chrissie Gregory, Susie Groeli, Niels Gutschow, Mangala Karanjit, Tom Kelly, the Lady Jaycees, Kunal Lama, Mani Lama, Hari Bahadur Limbu, the late Inger Lissanevitch, Guna Raj Luitel, Andrew and Malika McCosh, Andrew Mitchell, Usha Rajkarnikar, Dr Rohit Ranjitkar, Tsering Rita Sherpa, Laxman Shrestha, Omkareshwor Shrestha, Martin and Jenny Spice, Jwala Sthapit, Susan Stenson, Sue Vokes, Steve Webster, Frank Wiseman and the Committee of the Sri Kumari 250th Anniversary Celebrations, headed by Bikas Bhakta Shrestha.

In England and elsewhere, I would like to thank Will Douglas, Dr Hettie Elgood and all tutors and lecturers on the 2002 Classical Arts of India postgraduate diploma course at the British Museum, Dr Elizabeth English, Georgia Garrett, Peter Hogg, Mark Katzenellenbogen, John Mellowship and Alistair Shearer.

I am grateful to two highly talented film directors, Tassia Kobylinska of Roving Eye Films and Ishbel Whitaker of Dark Fibre Films, for generously sharing with me transcripts of their interviews with Kumaris. In particular, Ishbel's acclaimed documentary *Living Goddess*, shot during the turbulent uprisings of 2005 and focusing principally on the Bhaktapur Kumari, gave extraordinary insights into the daily life of a Living Goddess and revealed, much to general surprise, an eloquent outpouring from

Patan's adult Dhana Kumari – who was long thought to have taken a vow of silence.

This book has been through so many incarnations and taken such an inordinate amount of time – almost thirteen years – that there have inevitably been casualties along the way. I would like to thank Tatiana Wilde for all her support in the beginning. I know how disappointing it was, for all of us, when the contract deadline came upon us and I was still in the throes of discovery in Nepal.

It is with particular warmth, therefore, that I would like to thank my agent David Godwin and Chiki Sarkar at Penguin India for bringing the Living Goddess home. A book that has been thirteen years in gestation is not an easy one to edit and Chiki received the unwieldy, yawling bundle from me with firm and steady hands. I owe her a massive debt for honing and moulding the material into an immeasurably finer, brighter and lighter entity. I couldn't have wished for a more skilful editor but I would like to thank her most of all for believing in the book and for making it happen. Thanks, too, to Jaishree Ram Mohan for copy-editing.

I would also like to thank Barnaby Rogerson and Rose Baring at Eland for giving The Living Goddess a home in the UK; as well as Angela Martin, my publicist, and Panni Bharti for the cover design.

For reading drafts at various stages I am profoundly grateful to Lydia Conway, Olivia Dalrymple, William Dalrymple, Dominic Dromgoole, Jane Feaver, Ralph Fiennes, Sasha Hails, Anna O'Connell, Lorna Russell, Quentin and Rowena Seddon, my late dear friend Sophie Smith – and always for the encouragement that spurred me on.

I am particularly grateful to Phil Whitaker whose enthusiasm when The Living Goddess was just the germ of an idea – a *bindu* in the *yantra* – was an incredible boost, and for giving me such a thoughtful critique of the book years later.

There are, of course, numerous other friends and acquaintances over the years, too many to mention, who played a part in some way in bringing this book to fruition – sometimes complete strangers who, finding themselves stranded with me at dinner or in the next seat on a plane, kindly engaged with my Topic Number One and often produced unexpectedly helpful observations and insights. I hope they recognize who they are and how grateful I am for their indulgence.

Heartfelt gratitude, finally, to members of my family who saw me through Himalayan ups and downs – Esther Cayzer-Colvin, Penelope Tree and my mother Anne Tree who sadly did not live to see the elephant born; and especially to my children, Nancy and Ned, who grew up with the Kumari in their lives, and their mother either disappearing off on trips to Nepal or distracted at home with her head in Kathmandu – thank you for the little offerings for my writing shed, for gifts to take the 'little goddesses' and notes in my suitcase, and for sharing the adventure.

But most of all to my husband Charlie, who started this journey when we were teenagers together in a little flat in Freak Street and who has been with me ever since, every step of the way. I quite simply couldn't have done it without you.

Glossary

Adi Buddha   the original self-generated Buddha of Tantric Buddhism from whom the five Dhyani, or Transcendent, Buddhas emanated

agam   a secret shrine room on the top floor of a Buddhist house or *bahal* which may not be entered by anyone who has not taken tantric initiation

amrita   sacred elixir; also a euphemism for alcohol in tantric rituals

apsara   the female counterparts of the *gandharvas*, musician demigods

arati   the devotional waving of light in the form of a flame in front of a deity, an obligatory daily rite

asan   lit. 'seat'; yogic posture or throne

ashram   a hermitage or place of religious retreat

astamangala   the eight auspicious symbols: parasol, two fishes, conch, victory banner, endless knot, *kalash*, lotus and fly whisk

Astamatrika   the eight ferocious, protective 'Mother Goddesses' whose *pithas* ring the towns and cities of the valley

asuras   a class of powerful supernatural beings who are the enemies of the gods

avatar   an incarnation of a Buddha or other deity on Earth

baba   a term of respect usually applied to an older man, like 'father'

bahal   (Sanskrit: vihara) a Buddhist monastery, usually two-storeys high, built around a courtyard; usually located in the centres of the old towns in the Kathmandu Valley and traditionally lived in by the Newar Buddhist caste, with Mahayana and Vajrayana features

bahil Buddhist monastery, similar to a *bahal*, but usually located on the outskirts of towns, with Theravada features

bandh the severest form of strike where all shops, schools and offices are closed and vehicles are banned from roads

bara tayegu (New.) a Newar puberty rite in which girls are married to the sun after a period of confinement

bdellium a dark gum resin extracted from *Commiphora wightii*

Bhairab the 'terrific' or fearsome tantric form of Shiva with sixty-four manifestations

bhakta a devotee of a particular deity

bhakti loving devotion to a particular deity

bhavana lit. development, calling into existence; esp with ref to spiritual cultivation

bhoto a padded, sleeveless vest tied with strings at the shoulders, often offered to deities

bhuta a spirit, usually one that is not the ghost of a dead person

bodhisattva a being that has achieved *nirvana* but vowed to remain in the mundane world to assist others in gaining enlightenment

Buddha 'the enlightened'. The name refers either to the historical Buddha, or to the many Buddhas believed to have come before him

bura janko a Newar old-age ceremony

chaitya a Buddhist object of worship modelled on the *stupa*, but much smaller; found in the courtyard of all *bahals*

chakra lit. 'wheel; a common symbol of the Buddha's teaching. In tantric mystical physiology, centres of nervous energy in the body

chakravartin lit. 'turner of the wheel; a righteous world ruler

chaturmukha four-faced; referring to the carving of faces of deities on a *linga* or column, facing the four directions

Chaubisi Rajya a confederacy of fourteen hill-kingdoms of western Nepal

chema puja (New.) ritual of seeking permission from a deity for an event about to happen, or forgiveness for an oversight in the past

chen (New.) house

Chetri the upper level, non-Brahminical, section of Indo-Nepalese – or Parbatiya – society

chhyepu (New.) (Sanskrit 'kirtimukha') 'face of glory'; a motif most commonly at the apex of a *torana*, where a ferocious face grips snakes in its mouth and devours its own lower jaw; symbolic of the voracity of time

chinna (New.) astrological horoscope drawn up at birth

chipa (New.) food that has been contaminated by contact with some source of pollution

chowk a courtyard or quadrangle

dakini a tantric figure representing a female embodiment of enlightened energy, a 'sky-dancer'

dakshina lit. recompense, thanks; stipend or offering made to a priest for his services

daityas a race of giants who fought against the gods

damaru a double-headed hand-held drum

danava demons descended from Danu, a water goddess

dark fortnight two weeks of the waning moon

darshan lit. 'seeing'; visual connection with a deity

Devi the name of the Goddess as Supreme Creator deity

devas gods

dharma religion, law, proper conduct, destiny, ritual duty, righteousness

dharni a unit of mass used in Nepal, roughly equivalent to 2.33 kilos

dhyana deep contemplation, meditation; states achieved by meditation

diksha tantric initiation including the giving of a *mantra*

drishti focused gaze, vision, insight

durbar palace

dya (New.) god/goddess

Dya Maiju   honorific term for the Kumari meaning 'Mother Goddess'

gajura   bronze or gold temple finial

Gana Kumaris   the nine temporary Kumaris installed for the duration of the festival of Dasain

gandharva   a race of demi-gods, heavenly musicians said to haunt remote areas like forest glades and ponds

ghanta   tantric bell; the female equivalent of the *vajra*

ghat   steps leading down to the river, used for bathing, washing or cremations

Gorkha   the hill kingdom to the west of the Kathmandu Valley from which the conqueror Prithvi Narayan Shah came

Gurkhas   renowned fighting men recruited in the Nepalese, British and Indian Armies, enlisted mainly from mid-western and eastern Nepal. The name derives from the kingdom of Gorkha and the army originally conscripted by Prithvi Narayan Shah

gunas   (Sanskrit, lit. 'strand' or 'thread'); the primary sources of Creation associated with *sattva*, *rajas* and *tamas*

guru   a teacher of esoteric knowledge

harmika   a square platform surmounting the dome of a Buddhist *stupa*

homa   the ritual of offering grains, clarified butter, etc. into the sacred fire

ichingaa   (New.) pure, holy water

ihi   (New.) a Newar girl's mock marriage to a god

jal   pure/holy water

japamala   a rosary

jatra   a religious procession, or festival

joshi   astrologer

Jyapu   Newar farmer caste

kalash   a flask-like vessel used in worship

kanya puja   virgin girl worship

karma   a person's condition or destiny as affected by actions in that person's current or previous life; can also apply in broader terms to the destiny of a nation as a whole

Khasas hillmen

khat palanquin or portable shrine used for carrying a deity in procession

khata honorific silk scarf

khe sagan (New.) (see sagan)

khora heavy sickle-shaped sword used by the Gurkhas, larger than a *khukuri*

kinnara a mythical creature, half-human, half-horse or bird

kot fort

kotihoma a special sacrificial fire ceremony

kumara the boy equivalent of a Kumari

kundalini coiled snake of female energy at the base of the spine, aroused during tantric practice so it travels up through the *chakras* to unite with universal consciousness, thereby flooding the body with a feeling of supreme bliss

kurta suruwal traditional dress comprising long loose shirt/dress and leggings

kvahpah dya (New.) the guardian deity of a *bahal* who resides in the principal shrine on the ground floor; usually Shakyamuni Buddha, one of the five Transcendent Buddhas, or a *bodhisattva*

light fortnight two weeks of the waxing moon

linga a representation of the god Shiva in an abstract phallic form, mounted on a *yoni* base representing union with the female principle

maitritva bhavana the practice/feeling of unlimited loving kindness to all

makara a stylized crocodile, often represented in metal or stone, and used as a waterspout

mala a necklace or garland

mandala a circle or cosmic diagram with a principal deity at its centre and the other divinities of this deity's retinue arranged geometrically around it; an indispensable aid to tantric meditation.

mantra a sound, word or phrase with special power chanted in prayer

mit (New.) a sacred bond between friends

mit-bhai lit. 'mit-brother'; a friend who has undertaken the bond of *mit*

mitini lit. 'mit-sister'

mudra mystical hand-gesture used in rituals; lit. 'seal' – the seal of approval of the deity with whom the practitioner is identifying

mul main, principal

muri a Nepali weight measurement for cereals contained in a sack approx 4 ft tall by 1 ft diameter; roughly equivalent to 64 kilos

murti the manifest form or image of a deity

naga mala necklace in the form of a supernatural serpent

namaskar from Sanskrit 'namar' meaning 'reverent salutation' and 'kaar' meaning 'form' or 'shape'; lit. 'I salute your form (the entity you represent)'

namaste similar to the older *namaskar*, meaning 'salutation to you'; the customary greeting on meeting or parting, usually accompanied by a slight bow made with the hands pressed together

Nepal mandala the Kathmandu Valley conceived as a *mandala*

ninicha (New.) female ritual attendant

nirvana enlightenment; salvation from the endless wheel of rebirth

nitya puja obligatory daily worship

niyam rule, restraint of mind, self-discipline in accordance with resolve or ethical rules

pan betel nut

Pancha Buddha the five Transcendent Buddhas: Akshobhya, Amitabha, Amoghasiddhi, Ratnasambava and Vairochana; also refers to the Newar Vajracharyas who represent them during rituals

parikrama lit. 'path surrounding something'; the circumambulation of sacred places in Hinduism and Buddhism (same as *pradakashina*)

pataka (New: *patah*) a long cloth or metal banner that descends from the pinnacle of a temple down the roof. The end may bear the image of a deity

pati a simple colonnaded open-fronted building providing shelter for passing travellers and pilgrims *pitha* an open shrine, generally belonging to one of the Astamatrika, where the deity is depicted in aniconic form, usually a stone

pradakshina the circumambulation of a temple, *stupa*, or other sacred space

prasad food or other offerings that have been blessed by a deity and then taken back by a worshipper

pratima image, replica

preta a ghost of a dead person

puja religious offering or prayer

pujari a Hindu temple priest

Purana a class of Hindu texts, dating from the first millennium CE, recounting stories of the deities

purohit Hindu priest exclusively for a king or royal family

Raj Kumari royal Living Goddess

rajas passion, motion, energy (one of the three gunas)

raksha chakra the protective outer circles of a *mandala*

rath temple chariot in which a deity is conveyed in procession

rishi an inspired poet / sage

sadhana progressive spiritual discipline, or quest

sadhu a Hindu ascetic

sadya established

sagun (New.) ritual food consisting of the *panchakara* – the five tantric substances beginning with the letter 'm': *mamsa* (meat), *matysa* (fish), *mudra* (divine sign language) – represented by lentil cake; *madya* (alcohol) and *maithuna* (sexual intercourse) – represented by an egg.

sahasrara chakra the 7th chakra of the body which integrates all the chakras with their respective qualities. Also known as the 'crown' chakra.

samay baji beaten rice with meat and fish, eaten on festival occasions

samskara a rite of passage

sannyasin religious ascetic who has renounced all ties of society *sangha* the Buddhist community, referring to monasteries or families attached to a *bahal*

sardar military leader

sattva light, bliss, goodness (one of the three gunas)

shakti female power personified as a goddess; dynamic female element in male-female relationships

Shakya the lower of the two sections of the Newar priestly caste. They and the Vajracharyas are the 'married monks' of Newar Buddhism: only they may be initiated in Newar Buddhist monasteries

shanta puja puja for peace

shilpakar hasta puja lit. craftsman hand worship

shikara a style of temple architecture, usually in stone, with a tall spire symbolizing Mount Kailash

shraddha any act performed with all sincerity and faith, but often referring to the ritual paying of homage to ones ancestors or parents

Shrestha the large merchant middle-ranking Newar caste

siddha tantric adept who has acquired magical powers

Singhasan lion throne; also applies to the Lion Throne Room in the Kathmandu Kumari's house

sloka Sanskrit verses

stupa hemispherical Buddhist monument, originally shaped like a stylized tumulus, often containing relics

sukunda ritual oil lamp

Sutras Hindu or Buddhist texts originally written in palm leaf books

tamas inertia, darkness (one of the three gunas)

tapas austerities or deep meditation generating spiritual heat, or *shakti*

Tantra the esoteric path of Buddhism and Hinduism practiced only by initiates under the guidance of a guru

tantrika tantric practitioner

tapas heat; creative fervour; austerity

Tathagata title of a Buddha

tayo   gold lozenge-shaped amulet worn around the neck by married Newar women

tika   vermilion (or sometimes yellow–sandalwood) paste mark bestowed as a blessing on the forehead, or on images and *puja* vessels

tola   a Vedic measure traditionally the weight of 100 ratti seeds; equivalent to 11.7 grams

topi   traditional Nepali cap

torana   the semi-circular decorative panel in wood or bronze over the doorway and windows of a temple or *bahal.*

trisul   trident, representing creation, preservation and dissolution

vajra the thunderbolt symbol of Tantric Buddhism, associated with the male principle and used in Tantric rituals together with the 'female' *ghanta*

Vajracharya   lit. thunderbolt/diamond teacher; a Newar tantric Buddhist priest

Vajrayana   the 'Diamond Way' of Tantric Buddhism; the specialized esoteric path within Mahayana Buddhism

vetala   ghost or spirit inhabiting corpses and the cremation grounds

vishesh puja   lit. distinguished worship

vrata   an austerity, such as fasting

yachin lah   (New.) see *ichingaa*

yajna   fire sacrifice; Vedic fire altar, usually made from bricks laid out in a *mandala* on the ground

yaksha   attendant deity or benign nymph often associated with trees

yantra   a symbolic diagram representing a deity; in the case of the Goddess, a downward-facing triangle symbolizing a *yoni*

yogi(n)   a Hindu ascetic

yoni   female sexual symbol, equivalent of a *linga*

yugas   cosmic ages, aeons

Bibliography

Allen, Michael. 1975, reprint 1996. *The Cult of Kumari: Virgin Worship in Nepal*. Kathmandu: Mandala Book Point.

Allen, Michael. 2000. *Ritual, Power and Gender: Explorations in the Ethnography of Vanuatu, Nepal and Ireland*. New Delhi: Manohar.

Anderson, Mary. 1971. *The Festivals of Nepal*. London: George Allen & Unwin.

Bangdel, Dina. 1999. *Manifesting the Mandala: A Study of the Core Iconographic Program of Newar Buddhist Monasteries in Nepal*. PhD Thesis, Ohio State University. UMI: 9941281.

Bennett, Lynn. 1983. *Dangerous Wives and Sacred Sisters: Social and Symbolic Roles of High-caste Women in Nepal*. New York: Columbia University Press.

Blom, M.L.B. 1989. *Depicted Deities: Painters' Model Books in Nepal*. Netherlands: Egbert Forsten.

Brown, Percy. 1912. *Picturesque Nepal*. London: Adam and Charles Black.

Caldwell, Sarah. 1999. *Oh Terrifying Mother: Sexuality, Violence and Worship of the Goddess Kali*. New Delhi: Oxford University Press.

Dixit, Kanak Mani, and Shastri Rmachandaran (eds.). 2002. *The State of Nepal*. Nepal: Himal Books.

Dyczkowski, Mark S.G. 2004. *A Journey in the World of the Tantras*. Varanasi: Indica Books.

Eliade, Mircea. 1958, reprint 1969. *Yoga: Immortality and Freedom*. Princeton, New Jersey: Princeton University Press.

English, Elizabeth. 2002. *Vajrayogini: Her Visualizations, Rituals, and Forms*. Massachusetts, USA: Wisdom Publications.

Gabriel, Hannelore. 1999. *Jewelry of Nepal*. London: Thames & Hudson.

Gellner, David. 1992. *Monk, Householder and Tantric Priest: Newar Buddhism and Its Hierarchy of Ritual*. Cambridge: Cambridge University Press.

Glowski, Janice. 2002. *Protection, Power & Politics: An Iconographic Study of Kumari Baha Mandala in Kathmandu*. PhD Thesis, Ohio State University. UMI: 3059253.

Gray, David B. 2007. *The Cakrasamvara Tantra (The Discourse of Sri Heruka)* (A Study and Annotated Translation). New York: The American Institute of Buddhist Studies at Columbia University.

Gregson, Jonathan. 2002. *Blood Against the Snows: The Tragic Story of Nepal's Royal Dynasty*. London: Fourth Estate.

Gupta, Sanjukta, and Richard Gombrich. 1986. 'Kings, Power, and the Goddess'. South Asia Research 6(2).

Gutschow, Niels, and Axel Michaels (eds). 1987. *Heritage of the Kathmandu Valley*. (Nepalica 4.) Sankt Augustin: VGH Wissenschaftsverlag.

Gutschow, Niels, and Bernhard Kolver. 1975. *Ordered Space: Concepts and Functions in a Town of Nepal*. Nepal Research Centre Publications, no. 1. Wiesbaden: Franz Steiner Verlag.

Gutschow, Niels, and Manabajra Bajracharya. 1977. 'Ritual as Mediator of Space in Kathmandu'. *Journal of the Nepal Research Centre* 1(Humanities): 1–10.

Hasrat, Bikrama Jit. 1970. *History of Nepal: As Told by Its Own and Contemporary Chroniclers*. Hoshiapur: V.V. Research Institute.

Hilton, Isabel. 2001. 'Royal Blood: Letter from Kathmandu'. *The New Yorker* 30 July.

Hoek, Bert van den. July 1990. 'Does Divinity Protect the King? Ritual and Politics in Nepal'. Contributions to Nepalese Studies 17(2): 147–55.

Hodgson, Brian H. 1835. 'Account of a Visit to the Ruins of Simroun, Once the Capital of the Mithila Province'. *Journal of the Asiatic Society of Bengal* 4(39): 121–24.

Hodgson, Brian H. 1874. *Essays on the Languages, Literature and Religion of Nepal and Tibet together with Further Papers on the Geography, Ethnology and Commerce of Those Countries*. 2 parts. Reprint Varanasi: Bharat-Bharati.

Huntington, John, and Dina Bangdel. 2003. *The Circle of Bliss: Buddhist Meditational Art*. Chicago: Serindia.

Hutt, Michael, et al. 1994. *Nepal: A Guide to the Art and Architecture of the Kathmandu Valley*. Stirling, Scotland: Kiscadale Publications.

Hutt, Michael (ed.). 2004. *Himalayan People's War: Nepal's Maoist Rebellion*. London: Hurst & Co.

Iltis, L. 1985. *The Swasthani Vrata: Newar Women and Ritual in Nepal*. PhD Thesis, University of Wisconsin. UMI: 8528426.

Jayakar, Pupul. 1989. *The Earth Mother: Legends, Goddesses and Ritual Arts of India*. London: Penguin.

Kaji, Pandit Vaidya Asha Kaji. 2010. *The Dasakarma Vidhi: Fundamental Knowledge on Traditional Customs of Ten Rites of Passage amongst the Buddhist Newars*. (Translated into English by N.B. Bajracharya; edited & annotated by Michael Allen). Kathmandu: Mandala Book Point.

Kirkpatrick, Col. William. 1811, reprint 1969. *An Account of the Kingdom of Nepal*. Delhi: Manjusri Publishing House.

Levi, Sylvain. 1905. *Le Népal: Étude historique d'un royaume Hindou*. 3 vols. Paris: Leroux.

Levy, Robert I. 1990. *Mesocosm: Hinduism and the Organisation of a Traditional Newar City in Nepal*. Berkeley: University of California Press.

Lidke, Jeffrey Stephen. 2000. *The Goddess Within and Beyond the Three Cities: Sakta Tantra and the Paradox of Power in Nepala-Mandala*. PhD Thesis, University of California. UMI: 3020289.

Locke, Fr. John. 1985. *The Buddhist Monasteries of Nepal: A Survey of the Bahas and Bahis of the Kathmandu Valley*. Kathmandu: Sahayogi.

Lowdin, Per. 1985, reprint 1998. *Food, Ritual and Society among the Newars*. Kathmandu: Mandala Book Point.

Manandhar, J.B. 2002. 'Kumari gharka myuralharu'(Murals of Kumari Ghar). *Gorkhapatra* 21 October.

Mellowship, John. 2007. *The Enchanted World of Kumari*. Varanasi: Pilgrims Press.

Menzies, Jackie (ed.). 2006. *Goddess: Divine Energy*. Sydney, Australia: Art Gallery of New South Wales.

Michaels, Axel. 2008. *Siva in Trouble: Festivals and Rituals at the Pasupatinatha Temple of Deopatan* (esp. ch.7, 'The Goddess of the Secret and Her Procession, Guhyesvarijatra'). Oxford: Oxford University Press.

Michaels, Axel, Cornelia Vogelsanger, and Annette Wilke (eds.). 1996. *Wild Goddesses in India and Nepal*. Studia religiosa Helvetica vol. 2. Bern, Germany: Peter Lang.

Moaven, Niloufar. 1974. 'Enquête sur les Kumaris'. *Kailash*, 2(3): 167–87.

Nepali, Gopal Singh. 1965. *The Newars: An Ethno-sociological Study of a Himalayan Community*. Bombay: United Asia Publications.

Oldfield, Henry Ambrose. 1880, reprint 2005. *Sketches from Nipal*. 2 vols. New Delhi: Asian Educational Services.

Oliver, Paul (ed.). 1975. *Shelter, Sign and Symbol* (ch. on 'Three Cities of Nepal' by Jan Pieper). London: Barrie & Jenkins.

Pal, Pratapaditya. 1974. *The Arts of Nepal*. 3 parts. Leiden: E.J. Brill.

Pal, Pratapaditya. 1975. *Nepal: Where the Gods Are Young*. New York: Asia Society.

Pal, Pratapaditya (ed.). 2009. *Goddess Durga: The Power and the Glory*. Bombay: Marg Publications.

Petech, Luciano. 1984. *Medieval History of Nepal* (second, thoroughly revised edition). Serie Orientale Roma LIV. Materials for the Study of Nepalese History and Culture, Rome: Instituto Italiano per le Medio ed Estremo Oriente.

Rawson, Philip. 1972. *Tantra*. 2nd edition, revised and enlarged. London: Arts Council of Great Britain.

Regmi, Dilli Raman. 1961. *Modern Nepal*. Calcutta: Firma K.L. Mukhopadhyay.

Regmi, Dilli Raman. 1965 and 1966. *Medieval Nepal*. 4 vols. Calcutta: Firma K.L. Mukhopadhyay.

Regmi, Dilli Raman. 1969. *Ancient Nepal*. Calcutta: Firma K.L. Mukhopadhyay.

Riccardi, Theodore. 1975. 'Sylvain Levi: The History of Nepal, Part I'. *Kailash* 3(1): 5–60.

Rospatt, Alexander von. 2008. 'The Sacred Origins of the Svayambhucaitya and the Nepal Valley'. *Journal of the Nepal Research Center* 13:31–70.

Sanday, John. 1989. *An Illustrated Guide to the Kathmandu Valley*. Hong Kong: The Guidebook Company.

Sanderson, Alexis. 2004. 'Religion and the State: Saiva Officiants in the Territory of the King's Brahmanical Chaplain'. *Indo-Iranian Journal* 47: 229–300.

Shakya, Durga. 2013. *The Role of Goddess Tulaja and Kumari in Our Culture*. Kathmandu: Kumari Publications.

Shakya, Rashmila. 2005. *From Goddess to Mortal: The True-life Story of a Former Royal Kumari* (as told to Scott Berry). Thamel, Kathmandu: Vajra Publications.

Sharkey, Gregory. 2001. *Buddhist Daily Ritual: The Nitya Puja in Kathmandu Valley Shrines*. Bangkok: Orchid Press.

Sharma, Rama. 2000. *Kathmandaun vasantapurasthita jivita kumaripujako sanskritika evam aitihasika parampara* (The Cultural and Historical Traditions of Living Kumari Worship in Basantpur, Kathmandu). Unpublished PhD thesis submitted to the Dean's Office of Humanities and Social Sciences, Tribhuvan University.

Shaw, Miranda. 1994. *Passionate Enlightenment: Women in Tantric Buddhism*. Princeton, New Jersey: Princeton University Press.

Shrestha, D.B., and C.B. Singh. 1972. *The History of Ancient and Medieval Nepal*. Kathmandu: HMG Press.

Shrestha, Badrilal. 2001. *'Nepalay Kumari Jatraya Parampara'* (The Kumari Jatra Tradition in Nepal), *Kumari* pp. 86–130.

Shrestha, Narbada, et al. Vikram Samvat 2064. *Kumari Ghar.* Kathmandu: An Unpublished Research Report Produced by Nepal Research Group for the Kathmandu Metropolitan City.

Slusser, Mary. 1982. *Nepal Mandala: A Cultural Study of the Kathmandu Valley*. 2 vols. Princeton: Princeton University Press.

Stiller, Ludwig F. 1968. *Prithwinarayan Shah in the Light of 'Dibya Upadesh'*. Bihar, India: Catholic Press.

Stiller, Ludwig F. 1995 (revised edition). *The Rise of the House of Gorkha*. Nepal: Human Resources Development Research Centre.

Stiller, Ludwig F. June 1974. 'The Role of Fear in the Unification of Nepal'. *Contributions to Nepalese Studies* I, pp 42–89.

Tamot, Kashinath, 2007. *'Kumarimajuyata Chen dayakaya dharota'*. (Register of the house made for Mother Kumari). Dashaymaru Jhyah (Newar Weekly), 14:12 (April 12), p.3.

Tamot, Kashinath, 2007. *'Kumaripuja sanksepvidhi: Kumari sambandhi dakvasibay nhapangu saphu'*. (A short system of worshipping Kumari: the earliest booklet on Kumari). Kathmandu: Shubha Saphukuthi Publications.

Tingey, Carol. 1993. 'Auspicious Women, Auspicious Songs: Mangalini and Their Music at the Court of Kathmandu'. *British Journal of Ethnomusicology* 2: 55–74.

Toffin, Gerard. 1984. *Société et religion chez les Newar du Nepal*. Paris: Centre National de Recherche Scientifique.

Toffin, Gerard. 1993. *Le Palais et le Temple: La fonction royale dans la vallée du Nepal*. Paris: Centre National de Recherche Scientifique.

Toffin, Gerard (ed.). 1993. *Nepal: Past and Present*. New Delhi: Sterling.

Toffin, Gerard. 2007. *Newar Society: City, Village and Periphery*. Lalitpur, Nepal: Himal Books.

Tree, Isabella. 2014. 'A House for the Living Goddess: On the Dual Identity of the Kumari Chen in Kathmandu'. *South Asia: Journal of South Asian Studies*, vol. 37, no. 1.

Tuker, Francis. 1957. *Gorkha: the Story of the Gurkhas of Nepal*. London: Constable & Co.

Vaidya, T.R. 1996. *Jaya Prakash Malla: The Brave Malla King of Kantipur*. New Delhi: Anmol Publications.

Vajracarya, Dhanavajra, and Kamal P. Malla. 1985. *The Gopaalarajavamsavali*. Wiesbaden: Franz Stainer Verlag.

Vajracarya, Manabajra, tr., and Warren W. Smith, ed. 1978. *Mythological History of the Nepal Valley from Svayambhu Purana, and Naga and Serpent Symbolism*. Kathmandu: Avalok Publishers.

Vergati, Anne. 1979. 'Taleju, Sovereign Deity of Bhaktapur', *Colloques Internationaux du CNRS*, No 582 – Asie du Sud, Traditions et Changements, pp 163–67.

Wayman, Alex. 1971. 'Contributions on the Symbolism of the Mandala-palace'. In *Études tibetaines dediées à la memoire de Marcelle Lalou*, pp 557–66. Paris: Librarie d'Amerique et d'Orient.

Wayman, Alex. 1973. *The Buddhist Tantras: Light on Indo-Tibetan Esotericism*. New York: Samuel Weiser.

White, David Gordon. 2003. *Kiss of the Yogini: 'Tantric Sex' in Its South Asian Contexts*. Chicago: University of Chicago Press.

White, David Gordon (ed.). 2000. *Tantra in Practice* (esp. ch. 11, 'An Advertised Secret: The Goddess Taleju and the King of Kathmandu' by Bronwen Bledsoe). Princeton, New Jersey: Princeton University Press.

Willesee, Amy, and Mark Whittaker. 2003. *Love & Death in Kathmandu: A Strange Tale of Royal Murder.* Australia: Pan Macmillan.

Wright, Daniel (ed.). 1877, reprint 1972. *History of Nepal.* (Translated from the Parbatiya by Munshi Shew Shunder Singh and Pandit Sri Gunanand). Kathmandu: Nepal Antiquated Book Publishers.

Note on Sources for the Mythical Chapters

Ch. 2, 'The Jewel of Beginnings', is based on the *Swayambhu Purana*.

Ch. 4, 'The Supreme Goddess', is based on stories from the *Devi Mahatmya*.

Ch. 6, 'The Goddess's Yantra', and Ch. 8, 'Taleju's Flight from India', are based on stories told in Wright's Chronicle concerning the 'Dynasty of Harisimhadeva', in the *Gopalaraja Vamsavali* concerning the death of Harisimhadeva, and oral tradition (see Levy, ibid. pp 234–36); as well as historical accounts in Petech.

Ch. 10, 'Gorakhnath's Prophecy', related in Wright's Chronicle, is a popular story elaborated upon in oral tradition.

Ch. 15, 'A King Offends the Goddess', is inspired by oral tradition.

Ch. 20, 'Sati's Yoni Falls to Earth', is based on the Newar version of the famous legend as told in the *Swasthani Vrata Katha*.

ELAND

61 Exmouth Market, London EC1R 4QL
Email: info@travelbooks.co.uk

Eland was started thirty years ago to revive great travel books which had fallen out of print. Although the list soon diversified into biography and fiction, all the titles are chosen for their interest in spirit of place. One of our readers explained that for him reading an Eland is like listening to an experienced anthropologist at the bar – she's let her hair down and is telling all the stories that were just too good to go into the textbook.

Eland books are for travellers, and for those who are content to travel in their own minds. They open out our understanding of other cultures, interpret the unknown and reveal different environments, as well as celebrating the humour and occasional horrors of travel. We take immense trouble to select only the most readable books and many readers collect the entire series of well over one hundred titles.

Extracts from each and every one of our books can be read on our website, at www.travelbooks.co.uk. If you would like a free copy of our catalogue, please order it from the website, email us or send a postcard.